Canada Among

Canada Among Nations 2008

100 Years of Canadian Foreign Policy

EDITED BY
ROBERT BOTHWELL
AND JEAN DAUDELIN

Published for the Norman Paterson School of
International Affairs, Carleton University, in cooperation
with The Centre for International Governance Innovation

by McGill-Queen's University Press
Montreal & Kingston • London • Ithaca

© McGill-Queen's University Press 2009
ISBN 978-0-7735-3434-6 (cloth)
ISBN 978-0-7735-3438-4 (paper)

Legal deposit first quarter 2009
Bibliothèque nationale du Québec

Printed in Canada on acid-free paper that is 100% ancient forest free (100% post-consumer recycled), processed chlorine free

This book has been published with financial support from the Norman Paterson School of International Affairs, Carleton University, and The Centre for International Governance Innovation.

McGill-Queen's University Press acknowledges the support of the Canada Council for the Arts for our publishing program. We also acknowledge the financial support of the Government of Canada through the Book Publishing Industry Development Program (BPIDP) for our publishing activities.

Library and Archives Canada has catalogued this publication as follows:

Canada among nations.
    Annual.
    1984–
    Produced for the Norman Paterson School of International Affairs
    at Carleton University
    In cooperation with The Centre for International Governance Innovation.
    Publishers varies
    Each vol. also has a distinctive title.
    Includes bibliographical references
    ISSN 0832–0683

    ISBN 978-0-7735–3434-6 (bnd)
    ISBN 978-0-7735–3438-4 (pbk)

    1. Canada – Foreign relations – 1945–   – Periodicals.
    2. Canada – Politics and government – 1984–   – Periodicals.
    3. Canada – Politics and government – 1980–1984 – Periodicals.
    I. Noman Paterson School of International Affairs.

FC242.C345   327.71   C86–031285-2 rev

This book was typeset by Interscript in 10/12 Sabon.

Contents

Foreword   vii
Fen Osler Hampson

List of Acronyms   xi

Introduction: Managing Empires   3
Jean Daudelin

1 Foreign Affairs a Hundred Years On   19
   Robert Bothwell

PART ONE
THE MACHINE

2 "A Sad, General Decline?":
   The Canadian Diplomat in the 20th Century   41
   Greg Donaghy

3 Managers, Innovators and Diplomats: Canada's
   Foreign Ministers   61
   Gerald Wright

PART TWO
ISSUES

4 Old Wine, New Bottles: Canadian Economic
   Multilateralism and the North Atlantic Triangle,
   1941–1947   85
   Kathleen Rasmussen

5 The Interplay of Defence and Foreign Policy 111
  Roger Sarty

6 Canada's Contribution to International Law 142
  William A. Schabas

7 "And who is my neighbour?" Refugees, Public Opinion, and Policy in Canada since 1900 159
  Julie Gilmour

8 Foreign Aid and Canadian Purpose: Influence and Policy in Canada's International Development Assistance 183
  Ian Smillie

9 Tools and Levers: Energy as an Instrument of Canadian Foreign Policy 209
  Duane Bratt

PART THREE
"GEOGRAPHIC" FILES

10 A Special Relationship? The Importance of France in Canadian Foreign Policy 235
   Justin Massie

11 From King to Kandahar: Canada, Multilateralism and Conflict in the Pacific, 1909–2009 271
   John Meehan and David Webster

12 Chinese Shadows 293
   Fred Edwards

PART FOUR
IDENTITY

13 The Transatlantic Romance of the North Atlantic Triangle: Narratives of Autonomy and Empire in Canadian Foreign Relations 317
   Cara Spittal

14 And the Beat Goes On: "Identity" and Canadian Foreign Policy 343
   David G. Haglund

   Contributors 369

   Chronology 371

   Index 383

Foreword

This is a very special issue of *Canada Among Nations* because it celebrates the one-hundredth anniversary of the founding of Canada's Department of "External" Affairs (now known as the Department of Foreign Affairs and International Trade). This volume departs from the usual format of previous volumes because it takes the long view, assessing a full century of Canadian foreign policy making mostly through the eyes of historians. The editors have put together a remarkably talented and diverse team, drawing researchers, many of them young scholars, from several universities, the public service, the voluntary sector and the media. Together, they cover a vast historical canvas in extraordinary richness and detail. The story they tell is a fascinating and rewarding one for both the general reader and students of Canada's international relations.

Because of our unique bicultural legacy and the fact we share the continent with a much bigger and more powerful neighbour, Canada's history has been deeply intertwined with its foreign affairs. In fact, as Robert Bothwell suggests in his chapter, much of Canada's "foreign policy" over the last century has not really been "foreign" but "local" or "neighbourly," circumscribed by our North American and transatlantic ties. It is indeed appropriate that the department charged with the management of Canada's international relations was called for much of that period "External Affairs." Picking up a famous theme of Canadian foreign policy scholarship, Jean Daudelin rightly points out that much of this history had the familiar air of relations with "uncles." The book makes clear, however, that Canada has reached well beyond the North Atlantic community to other regions and corners of the globe. Significantly, however, few if any of our "foreign" adventures ever broke free from those original family ties.

Much of the book is devoted to the mechanics and the implications of that complex articulation of "imperial" linkages and the broader involvement of Canada in world politics: Kathleen Rasmussen on international economic institutions, Roger Sarty on defence policy and military alliances, Ian Smillie on foreign aid, and Duane Bratt on energy. All of these chapters demonstrate how constrained Canada's options have been. Their chapters also show how creative the best of its policy makers have been at transcending those constraints to create a remarkable new policy space for the country.

Greg Donaghy and Gerald Wright look at the past century of foreign policy from the standpoint of its makers. Wright's systematic presentation of the country's successive foreign ministers and Donaghy's examination of bureaucratic evolution of the department itself have a bittersweet quality to them. They recount remarkable achievements, and tell the story of some extraordinary individuals. But they also chronicle the progressive marginalization of an entity that lost all claims to what Daudelin calls a "monopoly on the means of diplomacy."

The book also looks beyond the "Empires" but finds little coherence in Canada's policies towards Japan and Indonesia (Meehan and Webster), China (Edwards), or developing countries more generally (Smillie). The constraints imposed by relations with major allies, particularly the United States, weigh heavily here, but so do deeply-held, euro-centric views of the world, coupled with an overwhelming preoccupation with trade-related issues.

Three chapters in the book address the thorny issue of national identity. David Haglund brings international relations theory to bear on Canada's role in the world, exploring the implications of *realist* and *constructivist* approaches to the way in which Canadian foreign policy is understood. Cara Spittal adroitly tackles the gorilla in the room, reconstructing through its various iterations, the debate opposing "narratives of autonomy and empire" that began a century ago, but whose loud and clear "echoes" resonate in today's discussions about Canada's mission in Afghanistan.

Justin Massie's contribution neatly complements that discussion, suggesting that widening the traditional North-Atlantic triangle to include France provides a more comprehensive and fulsome understanding of the way in which the North-Atlantic alliance has had a profound impact on how Canada defines its security and its place in the world.

This is the 24th instalment of *Canada Among Nations*. The volume offers an exceptionally comprehensive and challenging assessment of

Canadian foreign policy over a hundred-year span. The School is delighted to collaborate with the Centre for International Governance Innovation in publishing this volume. The book is one among a large number of "joint ventures" between NPSIA and CIGI. *Canada Among Nations* nonetheless certainly ranks among our jewels. Special thanks go to John English and Daniel Schwanen for their generous and unconditional support and to their dependable and extremely efficient editorial-support team, led by Andrew Thompson. We are also grateful to McGill-Queen's University Press and their splendid production and publishing team.

To close, let me wish our readers an interesting ride through time, and to our friends and colleagues at "External," a very happy anniversary!

Fen Osler Hampson
Chancellor's Professor & Director
The Norman Paterson School of International Affairs

List of Acronyms

AECL	Atomic Energy of Canada Limited
ASEAN	Association of Southeast Asian Nations
BCATP	British Commonwealth Air Training Plan
CAF	Canadian Armed Forces
CAPP	Canadian Association of Petroleum Producers
CDM	Kyoto Protocol's Clean Development Mechanism
CEF	Canadian Expeditionary Force
CEPA	Canadian Energy Pipeline Association
CGA	Canadian Gas Association
CID	Committee of Imperial Defence
CIDA	Canadian International Development Agency
CIEC	Conference on International Economic Cooperation
CIPMA	Canadian Independent Petroleum Marketers Association
CNRL	Canadian Natural Resources Limited
CSCE	Conference on Security and Co-operation in Europe
CUSFTA	Canada-U.S. Free Trade Agreement
DAC	Development Assistance Committee of the OECD
DFAIT	Department of Foreign Affairs and International Trade
DFID	U.K. Department for International Development
DPS	Displaced Persons
DPT	Democratic Peace Theory
EAO	External Aid Office
ECOSOC	United Nations Economic and Social Council
EDC	Export Development Canada
FDI	Foreign Direct Investment

FIRA	Foreign Investment Review Agency
GATT	General Agreement on Tariffs and Trade
IAE	International Assistance Envelope
IAEA	International Atomic Energy Agency
ICBM	Inter-continental Ballistic Missile
ICCS	International Commission of Control and Supervision
ICER	Interdepartmental Committee on External Relations
ICISS	International Commission on Intervention and State Sovereignty
IDRC	International Development Research Centre
IMF	International Monetary Fund
INC	Industrial Cooperation Program
IRD	Integrated Rural Development
IRO	International Refugee Organization
ITO	International Trade Organization
MDGS	Millennium Development Goals
NAFTA	North American Free Trade Agreement
NATO	North Atlantic Treaty Organization
NEP	National Energy Program
NIEO	New International Economic Order
NORAD	North American Air Defense Agreement
NSG	Nuclear Suppliers Group
ODA	Official Development Assistance
OECD	Organisation for Economic Co-operation and Development
PAHMD	Program against Hunger, Malnutrition and Disease
PJBD	Permanent Joint Board on Defence
PMO	Prime Minister's Office
POWs	Prisoners of War
PRC	People's Republic of China
RCAF	Royal Canadian Air Force
RCMP	Royal Canadian Mounted Police
RCN	Royal Canadian Navy
RTAA	Reciprocal Trade Agreements Act
SAC	U.S. Strategic Air Command
SDI	Strategic Defense Initiative
SEATO	Southeast Asia Treaty Organization
SEPA	Small Explorers and Producers Association
UNCED	United Nations Conference on Environment and Development
UNRRA	United Nations Relief and Rehabilitation Administration
USAID	United States Agency for International Development
WFP	World Food Programme
WID	Women in Development

Canada Among Nations 2008

Introduction: Managing Empires

JEAN DAUDELIN

This book could be called "Life with Uncles," in a paraphrase of John Holmes' famous title.[1] Its chapters tell very different stories but much of what they recount nonetheless revolves around Canada's handling of Britain and the United States. Holmes' words neatly convey the complexities of the relationship between a smaller, sometimes insecure, but nonetheless significant nation, and mostly benevolent superpowers, closely related but different, well-disposed but often overbearing and patronizing: never enemies, not always friendly either; more like family, with a history; uncles indeed, close and powerful uncles. The book tells a story of dependence and independence, of the conflicted demarcation of a space of one's own, literally in the middle of those powers, cuddling them, helping them, leveraging one, challenging the other, at times bridging them too. It is mostly the story of a "taker" nation, a story of constraints well managed and others bungled. It is not a morality tale: values have their place, but also greed, narrowly defined interests, and sometimes hypocrisy and cynicism. What "golden ages" there were had a pragmatic shine to them, and the country's best diplomats have never been starry-eyed idealists – notwithstanding the common image, as drawn even by critics.[2]

Unusually for *Canada Among Nations*, and beyond its "normal" multidisciplinary bent, historians make up most of the group brought together here. The departure was proper: our project was to celebrate the forthcoming one hundredth anniversary of Canada's department of foreign affairs by looking back at the full period. Authors were explicitly asked to cover, as much as possible, the whole century, something few political scientists usually engage in. At the risk of uttering clichés, I would say that bringing these historians on board gives the book a different tone, less focused on theory-building or -testing, and more sensitive to the peculiarities of the times examined. Detailed historical knowledge feeds this book's healthy scepticism towards overly "clean" narratives, emphasizing instead complexities, contradictions and discontinuities, thereby conveying more of the uncertainty that has confronted Canadian foreign policy makers.

In the next few pages, I will cede nonetheless to a very social-scientific disposition to parsimony, to identify a number of overlapping themes that still give this collection a remarkable coherence. This brief introduction will end with a short presentation of the book's various chapters.

LIFE WITH UNCLES

In his chapter on defence policy, Roger Sarty deftly encapsulates the country's existential predicament, which also happens to be the most basic datum of its foreign policy: "Canada's sprawling land mass and vast seaboards are indefensible by its tiny population without the assistance of strong allies." This was true a hundred years ago, and remains true today, and this is why Canada has always been a superpower's ally or more precisely an Empire's ally: Britain until World War II, and then the United States. The "management" of those empires has been the central task of its diplomacy. Directly or not, several chapters address the forms of that management. I suggest that the latter can be subsumed under three broad headings: balancing, bridging, and leveraging.

Balancing has been foundational for Canada. Sarty shows how the country's growing autonomy and relative defencelessness were used by the British and then by Canadian governments themselves to reassure the U.S. and thus sustain its "unprotected" Southern border. Canada's place at the heart of the British Empire and then the Commonwealth, by contrast, conveyed a clear imperial commitment to the independence of its Dominion. Canada's defence was thus served by the British making it look both weak and strong. Between the World Wars, Canada's growing assertiveness in its relationship with Britain was well-served by its increasingly close relationship with the U.S., defining Frank Underhill's famous "triangle," which Cara Spittal examines at length in her contribution to this book. After WWII, balancing took on a whole new meaning as the triangle collapsed into a very asymmetric figure, which in turn spurred in part Canada's multilateralist policy, as well as later attempts to "diversify" its economic and political relations, from Trudeau's Third Option to Chrétien's later aggressive courting of China (see Edwards' chapter) and possibly even Stephen

Harper's recent Latin American strategy. Canada, however, has never been very good at using the world to balance or even contain the United States, nor has it been really serious about it. Empire management would instead take different, less direct paths.

Canadian foreign policy's "Golden Age," those years in the 1950s and the early 1960s that are widely associated with influence through exceptional diplomatic skills, creative activism, and effective crisis management, had much to do with the aptitude of senior Canadian diplomats to protect and sometimes salvage the alliances on which the country's security depended so acutely. In their overview of Canada's Asian policy, Meehan and Webster bring an interesting twist to the story, by showing how such "bridging," has a longer, albeit less glorious, history. Their discussion of the 1931–33 Manchurian Crisis points to an instance where such a bridging role was to a large extent forced upon Canada by differences between the United States' increasingly confrontational policy towards Japan, and Britain's preference for appeasing the Japanese. Not much could be done in that instance, but a large part of Canada's post-War success would build on the ability of its diplomats to bring the United States and Britain together, along with an increasingly large group of lesser allies. Canada's contribution to the establishment of NATO (see Sarty's chapter), the construction of the post-War trade regime, from Bretton Woods on (see Rasmussen's chapter), and perhaps most memorably the resolution of the Suez Crisis (see Bothwell's chapter), very much revolved around the bridging of differences between its two key allies. As the range of its foreign policy expanded, however, Canada would discover that such bridging is easiest with "uncles." Even as close an ally as the Netherlands could barely be kept in NATO when Indonesia, with U.S. support, wanted to get rid of any post-colonial linkages (see Meehan and Webster). In the 1970s and 1980s, the Chinese and much of the developing world were left similarly tepid by Canada's entreaties and its "honest broker" claims (see Edwards' and Smillie's chapters), as would Latin America in the 1990s.

Canada's ability to leverage its imperial connections beyond the original "anglo" triangle is another side of its peculiar relationship with Britain and the U.S. Writing about sub-Saharan Africa, Patrick Chabal and Jean-Pascal Daloz discuss what they call "the bounties of dependence," that is, the flip side of most African states' reliance on Western countries' aid, military assistance and export markets, namely money for their rulers' pet projects and patronage networks, diplomatic or even military intervention to save their skin in times of crisis, or a guaranteed refuge when they are forced out of power.[3] The bounties of Canada's dependence on Britain and the United States have never been that perverse and dysfunctional, but they were certainly significant and possibly crucial not only to Canada's early survival as an independent entity, but also later to its security and to its international influence and prestige. Parallels can drawn between King's hoping that "Canada might benefit from its central position within the imperial network" (see Meehan and Webster's chapter), and Canada's leveraging its close relationship with the U.S. to join the G7 in spite of French scepticism and the relative indifference of Germany and Britain. With global governance moving away from formal institutions and towards more informal "clubs," Canada's reliance on powerful friends – primarily the United States – to get "a seat at the table," has become ever more critical.[4]

The close relationship that makes leveraging possible has its costs, however. Stephen Harper's decision to close off the breach opened between Canada and the U.S. by the Iraq war can be seen as an effort to re-establish the required strategic intimacy. In the words of Fred Edwards (this book): "Harper seeks to expand Canadian influence by being seen as a reliable ally of the United States." As he and Bob Bothwell (this book) suggest, however, such attempts may sometimes border on pandering, which is no way to increase one's own influence and power. Strict alignment, while it involves abandoning any attempt to "balance" the allied power, also impairs one's ability to serve as a bridge between it and outsiders. This policy would thus be quite a break for Canada. Yet, what many contributions to this book suggest, and contrary to much writing on Canadian foreign policy, such "changes of mind" have been far from unusual.

PRAGMATISM

The Canadian government's recent infatuation with "reviews" and "strategies" appears to assume that there is significant space for a proactive foreign policy and that Canada has enough leeway to shape its environment. Much of the material assembled here suggests instead that Canada's policy has been based on a much less sanguine reading of the country's scope for action. Through these analyses, one sees a Canadian foreign policy that has been very much reactive, whose makers were keenly aware of the fact that Canada was a "taker," and that their crucial skills lay precisely in their ability to deal creatively and effectively with a changing and uncertain environment. This is perhaps best conveyed by a quip attributed to then Secretary of State for External Affairs Lester Pearson, who is said to have replied, "[w]hen asked to define Canadian foreign policy (...): "Ask me at the end of the year and when I look back at what Canada has done, I'll tell you what our foreign policy is."[5] This, at a time when Canada was devoting more than 7 percent of its GDP to the military, when its relative economic weight in the world was essentially at its apex, and when its diplomatic corps was widely considered to be among the very best. A number of this book's chapters show indeed that muddling-through, without much dogmatism about means, and sometimes even principles, has more often than not been the name of Canada's game, which is arguably the proper way for a "taker" to make the most of its circumstances.

This is probably clearest in the many references to multilateralism, which is so often invoked to characterize the preferred Canadian way of conducting foreign policy. And yet, as Robert Bothwell put it, if Canada is "multilateralist by profession," it is also "muddled by nature."[6] Multilateralism appears never to have been valued as such. Roger Sarty, William Schabas and Kathleen Rasmussen show quite clearly that Canada's first major forays in multilateralism, with the Bretton Woods institutions, the UN and NATO, were primarily ways to deal with "triangular" challenges. Quoting Tom Keating,[7] Rasmussen (this book) points out that "[m]ultilateralism was Canada's best bet to achieve 'continuing prosperity, and harmony with both the United States and the Commonwealth'." If and when bilateralism worked better, for instance to deal with trade challenges in North America, then bilateralism was the way to go. And when neither multilateralism nor bilateralism worked, as in the case of the twelve-mile territorial sea, unilateralism was just fine (see Schabas' chapter).[8]

Canada has proven to be just as pragmatic in its commitment to the supposedly core values of its foreign policy, from respect to human rights to the defence of democracy against its foes from right or left. William Schabas (this book) reminds us that "[w]hen the negotiated text of the Universal Declaration of Human Rights came to a vote in the Third Committee of the General Assembly, Canada abstained, along with the Soviet Union and its five allies" … "shocking traditional allies like the United States and the United Kingdom." Julie Gilmour (this book) similarly points out that "it is not until 1969" that "Canada finally recognize[d] the 1951 and 1967 Geneva Conventions on Refugees." Meehan and Webster also show how Indonesian generals, either by virtue of their clear anti-communism, or because of the huge market they presided over, did literally get away with murder, without the Canadian government, in both cases under Trudeau, fretting about it. Canadians and their government ultimately ended up supporting much of the UN rights architecture and played a role, sometimes significant, in international campaigns against apartheid and more recently in a number of humanitarian endeavours. Yet from Diefenbaker's agricultural export agreements with Maoist China at the end of the 1950s, to Trudeau's sale of a CANDU reactor to Argentina's generals, or his dismissal of the repression of Poland's democracy movement by the Jaruzelski regime, and

Jean Chrétien's "realist" approach to human rights in China, there is clearly a tradition of largely "human rights-blind" foreign policy. Ian Smillie's analysis of Canada's aid policy also underline the highly conditional commitment of Canada to a principled foreign policy. In fact, Meehan and Webster's very specific characterization of Canada's policy should probably apply more broadly: "Canadian actions on East Timor, when they came, took place only in a narrow window when Indonesia's economic and strategic value, high in 1975, had both declined sharply." Canada' foreign policy has never systematically challenged democracy and human rights, but explicit and active support for those often appears to be confined to "ethical windows," where a narrow calculus of interest is irrelevant, or where political gains clearly outweigh any other costs.

Just like multilateralism, and "whether useful or futile, moralism and moralizing are part and parcel of [Canada's] ... international behaviour" (Bothwell, this book). Sometimes, as Julie Gilmour illustrates in the case of refugees, tensions between a very pragmatic behaviour and noisy righteousness border on – or cross into – hypocrisy. In many cases, however, such tensions may merely reflect Canada's somewhat confused sense of itself.

CONFLICTED IDENTITY

The question of identity comes up over and over again in this book. For a start, "empire management" has never been a purely detached endeavour involving the cold manipulation of larger allies for the sake of defending consensually articulated interests. The various options were much more deeply felt, never quite confined to a simple and short-term calculus of interest. Few historians of Canadian foreign relations would have problems with the now fashionable "constructivist" approach to international relations, according to which supposedly "national" interests are never really "given," being instead deeply woven into collectivities' understanding of who they are, who is close to them, and who is not. From that perspective, the "confused nature" of Canada's foreign policy can quite plainly be traced to a lack of clarity around its own identity.[9] Several chapters draw the picture of a nation sometimes unsure of itself, conflicted about who it really is collectively, and unclear about where it stands in the world, as if always aware of what Sarty (this book) calls its own "improbability."

Interestingly, the most important of those ambiguities have been with us for much of the period discussed here. Indeed, to a student of NAFTA and hemispheric integration like myself, there is something eerily familiar in the war of narratives that Cara Spittal chronicles here: between the Tory invocations of homely community, timeless fidelities, and the threat of Americanization, on one side, and the liberal ones of progress, modernity and ... continentalism, on the other. Ironically, and only adding to the confusion, it is striking that most "nationalists" have now found a home in today's Liberal party, albeit one they certainly do not dominate, while hard-core continentalists, though by no means a majority, are more at ease in Stephen Harper's Conservative party.

Reaching farther back, but no less relevant to this day, the nation's founding tensions between British and French-Canadians and their progressive mutations into more or less well-defined multicultural Canadian and nationalist Québécois identities also show up as significant constraints to foreign policy decision making. While those conflicting identifications clearly played a critical role in the "empire management" of the first half of the century, the more recent debates on the Canada-US FTA, the Iraq war, and Canada's military involvement in Afghanistan testify to their continued, if not always straightforward, relevance to the country's foreign policy.

Finally, there is also what one could call "thinner" identities, more narrowly related to foreign policy: from "middle power" to "multilateralism," "honest broker," and "humane internationalism," strong claims have been made about traits that would define a specifically "Canadian" foreign policy. Allan Gotlieb may have put it best: "Like the Danes who made good furniture, the French who made good wine, the Russians who made sputnik, Canada, as a specially endowed middle power, as the reasonable man's country, as the broker or the skilled intermediary, made peace."[10] This book contributes two main insights to that discussion. The first one, already introduced earlier, is that most of those claims can be shown to be true at times, false in others. The second one, most explicit in David Haglund's chapter, is that those representations nonetheless matter, that they structure Canadian perceptions of the world and of what can and should be done abroad. These tricky entities, call them "half-truths that matter," have recently been the focus of a debate that easily transcends the circle of foreign policy specialists: "While Canada Slept," Andrew Cohen argues, its influence and prestige in the world have declined precipitously, a decay he largely attributes to a dearth of commitment and will on the part of its elites and of its political leadership.[11] That discussion, again closely related to "who" Canada is, revolves to a large extent on the country's foreign policy capabilities and its point of reference, real or mythical,[12] is a post-war "Golden Age" that slowly faded, beginning in the 1960s, into this century's foreign policy grey times. Decline was not on this book's original agenda, but our group could not but address it.

AGES, GOLDEN AND DULL

In a recent column for the Globe and Mail, Michael Valpy decries the mythical picture that Canadians have of their country's influence in the world, pointing out, à-la-Cohen, that declining investments in capacity have weakened Canada's ability to influence the world.[13] This view is only partly borne out by the studies collected here: significant changes there have been, but the deliberate choices of policy makers may have mattered less than is often thought.

Nobody questions the quality of the Canada's post-War foreign service, but most of our contributors also describe circumstances that were extremely favourable to the deployment of their talents. Much of the gold was found, not mined. The war had destroyed Europe and the Japanese economy, China was in rubble and would remain so for many years still, the Soviet Union was clearly "on the other side" and no competition for relative prominence on "this" side, the "Third World," finally, was not yet much of a player. Canada meanwhile was prosperous, had resources aplenty and was devoting more than 7 percent of its GDP to its military (which today would mean $113bn!), and it had become a very close economic partner and an important military and diplomatic ally of the richest and powerful country of the planet.

The close relationship with the U.S. aside, none of those conditions would be sustained for long. In particular, not only did Europe re-emerge economically and, soon enough, militarily too, but also Canadian governments could hardly justify devoting such a large part of its resources to the military, nor did it try. It is ironical that Pearson himself would be the one to choose social programs over military capabilities: "[his] government's priority was funding for expanded national social welfare programmes, and particularly the implementation of universal medical care in 1965, which soon became the defining element of Canadian public policy, and indeed the nation's identity" (Sarty, this book). Trudeau and his successors, often credited with "killing" Foreign Affairs and the Canadian military, were arguably just widening a clearly laid out path when they deepened the cuts to consolidate Canada's welfare state. Admittedly, this was masked in Trudeau's case by his personal qualities which gave him prominence though perhaps not importance abroad. Even that cannot be said of his successors, however.

And yet it remains, as documented here by Greg Donaghy, that the foreign policy machinery was radically transformed in the process. The Golden Age was still a time when "external" affairs was tautly tied up to "the centre." As of 1946, prime ministers were no longer also secretary of state for external affairs, but those holding the job were very close to them, and very powerful in the cabinet (see Wright's chapter). It is no coincidence that both Louis St. Laurent and Lester Pearson first made their names as foreign ministers, and that Paul Martin Sr. also expected the job to launch him to the prime minister's office. Such centrality would disappear completely, as would the sense of stability and continuity that significant ministerial tenure could ensure, with an extreme of sorts being reached today: how not to be struck by the fact that Pearson led External Affairs for nine years, whereas seven different individuals have been responsible for "foreign affairs" over the last nine.

Donaghy also points out that the times called for generalists, while today foreign relations now often revolve around arcane matters and thus require extremely specialized knowledge, from environmental regulations to intellectual property rights, that one simply cannot expect to find in a generalist. The transformation of the department of foreign affairs, and the involvement of most other departments in the "file," in other words, could very well be seen as a functional adaptation to changes largely imposed from the outside, and thus not at all as the outcome of some wilful wrecking of an institution by reckless political leaders.[14]

Lastly, the implications of the reduction in Canada's foreign aid, especially in recent years, maybe much more ambiguous than the "declinists" would have it. Ian Smillie's examination of Canada's aid policy, if it shows that aid policy was rarely free of commercial or strategic undercurrents, is much more ambivalent about how effective it has been, even from those standpoints. The expertise of individual diplomats notwithstanding, our two chapters on Asia (see Edwards, and Meehan and Webster) reinforce the impression that, beyond "empires," Canadian foreign policy still relies more on superficial impressions than on sound and detailed knowledge. Afghanistan, where Canada's involvement is now larger than in any other developing country, ever, may be an extreme case of jumping in the dark, but the impression lingers that at best Southern adventures never really matter in themselves, and thus do not call for an intimate understanding. This maybe the flip side of Canada's colonial virginity: while the British, the French and the Dutch are investing massive amounts of public resources in the study and support of their former colonies, in Canada's policy towards Africa, Asia, and most of Latin America, the "disinterest" so often sought and evoked may well be counterproductive.

To conclude this section, I would only add that the stories this book tells all look to be ending. The next hundred-year tome will not tell the story of how Canada managed empires. Not that these will necessarily disappear, or that their importance for Canada will diminish, but the mix of intimacy and interdependence – however asymmetric – that defined the country's relations to Britain and the United States over the last century is most unlikely to occur again.

THE BOOK

Robert Bothwell, who has co-edited this collection, opens the book with a systematic overview of those hundred years of foreign policy. He chronicles Canada's journey from colony to an independence that at first was not sought, and then to what he calls "the endless reaffirmation of sovereignty." Relations with Great Britain first and then the United States take centre stage, and he shows how little has changed in the country's main foreign policy challenge, between a constant desire for autonomy and the rewards – and risks – that flow from aligning with a friendly empire.

Two chapters make up a section on the foreign policy "machinery." Greg Donaghy traces the history of the department itself, or more precisely of Canadian diplomats, since the establishment of the department in 1909. To the question raised by his title, "A Sad and General Decline?" he gives a measured answer: diplomacy has changed over time, and diplomats simply do not command the same influence or prestige as they did particularly during the so-called "Golden Age" of the 1950s and 1960s. He warns against a "vision of the distant past [that] is far too rosy and [a] view of the present too dim." Yet, he documents quite striking differences between the influential Skelton and Cadieux "generations," who prepared and reigned over the "Golden Age," their self-confident "Gotlieb" successors, who bought into Trudeau's changed idea of diplomacy, and today's "less ambitious," "world-weary," and "battered and bruised" diplomats, who are less clear about how they can serve their country at a time when "the new world order does not belong to Canada."

Gerald Wright looks at the department through the succession of ministers that led it. He sees most as the managers of a foreign policy that has never really taken a radical turn. Wright finds few innovators among them, with Louis St. Laurent and Lester Pearson as the most prominent, mostly for pushing Canada into actively engaging global politics, particularly around the UN and NATO. With the stage set, only Howard Green, on nuclear proliferation, and to some degree Lloyd Axworthy, with "human security," really brought significant changes of direction in the country's foreign policy. The prominence of managers, however, he traces in no small measure to the "relentless pressure" of everyday politics and to increasing "encroachment" of prime ministers into the direction of foreign policy. Foreign ministers remain diplomats nonetheless, and "husbanding relations with the United States," their main task; and, as Wright shows, this is a duty to which each brought his and her own peculiar disposition, with attitudes that oscillated quite widely, between Allan MacEachen, Barbara McDougall and John Manley's easy openness and personal comfort with the Americans, to Howard Green and Lloyd Axworthy's quasi-visceral mistrust.

The core part of the book breaks down Canadian diplomacy into "issue" files, looking at economic relations, defence policy, international law, refugee policy, aid and energy. Kathy Rasmussen opens that section with a revealing look at Canada's economic diplomacy, as it was inaugurated by its involvement in the establishment of the current trade regime and of the Bretton Woods institutions, the IMF in particular. What she describes is the deployment of an extremely pragmatic commitment to multilateralism, narrowly meant to ensure Canada's access to the American and British markets. The country's economic security depended on it, and traditional bilateral approaches simply were not adequate. There was never any abstract commitment to multilateralism. Her analysis points to an interesting continuity between these founding moments of Canada's economic diplomacy, and the much later Canada-U.S. free trade agreement: for its advocates, economic security was again at stake, and, this time, multilateralism was simply not the right tool.

Roger Sarty examines the interplay of Canada's defence and foreign policies, reminding his readers of how profoundly intertwined war and diplomacy have been in the history of the country. He argues that the evolution of Canada's relations with Britain and the U.S., and its ascendancy first to full independence and then to "quasi great power" status in the 1950s, are inextricably tied up to its involvement in imperial and "allied" wars, as is the beginning of Canada's intimate economic relationship with the U.S. His discussion of the domestic politics of Canada's participation to the Boer War or to the First World War also brings a strong sense of "déjà vu" to more recent debates about the Balkans, Iraq, and Afghanistan. As with Rasmussen's look at multilateralism, Sarty's chapter strongly questions a conventional wisdom in which Canada's military remains mostly associated with UN peacekeeping, and for whom the Afghan mission is an historical aberration. His argument suggests instead that, as in the past, war continues to play a fundamental role in Canada's influence and international stature.

William Schabas' overview of Canada's contribution to international law ranges broadly but is dominated by two themes: the Law of the Sea and human rights and humanitarian law broadly understood. Canada's contribution to the first was significant and derived from a very opportunistic mixture of multilateralism and unilateralism. Indeed, Schabas quotes a Canadian official's argument that the two are not "mutually exclusive" and that one could hardly be "doctrinaire" about their use. Such a tough, results-oriented and very "realist" approach Canada had learned early, in the difficult attempts to manage its asymmetric relationship with the U.S. by legal means. The prominence of a more idealistic outlook would come much later, as Canada contributed significantly to the extension of an international human rights regime towards which it had been at best indifferent or even, in the words of John Humphrey, "almost completely negative." In this survey, Lloyd

Axworthy's "human security agenda," from the landmines convention and the International Criminal Court, to "the responsibility to protect," looms very large, but is by no means typical of, once again, a most pragmatic approach to international affairs.

In her comprehensive review of Canada's refugee and immigration policy, Julie Gilmour makes a compelling case for considering the period between 1937 and 1951 as a pivotal moment in the construction of Canadians' perception of themselves and of their place in the world. She describes quite a sweeping shift between the restrictive and squarely racist outlook that prevailed before the war, towards the much more open and humane policies that prevail today. In the face of a reluctant public opinion, the confluence of international and domestic pressures (from ethnic and religious groups, but also from "railways and resource industry representatives,") good economic conditions at home, and the decisive actions of a small group of public officials led to policies have changed Canada's ethnic and religious make-up, and its attitude towards outsiders. The shift she documents appears irreversible, although, from a high point reached in the 1980s, episodes of economic downturns, some abuse of the refugee system, and the fall-out from September 11 have made the country's commitment to an open and humane refugee and immigration policy more tentative.

Ian Smillie recounts a more depressing tale: from its beginnings in the 1950s, Canada's aid policy has been plagued by a confused mandate, inconsistent management, excessive centralization, and lack of coherence and continuity in its action in the field. Caught between political expediency, the quest for international prestige and markets, Cold War and then "terrorism" security concerns, ever-changing development policy fads, fast-revolving presidents, and weak and marginal ministers, CIDA has become "an overloaded rickshaw," barely moving and always on the verge of collapsing. Smillie nonetheless finds a ray of hope in the adoption of Bill C-293 in May 2008, which for the first time gives the agency a mandate from Parliament to focus on poverty reduction. The tone of his chapter suggests, however, that he is not holding his breath.

Duane Bratt closes this "issue" section with a look at energy as an instrument of foreign policy, contrasting oil and gas, deeply intertwined with Canada-U.S. relations, and nuclear energy, which has played a significant role in the country's "third-world" diplomacy. In theory, energy should have endowed Canada with significant influence in the world, perhaps justifying Stephen Harper's recent claim that the country is an "energy superpower": the largest producer of hydro-electricity in the world, largest uranium exporter, primary gas supplier to the United States, seventh-largest oil producer and with the oil sands, home to the world's second- or third-largest oil reserves. Bratt shows, however, that the energy instrument has proven tricky to use, and his detailed survey suggests that it may well remain so in the future. "Oil and gas" is fully embedded in North-America's integrated economic structure, and its governance, within Canada through constitutional arrangements, and between Canada and the U.S. through the 1989 free trade agreement, largely neutralizes whatever potential it may hold as a political tool. The weight of U.S. investments in the sector, and political dynamics, once again domestic and bilateral, combine with these economic constraints and formal arrangements to make any attempt at manipulating oil and gas for diplomatic or even strategic purposes highly improbable. Nuclear technology, quite aggressively promoted among large third-world states in the 1950s, 1960s and 1970s, has proven to be easier to leverage. It no doubt played a role in Canada's relations with China, India and Pakistan, as well as in the country's prominence in the establishment of the non-proliferation regime. Bratt shows however that Canada's very success at exploiting some of those countries' dependence on its nuclear technology, to force them to comply with the non-proliferation regime, constrained its ability to keep using that technology as a policy tool. Today, the non-proliferation regime is under attack, with Canada's former partners as some of its key challengers, and the country's CANDU reactors do not look very well placed to compete in the forthcoming nuclear resurgence. Bratt's chapter suggests in sum that there are huge limits to Canada's ability to capitalize internationally on its massive energy resources.

This broad-ranging section is followed by a shorter one devoted to a few "geographic files." Justin Massie opens it by wondering if Canada has a special relationship with France. His analysis reaches beyond the Ottawa-Quebec-Paris triangle to which the discussion is often confined, and looks at the role of the bilateral relationship from the standpoint of Canada's place in the world. Even when factoring in "episodic hostility" and "periodic bitterness," his answer is a measured yes: France has indeed played a "special role" in Canada's security, in its independence and influence, and in its domestic harmony, essentially because it is a vital component of an Atlantic alliance that has been around since WWII and that remains to this day the central component of the country's international security. From that standpoint, "saving" the alliance, for instance during the Suez Crisis, was crucial for Canada because of its relationship with Britain, but also with France.

John Meehan and David Webster take us from these core, Atlantic, dimensions of Canada's foreign relations, to the latter's Pacific periphery, particularly Japan and Indonesia. The picture they draw shows a Canadian policy that, although far from automatically aligning with those of its allies, never frees itself from "the prism of the North Atlantic triangle."

From its officials' first ventures in Asia at the beginning of the twentieth century to today's massive military intervention in Afghanistan, they see a remarkable continuity in Canadian policy, from the "alliance thinking" that dominates its design, to a Eurocentrism that feeds on "vaguely formed images" of vast riches and limitless markets. Canada's policies remain driven by North Atlantic priorities, and "within those confines ... take advantage of trade opportunities." Behind Canada's increasingly strident claims to the status of a "Pacific nation," they see to this day little sign of a true awareness of Asia.

Fred Edwards' more specific look at Canada's China policy is no less severe: he describes a policy that is "rife with contradiction" and that oscillates over and again between engagement, Foreign Affairs' preferred course, and restraint, between almost cynical indifference to "Maoist totalitarianism" and forceful denunciations of human rights violations. He notes how baffling it is that Canada's policy has recently turned into outright – if mostly rhetorical – belligerence at the very moment when, for the first time ever, the economic and political relationship between the two countries, has also attained "real substance." To a large extent, Edwards traces these ambiguities to a relationship that never truly stood on its own, one that is profoundly embedded in Canada's relations with the United States, and for which "China has (rarely) just been China." In many ways, it is a case that embodies the tensions that pervade Canada's whole foreign policy, between morality and realism, and between alignment with the Empire and a quest for autonomy.

These tensions take us naturally to our last section, devoted to Canada's identity and its relevance to foreign policy. Cara Spittal tackles the very heart of the matter as she reconstructs the debate between the "narratives of empire and autonomy" that to this day have a bearing on Canadian foreign policy through their representation of Canada and of its place in the world. She considers various iterations of this debate through the writings of major English Canadian intellectual figures, from Peter C. Newman and George P. Grant in the 1960s, all the way back to Goldwin Smith and George M. Grant at the end of the nineteenth century. Along with the material, military and strategic dimensions of the North-Atlantic triangle, Spittal makes a compelling case for the critical importance of its psychological and philosophical representations. Her brief references to Stephen Harper and Stéphane Dion also make clear that these narratives continue to structure contemporary foreign policy debates.

In a discussion that, unlike the book's other chapters, explicitly engages international relations theory, David Haglund also tackles the problem of identity, trying to ascertain how it can be used to understand foreign policy. He distinguishes between two broad approaches. The first, which he terms "deductive" and associates with a more "realist" outlook, infers identity from a state's capacity relative to others. This approach, which for Canada has centred around the meaning and implications of being a "middle power," has been extremely influential. Yet it does not exhaust identity's potential as a heuristic tool and Haglund delves into a second, perhaps more ambitious approach, for which a state's interests are not given by its relative capability, but instead derive from a country's particular sense of itself and of the communities to which it partakes. From that perspective, it is Canada's "transnational identity," as a liberal democracy, as a North-American nation, and as a multicultural society, that structures the way in which its interests are defined. For all the distinctness of his analysis, Haglund's conclusion shores up a central theme of this book: through either of the theoretical lenses he deploys, the U.S. remains the most important point of reference for the definition of Canada's national identity, and as such, for the definition of its interests.

This elegant analysis neatly concludes a collection that puts the last hundred years under a soft but searching light, purposefully emphasizing neither dark nor bright areas. This group of authors engages instead in a measured conversation about the peculiar qualities, travails and contradictions of Canada's foreign policy history. "Critical" books may be fashionable, but this editor will only claim rigour and "intelligence" for this one.

ACKNOWLEDGEMENTS

As is usual for *Canada Among Nations,* this book has been produced under severe time constraints and Robert Bothwell and I would like to thank the contributors for delivering manuscripts of remarkable quality under significant pressure. Andrew Thompson at the Centre for International Governance Innovation provided discipline and spectacular support to the process, taking over the whole logistical side of the endeavour. His team in Waterloo and, for the authors' meeting, in Cambridge, also deserve our gratitude: Anne Blayney, Briton Dowhaniuk, Andrew Schrumm, and Robert Harvey. I would also like to give special thanks Charlotte Freeman-Shaw for compiling the chronology found at the back of this volume. We are also beholden to McGill-Queen's University Press for the continuing quality of their work both at the production and distribution ends. Our thanks also go to John English and Daniel Schwanen at CIGI for supporting financially and intellectually the whole process, and to Fen Hampson and his staff at the Norman Paterson School of International Affairs for their unfailing support. I also personally want to thank Robert Bothwell for the erudition, the humour, and the huge amount of time and effort he has brought to this project.

NOTES

1 John Holmes, *Life with Uncle* (Toronto, Buffalo, London: University of Toronto Press, 1981).
2 Most famously by Dean Acheson in "Canada: Stern Daughter of the Voice of God." Dean Acheson," "Canada: Stern Daughter of the Voice of God," in Livingston T. Merchant (ed.), *Neighbors Taken for Granted: Canada and the United States* (New York: Frederick A. Praeger; Toronto: Burns and MacEachern, 1966), 134–43.
3 Patrick Chabal and Jean-Pascal Daloz, *Africa Works: Disorder as Political Instrument* (London: James Currey Publishers, 1999).
4 Andrew Cooper, "Opening up Governance from the Top: The L20 as a project of 'New' Multilateralism and 'New' Regionalism," paper presented at the Hallsworth Governance Conference, 16 & 17 March 2006, Chancellors Conference Centre, The University of Manchester, http://www.ipeg.org.uk/papers/hallsworth_papers/a_cooper.pdf. See also, Robert Wolfe, "Canada's Adventures in Clubland: Trade Clubs and Political Influence," in Jean Daudelin and Daniel Schwanen (eds.), *What Room for Manoeuvre? Canada Among Nations 2007* (Montreal, Kingston: McGill-Queen's University Press, 2008), 181–97.
5 Allan Gotlieb, "Romanticism and Realism in Canada's Foreign Policy," *Policy Options*, February 2005, 24.
6 Robert Bothwell, *Alliance and Illusion: Canada and the World, 1945–1984* (Vancouver, BC: UBC Press, 2007).
7 Tom, Keating, "Multilateralism and Canadian Foreign Policy: A Reassessment" (Calgary: Canadian Defence and Foreign Affairs Institute, 2003).
8 Allan Gotlieb, "Romanticism and Realism in Canada's Foreign Policy."
9 Bothwell, *Alliance and Illusion.*
10 Michael Valpy, "The foreign policy myth," *The Globe and Mail*, 30 June 2008. http://www.theglobeandmail.com/servlet/story/RTGAM.20080630. wcandayvalpytw00630/BNStory/CanadaDay2008/home?cid=al_gam_ mostemail (consulted 080802)
11 Andrew Cohen, *While Canada Slept* (Toronto: McClelland & Steward, 2004).
12 Valpy, "The foreign policy myth."
13 Ibid.
14 Jean Daudelin, "Bubbling Up, Trickling Down, Seeping Out: The Transformation of Canadian Foreign Policy," in David Carment, Fen Osler Hampson and Norman Hillmer (eds.), *Setting Priorities Straight, Canada Among Nations 2004* (Montreal & Kingston: McGill-Queen's University Press); 103–23.

1 Foreign Affairs a Hundred Years On

ROBERT BOTHWELL[*]

The formal occasion for this book is the hundredth anniversary of Canada's Department of Foreign Affairs. More properly, it is the hundredth anniversary of an act establishing a department to deal with "external affairs," and for the first eighty-four of those hundred years that is what the department was called.[1] To explain how Canada's diplomacy has evolved, and what it has meant over a hundred years, it is necessary to go back to a time when Canada had a foreign policy institution, the Department of External Affairs, but not a foreign policy – back, in other words, to a time when Canada was a colony.

The fact that Canada evolved from a colony to independence is an obvious theme, and probably the most important theme, in the history of Canadian foreign policy. This process used to be described as "colony to nation," and was presented as an example of the working of the Law of Progress – in other words in the optimistic, whiggish terms of the nineteenth and early twentieth centuries. This formulation causes problems. Not only did Canadian colonial politicians from Macdonald to Laurier not seek "independence;" they asked nothing better than to be left alone – autonomy, not independence. And that leaves entirely apart the vexed question of what a nation is, and how many of them Canada may have.

Colonies do not always seek independence. Canada didn't. A colony had little control over a large and confusing world and, more important, could hope to have little control. It was not an uncomfortable situation, because Canada was in no particular danger, because its trading and investment links worked well enough, and, just as important, there was not a problem of cultural dissimilarity between Canada and the more powerful countries that surrounded it – Great Britain by water, and the United States by land. This was not Poland and Prussia, or Greece and Turkey, or Finland and Russia.

So Canada was an island in an English-speaking sea. In some respects it still is, though the English-speakers these days may well hail from Bangalore as much as from Ipswich or Atlanta. Cultural similarity does not always make for harmony; Anglo-Saxons are a quarrelsome lot. There is "the narcissism of small differences," a term from Freudian psychology, applied by the American historian David Potter to the relations of Canada and the United States,[2] but which might equally well apply to relations between Canada and Great Britain, or, at a slight remove, to relations between Canada and France.

As Louis St. Laurent, external affairs minister in 1947, pointed out in a lecture that year, Canada's cultural roots were in Western Europe and its traditions, especially (but not limited to) its liberal political and economic traditions.[3] These cultural resemblances made and make the other societies apparently comprehensible, though they do not always explain their behaviour. We should note the broad streak of liberal moralism that runs through Canadian pronouncements, official and unofficial, on international affairs. Whether useful or futile, moralism and moralizing are part and parcel of liberal international behaviour. As recently as the 1930s they were held, by people like Neville Chamberlain (himself a notable moralizer), to be characteristic of that irresponsible and irritating power, the United States.

Because Canada has been a distinct (though not independent) political entity since the 1840s, its politicians have consistently though not invariably tried to maximize its autonomy. This is in part because the more intelligent ones have suspected that Canada remains a work in progress, that its sense of national identity and thus national cohesion is fraught with difficulties – not least the fact that Canada was born, and remains, a bilingual nation and that it has at least two publics to satisfy, and often more than that.

The pursuit of autonomy, the desire to be left alone, is not unique in international relations. Small countries naturally seek it vis-à-vis their larger counterparts – especially when those counterparts are culturally similar. Canada's behaviour in international affairs would not have seemed strange to American politicians during the first fifty years of the republic, who specialized in distant and unhelpful comments on the failings of other countries, meaning, usually, their cultural cousin, Great Britain. We shall see this characteristic re-emerging in the twenty-first century.

THE COLONIAL PERIOD

But to begin at the beginning, in 1908 Canada was a large colony and part of the British Empire. In 1909, at the behest of the British ambassador in Washington and the British governor-general in Ottawa, the Canadian government created a new department of government. The title of the new department of External Affairs was carefully chosen by its legislative father, Liberal Prime Minister Sir Wilfrid Laurier. Laurier had thirteen years experience leading a bilingual, diverse and geographically scattered country. It made him cautious. He understood very well, as did his countrymen and -women, that not all affairs outside Canada were foreign. Canada was an upstanding member of the British Empire, and persons born in Canada were British subjects, not Canadian citizens. Legally, Canada was an imperial subdivision, and Canadians owed allegiance not to the senior governmental personage resident in Canada, the governor-general, Lord Grey, but to King Edward VII. Foreign affairs meant dealings with the United States, or with Germany, different sovereignties belonging to other monarchs, hereditary or, in the American case, elective.

This was not a mere matter of form. The best example of what Canadians thought of themselves occurred the previous year, 1908. Canada, led by Quebec City, had moved into an orgy of rejoicing and commemoration of the tercentenary of the country's first European settlement – everybody came, from the Prince of Wales and the American vice-president to thousands of ordinary Canadians, and they were greeted with displays and pageants that emphasized Canada's European past and its monarchical, British, present.[4]

The commemoration of a mere hundred years pales beside the three hundred years, now four hundred years, of Quebec City. But the contrast in lavish ceremonies and the parade of celebrities in 1908 with the less impressive and more local celebrations in 2008 does recall the adage that the past is another country, and they do things differently there.[5] It is important to remember that Canada was a part of a now vanished empire, and that Canadians of all varieties identified themselves differently, even if, in 1908 or 1909, they did not all agree on what they or their country might be.

This was something that Sir Wilfrid Laurier had to bear in mind. Imperialism was in flower in the early twentieth century, and the world was ordered through a series of empires, mostly based in Europe, of which the British Empire was the largest and most magnificent. To provincial British subjects, it looked very large and very fierce and very impressive and very rich, and they did not pause to consider whether the Empire might not also harbour very big problems.[6] In 1899, when the

Empire went to war in South Africa, the Laurier government was swept along by local imperial enthusiasm. Canada sent troops to South Africa as part of the British army – a precedent, whether Laurier acknowledged it or not.

Distant provinces also had their own identities, and Canada was no exception. There was a Canadian identity, existing side by side with linguistic identities, especially French Canadian. And there were provincial and regional identities too. Some called Canada a country, though the formal term was "dominion," which was interpreted to mean not a colony, but not an independent jurisdiction either. In fact, Canada *was* a colony, but a colony in an empire where the term conveyed a special meaning. To put it briefly, it was a liberal colony in a liberal empire; not a conservative or tory colony in a conservative empire.[7]

The liberal British Empire was run on the cheap, and it was that empire that was relevant to Canada. In 1909, the British taxpayer paid practically nothing to maintain British sovereignty in Canada, or Newfoundland, or Australia, or New Zealand. Those costs were cheerfully assumed by the Canadians and the others, though admittedly the costs were not many. Paying for something implied consenting to expenditures; and Britain had long since turned over the constitutional mechanism for securing consent to local politicians. Thus, Canada had its own autonomous political system, and had had one since the 1840s. It could not be argued that Canada was oppressed by the Empire, a point Laurier appreciated; he was determined to keep it that way. Laurier's approach was, arguably, a form of imperial patriotism, optimistic by nature, and committed to the liberal side of Britain's imperial heritage.

And, indeed, the highly devolved and decentralized nature of the liberal Empire was a factor in its survival, since there was usually not enough "Empire" to get in the way of local priorities in the self-governing colonies, including, and especially, Canada. It also allowed the Empire to represent liberal values – representative and responsible government, for example, hostility to privilege, and a commitment to equality.[8] But there were others who talked darkly of dangers abroad, and of expenses to meet them. The Empire was, according to them, in peril from roughly 1880 on.[9]

Canada's membership in the British Empire meant that, for most "external" issues, Great Britain was the primary focus of Canadian attention, whether or not one approved of the Empire, or felt any particular allegiance to it. The Empire, and Canada with it, came under great strain, economically, socially and politically, during the First World War, and there were some Canadians who concluded that the victorious Empire of 1918 could not stand another such victory. To support the Empire, Canada had voluntarily to commit to the war a huge outlay of money and manpower, which was secured by the wartime government of Sir Robert Borden lavishly expending its political capital in the dangerous and divisive election of 1917. Canada had divided along linguistic lines in terms of its support for the war. For many English Canadians, no sacrifice, whether of men or of money, was too much; to French Canadians, the limits of contribution were a great deal lower. This was a volatile confrontation, avoided, perhaps, only because the war came to an end in November 1918. As a result, Borden's successors at the head of the Canadian Conservative party found themselves politically embarrassed, if not politically bankrupt, especially in the province of Quebec.

The First World War demonstrated that Laurier's happy Empire, in which Canada was mostly left alone to pursue its own goals by its own means, had come to an end. The world had intruded, and it would, regrettably, not go away. Foreign policy had become an issue in Canadian politics, and could no longer be sloughed off on a distant Imperial government. The British had paid off Borden and his successors, Conservative Arthur Meighen and Liberal Mackenzie King, by conceding even more autonomy – so much autonomy as to establish Canada as a formally independent power in foreign affairs during the 1920s, culminating in the Statute of Westminster of 1931 – Canada's equivalent of a Declaration of Independence.

Colonial, pre-1931 or 1945 Canada may seem remote, quaint, and distant. But it left a legacy that informed how the country worked, and by extension how Canadian foreign policy was to be made. Most obviously, it left a linguistically divided polity, with a tradition of political accommodation that was usually honoured, and slightly less frequently applied. The danger of not applying it, however, had become evident when French and English Canadians quarrelled over the First World War. The colonial era also left a generation of Canadian nationalists, mainly English Canadian but including some French Canadians, who took Canadian sovereignty seriously, as being too recently won to be lightly abandoned.[10]

TRANSITION TO INDEPENDENCE

Mackenzie King was not inert during this process. His interpretation of the recent past – the First World War – was that foreign adventures were not to be lightly embarked upon. Another effect of the war was that, seen up close, British politicians lost much of the imperial lustre that had once served as a beacon to distant, awestruck, colonials. It was no longer enough for a British prime minister to beat the Empire's war drums. Many Canadians still hearkened to the sound, but not their prime minister. When in 1922 the British government proposed a hare-brained adventure which would have meant going to war with Turkey, King resisted. But

King's refusal to join in a lunatic war should not be interpreted as anti-British. King believed that Canada's refusal exemplified a better tradition of British thought and politics than the one represented by the British government; and he was probably right.

The response of the leader of the Conservative party, Arthur Meighen, was different. Canada should support Britain, as a matter of duty, and almost as a fact of life. In Meighen's mind, there was no need to think about it. British power must be sustained, and Britain's reasons for using that power must be right.

So the "other country" of the Canadian past persisted through the 1920s and 1930s. Canada remained part of the British Empire, and it is virtually certain that the Empire was not weakened by giving its self-governing colonies formal independence. Formal status was traded for informal but very real support.[11] Canada remained closely involved in the Empire's foreign affairs, even if Canada had little role in setting what Britain's foreign policy should be. Mackenzie King generally approved British foreign policy in the late 1930s, the period of "appeasement." King understood very well the technique of making concessions to satisfy your enemy or opponent, converting them into friends and even supporters for the future. It was, after all, what the British had been doing to Canada ever since the 1840s.

Appeasement was also politically astute, not merely in the short term but over the longer haul. When Great Britain did eventually go to war in 1939, there could be little doubt that the war was not of Britain's seeking, and that the British government had done all it could – and more – to avoid it. Behind such a policy, the imperially minded could find satisfaction in following British leadership, and expressing British solidarity. For those English Canadians more autonomously inclined (sometimes calling themselves "nationalists") there was limited satisfaction that the call to support Britain had not yet come, and perhaps never would. French Canadians, like these English Canadians, could take comfort in delay. Delay also spoke to reluctance, to prudence – desirable virtues when confronting the awful decision to go to war. King's political stock rose, not fell, with appeasement as a policy.

Canada's eventual decision to go along with Britain in declaring war on Germany in 1939 was reasonable enough as far as non-imperialists were concerned because they could see that everything else had been tried. Under the circumstances, the decision to go to war in 1939 would not diminish the ability of the Canadian government to be engaged abroad – constructively.

The impact of appeasement on French Canada must not be underestimated. It was already clear that Mackenzie King would not join a British war in the old imperial spirit. What appeasement showed was that King would go to war only very reluctantly and only when the political case for it was practically irrefutable, as King's interpretation of liberal ideology required. It was a sign that the country, and French Canadians' interest in it, were in good hands, or at any rate better hands than anyone else offered. It helped too that King had constructed a plausible political machine, strong in all parts of Canada, but particularly strong in the province of Quebec, and unlike the austere Borden during the First World War, King did not find politics beneath him.

The Second World War expressed English Canadians' continuing sense of British loyalty or identification. It expressed their conclusion, as a result of the events of the 1930s with the rise of Germany and Nazism, that going to war was something that could not be avoided, or, in retrospect, could not have been avoided. For the more realistically inclined, and also the more nationalist, it also expressed the fact that Great Britain in the 1930s was still a first class power, economically, diplomatically and militarily. It was not hard to pay attention to things British because British affairs were both notable and important, not just to Canada, but to the world.

The strain of the Second World War undermined British strength. Britain was bankrupt, a horrified Mackenzie King learned in 1941. Canada would have to look elsewhere for strength, at least some of the time. Fortunately, as a prudent politician, King had already found an alternative – Franklin D. Roosevelt and the United States.

King must have found the legacy of the war curious; if he had had a sense of irony he might have reached for the term. His political leadership was successful. He had kept his party united, and with it the country. He won the first postwar election, though he lost his own seat. Despite that minor embarrassment, he was both clever and lucky as a political leader. As a result, he was able to achieve his lifelong ambition of extreme political longevity.

But what kind of country had emerged from the war? When a group of Ontarians decided to commemorate the war and its leadership, they dedicated a carillon at Niagara to "our nation's leaders" – Britain's Winston Churchill and the United States' Franklin D. Roosevelt.[12] Even sixty years later, you would be hard pressed to find a memorial to King, outside the precincts of Parliament in Ottawa, while Churchill commemorations abound.

INDEPENDENCE AND RESEMBLANCE – CANADA AND THE UNITED STATES

It was doubtful that Canadians of an earlier time would have erected a monument to Woodrow Wilson as their nation's "leader" in the First

World War.[13] It was a very different thing to be an ally of the United States than it was to be an ally of Great Britain. For one thing, there was no constitutional connection to the United States. While Canada might be an issue in American politics, it could not be part of those politics. Canada had no constitutional standing in Washington as it did in Great Britain. Having "a seat at the table," in the tired old diplomatic formula, meant one thing in London, but something quite different in Washington.

There was also a problem of proportion: Canada was very important to Great Britain, because in time of war, from South Africa in 1899 to Korea in 1950, Canada's armed forces contributed substantially to the ability of the British Empire to make a showing, while Canada's financial and material aid to the British cause in the First and Second World Wars made a difference to Britain's economic fortunes, lessening the strain on the British economy and taxpayers when they needed help most.

The United States did not depend on Canada to shore up its strategic or political position among the great powers. American relations with Canada lacked most – though not all – of the positive sentimentality that accompanied the British connection. Admittedly, there was less of the negative side too. The American government had not sought to dominate Canada, or to intervene in its affairs. The last official war along the Canadian-American border had ended in 1814, and the depredations and atrocities of that distant conflict seemed evenly balanced.[14]

In the aftermath of 1814, Americans had turned their interests elsewhere, to slavery, to Mexico, to their Civil War, to the annexation of Hawaii and the conquest of the Philippines, Cuba and Puerto Rico, to the settlement of the prairies, leaving Canada to its own devices. The United States had nothing to fear from Canada and nothing from Great Britain either.

Though Britain remained a first-class military power at sea, with the capacity to blockade American ports, its army could do little more than offer pinpricks – or more likely, prisoners – to the Americans. British generals had long since concluded that a serious land war in North America – especially one in defence of Canada – was folly.[15] Canada did not menace the liberty, prosperity or security of the United States; and it could be argued that the presence of the Royal Navy in the ocean between Europe and the Americas did a great deal to guarantee all three. So both as part of a great Empire and as a small and underpopulated, though culturally similar, neighbour, an independent Canada may even have served American interests, by keeping Britain vulnerable to American pressures.[16]

Canadians could be of assistance to the American settlement enterprise. At home, times were tough, and as a result hundreds of thousands of Canadians – English- and French-speaking – decamped for the

United States. As a result, few Canadian families were without their American members, and those new Americans were swallowed up, virtually without trace, into the republic. It was hardly surprising if Canada seemed like a stagnant backwater to American politicians. The young Theodore Roosevelt easily and patronizingly wrote that "The American ... regards the Canadian with the good-natured condescension always felt by the free man for the man who is not free."[17]

It followed from Roosevelt's observation that Canadians could remedy the situation, and, if they did, would immeasurably improve their prospects and perhaps even their characters. In the late 1880s and 1890s, as the historian Chris Pennington has shown, people like Roosevelt took up the cause of commercial or continental union between Canada and the United States. Although its Canadian supporters tended to believe that "commercial" and "continental" unions were not really the same thing, their American associates were, on the whole, free of such illusions. What these Americans wanted, and expected, was "annexation" – once the Canadians themselves had paved the way.[18] When Canadians rejected that option in the election of 1891, the Americans did not insist and retreated, like Roosevelt, into "good-natured condescension."

Theodore Roosevelt's cousin, Franklin, occupied the White House for much of Mackenzie King's time as Prime Minister, and the two men achieved a relationship that is probably as close to friendship as is possible between two heads of government. Roosevelt cheerfully advised his friend on the "solution" for the French Canadian problem, pointing to the accelerating rate of assimilation of Franco-Americans into the larger English-speaking society around them. King, always prudent, does not seem to have replied.[19]

More constructively, the two men whiled away their evenings over cocktails, expounding plans for social security and for improving the press. The press was beyond their reach, but it is not hard to discern a similarity in their views on social welfare, and their connection to a larger current of ideas circulating in the mid-1940s. On the other hand, King was aware that his was a more conservative country than Roosevelt's America, less malleable and less tractable in terms of government initiatives. King had to be concerned with his country's political balance, poised between English and French, West and East, cities and farmers. It would be so easy for the larger power to upset Canada's necessary compromises; that was something to be guarded against. Or so Canadian history, quite recent history from the time of Laurier and Borden, seemed to teach.

There was also a lesson that *American* history might have taught. The United States had once been overshadowed by Great Britain, and American leaders down to the mid-nineteenth century had drawn back from the hint of alliance with Great Britain. Alliance, after all, might mean, probably would mean, subordination – being drawn, in John Quincy Adams' metaphor, "as a cockboat in the wake of the British man-of-war." And because American nationalism, or sense of nationality, was recent and fragile, he and his contemporaries gave it fierce expression.

The British did not mind all that much. Through the nineteenth century they poured investment into the United States, and Britain remained the Americans' main trading partner from the eighteenth century through the 1920s. Relations were never entirely smooth, but they were never truly hostile. And given the international situation through the nineteenth century, the question of alliance never surfaced again, until the world wars of the twentieth.

The Canadian government gave great value to exports and investment. It was well aware that Canada's economic viability depended on a steady flow of American money, but it was equally clear that economic survival should not be purchased at the price of political subordination. It was already obvious to Canadians that great decisions were being taken elsewhere, by the greater powers, in the interest of a cause to which most Canadians subscribed. The result was a fine balance between alliance and independence. If it became clear that no major decisions were being taken in Canada, it might not be long before Canadians questioned the viability or even the existence of the Ottawa government. Yet paradoxically, the viability of that government would come into question among its own citizens if it did not pursue the interests – ideological, strategic and economic – that bound Canada to the Americans. The commemoration of the "nation's leaders" at the Niagara carillon well illustrated *that* danger.

THE ENDLESS REAFFIRMATION OF SOVEREIGNTY

The generation that came to power after 1945 in Canada had fought the First World War, lived through the depressing decline of diplomacy into war during the 1930s, and managed, in some cases, the war effort between 1939 and 1945; they were symbolized by Lester Pearson and John Diefenbaker. Pearson's successor, Pierre Trudeau, continued on in the same mould, though a younger man with a different background. Yet in foreign policy the resemblances between Trudeau and Pearson/Diefenbaker are stronger than the contrasts.

The great issue of the forty years after 1945 was the Cold War and anti-communism; and at the forefront was the alliance with the United States that the Cold War necessitated. The alliance was the great fact of Canada's foreign affairs, and there was never any serious question that it would end; but that fact magnified discrepancies between the two countries on lesser issues – issues that played into the older theme of sovereignty, imperialism, and even colonialism that lay not far under the surface and within the experience of the older generations of Canadians.

Speaking in 1951, External Affairs Minister Lester Pearson stated that the era of "easy and automatic political relations" with the United States had come to an end.[20] It seemed an odd time to be saying so. The Korean War was on, in which both countries were fighting side by side under the auspices of the United Nations, Canada and the United States were allies in NATO, and the Canadian economy was booming, thanks to an inflow of American investment.

Pearson was not denouncing any specific American policy, or targeting any particular American politician or diplomat. He was objecting to the Americans "taking Canada for granted," to use the expression of the day.[21] It was easy enough to do. Canada and the United States shared a liberal-capitalist, anti-communist ideology. The differences that existed were matters of degree: the United States had a better social security net than Canada's, but neither country needed it much, because of abounding prosperity and low unemployment.

Pearson's generation, it should be remembered, were Canada's first diplomats. Pearson himself had moved from the simple imperial patriotism of his youth, the sentiment that had taken him to Europe to fight for the Empire, to a conviction that in the final analysis, only Canadians would look out for Canada – a recognizable form of Canadian nationalism. Yet if Canadian sovereignty were to mean anything, it must be protected from serious external harm from hostile powers – through alliance with like-minded countries, especially the United States.[22]

But what was an alliance? Classically an alliance was not a surrogate country or a super-state like the British Empire, but an expedient, an embodiment of converging views and interests. By that definition, alliances were temporary; only national interests were eternal.[23] Pearson did want the former, but he was disquieted by the notion that an alliance would last only so long as it was also a convenience. For Pearson, the pay-off of alliance should be in the longer term, while in the immediate future it should at least allow for consultation and consensus, giving Canada a say in its fate as well as the much cherished "seat at the table," a consideration that was then and remains now a staple of Canadian discussion on foreign policy.[24] A seat at the table should, however, be more than a geographical description.

Pearson, as is well known, wanted more. Supported by his prime minister, Louis St. Laurent, and sustained by a disciplined Liberal majority in Parliament, Pearson had unusual political latitude as external affairs minister. Thanks to the careful management of a professional foreign service, his subordinates knew that they had their minister's support and confidence, making for high morale and high performance. Rearmament in the 1950s gave Canada a streamlined but effective armed force, which prosperity paid for. And there was the recent experience and fresh memory of Canada's contribution to the Second World War, meaning that if war came again, and took the same form as the previous conflict, Canada could be relied on for a significant contribution.

In Pearson's time, Canada had a seat at many tables: at the League of Nations in the 1920s and 1930s, on a number of inter-allied boards during the Second World War, and at the United Nations and its organs after 1945. Canada remained a member of the Commonwealth, as the Empire had been renamed. And beginning in 1949 there was the North Atlantic Treaty Organization, in which every member had a seat at a table, but in which one member, the United States, was more equal than others. Because the Americans were making by far the largest contribution to the alliance, this was natural. Yet in practice many professional Canadian observers at least found American leadership flawed. "The United States does not apprehend the nature of the alliance of which it is the principal member," a senior Canadian diplomat wrote. "The United States is often intolerant of any line of thought or action which does not coincide with its own." Worse, it was "at times unduly hasty in its diplomacy," producing "lack of confidence" in its "policy and leadership."[25]

These severe comments were not uttered in public, to be sure. They did little justice to the complexity of American politics, even American diplomatic politics, a point Dean Acheson tried to explain to his Canadian friends. They understood the explanation well enough: there were so many interests, and so many checks and balances in American politics, that coming up with any policy or conclusion was sometimes a notable feat; and the authors of such a feat did not wish to see their finely balanced product disturbed. But Canadian interests were not directly represented in the process, whether the subject was the use of atomic weapons, wheat subsidies, or quotas for Canadian oil and natural gas.

The economic issues were real, and for the most part intractable, because they impinged on important American economic interests. But economic interests are difficult to translate into operational political terms. Although it is arguable that the St. Laurent government suffered at the hands of enraged farmer-voters in 1957 for their inability to persuade the Americans to modify their wheat-subsidy program that undermined Canadian markets, but that was a matter of indifference to competing American farmers or their representatives in Congress. The difficulty of negotiating economic differences with the United States played a significant part in feeding Canadian economic nationalism in the 1960s and 1970s.[26]

So it was the political and strategic issues that lingered and obviously festered. What was most disturbing was that Pearson (and with him the Canadian government and its military staff) had no clear idea of American plans to use the atomic weapon. The atomic deterrent – the US Strategic Air Command or SAC – resided outside NATO, in the hands of the US military and a narrow circle of civilian overseers. Some of it was based on Canadian territory, thanks to wartime agreements between Great Britain and the United States over Newfoundland (not then part of Canada), and some of it moved up above, overflying Canadian territory on patrols, or on practice runs. Some of the bombs, at least, were made from Canadian uranium, a lucrative export to what was, through the 1950s, an insatiable American bomb-production complex. Meanwhile, developments in weaponry made it possible for NATO units, including Canadian, to use American tactical nuclear weapons. By land, sea and air Canada was a part of a western defence structure, ultimately under American command through NATO, or through the North American Air Defense Agreement (NORAD) of 1957. And SAC was guarded from Soviet attack by three radar fences arrayed across Canada's land mass.

Canada was, through the 1960s, fully integrated into the US defensive and deterrence systems, both in Europe and in North America. It certainly made for a high level of confidence between the two countries' militaries; but the confidence ebbed on the diplomatic side in Canada. The differing views would eventually explode under the Progressive Conservative government of John Diefenbaker, and the Liberals, by then under Pearson's leadership, harvested the political results, returning to power in 1963 over the "nuclear weapons" issue.

"Nukes" and atomic questions generally suggest that there were continuities between Canadian nationalism, Liberal-style, and the Progressive Conservative version of the same thing.[27] Consciously or not, Liberal and Progressive Conservative ministers often pursued the same policies on the same issues; thus, the Progressive Conservative interlude from 1957 to 1963 is less different from Liberal policy than is often believed. That was true in other issues too. Recall the 1951 description of American diplomacy as "unduly hasty." Hasty could also mean rash, unwise, even intemperate and short-sighted. It is of course true that the diplomacies of two sovereign countries must differ to some degree, the more so because of the disparity in power, wealth and population between the two. Canadians could sometimes go where Americans could not, either as a smaller and thus less threatening member of the western alliance, or as a disinterested party. In 1954, for example, Canada went to Indochina on trilateral truce supervisory commissions in both capacities.[28] Canada was appointed in the first place because it was a western ally and thus represented a western point of view; on the commissions India was neutral or non-aligned, while Poland, a communist country, balanced Canada. Pearson instructed Canada's representatives to be impartial and non-committal, in the hope that the commission's members could actually work together, and effectively. Given that the communist side had a military preponderance in Indochina, this was a sensible point. It was hardly in the western interest for the commissions to break down, since the alternative might well have been a communist conquest of Indochina, or a more general war involving the United States.

Pearson's strictures did not prevent the Canadians on the commissions from working with the Americans, as it turned out, but they did encourage a less committed and more cautious point of view. There were many American diplomats who preached caution as well, but the mix in US policy formulation was different, and it is not surprising that the same ingredients in different proportions produced a different result. For Canadians on the commissions, life consisted in submerging small differences with the Indians and the Poles; and life was not easy. The commissions survived because nobody wanted to take the responsibility of admitting that they were a failure, and that war, not peace, was at hand. The experience gave peacekeeping an air of unreality.

There were other, better known, adventures in peacekeeping. Many if not most were undertaken because western interests generally called for the maintenance of a series of temporary truces – in Sinai, the Congo, and Cyprus, again and again. The instrument, a peacekeeping force with Canada as a major contributor, survived the purposes that had called peacekeeping into being in the first place.

Coupled with Pearson's original, and originally sensible, desire for Canada to be diplomatically effective through objectivity and impartiality, peacekeeping eventually contributed to a certain distance between Canada and some of its allies, including the principal ally, the United States. Personal style, under Pierre Trudeau, seemed to increase the distance – though not always. To many Americans, and to traditional Canadians, Canada seemed to be drifting away from a real world into an idealized cosmos. They believed that Canada was drifting away from its roots – away from history into fantasy. Because to most (though not all) American observers American history is unique, special and providential, they did not detect the similarity of Canadian behaviour to their own, especially in the historical past.

CONCLUSION

The distinction between history and fantasy is a matter of opinion. Many subjects of historical study are indeed fantastical – harmless if recognized as such, dangerous if they tip the historian over into the recreation of a past that is better, more complete, and altogether more satisfactory than what really happened.

Dean Acheson, whose memories of Canada stretched back through his family to the mid-nineteenth century, definitely preferred an older, more robust and traditional Canada – the one that his father had fought for at the battle of Batoche in 1885, when Canada was subduing the distant frontier of Empire. Latter-day Canadians like Pearson he found too finicky, and gave expression to his feelings in a 1966 essay, "Stern Daughter of the Voice of God." He once quipped of the British, that they had lost an empire and not yet found a role, but he might have applied the same sentiment to Canada. It is possible that he would have added that the Canadians had found a role – to be the public scolds of the western alliance. And, of course, it was Acheson whom the Canadians of the 1950s had found "too hasty."[29]

Americans of the Acheson school found the Canadians too slow. This brings us back to the question of alliances. Large leaders are almost always impatient with small followers, especially small followers whom they cannot coerce, or cannot coerce without inconvenience or even harm to themselves. Such Americans are not without Canadian friends and admirers – Canadians who admire "haste" and see it as a cardinal virtue. Conservative leader Stephen Harper, in 2003, called on the Jean Chrétien government to snap to it, and accept the wise judgement of the American and British governments who were going to war in Iraq. He emphasized the security of the world, and "the collective interests of our historic allies," which made joining the invasion "manifestly in the national interest of this country."[30]

Some years later, another acerbic American commentator, Walter Russell Mead, described Canada as a member of an international "Party of Heaven," committed to broadening and thickening international institutions so as to create permanent peace. Diplomats from other countries – countries like France and Russia – might "roll their eyes" as Canadians lobbied them for "tougher global regulations against cruelty to animals" and other subjects dear to the Canadian heart.[31]

Mead is ordinarily a perceptive historian, whose elegant prose style recalls Acheson's own. Mead recalls Acheson in another sense. Like Acheson a Tory, of a kind very recognizable in Canada, either today or throughout Canadian history, he is a friend to power and an enemy to idealism. Mead has his reasons, by no means all bad.

But they are reasons that Canadians should examine carefully. Citizens of a country that is *not* powerful, with its own distinctive traditions deriving mostly though not unanimously from nineteenth-century liberalism, with its own set of compromising institutions, Canada does not bask in the light cast by Mead's imperial flame. Following the Empire, British or American, can be a rewarding experience, if the Empire is going in the right direction. It is important to ask, as Laurier did in the 1900s, as Mackenzie King did in the 1920s and 1930s, as Pearson did in the 1950s and 1960s. It is not an especially good idea to invoke the other, Tory tradition, and shout ready aye ready, as Arthur Meighen did in 1922, and Stephen Harper did in 2003.

NOTES

* I would like to thank my research assistant, Charlotte Freeman-Shaw, for her assistance and persistence in researching this paper.

1 It was not the first department to deal with foreign affairs, however. There was a Department of Militia and Defence, whose origins went back before Confederation, and a Department of Trade and Commerce, dealing, naturally, with trade. The latter department would eventually be merged with the external affairs department in the 1980s, and despite attempts to separate them, merged they remain.

2 David Potter, "Canada Views the United States as a Reflex of Canadian Values: A Commentary," in R.C. Brown and S.F. Wise, *Canada Views the United States* (Seattle: University of Washington Press, 1967), 121–30.

3 St. Laurent, Gray lecture, 13 January 1947. Originally delivered to an audience at the University of Toronto, the Gray lecture outlined the principles of an active Canadian foreign policy. In particular, it upheld the importance of national unity and recognized Canada's unique international status as neither a great power nor a developing nation.

4 On the Quebec Tercentenary, see H.V. Nelles, *The Art of Nation-Building: Pageantry and Spectacle at Quebec's Tercentenary* (Toronto: UTP, 1999). For an earlier orgy of representatively loyal pageantry, surrounding the visit of the Prince of Wales (later Edward VII) in 1860, see Ian Radforth, *Royal Spectacle* (Toronto: UTP, 2000). The visit of King George VI and his consort, Queen Elizabeth, in 1939, produced huge crowds and effusive displays of loyalty and affection. See also David Cannadine's lively and amusing analysis, *Ornamentalism: How the British Saw their Empire* (Oxford: OUP, 2001).

5 This is not a very old adage, and seems to derive from a misquotation of a phrase by the novelist L.P. Hartley. Nevertheless historians, amateur and professional, have adopted it with enthusiasm.

6 Again, see Cannadine's *Ornamentalism*, passim, in which pomp and ceremony create not unreality, but an alternate reality.

7 Max Beloff catches the idea in his book, *Imperial Sunset*, vol. 1, *Britain's Liberal Empire, 1897–1921* (London: Methuen, 1969).

8 Robert L. Kelley, *The Transatlantic Persuasion: The Liberal-Democratic Mind in the Age of Gladstone* (first edition, New York: Knopf, 1969; second edition, New York: Transaction Books, 1989), especially in the Introduction to the second edition, makes a strong case for "cosmopolitan values" as fundamentally shaping political (and consequently foreign-political) attitudes.

9 There was a profoundly pessimistic streak to turn-of-the-century British imperialism: on this point, see Bernard Potter's extended essay, *Empire and Superempire: Britain, America and the World* (New Haven: Yale UP, 2006), 31–2.

10 The English-Canadian figures are well known – Lester Pearson, Hume Wrong, Norman Robertson, and Escott Reid. On the French-Canadian side, slightly younger, there were Marcel Cadieux, Paul Tremblay and Jules Léger. For Cadieux's and Tremblay's views, see Marcel Cadieux and Paul Tremblay, "Notre fédéralisme est-il viable?" *Quartier Latin*, undated but 1941, enclosed in Marcel Cadieux to Allan Gotlieb, 8 January 1968, Library Archives Canada, Marcel Cadieux Papers, file 8–15.

11 There is a certain confusion on this point among British historians. Bernard Potter, *Empire and Superempire*, (New Haven: Yale University Press, 2006), repeats the canard, found originally in Robert Holland's *The Commonwealth Alliance*, (London: Macmillan, 1981), that the dominions and especially Canada discouraged Britain from war with Germany at the time of Munich in 1938. In fact, as two historians showed in 1975, and as the internet version of King's diary confirms, the Canadian government would have gone to war at Britain's side in 1938: Robert Bothwell and J.L. Granatstein, "'A Self-evident National Duty': Canadian Foreign Policy, 1935–1939," *Journal of Imperial and Commonwealth History*, III, 1975, 212–33.

12 The Mackenzie King diary documents King's fulminations on the subject. An edited version is available in J.W. Pickersgill and Donald Forster, eds., *The Mackenzie King Record*, vol. 4 (Toronto: UTP, 1970), 38–42.

13 Though Wilson is not commemorated, Warren G. Harding, his undistinguished Republican successor, does have a prominent memorial in Vancouver's Stanley Park.

14 On this point I think that Robert E. Hannigan, *The New World Power: American Foreign Policy, 1898–1917* (Philadelphia: University of Pennsylvania Press, 2002), though not without foundation, exaggerates American attitudes and American policy toward Canada.

15 Robert Kagan, *Dangerous Nation: America's Place in the World from its Earliest Days to the Dawn of the Twentieth Century* (New York: Knopf, 2006), 302.

16 There is an admirable summary of the relationship between the United States and the British Empire in Walter Russell Mead, *Special Providence: American Foreign Policy and How it Changed the World* (New York and London: Routledge, 2002), 82–3.

17 Quoted in Hannigan, *New World Power*, 144.

18 C.J. Pennington, "The Continentalist Movement in the Politics of Canada and the United States, 1887–1894," unpublished PhD thesis, University of Toronto, 2007, 235. As Pennington points out, even a few prominent politicians like the ex-premier of Quebec, Honoré Mercier, favoured not merely commercial union, but annexation: ibid., 262.
19 Roosevelt's letter to King on the subject of assimilation, dated 18 May 1942, is reproduced in full in Jean-François Lisée, *Dans l'oeil de l'aigle: Washington face au Québec* (Montréal: Boréal, 1990), 454–5.
20 Pearson's speech is summarized in John English, *The Life of Lester B. Pearson, vol. 2, The Worldly years, 1949–1972* (Toronto: Knopf Canada, 1992), 59.
21 Not every American took Canada for granted, or underestimated the complexities of the relationship. In 1957–58 the U.S. embassy in Ottawa encouraged an American journalist, Joseph Barber to travel across the country and to summarize his experiences for an American audience (and a Canadian one too): Joseph Barber, *Good Fences Make Good Neighbors* (Toronto: M&S, 1958). Some time later, one of the most distinguished American ambassadors to Canada, Livingston Merchant, edited a collection of essays, *Neighbors Taken for Granted: Canada and the United States* (New York: Praeger, 1966).
22 Geoffrey Pearson draws attention to Pearson's "anti-colonial instinct," honed by long years in London before and during the Second World War, and his determination not to repeat the experience in the new alliance with the United States: Geoffrey Pearson, *Seize the Day: Lester B. Pearson and Crisis Diplomacy* (Ottawa: Carleton University Press, 1993), 91.
23 Dean Acheson, the American secretary of state, argued that position.
24 There is a classic statement of the "seat at the table" case in J.L. Granatstein, *Who Killed the Canadian Military?* (Toronto: Harper, 2008), 210–11.
25 R.L. Rogers, memorandum of 30 March 1951, quoted in English, *Worldly Years*, 57–8.
26 In this period Canadian and American cabinet members met in regular annual sessions. After one of them Pearson was so disturbed that he helped sponsor his friend Walter Gordon to a royal commission that investigated "Canada's economic prospects," meaning, in Gordon's terms, how Canada could increase its sovereignty in the area of economics and investment.
27 From 1943 to 2003 the Progressive Conservatives had a different name and, arguably, a different identity than the preceding or subsequent "Conservative" parties.
28 The proper title was International Commissions for Supervision and Control – ICSCS. There were three commissions, one each for Vietnam, Laos and Cambodia.
29 Acheson was of course a very Canadian or British-Canadian type, of the Anglican variety. He was impatient with the miniaturized moral world of the Methodists, those fallen Anglicans. Acheson's father was an Anglican parson, even a bishop, while Pearson's was a Methodist. Acheson would, however, have been satisfied that Pearson was ultimately buried from an Anglican church.

Acheson did believe in the certainties of British imperialism, though when he met a proconsul up close, like General Douglas MacArthur, he was not entirely appreciative. Oversimplifying a bit, one could argue that Pearson was or had become a Gladstonian Liberal, while Acheson was a Disraelian Tory.

30 Canada, 37th Parliament, second session, 20 March 2003, Online Edited Hansard Number 74, 1130. In invoking Canada's "historic allies," Harper did not mention that they were closer than anyone might have imagined – indeed present in his oration. Large sections of his speech had been copied from one given by the Australian prime minister, John Howard, to the Australian parliament, two days earlier: Carly Weeks, "Liberals accuse Harper of plagiarism," *Globe and Mail* online, 30 September 2008, http://www.theglobeandmail.com/servlet/story/RTGAM.20080930.welexnplagiarism0930/BNStory/politics/home. Despite the rather tentative title of Weeks' piece, the identical quality of much of Harper's speech is quite clear.

31 Walter Russell Mead, *Power, Terror, Peace and War: America's Grand Strategy in a World at Risk* (New York: Knopf, 2004), 65. One is reminded of H.L. Mencken's phase about "the bilge of idealism flowing through the veins" of 1920s populists.

PART ONE
The Machine

2 "A Sad, General Decline?": The Canadian Diplomat in the 20th Century

GREG DONAGHY[1]

On the eve of the 1969 Commonwealth Heads of Government Meeting, Prime Minister Pierre Trudeau faced his advisors from the Department of External Affairs. Only a year or so in office, Trudeau questioned the value of the Commonwealth gatherings and the diplomatic advisors who cajoled him into attending. He surveyed the room and neatly skewered both with a single barb. "I'm depending on you guys and my hairdresser," he quipped, "to get me through this."[2]

Canada's diplomats, and the people who study them, were not amused, and they have since fingered Trudeau as the principal villain in their accounts of the country's foreign service. This once noble body, they argue, staffed by far-sighted giants, bestrode the global stage and shaped a new world order in the two golden decades after 1945. And doubtless, they insist, it would have continued apace had Trudeau not destroyed the foreign service with his constant and irreverent meddling. Demoralized and weakened, Canada's diplomats steadily faded, increasingly marginalized, pale reflections of their former selves. Looking backwards, as Andrew Cohen does in his best-selling polemic, *While Canada Slept*, the critics wring their hands, bemoaning the "sad, general decline."[3]

There are elements of this narrative of rise and fall that are grimly satisfying, though its vision of the distant past is far too rosy and its view of the present too dim. The foreign service that emerged in the 1920s was certainly talented, but its effectiveness and its professionalism, if by that is meant a clearly defined career path with an established set of professional standards, were constrained by bureaucratic and political considerations.

This only changed during the Second World War, when administrative improvements and political engagement forged a diplomatic corps that was relevant and certain of its professional standing. The strong *esprit de corps* and clear standards that marked this generation, long-reigning survivors of depression and war, meant that change, when it finally came in the 1970s, would be difficult. But a sad general decline? Hardly. Their successors, products of the 1950s and 1960s, confronted changes in the global order and Canadian society, redefined what it meant to be a Canadian diplomat, and gave their political masters the kind of representation abroad and advice at home that they demanded.

When the Department of External Affairs was established in June 1909, its first under-secretary, Joseph Pope, possibly foresaw a career foreign service for Canada. Certainly, as he explained to the 1907 royal commission on the civil service, the department should be staffed with "well educated and carefully selected" young men, who were trained "in the conduct of diplomatic correspondence."[4] But Tory to the core and lacking the autonomist aspirations that might threaten the unity of the British Empire, where young Canada nestled safely, Pope had only modest ambitions for his department and little immediate need for a foreign service. Under Pope, and the two Conservative prime ministers he served, Robert Borden and Arthur Meighen, the department functioned as a "post office" and archive. When Borden wanted policy advice, he turned not to Pope, but to Loring Christie, whom he installed in 1913 as the department's first legal advisor. A graduate of Harvard Law School, where he edited its law review, Christie, at 28, was already a senior official in the U.S. Department of Justice when the prime minister's call came.[5]

Meighen's successor had different objectives. Liberal Prime Minister William Lyon Mackenzie King, elected in 1921, was leery of imperial entanglements that might tear at Canada's national fabric. He was determined to seek greater freedom from London and sought an advisor to help. His eye fell on Oscar Douglas Skelton. A prominent political economist and dean of arts from Queen's University in Kingston, Skelton impressed the prime minister with a speech to the Canadian Club in January 1922 that outlined a strategy for obtaining greater dominion autonomy. Already in his mid-40s, shy but self-confident, Skelton was looking for a career change that would provide him with an opportunity to translate his ideas into policy. He welcomed the prime minister's invitation to attend the 1923 Imperial Conference, replaced Pope as under-secretary in 1925, and was King's main advisor at the 1926 Imperial Conference where Canada secured the right to establish real diplomatic missions.

Skelton's views on the foreign service he wanted for Canada's new missions were naturally influenced by his early ventures in policy making. The preparations for the 1923 Imperial Conference exposed him to the Department of External Affairs, where he found little of worth. Imperial diplomacy introduced him to the Foreign Office and London's bureaucracy; there he encountered an admirable "tradition of efficiency, culture & responsibility" which he hoped to emulate.[6]

He was also influenced by the young American consul in Ottawa, Jack Hickerson, whom he met regularly for lunch in 1925–26 to discuss how best to organize a foreign ministry. The brash Texan provided him with a bootleg copy of the U.S. foreign service regulations, revised to reflect recent American efforts to establish their own career service. Hickerson impressed on the Canadian the need for reasonable salaries and generous allowances if the service was to remain open to any but the very rich.[7] An ardent democrat, Skelton was easily convinced, at least in principle. "The state," he would later observe, "should foot its own bills," adding that "it should provide as much for a rich man as for a poor man."

Salaries and allowances in the new service fell between those paid by London and Washington, a happy compromise that suited the national character. Conscious of uncertain support among both government and opposition politicians for his "noble experiment," Skelton's approach to building his new foreign service was just as pragmatic and flexible. He accepted that appointments as heads of mission would remain, at least for the moment, the preserve of the rich and politically connected. "There is a need," he admitted when pressed, "for promoting men from the ranks ... if you are to have an effective, keen, and active service," but these should be offset by "men of political and business experience."[8] The under-secretary was prepared as well to appoint officers at a variety of levels without formal competition if required, a course he followed in staffing the legation in Washington and an expedient he retained and used "from time to time" throughout his tenure.[9]

Like most progressives of his generation, who attacked patronage in the name of "decency, civic-mindedness and efficiency," Skelton supported the merit principle, which he thought accounted for his own successful career.[10] He favoured recruitment by competitive examination and organized the first real foreign service competitions in 1927 and 1928. He knew what kind of men he wanted as candidates (the service was open only to men until 1947) and used his extensive contacts in Canadian universities to recruit them. His criteria were broad, and appropriately for a small department, favoured flexible generalists over specialists. There was no age limit for applicants, who were expected to have a degree in history, political economy or international law, and to possess "undoubted integrity; tact; astuteness; keen perception; good judgement; and good address."[11]

For a two-dollar fee, the qualified sat a four-part exam, stretched over several days. Set by the under-secretary himself, it included an essay question on imperial relations designed to solicit the autonomist views that Skelton favoured. There were additional papers on Canadian affairs and the candidate's own field of study, as well as a precis-writing exercise. Successful candidates who scored over 70 percent faced an interview board, which was often chaired by Skelton, sometimes followed by lunch with the under-secretary at the Rideau Club, or even an encounter with the prime minister.[12]

Between 1926 and 1941, when he died, Skelton recruited 43 foreign service officers, most by exam. The group, which included five future under-secretaries – Hume Wrong, L.B. Pearson, Norman Robertson, Jules Léger, and Marcel Cadieux – was undoubtedly well-qualified. Those appointed without competition, including Hume Wrong, Georges Vanier, and Escott Reid, were equally distinguished. Like Skelton himself, the group had strong academic credentials. Nine were Rhodes scholars, and most had pursued graduate studies abroad: 26 had studied in Britain, 19 at Oxford or Cambridge; 12 had studied in the U.S.; and nine in France. Twelve of the 43 were francophone, a respectable proportion for the period, when English was virtually the only language of business used in the federal public service.[13]

Like Skelton his recruits were inclined to be thoughtful and reflective, with perhaps a whiff of the distracted academic about them. This legacy lingered, and even those joining in the 1940s recalled the "university-like atmosphere of the Department. Work stopped for tea at four o'clock."[14] They were also broad-minded and tolerant. As the under-secretary told Hickerson in 1940, "[w]hen we take a young man into the foreign service ... I think we ought to look at, not just what he is at that time, but what his philosophy of government will be when he is 40 ... if a young man of 23 to 25 isn't a little, by U.S., Canadian and British standards, a little 'radical', he's no damn good."[15] Skelton, Carleton University historian Norman Hillmer argues, had created a foreign service largely "in his own image."[16]

The new service was an informal affair. Neither King nor Skelton knew precisely what they wanted from it nor how to deploy its resources most effectively. Skelton himself took a close and fatherly interest in the careers of his young charges, earning their deep affection. "He was one of the best," Escott Reid wrote in 1941, "wise and whimsical and kind ... He was also courteous, never hurried."[17] Yet he controlled the department too tightly. The prime minister and his under-secretary insisted that all department business pass through Skelton's hands and he delegated little authority to his staff. As a result, experienced and trusted officers were over-worked, while junior officers were often under-employed.

New recruits started out doubled-up in a "cramped" East Block attic office, where it was cold in the winter and "hot as hell" in the summer.[18] They spent their first months on the job sorting files and coding telegrams, routine work that often left them frustrated and unhappy. As Jack Pickersgill, a Rhodes scholar who joined External Affairs in 1937 but left for the greener pastures of the prime minister's office, recalled: "There wasn't all that [much] work ... When I went into External Affairs ... after I read the *New York Times* through in the morning and decoded a couple of telegrams ... I wondered what to do next. I gathered that there was a sort of ripening process that went on ... but you didn't ripen much if you never saw anybody."[19]

The young foreign service laboured under similarly restricted conditions outside the country. Though recruits were expected to serve abroad, it was unclear when (or even if) they would change, or rotate, assignments. Posted to Washington in 1927, Wrong lingered abroad, increasingly unhappy, until 1941, a common enough experience. The government's reluctance to open new posts in the 1930s for fiscal and political reasons limited opportunities for promotion. With the exception of the legation that opened in The Hague in 1938, the top positions remained political appointments. "I am sorry," a saddened Mike Pearson wrote in 1941, "that the PM found it necessary to send a 71-year old millionaire to Washington. That sort of thing is pretty discouraging for the Service."[20]

A lack of substantive work abroad was discouraging too. Beyond their obvious role as physical monuments to the country's growing independence, Canada's diplomatic posts enjoyed poorly-defined and uncertain mandates. Officers, even heads of mission, were often posted without formal instructions or briefings. When Hugh Keenleyside set out to open the Tokyo legation after just a year in the department, he received no guidelines beyond the under-secretary's parting admonition "to use my head and if any difficulties arose to send him a cable."[21] Without significant work, the minutiae of diplomatic life were dull fare. "Oh I am so bored," wailed Wrong from Washington in 1936. "If I can't get something better to do than the dreary routine of the Legation ... I'm going to explode ... About 95% of it I can do while thinking of something else & the rest is just dull – like international double taxation & similar monstrosities."[22]

Wrong could expect little relief from the ever-cautious Prime Minister Mackenzie King, who was determined to do nothing abroad that might provoke divisive domestic debate as war loomed in Europe and Asia. Posted to the increasingly somnolent League of Nations in 1937, Wrong regaled Pearson with a plan for "the perfect representative." Canada's delegate, he sneered, "will have a name, even a photograph, and a distinguished record, and an actual secretary – but he will have no corporal existence and no one will ever notice that he isn't there."[23]

The outbreak of the Second World War in September 1939 produced more work, but few other changes in the Department of External Affairs. These would have to wait until 1941 when Skelton's death opened the department to change under his successor, Norman Robertson. Like his mentor, Robertson was a ready source of policy advice, but a poor administrator. In contrast to Skelton, however, he was, at 37, still a young man, and open to change. Encouraged by Wrong and Keenleyside, the under-secretary re-organized the department, creating small units based on geographic and functional duties and introducing a chain of command that made delegation possible. This was made easier as the department's middle ranks were strengthened by the appointment (without competition) of special wartime assistants, drawn from business, journalism, and, mostly, the universities. With reorganization, junior officers were given more coherent assignments and established duties. Moreover, their work and progress were subject to continuing direction and guidance from more experienced officers.[24]

Following hard on these changes, the department began to consider in a systematic way how to train, develop, and promote its foreign service officers. A new personnel board, created in March 1941 to advise the under-secretary on recruitment and training, persuaded him to adopt a policy "of diversifying the work of junior members as much as possible" to expose them on the job to the range of issues they would confront.[25] But further progress was slow, not surprising in a department where some of its senior members doubted the underlying premise. "Diplomacy is not a science, but an art," Pearson liked to declare, "– you can't teach it."[26] Training remained the responsibility of the individual recruit, who was urged to learn on the job, and reminded of his duty to "constantly improve" his second official language, to learn a third language in his spare time, and to use his annual leave to discover Canada through travel.[27]

As External Affairs grew quickly at the end of the war, this basic model was refined in two important respects. First, two young officers, John Holmes and Gordon Robertson, developed a formal training program in late 1944. Dubbed the University of the East Block, it consisted of a dozen informal talks by departmental experts on the work of foreign service officers, supplemented by a series of policy seminars by senior officials from external affairs and other government agencies.[28] Second, the department appointed a full-time personnel officer in early 1947 to handle the recruitment, promotion, and "general well-being" of its foreign service officers.[29] A high-school headmaster by profession, Terry McDermott worried that the department expected too much from its recruits and insisted that it assume greater responsibility for training them. "Junior officers should be considered frankly as a liability," he observed, "and accepted by the head of division (or head of mission) as a charge on his time."[30]

Under McDermott, and his successor, Marcel Cadieux, the department developed a formal process for training its recruits "on the job." Ideally, "newbies" would spend 12–18 months in Ottawa, where they would rotate through a number of divisions for periods of three or four months, regularly attending sessions of the "University of the East Block." As they moved, their work and abilities would be assessed by their supervisors and the reports added quietly to their personnel file. Only if a problem emerged would officers ever learn how they fared. In addition, recruits were expected to spend short periods of time learning about filing and administration, passports and consular affairs, security and codes, and information work.[31]

The training program was admittedly imperfect. While some enjoyed the lectures and seminars, many complained that the talks "were so frequent and the topics so diverse, that the saturation point ... [was] reached early on."[32] On-the-job training also had its problems. "The lessons were often as varied as the mentors," one novice recorded later.[33] The department was aware of these shortcomings, and improvements were made, most notably in 1967, when a cross-Canada tour was introduced to expose recruits to life in all parts of the country. Yet internal reviewers, Archibald Day in 1962 and Jack Maybee in 1969, were unimpressed, and they harshly condemned the department's training program as an "unplanned series of stop-gap placements."[34]

For good reasons, the system survived. It represented a workable compromise between the demands of busy senior officials for new bodies to fill vacant positions and the needs of those young employees for some kind of training. It reflected as well a rough balance between those who thought diplomats could be trained and those who considered them bred in the bone. And despite its problems, the model worked. At a minimum, it gave most young foreign service officers a basic introduction to the techniques and skills they would need in order to succeed at their new careers. For many, like the young David Reece, who was apprenticed to the formidable Escott Reid, it gave much more. "[I]f he liked your flavour," Reece recalled, "you were given much rope and long rein. [Reid] taught me how to write political and economic reports. He cut my long wind and long sentences. He encouraged enthusiasm. He improved my social graces."[35] Just as important, the training program introduced the large stream of postwar recruits to – and socialized them into – the increasingly explicit professional standards expected of a Canadian diplomat.

Recruited in 1941 from his family's legal practice in Montreal, Marcel Cadieux was the member of his generation who most clearly articulated what it meant to be a Canadian diplomat. His views were not fully shared throughout the department and they were often honoured only in the breach. Nevertheless, his writings on Canadian diplomacy reflected the views and attitudes of the generation which joined External Affairs between the late 1920s and the late 1940s, and dominated the department until the early 1970s. Moreover, as head of personnel in the early 1950s, and then deputy under-secretary and under-secretary from 1960 to 1970, Cadieux was well placed to make his views count among the growing pool of new recruits.

Like Skelton and Robertson, whom he embraced as fatherly exemplars, Cadieux thought of the foreign service as "deeply democratic," an impulse reflected in its modest style at home and abroad, and in its commitment to the merit principle in recruitment and promotion.[36] New recruits were warned against becoming "high-hat" and urged to adopt Skelton's "way of communicating a sense of restraint about promoting one's own interest."[37] In Ottawa, the diplomat was simply another public servant, distinguished by his non-partisan character and a lofty disdain for politicians, whom Cadieux greatly distrusted. Foreign policy was too important to be left in their hands. When Mike Pearson joined King's cabinet in 1948, many young officers "considered it to be something between desertion and a display of bad taste."[38]

Abroad, however, the foreign service officer came into his own. A bright generalist to begin with, Cadieux's diplomat was further refined by the rotational nature of his calling. By the end of the war, movement between missions and headquarters had been regularized, with most assignments of a set duration. Rotating officers was seen as helpful in breaking down divisions between Ottawa and missions, and in sharing tough assignments in an equitable fashion. The constant movement had a professional benefit as well, enhancing an officer's flexibility and transforming him into "a specialist of quite another kind."[39]

Like the Canadian mission itself, these "specialists" had a variety of roles in a world where diplomacy was still mainly defined by its traditional 19th-century preoccupation with managing relations between sovereign states. Clearly, they represented Canada and its government to the government of the host state, a task requiring an intimate knowledge of their homeland, and its political, economic, and cultural institutions. The diplomat had a responsibility to protect and defend Canadian interests, including its commercial interests. The foreign service officer might occasionally be required to negotiate with a foreign government as well, though Cadieux thought that most serious issues would surely be handled directly by Ottawa. In Cadieux's view, the most important duty for the diplomat abroad was to provide his government with advice on Canadian foreign policy.

At the core of this policy advisory function was the diplomatic dispatch, where foreign service officers came to terms with and assessed events in their host country, and, ideally at least, made a contribution to the shaping of Canadian policy. For Cadieux and his contemporaries, the dispatch – "infinitely ... creative, complex, time-consuming, and subtle" – was "the synthesis of the combined knowledge of a mission and ... the beacon which guides and illuminates all its activities."[40] Its importance was accepted throughout the service, and it was readily acknowledged that "careers were made largely on the basis of the relevance, timeliness, and readability of your *reporting* on internal political and foreign policy questions."[41] The preparation of the dispatch mobilized a diplomat's academic training and his political judgment. Its intellectual demands meant that the diplomat must be freed from mundane operational and administrative chores, and be given the "necessary leisure to know and to understand a country."[42] Indeed, argued Cadieux, this detached and leisurely process of study and reflection gave the profession its inherent dignity.

Professional dignity was reinforced further by an ideal of public service that transformed the foreign service from a mere career into a lifelong vocation. Cadieux considered it "part of a priesthood," whose gothic East Block headquarters appropriately echoed "l'esprit de monastère."[43] Once abroad in a representative capacity and entrusted with the cares of the Canadian state, the Canadian diplomat's most important qualities were moral and spiritual. Honest and virtuous, he embraced the society around him, not mechanically, but moved by "l'esprit qui est fait de charité au sens chrétien du mot."[44] Cadieux recognized the professional and personal challenges associated with frequent movement between posts, but was unsympathetic. "[J]ustement, pour ceux qui ont la vocation," he wrote, "il n'y a pas de sacrifices."[45]

A number of factors made such demands possible in the 1950s and into the 1960s. The military training of so many of this group disposed them to accept the prevailing order. Products of depression and war, their expectations were modest and their fiscal values conservative. Moreover, the steady growth of the department from 26 posts in 1946 to 93 by 1967 promised rapid promotion for the diligent. Indeed, Cadieux argued that it was explicit in the "hiring contract that the officer will advance in rank, and that ultimately he will become minister or ambassador."[46] Even the mediocre, provided they kept out of trouble, could often be assured a final head of post assignment in some obscure corner of the world and the gratifying title of "Your Excellency." The department's small size helped too and provided a supportive working environment. Despite two decades of expansion, there were still only 705 officers in the foreign service by 1967. "This wasn't just a team," enthused British High Commissioner Malcolm MacDonald, "it was almost like a big family."[47]

Just as important, during the postwar era, domestic and international circumstances favoured Canada and its diplomats. The relative weakness of war-ravaged Europe and Asia allowed this small northern country, with its booming resource economy and a Cold War military that accounted for 8.8% of GNP in 1952–53, to play a role out of proportion to its size.[48] The global agenda was focused on peace and security, on decolonization, and on building an institutional framework for the postwar world. These were traditional, political questions on which bright, well-educated generalists might have something to say. They were also the broad questions that engaged the interest of a succession of prime ministers and ministers. Louis St. Laurent and Pearson, John Diefenbaker and Howard Green, and then again Pearson and Foreign Minister Paul Martin mobilized diplomats in pursuit of their objectives and made sure their views were taken into account. Those views were reinforced by a broad national consensus on foreign policy, which freed Canada's diplomats from critical oversight and public challenges to their policy prescriptions. Together, these conditions gave Canada's professional diplomats a strong sense of relevance, purpose, and meaning.

Change, however, was coming. Though the pressures had already been evident in the early 1960s, they seemed to erupt in an all-out assault on External Affairs and its diplomats soon after Trudeau's triumph in the 1968 federal election. Traditional diplomacy was suddenly old-fashioned and dated. For a growing number of younger observers, the cautious and aging "men of External," wrote journalist Charles Taylor, seemed "tame and uninspired."[49] Their failure to end the brutal wars in Vietnam and Biafra angered the young and their gurus. From his perch at the University of Toronto, Professor James Eayrs denounced diplomacy as "an immoral profession, full of hypocrisy."[50]

Diplomacy seemed incapable too of keeping up as the global agenda was transformed: women's rights and human rights, the environment and energy policy, all competed for attention. Domestic departments and provincial governments sprouted international offices, sending waves of officials and ministers abroad. Business and non-government organizations (NGOs) followed. The "new diplomacy" challenged the diplomat's monopoly over international interaction. Faster communications – cheap phones and low-cost jet travel – encouraged many to question the diplomat's relevance. Trudeau did. "I think the whole concept of diplomacy today ... is a little outmoded," he told an interviewer in January 1969. "I believe much of it goes back to the early days of the telegraph, when you needed a dispatch to know what was happening in country A, whereas now you can read it in a good newspaper."[51]

Trudeau's questions went deeper. He knew that postwar reconstruction in Europe and Asia had restored the global balance of power, and not in Canada's favour. He questioned the country's attachment to the broad internationalism of the postwar decades and to a diplomacy that was defined by a network of US-led military alliances. He wanted a more modest foreign policy, rooted in a narrower, often economic, definition of Canada's national interest. The prime minister wondered about the foreign policy-making process, from which he had been excluded as a cabinet minister under Pearson. He opened up the process, exposing international policy to closer oversight by other departments, the central agencies, and cabinet. He sought to rationalize it as well. He invited departments with overseas responsibilities, mainly trade and commerce, immigration, finance, and the Canadian International Development Agency (CIDA) to join External Affairs on an Interdepartmental Committee on External Relations (ICER). An incomplete experiment that left External Affairs responsible for much overseas administration (but not programs) and gave other departments an increased voice in senior diplomatic appointments, ICER would change both the duties of Canadian diplomats, and increasingly, their make-up. To help keep track of these changes, Trudeau appointed Ivan Head, a member of his staff, as his foreign policy advisor, a "Mini-Kissinger" in direct competition with the country's professional diplomats.

Understandably, Cadieux and most of his contemporaries reacted with dismay to these developments. Over the next few years, however, they departed and their influence waned. Cadieux was posted in 1970 to Washington, where a stream of visiting cabinet ministers came to try their hand at the "new diplomacy." As they regularly by-passed the embassy, Cadieux fumed: "I don't run an embassy here. I run a *pissoir* and a hot dog stand, and no one comes near me unless they want to use one or the other."[52] In Ottawa, Ed Ritchie, and then Basil Robinson, took over the department. Drawn from Cadieux's cohort, they were more open to and tolerant of change, though neither under-secretary was inclined to create the kind of department staffed with the sort of diplomat that the prime minister wanted. That was left to Allan Gotlieb, who was appointed under-secretary in May 1977. Eleven years younger than Robinson, Gotlieb signalled the coming to prominence of a new generation.

Recruited between the early 1950s and the early 1970s, they met the criteria for the Canadian diplomat set out by the earlier generation and they resembled it closely. New recruits continued to sit a foreign service exam, which retained its reputation for being tough and exacting. It did so even when the public service commission forced the department in 1967 to replace its essay question format with an "objective" multiple-choice test on Canadian and international affairs. Those who passed faced the familiar interview, which weighed their academic credentials, assessed their personal suitability, and weeded out the unsuitable.

That was the theory and it largely worked. The department continued to recruit more than its share of bright, well-educated candidates. Just over half the new officers recruited between 1951 and 1957, 51%, had graduate degrees; in the group recruited between 1958 and 1964, when a strong economy provided an attractive alternative, the figure remained a respectable 36%. Most anglophones with graduate degrees who joined between 1951 and 1964 were still educated in England, and a third of that number attended Oxford. Their francophone counterparts headed to Europe as well, and were divided almost equally between the University of Paris and Oxford.[53]

Flexible generalists continued to dominate among the recruits. Of those responding to a 1972–73 survey, almost 60 percent of those hired between 1950 and 1969 claimed to be educated in either the general arts, history, political science, or languages. Almost another 17 percent were trained in law. These responses were virtually identical to those supplied by officers who joined before 1950.[54]

There were other similarities. Francophones remained under-represented. A 1965 survey indicated that only 21% of foreign service officers who joined the department between 1949 and 1965 were francophone, well below the 28 percent of francophones in the general population.[55] This was changing – francophones made up almost 28% of those recruited between 1962–68 – but not enough to alter the character of the department until well into the 1970s. Women, though they were finally permitted to join the foreign service in 1947, remained a very small group. In 1962, for instance, only 16 out of 444 officers were women, and they were expected to leave the service if they married, a rule that remained in place until the early 1970s. This was changing, but slowly; by the mid-1970s, only 8% of foreign service officers were women.[56] For the most part, the generation that arrived in the mid-1970s to dominate the department for the next twenty years, shared a demographic profile with the generation that hired them. They were well-educated, white men, drawn mostly from mainstream English Canada.

There were important differences. Gotlieb, and the officers who followed him into the department's senior ranks in the mid-1970s, were the products of a different era and it showed. Raised in the united, prosperous, and confident Canada of the postwar years, they welcomed Trudeau's desire for a better defined foreign policy, one explicitly rooted in the national interest. Despite the economic upheavals of the 1970s and 1980s, separatism and constitutional deadlock, energy crises and deficits, they were optimists to the core, sure of Canada's capacity to take on the world and win. Many were sceptical of the postwar "golden age," and suspected St. Laurent and Pearson of not exploiting its opportunities to the fullest. That would not happen on their watch. The G-7, which Canada joined in 1976, as Derek Burney later recalled, gave "us a relevancy and recognition globally on a level we did not receive at the end of World War Two."[57] They planned to make the most of it.

Not surprisingly, this generation was sometimes impatient with the department they encountered in the 1950s and 1960s. The "regal ambassadors," who populated Canadian embassies during their apprenticeship and "put on airs about their erudition and genteel tastes" were dismissed as "ridiculous and offensive."[58] Young diplomats resented being forced to draft and re-draft reports and telegrams, and exploded with irritation at being shown the proper use of the paper-clip. For Paul Heinbecker, who joined the tail-end of this cohort in 1965, this was "a made-in-Canada generation, tough-minded, self-confident and savvy, even a little ruthless, neither to the manor nor to the manse born, contemptuous of the fake Oxford accents and Ivy League preciousness that many predecessors had cultivated."[59]

The new generation embraced the possibilities for job mobility that Trudeau introduced into the bureaucracy. Many of the group were deeply shocked when the government's 1969 austerity measures included cuts to the foreign service; diplomatic life was not a religious vocation, it turned out, but simply another career. Faced with the stark reality that the number of attractive posts abroad had remained more or less static since the late 1940s, while the foreign service had tripled in size, many were prepared to try their luck elsewhere, in domestic departments and the increasingly powerful central agencies. Trudeau, who considered the department top-heavy with talent, was happy to oblige, moving many to senior positions elsewhere in Ottawa. Indeed, Gotlieb himself left external affairs in 1968 to serve as deputy minister in the new department of communications, a departure that strained relations with his mentor, Marcel Cadieux. For many, a successful foreign service career now included stints with a domestic department or agency or even a foreign NGO.

This group came to see its diplomatic responsibilities in terms very different than those of Cadieux's generation. While they continued to represent Canada abroad, they did so in different ways and often in different fora. Many recognized a core truth in the prime minister's barb about the usefulness of diplomatic dispatches that echoed their own experience. "Reporting on political and economic change was so ephemeral," recalled future ambassador Earl Drake about his early days in the department. "The analytical pieces which one thought so brilliant just disappeared, without a trace, into the great maw of External Affairs."[60]

By the mid-1970s, the dispatch had been replaced by shorter reporting telegrams, rushed and inelegant things, crammed with oddly-contracted words and mystifying abbreviations. These too passed away, unread and unmourned by the mid-1980s, as harried diplomats relied more on personal encounters with headquarters and the oral brief. Amassing frequent-flyers points, the Canadian diplomat returned to Ottawa more frequently than ever to join the policy-making fray. Gotlieb recognized this reality and created a committee of senior heads of missions in 1980, who met regularly to advise him on policy. The oral brief, and the ability to deliver it succinctly and convincingly, were increasingly important skills in the diplomat's toolkit. "I earned my salary on the way in from the airport," recalled Bob Fowler, Canada's ambassador to the UN in the late 1990s. Drawing on a network that would be familiar to his predecessors in the 1950s, Fowler offered visitors from Ottawa a lift into town and a concentrated "20 minute brief."[61]

There was another important difference. They accepted the new emphasis on management and its implications for the diplomat. They were often scornful of the excesses of contemporary management theory and they hooted with derision when the clerk of the privy council assured them that "if they got the process right, the policy would be right." However, they understood the importance of reconciling resources with programs and making sure they were related to the government's priorities. "I don't think that we could any longer have heads of mission who spent their time cultivating VIPs, greeting visitors, and writing 'think pieces,'" recalled one of this generation, "while leaving the operation of the embassy to an administrative officer." To the disgust of romantics, "management skills" were to become one of the signal characteristics of the contemporary Canadian diplomat.[62] "[T]he buck stops at the head of mission's desk when it comes to financial responsibility and accountability," declared ambassador Dilys Buckley-Jones, emphasizing the shift in the diplomat's priorities.[63]

Unlike Cadieux's foreign service, this new generation embraced the more concrete and economic-centered diplomacy that emerged under Trudeau. They did so for a variety of reasons. By the 1970s, the institutional framework of the postwar world had long been completed, leaving behind long-term and increasingly intractable problems. Promoting trade or managing aid, as many of their recollections make clear, was a "tangible and satisfying" alternative, whose value both the government and Canadians could readily understand. Selling Canadian exports,

Burney writes of his ambassadorial experiences in Korea during the late 1970s, meant that "[w]e were relevant and we could help and that made our task meaningful as well as satisfying."[64]

The willingness shown by some diplomats to embrace trade promotion was given bureaucratic sanction in January 1982 when Trudeau merged the trade commissioner service and the government's trade policy functions into External Affairs. The new department, eventually named the Department of Foreign Affairs and International Trade, brought trade to the core of Canada's foreign policy. Foreign service officers were aghast as trade commissioners in their "white belts and white shoes" moved into the department. Trade commissioners in turn grumbled at sharing their space with the "fancy pants" from External. Still, the two groups – diplomats and traders – found enough common ground to begin realigning Canada's foreign and trade policy in the 1980s.

With Burney at their head, they seized trade policy and backed freer trade with the U.S. as the centerpiece in a renewed diplomatic strategy toward Washington. It was the start of a "revolution" in Canadian external trade policy that stretched from CUSFTA to NAFTA to the WTO. As the Cold War faded late in the 1980s and globalization picked up speed, Canadian diplomats embraced their new duties. Paul Heinbecker, who served as ambassador to Germany from 1992 to 1996, was clear on why he was there. "My number one priority," he recalled, "was investment advocacy ... retail work, best pursued one company at a time."[65] The ambassador, echoed Anthony Eyton, who served as Canada's representative in Brazil and Bermuda in the late 1980s, was now the "senior trade commissioner" at posts.[66]

Gotlieb's generation not only embraced trade and economic issues as the proper objects of their diplomacy, but they pursued new forms of diplomatic activity to address them. The eclipse of the sovereign state and its foreign ministry as the sole source of international activity in the 1970s forced Canadian diplomats to move into the public realm. Though clearly not applicable everywhere, public diplomacy became a vital skill for the Canadian diplomat in Europe, and especially, in the United States. The major efforts by Canada's mission in Europe to defend the seal hunt in the 1980s and to challenge European environmentalists outraged by Canadian clear-cutting in the 1990s forced diplomats onto unfamiliar territory.

In Washington, where the imperial presidency collapsed after Watergate and policy making shifted to an insurgent Congress, the change was dramatic and illustrated in the fight to control cross-border acid rain. With Congressional interests blocking progress with the U.S. administration, the embassy was forced to develop a public strategy to rally popular support in the United States to Canada's cause. "The new diplomacy," wrote Allan Gotlieb, who served as ambassador in Washington from 1981 to 1989, was "public diplomacy and requires different skills, techniques, and attitudes than those found in traditional diplomacy."[67]

These were skills that this generation proved quick to incorporate into their diplomacy. Liberal Lloyd Axworthy happily exploited them when he became foreign minister in 1996. Under Axworthy, the foreign service successfully played an important role in a series of public diplomatic initiatives that mobilized states as well as NGOs and other nontraditional actors in support of an ambitious human security agenda, which included: the landmines treaty, the International Criminal Court, and initiatives to limit the spread of small arms, curb the use of child soldiers, and restrict the sale of "conflict diamonds."[68]

CONCLUSION

Most of the senior diplomats who backstopped Axworthy, recruits of the confident Canada of the 1960s and early 1970s, have now departed. Rising to replace them and to define the Canadian diplomat for the 21st century, is a generation largely hired and trained in the 1970s and 1980s. Nurtured on a steady diet of separatist threats, recessions and deficits, rapid technological change and globalization, its middle-aged members are a world-weary, suspicious, and sceptical crew. Battered and bruised, they survived no less than 15 rounds of budget cuts between 1984 and 1993, before they finally lost count. They watched – amazed and bewildered – as capital and information moved with breathtaking speed throughout the globalized world. Here, it seemed, there was less of a role for government, and they were content to embrace the notion of "smaller and perhaps less ambitious public sectors."[69] They were less ambitious too in advancing Canada's claim to global status. Indeed, as they (and most Canadians) would soon learn, the new world order did not belong to Canada, notwithstanding its membership in the G-7 or the G-8 or the G-20. Under governments both Liberal and Conservative, the country's diplomats were urged to come to terms with a "harsher and more complex and competitive environment"[70] and "evermore unforgiving competitive forces."[71]

Precisely how this generation will shape and redefine the nature and functions of the Canadian diplomat in the coming decades is still unclear. As befits a group that has matured professionally under difficult circumstances, its efforts to re-imagine the diplomatic role have been cautious and incremental. Building on Trudeau's earlier reforms, it has embraced service delivery, especially consular and business activities, as central to the diplomatic function. "Serving Canadians," as their department's slogan has it, is at once politically popular and demonstrably useful. Recent decisions to move staff and resources from headquarters to the "platform abroad," seen once again as the place where the Canadian diplomat makes his or her distinct contribution, may well reinforce this orientation. And over time, perhaps, this change in focus will encourage another generation of Canadian diplomats to re-think what it means to be a professional. But this is hardly a surprise or a cause for alarm. For almost a century, led by men like Skelton, Cadieux, or Gotlieb, Canada's diplomats have constantly reinvented themselves, giving their political masters the service they wanted and the advice they needed.

NOTES

1 The author would like to thank Norman Hillmer, Mary Halloran, Mark Eaton, Daryl Copeland, and Adam Chapnick for their help with this article. The views expressed are the author's alone and do not represent the views of Foreign Affairs and International Trade Canada or the Government of Canada.
2 Cited in Allan McGill, *My Life As I Remember It* (Vancouver: Granville Island Publishing, 2004), 244.
3 Andrew Cohen, *While Canada Slept: How We Lost Our Place in the World* (Toronto: McClelland and Stewart, 2003), 23.
4 Cited in R. Barry Farrell, *The Making of Canadian Foreign Policy* (Scarborough, ON: 1969), 36–7.
5 Robert Bothwell, *Loring Christie: The Failure of Bureaucratic Imperialism* (New York: Garland Publishing, 1988).
6 Cited by Norman Hillmer in the draft manuscript of his biography of O.D. Skelton.
7 Ruth Smith interview with Jack D. Hickerson, 17 February 1971, and Don Page interview with Jack D. Hickerson, 27 September 1979, Historical Section, Department of Foreign Affairs and International Trade [DFAIT].
8 Canada, House of Commons, *Minutes of Proceedings and Evidence, Select Standing Committee on Industrial and International Relations*, 20 and 25 March 1930.
9 O.D. Skelton to Hume Wrong, 10 November 1938, RG 25, Vol 2961, File 56, Library and Archives Canada [LAC].
10 Cited in John Hilliker, *Canada's Department of External Affairs, Volume 1: The Early Years* (Montreal & Kingston: McGill-Queen's University Press, 1990), 118.
11 J.L. Granatstein, *A Man of Influence: Norman A. Robertson and Canadian Statecraft, 1929–1968* (Ottawa, Deneau, 1981), 25.
12 See, for example, Hugh Keenleyside, *Hammer the Golden Day: The Memoirs of Hugh L. Keenleyside* (Toronto: McClelland and Stewart, 1981), 217; Norman Hillmer, "O.D. Skelton: Called and Chosen," *Dialogue*.

13 Hilliker, *The Early Years*, 237.
14 John Hilliker interview with Freeman Tovell, 4 March 1980, Historical Section, DFAIT.
15 Smith interview with Hickerson, 17 February 1971, Historical Section, DFAIT.
16 Norman Hillmer, "O.D. Skelton: The Scholar Who Set a Future Pattern," *International Perspectives* (September-October 1973): 46–9.
17 Escott Reid, *Radical Mandarin: The Memoirs of Escott Reid* (Toronto, University of Toronto Press, 1889), 144.
18 Ruth Smith interview with Fred Soward, 14 September 1971, Historical Section, DFAIT; see also Hugh Keenleyside, *Hammer the Golden Day: The Memoirs of Hugh L. Keenleyside* (Toronto: McClelland and Stewart, 1981), Vol 1, 217.
19 Cited in Hilliker, *The Early Years*, 194.
20 L.B. Pearson to Norman Robertson, 4 March 1941, Pearson Papers, Volume 17, LAC.
21 Keenleyside, *Hammer the Golden Day*, 263.
22 Hume Wrong to Pearson, 15 July 1936, Pearson Papers, Vol 17, LAC.
23 Wrong to Pearson, 7 November 1937, Pearson Papers, Vol 17, LAC.
24 Hilliker, *The Early Years*, 241–4.
25 Hugh Keenleyside, Memorandum for the Members of the External Service, 7 March 1941, and Memorandum to Chris Eberts, 22 May 1941, RG 25, Vol 2814, File 1086–40, LAC.
26 Pearson, "The Nature of Canada's External Relations," [1931–32], Pearson Papers, Volume 31, File: Organization, 1929–41, LAC.
27 "Draft Instructions and information for Junior Members of the Staff," [1941], RG 25, Vol 686, File 158-D, LAC.
28 John Holmes, Memorandum for R.G. Robertson, 30 November 1944, and Robertson to Leighton McCarthy, 21 December 1944, RG 25, Vol 2814, File 1086–40, LAC.
29 Under-Secretary of State for External Affairs to Heads of Mission, 9 January 1947, RG 25, Vol 3559, File 1086–40, LAC.
30 Terry MacDermot to Heads of Divisions, 18 August 1948, RG 25, Vol 687, File 158-J, LAC.
31 Terry McDermott, "Training of New Officers in the Department of External Affairs," 14 May 1947, RG 25, Vol 687, File 158-J, LAC. See also, Marcel Cadieux, *Le Ministere des Affaires Exterieures: Conseils aux étudient qui se destinent a la carrière* (1948), 34–36.
32 J.D. Turner to Personal Division, 7 September 1962, RG 25, Vol 2489, File 158-J-40, LAC.
33 Derek Burney, *Getting it Done: A Memoir* (Toronto: University of Toronto Press, 2004), 13.
34 John Hilliker and Donald Barry, *Canada's Department of External Affairs, Vol 2, Coming of Age* (Montreal and Kingston: McGill Queen's University Press,

1995), 188, and "Summary Record of a Meeting of the Sr. Committee," 29 July 1970, RG 25, Vol 10233, File 12-4-4-, LAC.
35 David Reece, *A Rich Broth: Memoirs of a Canadian Diplomat*, (Ottawa: Carleton University Press, 1993), 36–7.
36 Marcel Cadieux, *The Canadian Diplomat: An Essay in Definition*, (Toronto: University of Toronto Press, 1963), 111.
37 T.W.L. MacDermot, University of the East Block Lecture, 25 June 1947, RG 25, Vol 3812, File 8484–40, LAC.
38 Arthur Andrew, *The Rise and Fall of a Middle Power* (Toronto: James Lormier and Co., 1993), 45.
39 Cadieux, *Canadian Diplomat*, 106.
40 *Ibid*, 47–8.
41 Earl Drake, *A Stubble-Jumper in Striped Pants: Memoirs of a Prairie Diplomat* (Toronto: University of Toronto Press, 1999), 35.
42 Cadieux, *Canadian Diplomat*, 33.
43 Cadieux, *Le Ministère des Affaires extérieures*, 33.
44 *Ibid*, 61.
45 *Ibid*, 96. Above all, insisted Cadieux, "[l]e soldat obéit ... Il abandonne sa famille, ses amis, sa patrie pour aller où le devoir l'appelle." (p. 82).
46 Cadieux, *Canadian Diplomat*, p. 89, 92.
47 Ruth Smith, Interview with Malcolm MacDonald, 3 August 1970, Historical Section, DFAIT.
48 Figure cited in David J. Bercuson, "Canada, NATO and Rearmament, 1950–1954: (Why Canada Made a Difference (But Not for Very Long)," in John English and Norman Hillmer (eds.), *Making a Difference? Canada's Foreign Policy in a Changing World Order* (Toronto: Lester Publishing, 1992), 104.
49 Cited in Hilliker and Barry, *Canada's Department of External Affaires*, 404.
50 Cited in Walter Stewart, "Should We Haul Down the Flag in Addis Ababa?," *Maclean's Magazine*, December 1969, 42.
51 *Ibid*, 35.
52 Andrew, *Rise and Fall*, 122.
53 Gilles Lalonde, *The Department of External Affairs and Biculturalism* (Ottawa: Queen's Printer, 1969), 80–6.
54 T.A. Keenleyside, "The generalist versus the specialist: the Department of External Affairs," *Canadian Public Administration* 22 (Spring 1979), 57.
55 Gilles Lalonde, 28–29. The overall percentage of francophones moved to 24.8% by the 1970s. T.A. Keenleyside, "Career attitudes of Canadian foreign service officers," *Canadian Public Administration*, 19, No 2 (Summer 1976), 211.
56 Canada, Department of External Affairs, *Annual Report on Equal Opportunities for Women* (Ottawa: Department of External Affairs, mimeo), 4.
57 Burney, *Memoirs*, 186.
58 Drake, *Stubble-Jumper*, 39, and Confidential Interviews.

59 Paul Heinbecker, "Burney's prescription is not a good fit for today's Washington," *Diplomat and International Canada Magazine* (May-June 2005).
60 Drake, *Stubble-Jumper*, 93.
61 Author interview with Bob Fowler, 20 May 2008.
62 Paul Heinbecker, "Fish, Forests, Furs and Canada's Fortunes in Bonn," in Robert Wolfe (ed.), *Diplomatic Missions: The Ambassador in Canadian Foreign Policy* (Kingston, Ont.: School of Policy Studies, Queen's University, 1998), 77.
63 Michelle Brisson, Interview with Dilys Buckley-Jones, Historical Section, DFAIT.
64 Drake, *Stubble-Jumper*, 39; Burney, *Memoirs*, 46.
65 Heinbecker, "Fish, Forests, Furs and Canada's Fortunes in Bonn," 73.
66 Antony Eyton, "The Ambassador as Senior Trade Commissioner," in *ibid*, 135.
67 Allan Gotlieb, *I'll be with you in a minute, Mr. Ambassador: The Education of a Canadian Diplomat in Washington* (Toronto: University of Toronto Press, 1991), vii.
68 Greg Donaghy, "All God's Children: Lloyd Axworthy, Human Security and Canadian Foreign Policy," *Canadian Foreign Policy* 10, no. 2 (Winter 2003): 39–58.
69 Under-Secretary of State for External Affairs to General Distribution, BML-0344, 25 June 1993, and attachment, Reid Morden, "The Foreign Service of the Future," DFAIT Library, Vertical File: Department of External Affairs.
70 V. Peter Harder, "Building a 21st Century Foreign Ministry," 18 January 2005, DFAIT Library, Vertical File: Department of External Affairs.
71 "DFAIT 2020: Serving Canadians, Engaging the World," 9 November 2007.

3 Managers, Innovators and Diplomats: Canada's Foreign Ministers

GERALD WRIGHT

Allan MacEachen, who was foreign minister twice, thought it was the best job a minister could have. Ambitious politicians, even those who have cut their teeth on domestic issues, would say the same. The foreign minister has traditionally stood apart from others in cabinet, enjoying the esteem that comes from representing Canada in international councils. No wonder that foreign ministers exude euphoria when they are sworn in.

Has their enthusiasm at the beginning been matched by their accomplishments in office? This is hard to answer because ministers are judged according to many different standards. The verdict of officials in Foreign Affairs and International Trade Canada will depend on whether the minister is pushing their agenda. Lloyd Axworthy was looked on admiringly by those working on human security and tepidly by those working in policy areas he ignored. Members of the parliamentary caucus will measure a minister's statements and actions against their bedrock opinions. Is Canada positioning itself too close to or too far from the United States? What will be the effect on our allies? Interest groups will want to see if the minister delivers, for example, export permits for military goods or statements on the Middle East that hew to the correct path. As for a wider group of foreign policy watchers, it may come down to whether the individual handling Canada's foreign relations projects a reassuring gravitas.

Ministerial reputations are a crude amalgam of some or all of these, mostly parochial, judgements. Disputing them can generate a lot of heat but not much insight. A more constructive discussion of ministerial performance can be had by breaking the job down into three broad, sometimes overlapping, roles:

Manager. Every day the foreign minister confronts a plethora of issues ranging from high politics to the plight of a Canadian incarcerated in a foreign jail. Managing these issues means ensuring that desired goals are pursued without needlessly irritating other countries or jeopardizing other interests, that policy is coherent and balanced and consistent with domestic interests, that the image and reputation of the country are safeguarded, that alliances are in good repair, and that foreign policy commands the support of a strong domestic constituency.

Innovator. The foreign minister is held responsible for foreign policy. Whatever the actual capabilities of the office, we think of an effective foreign minister as one who sets new directions, mobilizes governmental resources to tackle emerging issues and imparts impetus to the bureaucracy and the foreign policy community at large. If these things don't happen we are tempted to conclude that the minister has fallen down on the job.

Diplomat. The minister is the point of contact with other foreign ministers and is empowered to "conduct all diplomatic and consular relations on behalf of Canada."[1] Important negotiations can be pushed up to the ministerial level and ministers represent Canada in bilateral and multilateral meetings. Furthermore, a negotiator, unless the mandate is extraordinarily restricted, can gain a measure of autonomy, making on-the-spot decisions to which the government finds itself committed.[2]

In Canada's history there have technically been twenty-nine foreign ministers, including David Emerson, the present (July, 2008) incumbent. The list includes two secretaries of state, Charles Murphy, an Ontario lawyer in the Laurier government, and William James Roche, a Manitoba medical doctor in the first year of the Borden government. They were assigned superintendence of the Department of External Affairs by the 1909 Act that set it up.[3] The Office of Secretary of State for External Affairs was created by statute in 1912 and assigned to the prime minister. Sir Robert Borden, Arthur Meighen, William Lyon Mackenzie King and R.B. Bennett all held the office along with their prime ministerial duties. The department began providing foreign policy advice to its minister under Borden, a practice which continued under Meighen. A major stride forward was taken under King with the establishment of a professional foreign service, a development that Bennett fortunately endorsed. Meanwhile, Canada was beginning to exercise its full autonomy in international affairs and, fittingly, an independent portfolio was established by legislation in 1946.

COLD WAR MINISTERS

Louis St. Laurent served as secretary of state for External Affairs from 1946 to 1948. He set a course for Canada's postwar foreign policy, an accomplishment that looms larger if it is realized that the course was hardly foreordained. He rejected the notion that because Canada could not frame the international agenda it was better to stand aside. With the cooperation of his under-secretary, Lester Pearson, he tactfully pushed back against Prime Minister Mackenzie King's inclination to shrink from commitments to allies. He prevailed over King on the issue of Canadian membership of the United Nations (UN) Temporary Commission to supervise elections in Korea. He showed firmness towards the Soviet Union and lent his weight to the idea of a defensive alliance that was enshrined in the North Atlantic Treaty. Signifying an ambitious reach, he agreed that Canada should run for a seat on the UN Security Council.

St. Laurent had presence. None of his successors has equaled him in that regard. Combined with his mental abilities, it made him an effective actor in cabinet and on political platforms. He quickly established a relationship of loyalty and respect with his subordinates in the department. This would continue when he became prime minister. He was particularly sensitive to the relationship between foreign policy and national unity. The fact that a francophone held the External Affairs portfolio mattered in the battle to keep Québec from adopting an insular mentality – a mentality incarnated in Québec's belligerently nationalist premier, and St. Laurent's deadly rival, Maurice Duplessis. He spoke to Quebecers on foreign policy and, unlike Mackenzie King, he took steps to develop public support. His 1947 Gray Lecture set out the principles underlying Canadian policy in a way that lent lasting impetus and direction to Canada's engagement in the world. (John Manley, in fact, invoked the Gray Lecture in remarks to his assembled officials when he became foreign minister in 2000.)

When St. Laurent replaced King, the new minister, Lester Pearson, continued to play the central role he was already playing, defining Canada's role in the postwar world. Yet it is Pearson's diplomacy that stands out, informed as it was by a pragmatic approach to the resolution of disputes, an appreciation of the complex motives underlying state behaviour, and a willingness to try to understand the other side. He broke new ground with visits to Asia and the Soviet Union. As far as Canadian interests were concerned, he kept relations with Democratic and Republican administrations in Washington in good repair. He deserves some credit for getting the Americans enmeshed in international institutions and commitments. He tried but failed to convince them that UN forces fighting in Korea should be stopped at the thirty-eighth parallel. His Nobel Prize-winning achievement, a resolution of the 1956 Suez Crisis through the UN, can be ascribed to relentless diplomacy.

There are startling contrasts between Pearson's tenure, the longest of any foreign minister (1948–1957), and those of his more recent successors. The foreign policy agenda was heavily, though not exclusively, focused on Europe. "In the view of the Canadian Government, Western Europe is of greater strategic importance than any other area in the world," wrote Pearson in 1951.[4] Managing Canada's foreign relations was a lighter task. There was periodic high-level dialogue with Washington on how the U.S. should handle its superpower responsibilities, much more than is likely to have occurred since 9/11. As for Pearson himself, his biographer has drawn attention to the freedom he enjoyed as foreign minister.[5] That included freedom from most of the laborious chores of domestic politics. He also worked under a prime minister who did not seek the international limelight, another circumstance that made his tenure unique in the period since 1946.

The legacy of the Pearson era was that the primary importance of western unity, the necessity of strengthening international institutions and rule-based systems for the management of conflict, the strong preference for multilateral over bilateral settings for dealing with the United States and the inclination to refrain, in almost all circumstances, from public airing of disputes with the U.S., were deeply embedded in the culture of Canadian foreign policy. It has been hard to argue against the lessons drawn from the forties and fifties because Canada then enjoyed such remarkable success on the world stage. Perversely, the idea that we could "punch above our weight" by sharpening our diplomatic skills has been one of a number of factors encouraging governments to believe that they could invest less and less in foreign policy resources. At the same time, a desire to recapture the clarity of purpose and excellence in execution associated with Pearson has driven periodic efforts to review and reform foreign policy. "We are still searching for a Canadian role or, more accurately, the big Canadian initiative, the one that's going to win our minister, whoever he is, a Nobel peace prize," wrote Allan Gotlieb in 1985.[6]

We have also inherited a public standard by which foreign ministers can be, and often are, measured. The clear articulation of foreign policy principles, the status accorded Canada in international forums, the buoyant morale of a foreign service that dared to think about great issues and inventive diplomacy culminating in a Nobel Prize, have been identified with the way foreign policy ought to be handled. Even Tory foreign ministers, Flora MacDonald, Joe Clark and Barbara McDougall, have been exponents of such Pearsonian principles as multilateralism and the centrality of the UN. Though it is easy to discount Canada's slippage in the ranking of states since Pearson's day and to exaggerate his accomplishments, the postwar period retains its halcyon aura. A politician decrying Canada's current performance can always strike a sympathetic chord with an audience by asking, "Why don't we command the respect in the world that we did when Mr. Pearson was foreign minister?"

Pearson, whose personality had become indistinguishable from his role, was dislodged by the Progressive Conservative victory in June 1957. The new prime minister, John Diefenbaker, held the portfolio himself until September, when he plucked Sidney Smith from the presidency of the University of Toronto. It was an audacious attempt to match Pearson's lustre. Smith, however, was fated to join the long line of Canadians who, having distinguished themselves in one walk of life and then been lured into politics, find themselves tripped up by inexperience. Diefenbaker took a considerable interest in foreign policy and Smith's life cannot have been made any easier by difficulties that the prime minister had with senior levels of External Affairs. Sidney Smith died on 17 March 1959.

The second Progressive Conservative minister, Howard Green, was a shock to foreign policy watchers. He had been immersed in British Columbia and national, not international, politics and his manner was direct and seemingly naïve. His reputation has grown in the years since his tenure (1959–1963), partly because it has been realized that Pearson's background and attainments made him an exception and Green was closer to the kind of foreign minister we might normally expect to have.

By doggedly pressing his "crusade" for disarmament and against nuclear testing in Geneva, New York and other world capitals, Green evoked the issue of the age, an issue that connected him to millions of households apprehensive about the effects of atomic radiation. No other foreign minister has established such a bond with Canadians. He was a policy innovator, the more effective because his officials developed the bureaucratic machinery needed to give his efforts back-up and follow-through. The Disarmament Division was set up while he was minister and the Disarmament Mission to the UN commanded some of the best talents in his department. His attention was not totally consumed by disarmament. He lent strong support to the aid program then housed in the External Aid Office, one of the first bilateral aid agencies to be established by a western country. He was the first foreign minister to visit Latin America and the Latin American Division of External Affairs came into existence under him.

Prime Minister John Diefenbaker decided the Canadian position on South Africa's continued membership in the Commonwealth and managed his government's reaction to the Cuban Missile Crisis. It is noteworthy that the paper flow between Diefenbaker and External Affairs continued to go through the Minister's office. Green, who had been elected to the House of Commons five years earlier than Diefenbaker, was unafraid of the prime minister. Diefenbaker gave him a fairly free rein and, in fact, Green's disarmament crusade pushed the Conservative government to drag its feet on arming Canada's Bomarc missiles and Voodoo jets with nuclear warheads. How, after all, could Canada press for nuclear disarmament globally and, at the same time, accept nuclear weapons on its own territory?

Howard Green has been criticized for antagonizing the United States by his unqualified opposition to nuclear testing without recognition of the need for onsite inspections to check on the possible occurrence of underground tests. His outspoken moralizing is held to have lost Canada influence with major powers and damaged its effectiveness in international forums.[7] He did alienate U.S. Secretary of State Dean Rusk. The initiatives he sponsored at the United Nations were sometimes amateurish.[8] Yet he was, in many respects, extraordinarily prescient. He advocated, for example, a disarmament role for the North Atlantic Treaty Organization (NATO) and his prescription for how the West should deal with the Soviet Bloc was a harbinger of what later became détente. Furthermore, principle trumped pragmatism for millions of people made uneasy by the dawn of the nuclear age. Green articulated this unease and contributed to a mounting demand for taming east-west competition, which began to bear fruit when the Partial Test Ban Treaty was concluded in August 1963.

The Liberals' election victory of 1963 made Lester Pearson prime minister and propelled Paul Martin, Sr., a veteran Liberal minister who had helped break the impasse over the admission of new members to the United Nations in 1955, into External Affairs. Martin moved quickly to repair damage that he thought Diefenbaker had done to relations with London and Washington. He was strongly alliance-minded, always zealous to keep communication lines open with Washington and the last foreign minister for whom the United Kingdom served as an anchor of Canada's foreign relations. He had a reputation for mastery of his files. The stature Canada had acquired during World War Two had not yet evaporated and during his term (1963–1968) he enjoyed access in foreign capitals that recent foreign ministers might envy.

Martin was more inclined than Pearson to temporize over President Charles de Gaulle's incursions into Canadian affairs. There was a heated disagreement between the two over the advisability of Pearson's Temple University speech in 1965 requesting a temporary halt to U.S. bombing in Vietnam. Yet the lines of responsibility were clear. The prime minister took on the tasks that flowed from his role as head of government, such as representing Canada in Commonwealth meetings on Rhodesia. The External Affairs minister exercised a degree of autonomy greater than that possessed by his successors, dealing with U.S. unhappiness over Canada's trade with Cuba, the Columbia River Treaty, the financing of United Nations peacekeeping operations, France's continuing membership in NATO and the organization of the Cyprus peacekeeping force. That Martin could send Chester Ronning as an emissary to the North Vietnamese over the prime minister's protest bears witness to the minister's independence.[9]

An effective diplomat, a consummate politician, and yet the domestic constituency for Canada's foreign policy began to develop fissures during Paul Martin's tenure. He had internalized the principles of Canadian policy too well to realize that they needed advocacy. He did not even want foreign policy to be discussed in cabinet. Academics were calling for a more independent foreign policy, there was a rising mood of nationalism in the country that fed off the increasingly unfavourable image of the U.S. and within External Affairs itself there was a feeling that Pearsonian thinking had become calcified.

Paul Martin's too evident ambition to succeed Pearson undermined his stature and he came to symbolize policy stagnation. He was also at a disadvantage, caught between his attachment to Canada's traditional allies and his agreement with some of the critical views that were being expressed. He favoured recognition of the People's Republic of China and tried to influence the thinking of the Johnson administration on China. He got as far as engineering a Canadian abstention on the Albanian resolution that would have seated the Beijing government in the UN in place of Taiwan, but there were always overriding considerations, not least being the Cultural Revolution then under way in China, which made it impossible to go further.[10] He became an opponent of the bombing of North Vietnam, but he insisted on handling differences with Washington discreetly and the government never shook the charge of complicity with U.S. policy in Southeast Asia. By the time Martin handed over his portfolio the mood of dissatisfaction made Canada's foreign policy ripe for change.

Mitchell Sharp became foreign minister in 1968, his reward for having thrown his support to Pierre Trudeau in the Liberal leadership contest. His six-year tenure witnessed the first steps towards east-west détente, the concluding convulsions of the Vietnam War, the Yom Kippur War of 1973 and the Arab oil embargo, rising militancy among developing countries and signs that the Canada-U.S. agenda was becoming increasingly complex and demanding of the foreign minister's time. He was the quintessential manager and the initiatives and issues with which he occupied himself were well managed. He negotiated the tricky path to recognition of the People's Republic of China, which included tense interchanges with a sceptical U.S. secretary of state, William Rogers. He managed to preserve more or less intact the principle of the indivisibility of foreign policy when Québec sought separate representation at international conferences. He agreed to Canada's participation in the International Commission of Control and Supervision (ICCS) for Vietnam but ensured that it was of short duration, thus helping the Americans extricate themselves from the morass while avoiding a long and undoubtedly frustrating commitment.

This went on against the backdrop of a major upheaval. Pierre Trudeau's foreign policy review tied Canada's foreign policy goals to its domestic interests. After the dust settled there were new rules of the game. There was a foreign policy advisor in the Prime Minister's Office (PMO), officials in the Department of External Affairs began taking instructions directly from that office and, later in the Trudeau era, a "mirror committee" of deputies enabled the PMO to have input into the decision making of the Cabinet Committee on Foreign and Defence Policy. The prime minister was no longer just a distant figure giving approval to the general direction of foreign policy.

Sharp was at a disadvantage, at times admiring, at times aghast at what Trudeau was doing. As a loyal lieutenant he tried not to show his dislike of being upstaged, particularly by a prime minister who enjoyed breaking the rules. Supporters of the foreign service thought him feeble for knuckling under when Trudeau pruned posts and positions. Together with cabinet colleagues he did succeed in beating back a 1969 attempt to fundamentally redirect Canadian policy with respect to NATO but it was too hard-won a victory to strengthen his position vis-à-vis the prime minister. His single attempt at policy innovation, the Third Option, intended to shore up Canada's independence from the U.S., was a dismal failure. To have been successful the strategy would have required careful coordination of domestic departments of government, but Sharp was in no position to elicit this kind of cooperation from his cabinet colleagues. The well-honed instincts that made the longtime civil servant an effective manager of foreign policy made him less capable as a politician.

"Nice to see a foreign minister with whom we are not locked in mortal combat," was U.S. Secretary of State Henry Kissinger's greeting to Sharp's successor, Allan MacEachen, when they first met.[11] In fact, the bilateral agenda had grown fractious but in both his first (1974–1976) and second (1982–1984) terms MacEachen understood that to reach the Americans it was necessary to address their agenda, which meant discussing such issues as nuclear proliferation and the Middle East. He also understood that with the relationship now clearly exposed to the vagaries of Washington politicking, good relations at the top were vital. During his second term, prickliness between President Reagan and Prime Minister Trudeau made all the more important MacEachen's initiative to set up regular bilaterals with Secretary of State George Shultz. One of his achievements was to fashion an independent Canadian position on Central America, where the Reagan Administration discerned the spectre of communism in social unrest, and maintain this position while keeping workable relations with the Americans.

It is plausible to link Allan MacEachen's youthful involvement in Moses Coady's Antigonish Movement with his later interest in international development but he was essentially a pragmatist. As co-chair of the Conference on International Economic Cooperation (CIEC) in the mid-seventies, he tried to work out positions on commodities, debt relief and official development assistance that could be accepted by eight industrial countries and nineteen developing states. Pragmatism was the hallmark of his undertakings as minister, whether trying to find an accommodation with the demand for a New International Economic Order (NIEO), pursuing a contractual link with the European Community, superintending Canada's participation in the Geneva Law of the Sea Conference or working to overcome French objections to Canada's participation in the G7 economic summit.

MacEachen's slow, deliberate style and his contributions to policy discussions conveyed seriousness of purpose. He had an understanding of policy much broader than the subject at hand. Officials likened the experience of briefing him to the Inquisition. He was a strong negotiator and acquitted himself well in bilateral meetings. Questionable aspects of his management style were his slowness in making decisions and his penchant for restricting decision making to a small number. He took issues to the prime minister for resolution before they had been to cabinet committee. He was unhelpful when it came to mandating parliamentary committees to study foreign policy issues.

He held the additional title of deputy prime minister during his second tour of duty, indicating that he possessed a foreign minister's most valuable asset, the prime minister's confidence. This could be accounted to his experience (he had been first elected to the House of Commons in 1953), his intelligence, his orchestration of Pierre Trudeau's political resurrection in 1980 and his regional base as senior minister for Nova Scotia. He was an effective advocate for Trudeau's policy of testing cruise missiles, both in cabinet and in the House. He pushed back, however, against prime ministerial appropriation of the foreign policy field.[12] He loyally supported the last hurrah of the Trudeau government, the prime minister's peace initiative, but he regarded it with skepticism.

Although not an originator of policy, Allan MacEachen came closer than any foreign minister to exercising the powers of his office across the full spectrum of Canada's foreign relations. He retained responsibility for the Canadian International Development Agency (CIDA), successor to the External Aid Office. Following Trudeau's 1982 decision to integrate the trade commissioner service and trade policy in External Affairs, he oversaw the integration process and made it work as it was intended to work. It was patently clear that he was senior to the trade minister, though they shared a department.[13] None of his successors has been able to say the same.

Some foreign ministers have deliberately sought to make personal relationships the basis of their diplomacy. Don Jamieson's unique ability to get along with people made him the nonpareil in that regard. The former Coca-Cola distributor and radio announcer from St. John's, who had once wanted to take Newfoundland into an economic union with the U.S., filled the corner office in the Pearson Building from 1976 to 1979. He built close ties with Secretary of State Cyrus Vance and United Kingdom Foreign Secretary David Owen in the five-nation Contact Group on Namibia. He could get Vance to discuss bilateral problems that had caused Kissinger's eyes to glaze over and he could charm confidences out of Jimmy Carter at a G7 meeting.[14] His gregarious approach compensated for that of Pierre Trudeau, whose major foreign policy interest was north-south relations and who was rarely at ease with British and American leaders. Jamieson was an orator and his language could be pungent, as when he signaled Canada's growing disillusionment with the UN in a 1977 address to the General Assembly. "I have concluded that I could read my last year's speech again word for word and no one would notice the repetition nor would they care!"[15]

Flora MacDonald, who became the Clark government's foreign minister (1979–1980), was determined not to be overwhelmed by her officials.[16] She was uneasy because the flow of advice appeared to be structured to confine her options. If other ministers have felt the same way, which they probably have, they have judged it wise not to stir up a hornets' nest. MacDonald went so far as to begin assembling a team of outside advisors. Her inexperience might well have doomed this initiative had the curtain not fallen on the government. Her tenure will nonetheless be remembered for the bold and generous decision that she and Employment and Immigration Minister Ron Atkey took to take in up to 50,000 Indochinese refugees.

Mark MacGuigan was Trudeau's choice for the portfolio after the Liberals returned in 1980 and he remained in it until MacEachen took it back in 1982. MacGuigan, whose unassertive personality belied his intellect, co-existed uneasily with a prime minister who did not show much regard for his opinions. The Cold War was being renewed. Differences in the way they approached east-west issues occasionally popped up, especially when Trudeau refused to condemn the imposition of martial law by General Jaruzelski's government in Poland. MacGuigan was more closely attuned to the Helsinki Final Act of 1975 and the Conference on Security and Co-operation in Europe (CSCE) process then under way. The failure of the Fisheries Resources Agreement in the Senate, trans-boundary air and water issues and American abhorrence of the Foreign Investment Review Agency (FIRA) and the National Energy Program (NEP) required urgent attention to bilateral relations. The Washington embassy began to practice what MacGuigan terms in his memoirs a "New Diplomacy."[17] Again, the prime minister made life difficult by his nose-thumbing approach to the Reagan administration. MacGuigan worried that the bilateral relationship was in disrepair but his own nationalist views made it hard to forge a bond with the Americans.

In June 1984, Prime Minister Turner handed External Affairs to his leadership rival, Jean Chrétien, who served until Brian Mulroney's Conservatives were elected in September. Mulroney extended the same favour to his rival, Joe Clark, who served in the portfolio until 1991. Clark's foreign policy principles were rooted in his political instincts. Keeping Canada-U.S. relations in good repair was of first importance not just because of Canada's dependence on its southern neighbour but because Canada might on occasion have to differ from the U.S. – as Clark differed from Secretary Shultz over aid to the Nicaraguan contras. Moreover, he believed that Canada should act where it could make a difference, South African apartheid and the "Open Skies" initiative,[18] and should devote more attention to areas of growing importance, the Arctic and the Pacific Rim. He was also convinced that Canadians possessed a bent for activism in international affairs.

Joe Clark belonged to the progressive wing of his party and he had to battle for his views in cabinet debates on the aid budget, cultural sovereignty and advanced cruise missile testing. His influence over his colleagues waxed and waned.[19] He was marginalized in the free trade negotiations. Yet he was active on a very wide range of files. The foreign minister did not always prevail but he usually made his influence felt. The North Pacific Cooperative Security Dialogue he initiated would have laid the foundation of a more intensive Canadian involvement with Asia had it not fallen victim to later austerity measures.

The proliferation of summit meetings propelled the prime minister's appropriation of foreign affairs, continuing the pattern established by Trudeau. Mulroney could defer to Clark's judgement as he did on the language of the 1985 Shamrock Summit communiqué regarding President Reagan's Strategic Defense Initiative (SDI). The public saw a divergence in 1988 when Clark criticized Israel's use of force to put down Palestinian uprisings in the occupied territories and Mulroney sought to quell the uproar. In general, they achieved a remarkable *modus vivendi*.[20] The effort to rally the Commonwealth against apartheid saw them working together, with Brian Mulroney confronting the redoubtable Margaret Thatcher, and Joe Clark serving as chairman of the Committee of Commonwealth Foreign Ministers considering how to keep pressure on Pretoria.

Partisan at an early age, Joe Clark knew when it was possible to set partisanship aside. In contrast to MacEachen he wanted to open up the policy process and, in particular, to strengthen Parliament's role. He initiated a foreign policy review which led to a special joint committee of the two houses of Parliament travelling across the country and listening to each and every citizen who had a point to make. His political value to the Mulroney government was that he protected it from attack by the foreign policy community which, though not a large constituency, exercised a disproportionate influence on public opinion.

POST-COLD WAR MINISTERS

"We are at the dawn of a new era, an era of extraordinary promise and profound challenge for Canada and the world," said Minister Clark in September 1990, in the aftermath of the collapse of the Berlin Wall.[21] Foreign ministers now had to cope with a world in which the threat of an exchange of strategic missiles was replaced by more elusive problems of ethnic strife, the abuse of citizens by their governments and terrorism.

As Pierre Trudeau had done, Prime Minister Mulroney stepped up his foreign policy activity as his term neared its end. In the face of enormous fiscal pressures, he insisted on Canada playing a significant international role in Haiti, the former Yugoslavia and Somalia, and in mobilizing aid to Russia. Barbara McDougall, who was minister from 1991 to 1993, carved out a niche for herself as the government's communicator, striving to convince the public that the government was carrying out its responsibility for the safety of Canadian peacekeepers. At the same time, Mulroney's activism enhanced her diplomatic role. She got a hearing from her opposite numbers and in international meetings grappling with the unfamiliar problem of how to restrain ethnic conflict. Her capacity for decisiveness at a time when decisiveness was in short supply won the respect of British, American and Russian colleagues, with whom she avidly worked the phones. In keeping with her progressive views, she battled both colleagues and bureaucrats to reduce military exports to South Asia and oversaw Canadian efforts to refine the concept of an international criminal court.

Perrin Beatty held the foreign affairs portfolio during the 1993 Kim Campbell interregnum, not long enough, he admitted, to discover the auditorium in the Pearson Building.[22] André Ouellet took over with the election of the Chrétien government and served from 1993 to 1996. Since MacEachen, CIDA had usually had its own minister (a practice that continues in the present) but, on account of cabinet down-sizing, Ouellet was also responsible for that agency. He initiated a public consultation and foreign policy review that was a harbinger of the human security agenda. A stiffer test was the question of air strikes against the Serbs in Bosnia and participation in the Implementation Force set up after the Dayton Accords. Both prime minister and foreign minister dithered, provoking the anger of allies.[23] Coming after a period of foreign policy activism a letdown was to be expected, especially given cuts to the foreign affairs and international assistance envelope and the distraction posed by the impending Québec referendum. André Ouellet was too much the machine politician to go against the prevailing current.

"You have to ask what will be the impact on people."[24] With that injunction, Lloyd Axworthy, who replaced Ouellet in 1996 and served until 2000, shook up Canadian foreign policy. Axworthy came to the portfolio with experience as a minister and opposition critic and with a concept of security attuned to post-Cold War threats. He sponsored or encouraged major initiatives: launching the Ottawa Process on Landmines, which led to a treaty banning anti-personnel landmines signed by representatives of 122 countries in December 1997; taking a leading role in preparatory work for the Rome Statute of the International Criminal Court, which was approved in June 1998; and setting up the International Commission on Intervention and State Sovereignty (ICISS), which re-formulated the concept of state sovereignty into the "Responsibility to Protect." These initiatives were backed by speeches and documents composing what observers dubbed the Axworthy doctrine. The individual strands of the human security "package" were not original, not all his ideas worked and his advocacy of human security lacked rigour.[25] At least temporarily, however, Canada was cast as an independent actor in international affairs, a builder of coalitions and a forward thinking country prepared to cut loose from national interest and power politics.

Axworthy combined an intellectual's grasp of principles with a ward politician's understanding of how to get things done. Sometimes moody and erratic himself, he employed a pushy staff. He could go around his officials with unorthodox stratagems, some of which, like the Canadian Centre for Foreign Policy Development, a new instrument of public diplomacy, were to go awry in the end. He sought advice from academics and human-rights specialists outside government.

At the same time, some of his acolytes came from the ranks of officialdom. Seeing that NGOs were becoming influential actors in their own right, he forged alliances with them and, somewhat too enthusiastically, welcomed a new form of global democracy. The capstone of his crusade was Security Council membership, to which Canada was elected for the 1999–2000 term and which proved an effective instrument to advance the cause of protecting the individual. He was lucky in having a prime minister who would cut him some slack.

Jean Chrétien did nevertheless hold major foreign policy files, driving the eventually aborted effort to mobilize international action for the protection of refugees in Zaire (now the Democratic Republic of the Congo). He showed considerable interest in trade and personally led Team Canada missions overseas. The way in which his government downgraded the priority accorded to human rights undermined the foreign minister. The finance minister's fiscal belt-tightening reduced Axworthy's room for manoeuvre even further.

Axworthy's handicaps make the lesson to be drawn from his experience all the more compelling. An ambitious foreign minister can leave an imprint on policy. Axworthy demonstrated that a minister with energy, determination and ideas can innovate, and his major achievements – though humanitarian intervention is presently under attack – have a good chance of being sustained.

Critics argue that if only Axworthy could have put a little water in his wine, qualifying the jurisdiction of the International Criminal Court and the application of the Landmines Convention, he could have ensured U.S. participation in these new multilateral instruments.[26] That argument discounts strong opposition to both the Court and the Landmines Treaty in the Pentagon and the Congress. The U.S. would have made every effort to widen any exemptions. Axworthy was right not to bend.

A more powerful criticism is that he skewed Canada's foreign policy. His agenda was too limited. He got along with U.S. Secretary of State Madeleine Albright but, on occasion, he antagonized the Americans. The parallel with Howard Green is inescapable but it has to be remembered that, in the interval between the two, Canada had acquired a broader set of international relationships needing constant tending. Axworthy aroused the concern that Canada was not investing its foreign policy resources in a manner roughly proportionate to its interests. Of course, outside the area that Axworthy sought to influence, things went on much the same as before. The prime minister put economic interests front and centre. Canada had, in effect, two foreign policies.

John Manley, who served as minister from the fall of 2000 to early 2002, began to go in a very different direction from Axworthy. Coming from Industry Canada, he wanted Canada's strategic economic interest to be reflected in its foreign policy. Manley soon dropped the term "human security." He was also dissatisfied with the organization of his department and its lack of priorities. His dissatisfaction mounted when officials bobbled the case of a Russian diplomat who, driving while intoxicated, killed an Ottawa lawyer. Then 9/11 shoved everything else aside and border and security issues, together with Canada's responsibilities to its allies, became the sole priority. Manley, who was popularly identified as pro-American, considered rather that it was his professional responsibility to address President Bush's preoccupations and get Canada back into a special relationship with Washington. "You can't just sit at the G8 table and then, when the bill comes, go to the washroom," he famously said, triggering an enthusiastic response in the country. Jean Chrétien, who was inclined to distance himself from the U.S. administration, took a while to catch up to Manley's and the prevailing view, an unusual example of a foreign minister leading a prime minister.

A former chair of the House of Commons Standing Committee on Foreign Affairs and International Trade, Bill Graham (2002–2004) confronted a problem familiar to incoming foreign ministers: trying to impose a set of priorities on a volatile agenda. After the convulsive developments of the preceding years it was important to restore a sense of balance to Canadian foreign policy. Endowed with personality and intellect, Graham had some success at this but events soon took command of his time. He made his mark by setting a torrid pace. His first task was to back up Prime Minister Chrétien's intention to make the New Partnership for Africa's Development a centrepiece of the G8 meeting in Kananaskis in June 2002. The impending U.S. invasion of Iraq saw him thrown into a furious round of diplomacy with Joschka Fischer, Colin Powell, Javier Solana, Jack Straw and Dominique de Villepin. He supported the prime minister's decision not to participate in the invasion on the ground that "resorting to war required a clear international mandate: the sanction of the Security Council."[27] He had to contend with the fall of President Jean-Bertrand Aristide in Haiti and with draining consular cases.[28] He shared with Joe Clark an interest in the democratization of foreign policy and got a mandate from the prime minister to conduct a foreign policy review. There ensued a tug of war with an unenthusiastic bureaucracy but Graham was able to conduct a series of town hall meetings across the country. He was too much a team player to sustain the unpredictability that is an ingredient of political clout. He went unwillingly to the defence portfolio.

Paul Martin, Jr.'s aspiration to leave a mark in international affairs almost smothered his choice as foreign minister, Pierre Pettigrew, who served from mid-2004 until the victory of the Harper Conservatives in early 2006. A longtime Liberal, he was made to look weaker by the eventually reversed decision to split Foreign Affairs and International Trade, and by reports that he would be unable to win his constituency again, which proved to be correct. With his support, the minority Liberal government defined a wary stance vis-à-vis the U.S. by declining Washington's invitation to participate in ballistic missile defence. He undertook a review of how well Canada's resources were being applied to further peace in the Middle East, but was never able to follow through. He was one of many midwives at the birth of *Canada's International Policy Statement*, the Martin government's foreign policy review, the negotiation of which illustrated the difficulty of integrating the three "Ds," defence, development and diplomacy. His tenure was unremarkable because he either could not or would not find a way to distinguish his own role or convince foreign policy watchers that he had thought through an approach to his job.

History repeated itself as Stephen Harper handed the foreign affairs portfolio to his erstwhile rival, Peter MacKay. The Harper government started out as the most centrally controlled in Canadian history – MacKay could not select his own chief of staff[29] – and the prime minister boldly revised time-tested Canadian policy. The importance of good relations with the People's Republic of China was downgraded and any pretence at an even-handed approach to Israel and the Palestinians was abandoned. Whether or not MacKay fully agreed with Harper's views, he was saddled with the image of a hapless apparatchik, which cannot have enhanced his effectiveness. He got better as he acquired ministerial experience. He gained kudos by hosting Secretary of State Condoleezza Rice in Nova Scotia. He did a good job of defending the Canadian role in Afghanistan, the government's number one policy priority, and was an effective regional minister for Nova Scotia, taking some heat out of the quarrel between the prime minister and Nova Scotia Premier Rodney MacDonald over off-shore oil revenues and the Atlantic Accord. These are accomplishments that count and when he was moved to Defence it was not just to make room for a Quebecer but also to place a good performer in what had become a highly sensitive position.

The most noteworthy aspect of Maxime Bernier's tenure (2007–2008) was its ignominious end after a series of blunders and indiscretions had made his position untenable. Bernier's forced resignation graphically made the point that the turnover of foreign ministers was becoming far too rapid. Bernier was the sixth minister in eight years and, at the time of his appointment, he had been a minister and member of parliament for only eighteen months. With any luck, his departure marked the nadir of the foreign affairs portfolio.

WHAT FUTURE FOR THE FOREIGN MINISTER?

"I was in a G8 foreign ministers' meeting and it occurred to me that only one (the Canadian foreign minister) of these eleven guys has to get elected and has to go to Question Period every day,"[30] recalled a former ministerial advisor. Unlike many of their opposite numbers in other governments, Canadian foreign ministers endure the relentless pressure of parliamentary, caucus and constituency obligations. They have to shift gears in an instant, switching their attention from the fate of millions to a problem preoccupying a single voter. Few were foreign policy specialists before and they have little opportunity to develop expertise in office. They are first and foremost managers of foreign relations. If they have shortcomings as managers, these are chiefly due to lack of political skills, clout or experience. Lack of foreign policy acumen is a handicap but not a serious one. Most do not view themselves as setting a radically new course for Canada. Not surprisingly, none of the twenty-three ministers since 1946 has resigned over a policy issue.

Innovators have been far fewer in number than managers. After St. Laurent and Pearson had charted the course, Green and Axworthy effected significant changes of direction. They stand out as having tested the potential of their office but their experience demonstrates that innovation comes at a cost. Axworthy's initiatives, in particular, detracted from the coherence and balance of Canadian foreign policy.

Diplomacy is a subsidiary role but all foreign ministers are part-time diplomats. Husbanding relations with the United States is the central task but there have only been intermittent efforts to maintain or rebuild the personal ties that have on occasion contributed depth and substance to the relationship. There appears to be no serious Canada-U.S. dialogue on how Americans should exercise their leadership, though Canada has a major stake in that. Bilateral problems, especially the border, have pushed any such dialogue out of the way and, in other respects, Canada's relevance to Washington in terms of security has declined. Nevertheless, a future foreign minister might be wise to try capturing the attention of U.S. decision makers by broaching a discussion on their global agenda.

Does the office of foreign minister have a future? That depends on the prime minister. In most of the cases we have studied the minister has been, as Denis Stairs has put it, "rivalled by his boss."[31] Over forty years ago James Eayrs could write of the prime minister, "Foreign policy is his prerogative; the range and intimacy of his concern are rarely matched by any of his colleagues, even by his foreign secretary."[32] Prime minister and foreign minister have shared the field amicably or not so amicably, complemented one another or fashioned separate solitudes.

In recent years prime ministerial encroachments on the foreign minister's territory have gone far beyond setting the main lines of policy. Today we observe the bifurcation of the foreign ministry. The prime minister's role has been enormously expanded as part of the centralization of power in the office, a process furthered by the proliferation of summit meetings and the ease of telephone contact with other government leaders. Having to cajole, impress and debate with other heads of government leads to a growing requirement for support from the bureaucracy. Thus, at any one time, a part of Foreign Affairs and International Trade Canada is working directly for the prime minister, receiving instructions from the Langevin Building (which houses both the Prime Minister's Office and the Privy Council Office) and funneling memoranda to it in return. Even this splitting of departmental loyalties does not fully convey the weakness of the foreign minister's position. The ability to go around the minister means that officials can seek prime ministerial rulings effectively countermanding what the minister wants.

Formulating foreign policy will continue to be the prime minister's prerogative and prime ministerial involvement in summitry cannot be expected to diminish. Most foreign ministers will, grudgingly or not, defer to the policy leadership of their boss. A dose of political realism leads us to conclude that two ambitious politicians, one headstrong, the other wary, will not do much to correct the bifurcation of the bureaucracy and even, at times, of policy.

It is possible to imagine another scenario in which the prime minister, while by no means withdrawing from the field, brings an end to the bifurcation of the Foreign Affairs Department and makes the foreign minister a single focal point for foreign policy. The prime minister will have recognized that a coherent and credible foreign policy reflects well on the government and the country. Managing alliances, negotiating agreements, mobilizing domestic support and all the other actions of a foreign minister are performed more effectively if the incumbent *knows* that he or she possesses the confidence of the head of government and a substantial margin of manoeuvre.

With a longer tenure and freer rein a foreign minister could be active internationally in a way that would strengthen Canada's access in foreign capitals, advancing Canadian interests. At home, an effective minister could impose a framework of political objectives on the competing interests of domestic departments. There should be a powerful figure in cabinet keeping Canada's political interest to the fore in a way that prime ministers, who conserve their energies for a crisis, cannot be expected to do. The supposedly immutable laws of politics may never let this happen but the alternative is to devalue a great office of state.

NOTES

The author would like to thank a number of individuals who have taken the time to discuss the role of foreign minister with him: Eric Bergbusch, Derek Burney, Tom Delworth, Greg Donaghy, John Graham, Francis LeBlanc, Hector Mackenzie, Tony Macerollo, Peggy Mason, James R. Mitchell, John Noble, Julie Rickerd and Colin Robertson. The views expressed here are solely the author's.

1 Canada, *Department of Foreign Affairs and International Trade Act* (R.S., 1985, c. E-22) (Ottawa: 1995). Available at: <http://laws.justice.gc.ca>
2 An example is Barbara McDougall's agreement at the Moscow talks in 1992 that Canada should handle the Refugee Working Group of the Middle East Peace Process. Prime Minister Mulroney was at first skeptical that this was a role that Canada should take on.
3 The Department was called "External Affairs" until 1989 when the name was changed to "External Affairs and International Trade." In November, 1993 the Chrétien government changed the name again to "Foreign Affairs and International Trade" and the minister's title from "Secretary of State for External Affairs" to "Minister of Foreign Affairs."
4 Lester B. Pearson, "The Development of Canadian Foreign Policy," *Foreign Affairs* 30, no. 1 (1951): 27.
5 John English, *The Worldly Years: The Life of Lester Pearson 1949–1972* (Toronto: Alfred A. Knopf Canada, 1992), 49.
6 Allan Gotlieb, *The Washington Diaries 1981–1989* (Toronto: McClelland & Stewart Ltd., 2006), 339.
7 For a critical assessment of Howard Green see Peyton V. Lyon, *Canada in World Affairs XII 1963–1968* (Toronto: Oxford University Press, 1968), 276–79.
8 A resolution introduced by Canada at the 16th General Assembly called for an international program to measure radioactive fallout from nuclear explosions. Had it been put into effect international communications facilities would have been clogged. See Peter C. Dobell, *Canada's search for new roles: Foreign Policy in the Trudeau Era* (London: Oxford University Press, 1972), 144.
9 English, *The Worldly Years*, 371.
10 Interview, Hon. Paul Martin, 23 April 1971.
11 Remarks by the Hon. Allan MacEachen, Foreign Ministers' Forum, Ottawa, 30 January 2003.
12 He appears to have won support from Privy Council Clerk Gordon Osbaldeston in this effort. Allan Gotlieb records being counseled by Osbaldeston, "don't go around MacEachen." Gotlieb was Ambassador to Washington at the time. Gotlieb, *The Washington Diaries*, 172. One historian asserts that MacEachen got Ivan Head moved out as Foreign Policy Advisor in the P.M.O. Robert Bothwell, *Alliances and Illusions: Canada and the World 1945–1984* (Vancouver: University of British Columbia Press, 2007), 376.

13 An example of MacEachen's predominance over the integrated department was that he chaired the 1982 GATT ministerial meeting in Geneva while the trade minister, Gerald Regan, led the Canadian delegation. MacEachen was also instrumental in getting Sylvia Ostry appointed deputy minister of trade.
14 Derek H. Burney, *Getting It Done: A Memoir* (Montreal & Kingston: McGill-Queen's University Press, 2005), 42.
15 Notes for a Speech by the Secretary of State for External Affairs of Canada, the Honourable Don Jamieson, to the XXXII Regular Session of the United Nations General Assembly, New York, 26 September 1977.
16 See Flora MacDonald, "The Minister and the Mandarins: How a new minister copes with the entrapment devices of bureaucracy," *Policy Options* 1, no. 3 (September/October 1981): 29–31.
17 "... an in-their-face representation of our interests by which we would press our case on any issue unremittingly and in all directions." Mark MacGuigan, *An inside look at External Affairs during the Trudeau years*, P. Whitney Lackenbauer, ed. (Calgary: University of Calgary Press, 2002), 114.
18 In 1992 twenty-seven nations signed the Treaty on Open Skies, allowing former Cold War enemies to conduct aerial observation over each other's territories. Canada played a major role in achieving the Treaty.
19 See John Kirton, "The Foreign Policy Decision Process," in Maureen Appel Molot and Brian W. Tomlin, eds. *Canada Among Nations 1985: The Conservative Agenda* (Toronto: James Lorimer & Company, 1986), 25–45; John Kirton, "Foreign Policy Decision Making in the Mulroney Government," in Brian W. Tomlin and Maureen Appel Molot, eds. *Canada Among Nations 1988: The Tory Record* (Toronto: James Lorimer & Company, 1989), 21–38.
20 "I always treated Joe Clark with the greatest of respect. He was the only one I treated differently in cabinet. I always gave him more accord. He was the only one I deferred to, because he was a former leader, former prime minister, and indeed I kept it going right to the end." Brian Mulroney, quoted in Peter C. Newman, *The Secret Mulroney Tapes: Unguarded Confessions of a Prime Minister* (Random House Canada, 2005), 343.
21 Notes for an Address by the Secretary of State for External Affairs, the Right Honourable Joe Clark, on the occasion of the 66th meeting of the Canada-America Committee of the C.D. Howe Institute, 13 September 1990.
22 Remarks by the Hon. Perrin Beatty, Foreign Ministers' Forum, Ottawa, 30 January 2003.
23 Dean Oliver, "External affairs and defence," in David Leyton-Brown ed. *Canadian Annual Review of Politics and Public Affairs 1994* (Toronto: University of Toronto Press, 2000), 92–7.
24 Remarks by the Hon. Lloyd Axworthy, Foreign Ministers' Forum, Ottawa, 30 January 2003.
25 Fen Osler Hampson and Dean Oliver, "Pulpit Diplomacy: a critical assessment of the Axworthy doctrine," *International Journal* 53, no. 3 (Summer 1998): 379–406.

26 In his memoirs Axworthy says that the sticking point on the Landmines Convention was the Pentagon's insistence on retaining an anti-tank mine system that used unconnected anti-personnel mines as guards. Lloyd Axworthy, *Navigating a New World: Canada's Global Future* (Toronto: Alfred A. Knopf Canada, 2003), 147. President Clinton did eventually sign the Rome Statute of the International Criminal Court but President Bush has been totally opposed to the idea.

27 Notes for an Address by the Honourable Bill Graham, Minister of Foreign Affairs, to the Canadian Club on "Sovereignty, Interdependence and Canada – U.S. Relations," Vancouver, British Columbia, 15 April 2003.

28 The cases of Maher Arar, Bill Sampson and Zahra Kazemi.

29 Lawrence Martin, *Globe and Mail*, 30 March 2006.

30 In addition to the eight foreign ministers three representatives of the European Union normally attend these meetings: the Commissioner for External Relations, a representative of the EU Presidency and the High Representative of the Council for the Common Foreign and Security Policy.

31 Denis Stairs, "The Changing Office and the Changing Environment of the Minister of Foreign Affairs in the Axworthy Era," in Fen Osler Hampson, Norman Hillmer, and Maureen Appel Molot, eds., *Canada Among Nations 2001: The Axworthy Legacy* (Toronto: Oxford University Press, 2001), 26.

32 James Eayrs, *The Art of the Possible: Government and Foreign Policy in Canada* (Toronto: University of Toronto Press, 1961), 4.

PART TWO
Issues

4 Old Wine, New Bottles: Canadian Economic Multilateralism and the North Atlantic Triangle, 1941–1947

KATHLEEN RASMUSSEN[*]

The 1940s are widely regarded as a turning point in the history of Canadian diplomacy. It was during this decade, after all, that Ottawa shed the isolationism of the past in favour of a broader and deeper engagement with the affairs of the world. During these years, the country gave its all to win not only the war, but also the peace, as Canadians traveled the globe to take part in the negotiations that laid the foundations of the postwar world. When the last conference was through – the ashtrays emptied, surplus agendas discarded, conference room chairs stacked – what remained was a new international system that reflected such multilateralist principles as consultation, cooperation, and collective action. Canada was an active supporter of this endeavour, a champion of the cause of multilateralism.

In the realm of international economics, the government of William Lyon Mackenzie King offered enthusiastic support to the effort to craft a multilateral economic order based upon freer trade and currency convertibility. It did so because multilateralism appeared to be the best way to meet the country's pressing need for export markets in the postwar world. However, as Robert Bothwell and John English have shown, Canada's commitment to economic multilateralism was far from absolute. Asserting that Ottawa "was reactive, not creative, and common prudence dictated a policy for each possible circumstance," they conclude that "there was no fixed Canadian position on international trade between 1942 and 1947."[1] Tom Keating and Michael Hart also note Canada's pragmatic approach to foreign economic policy in the 1940s. To Keating, economic multilateralism was "intended to serve

Canadian interests first,"[2] while Hart suggests that "[e]conomic security was the priority, wherever it could be found."[3]

The King government was motivated by interests, rather than ideals, in its approach to postwar economic planning. At the heart of this approach lay not a general interest in the undifferentiated expansion of world trade, but a very specific interest in the expansion of a particular subset of world trade, namely, trade among the countries of the North Atlantic triangle. Multilateralism offered the promise of the free flow of Canadian goods not simply to the rest of the world in general, but to the United States and the United Kingdom in particular. These countries had been the two most important destinations for Canada's exports, by large margins, for years. The Second World War did not change this basic fact; in fact, it reinforced it. What did change during the war – to a certain extent and by no means fully – was the way in which Ottawa sought to secure the country's access to these critical markets. Before 1941, it endeavoured to do so through the bilateralism of imperial preferences and reciprocity. After 1941, Ottawa put its faith in multilateralism as the best means of ensuring a functioning and prosperous North Atlantic triangle. And when it seemed possible that multilateralism might not fill the bill, Ottawa explored other means of achieving this same end.[4]

In this respect, the King government's embrace of economic multilateralism during the 1940s did not represent a break with the past. Multilateralism was an innovation only in the style of Canadian foreign economic policy, not its substance. In its approach to the postwar world, the King government was not motivated by the means of multilateralism, but the end of ensuring the continued flow of Canadian exports to the United States and the United Kingdom.[5] Canadian foreign economic policy during the 1940s was, in other words, very much an old North Atlantic wine in a new multilateral bottle. The basic goals of that policy had not changed, so much as had the means to achieve them.

John Gerard Ruggie, the international relations theorist, reminds us that multilateralism has several meanings. In its most literal sense, it refers to a relationship among three or more states. This, however, is rarely what we mean when we speak of multilateralism in foreign policy. Instead, support for multilateralism usually involves adherence to a code of conduct that, in the economic realm, includes non-discrimination and liberalized trade and currency flows, as well as support for the international institutions created to oversee these principles.[6] In August 1941, U.S. President Franklin D. Roosevelt and U.K. Prime Minister Winston Churchill described their vision of a multilateral world order in the statement of postwar aspirations that has come to be known as the Atlantic Charter. In the economic realm, Roosevelt and Churchill promised to promote "the enjoyment by all States, great or small, victor or vanquished, of access, on equal terms, to the trade and to the raw materials of the world which are needed for their economic prosperity," as well as "the fullest collaboration between all nations in the economic field with the object of securing, for all, improved labour standards, economic advancement, and social security."

As every student of Canadian diplomacy knows, Ottawa actively supported the reconstruction of the post-World War Two global economy along multilateral lines. Prime Minister William Lyon Mackenzie King quickly associated Canada with the Atlantic Charter, despite his chagrin that neither Roosevelt nor Churchill had consulted him on its wording.[7] Canadian officials participated in the two years of negotiations that led to the founding of the International Monetary Fund (IMF); Louis Rasminsky, an official with the Bank of Canada, even drafted his own proposal for postwar monetary stabilization, which was submitted for international consideration alongside the American and British plans prepared by Harry Dexter White and John Maynard Keynes, respectively. Canada participated in the very first round of international tariff-cutting negotiations after the war and contributed to the drafting of the General Agreement on Tariffs and Trade (GATT). And, of course, in 1946 the Canadian government provided Great Britain with a $1.25 billion loan to help it resume its position as one of the two pillars of the global economy. On its surface, Ottawa's support for economic multilateralism during the 1940s suggests a break with decades of protectionism and bilateralism. But this break was more one of style than substance. The means had changed, but the end remained what it had been for decades: secure access to the American and British markets.

Long before the Statute of Westminster in 1931, Canada enjoyed almost total freedom of action in its foreign economic policy. The British North America Act authorized the federal government to issue currency and determine its external value. Like much the rest of the world, however, Canada adhered to the gold standard both before the First World War and for a brief time after it, surrendering its power to manipulate the exchange rate so as to encourage exports. While Ottawa could not independently sign off on trade agreements, the BNA Act did give it the right to set tariffs, a right it exercised with considerable enthusiasm for six and a half decades after Confederation. After the 1878 election the National Policy of Sir John A. Macdonald ruled the day, providing Canada's manufacturing industries with ample protection and the federal government with ample revenue. For the producers of primary products – the farmers, the lumberjacks, the fishermen – Ottawa welcomed markets anywhere it could find them, but concentrated its efforts on improving

Canada's access to the markets of its two largest trading partners, the United Kingdom and the United States.[8]

From the United Kingdom, Ottawa hoped to secure preferential market access based upon imperial kinship. Canada first extended preferential treatment to British exports in 1897, a policy adopted by the Liberal government of Sir Wilfrid Laurier in part to curry favour among English Canadian imperialists.[9] While these preferential tariffs, as well as the ones that followed, were extended unilaterally, Ottawa never lost hope that London would one day reciprocate, according Canadian primary producers a privileged place in British markets. But for years London would not return the favour, instead standing firm in the commitment to free trade that it had maintained since the 1840s. The United Kingdom only began to edge away from free trade at the end of the First World War, when, in a nod to imperial unity, it accorded the dominions limited preferential access to its markets. With one important exception, Canada did not greatly benefit from these preferences; the single exception was the automotive sector, where Canadian exports to Britain and the rest of the Empire increased substantially during the 1920s. Canadian primary producers, however, continued to compete in British markets on the same terms as non-Commonwealth producers.[10]

From the United States, Ottawa hoped to secure improved market access through reciprocity. Despite his status as the author of the National Policy, Macdonald avidly sought reciprocity with the United States both before and after he began erecting a high tariff wall around the country; indeed, Macdonald believed that high tariffs might one day bring the Americans to the negotiating table. After his final failed attempt to strike a deal with the United States, Macdonald made a virtue out of a necessity, winning the 1891 election on the anti-reciprocity platform of "The Old Flag, the Old Policy, the Old Leader."[11] Two decades later, Laurier succeeded where Macdonald had so often failed, concluding a reciprocity agreement with the United States in 1911. For his efforts, voters tossed him out on his ear later that year and the deal died. After the First World War, the King government signalled its interest in reaching an arrangement with the United States by including a call for reciprocity in its 1923 budget.[12] That Mackenzie King, for whom the Liberal defeat in 1911 was both a personal and political formative experience, was willing to put out reciprocity feelers a year and a half into his first turn as prime minister – tentative though those feelers may have been – speaks volumes about Canada's abiding interest in improving its presence in the American market.

Despite their lack of privileged access to either the British or the American market, Canadian exporters did just fine for themselves. As they had been before 1914, the United States and the United Kingdom were by far Canada's two best customers for much of the interwar period. Together they took at least 69 percent of Canada's exports from 1926 to 1928. Exports to all countries continued to be a critical component of prosperity. From 1926 to 1928, more than 20 percent of gross national product was attributable to exports; exports to the United States and the United Kingdom alone produced at least 15 percent of national income.[13] Such a heavy reliance upon foreign markets was, however, a mixed blessing. When international demand was high, times were good. But when international demand was low, times were bad. And by 1929, times were about to become very bad indeed. As global trade declined during the Great Depression, so did Canada's fortunes. Exports to all countries plummeted from $1.33 billion in 1928, the last non-Depression year, to $487 million just four years later. In that same year of 1932, exports to all countries contributed a little less than 13 percent of the nation's income, with exports to the United States and the United Kingdom accounting for a little less than 9 percent.[14]

Ottawa's *sauve qui peut* response to this catastrophe mirrored that of most governments. It was also in keeping with the direction of Canadian trade policy for decades, with its faith in high tariffs, imperial preferences, and reciprocity as the path to prosperity. R. B. Bennett's Conservatives won the 1930 federal election in part by promising that higher tariffs would "blast" Canada's way out of the Depression. Within weeks of becoming Prime Minister, Bennett introduced legislation effecting an immediate tariff increase; more increases followed in his budget of June 1931.[15] Like Macdonald, Bennett reasoned that higher tariffs would give his government the leverage it needed to pry open foreign markets.[16]

Also like his predecessors, Bennett sought to improve Canada's access to the British market. He pushed for the creation of a preferential trading bloc at the October 1930 Commonwealth conference in London, but Britain would have none of it. London was more open to the idea at the 1932 Commonwealth conference in Ottawa, where the imperial preference system was vastly expanded. The preferences agreed to at Ottawa differed from previous preferences in several important respects. First, they were reciprocal, as Britain abandoned free trade and extended preferences to the dominions. Second, they were bound, meaning they could not be modified without the consent of the country that benefited from them. Finally, Britain agreed to implement preferences on products of interest to Canadian exporters, such as wheat. This exercise in economic regionalism came at the expense of the rest of the world, as many of the preferences were achieved by raising tariffs against goods sold by non-Commonwealth countries, rather than lowering tariffs on goods sold by Commonwealth nations.[17]

Bennett also tried to beat back the Depression by improving Canada's access to the American market. In February 1933, a month before Roosevelt's presidential inauguration, Bennett told the House of Commons that he would welcome reciprocity with the United States. He personally delivered the same message to Roosevelt in Washington two months later.[18] In 1935, taking advantage of the newly-enacted Reciprocal Trade Agreements Act (RTAA) – the 1934 U.S. law that authorized the president to reduce tariffs by up to 50 percent in exchange for tariff concessions by other countries – Canada and the United States began negotiating a trade agreement. After his victory in the October 1935 election, Mackenzie King quickly finished what his predecessor had started and concluded the negotiations with the United States. The resulting agreement, which was signed in 1935, was followed by a second one three years later. The 1938 U.S.-Canadian trade agreement was actually one of three separate, but linked, bilateral deals among the United States, the United Kingdom, and Canada. Washington had initially sought just an agreement with London, but given that it wanted concessions affecting bound preferences granted to Canada, Ottawa was brought into the negotiations. The 1938 agreement between the United States and Canada both clarified and expanded the 1935 deal.[19]

On the eve of the Second World War, therefore, Ottawa had succeeded in achieving two long-pursued goals, preferential access to the markets of the British Commonwealth and a bilateral trade pact with the United States.[20] Canadian policy makers had also witnessed firsthand the dependence of their nation's prosperity upon foreign trade. And as important as trade had been before the advent of war in 1939, the King government believed it would be even more important once the fighting had stopped. Just as for the United States, it was the Second World War that finally hoisted Canada out of the Great Depression. The massive effort to rearm and to meet the urgent demand for food and materiel from Britain after the fall of France in 1940 provided the stimulus that got the farms and factories of North America up and running again.[21] In 1940, Canadian exports to the United Kingdom had risen by 50 percent of their 1938 levels; by 1942, they had doubled. In 1944, the last full year of the war, Canada exported nearly $1.2 billion worth of goods to Britain, more than a trebling of the 1938 value of $339 million. Trade with the United States also soared. In 1938, Canada sent $270 million worth of goods south of the border; by 1944, that figure had reached nearly $1.3 billion.[22]

The Second World War did more than just lift the country out of the Depression. It changed the very structure of Canada's economy. Under the resolute direction of C. D. Howe – officially the Minister of Munitions and

Supply, but unofficially the "minister of everything" – Canada's industrial base was modernized and expanded, such that by war's end it was a bona fide industrial power.[23] These changes shaped the King government's approach to the postwar world. The revitalization of the primary products sector inspired a determination to hold on to markets established before the war; that is to say, markets in the United Kingdom and the United States. The emergence of a robust manufactured goods sector suggested the need to seek out new markets; the most likely candidate in this category was the world's largest economy, the United States.[24]

As Canadian policy makers in the 1940s thought about the postwar world, therefore, they faced much the same dilemma as had their predecessors. To prosper, Canada had to trade. Canadian exports overwhelmingly went to two countries, the United States and the United Kingdom. How best to ensure that Canadian producers could continue to sell their wares abroad, particularly in these two markets? The King government's response to this old dilemma was to embrace a new policy, rejecting the bilateralism of the past in favour of multilateralism. Why the change?

Multilateralism was in the air during the Second World War. As Wendell Willkie, the 1940 Republican U.S. presidential nominee, put it in his best-selling 1943 book, there was just *One World*. The belief that the fates of all countries were inextricably linked, that the United Nations – as Roosevelt dubbed the wartime anti-fascist alliance, the name itself a nod to the prevailing spirit – would have to work together to secure the peace as they were working together to win the war, informed the postwar planning process. To a certain extent, then, Ottawa's support for multilateralism was simply in keeping with the times. Put another way, Ottawa embraced multilateralism because that was what was on offer. From August 1941, when they signed the Atlantic Charter, until October 1947, when they, along with twenty-one other countries, signed the General Agreement on Tariffs and Trade, the United States and the United Kingdom – with varying and variable degrees of enthusiasm – worked to rebuild the global economy along multilateral lines. The IMF, the World Bank, the GATT, the stillborn International Trade Organization (ITO): each of these institutions was the product of proposals originating in either Washington or London. Ottawa pursued the nation's interest in an international environment largely not of its own making. It had to work with what it had. And what the King government had was Canada's two largest trading partners, the United States and, to a lesser degree, the United Kingdom, working toward multilateralism. Unless Canada wanted to go it alone after the war, turning its back on its two most important relationships, it had little choice but to support multilateralism too. As J. Scott Macdonald, a long-time Department of External Affairs economics specialist, observed in March 1943, "While we cannot set ourselves up in opposition to the 'Great Powers', we can try to influence their programmes, while they are still in the formative stage, in a sense favourable to ourselves."[25]

But this does not explain the enthusiasm with which Canada signed on to the multilateralist project. Ottawa could have been a far more reluctant or obstructionist participant in the postwar negotiations. Australia, for example, was very sceptical of the proposed new global economic order and was, as historian Ann Capling puts it, very much the *enfant terrible* of the postwar planning process.[26] Indeed, Australia's reluctance to offer its unreserved support for freer trade and currency convertibility was a source of frequent frustration for Canadian policy makers. At one point their differences resulted in a bitter row, when Canberra baulked at committing to postwar economic multilateralism as a condition for receiving wartime assistance from Canada. The dispute grew so sharp that the King government threatened to exclude Australia from the Mutual Aid program altogether, as well as announce the reason for its exclusion.[27] The two countries eventually came to terms and the flow of aid was not disrupted, but the episode throws into sharp relief Ottawa's enthusiasm for economic multilateralism.

Why was Ottawa so enthusiastic? In short, because multilateralism seemed likely to secure Canada's place within a prosperous North Atlantic triangle. In the realm of international monetary policy, Canada's support for the creation of the IMF was driven by its historic pattern of trade. Before 1939, Canada had usually enjoyed a trade surplus with Britain and a trade deficit with America. It used the proceeds of its surplus with the United Kingdom, as well as, to a lesser extent, with the rest of the Commonwealth and the non-Anglo-American world, to pay for its deficit with the United States. Canada thus needed a world in which British pounds could be converted into American dollars, a world characterized by multilateral, rather than bilateral, settlements. Both Keynes' clearing union and White's stabilization fund looked to such a world and, as such, both plans commanded Canadian support. As Graham Towers, the governor of the Bank of Canada, noted of Keynes' proposal, "Canada's position will be so unsatisfactory, if the sterling area and the U.S. dollar area are separated by a stone wall, we are almost bound to give support to the Clearing Union idea."[28] In this light, it becomes clear that Ottawa's general support for multilateral currency convertibility was driven in large part by a very specific interest in sterling-dollar convertibility. While the ability to convert French francs or Dutch guilder or Mexican pesos was certainly desirable, francs and guilder and pesos alone would not go very far in paying for Canada's imports from the United States. Above all else, Canada needed sterling-dollar convertibility; it needed, as it were, to square the North Atlantic monetary triangle. That meant that it needed an international monetary regime to which both the United Kingdom and the United States could commit.[29]

Canada's diplomacy reflected its need for a postwar monetary regime that included both the United States and the United Kingdom. In talks with the British, Canadian officials offered amendments that would make Keynes' highly expansionist clearing union plan more attractive to a creditor nation such as the United States. In talks with the Americans, they urged the augmentation of the stabilization fund's financial resources and the dilution of American influence in favour of a more truly multilateral institution, changes that would appeal to likely debtor nations such as Great Britain. The famous Rasminsky plan was specifically designed to bridge the gap between the British and American approaches; Rasminsky himself noted that his proposal melded "some of the essential features of the Keynes plan and the White plan."[30] When, in June 1943, Rasminsky's plan was submitted for consideration to a group of international experts at a meeting in Washington, Ottawa hoped that it would serve to break an Anglo-American impasse in the negotiations.[31] While this initiative failed to bring the two sides together – British and American officials had to find their own way to a compromise – it does illustrate Canada's stake in Anglo-American agreement. As L. P. Thompson-McCausland, an official with the Bank of England, noted after a conversation with him in the autumn of 1943, Rasminsky, "like all Canadians, is anxious above all for Washington and London to agree."[32]

But Ottawa did not confine itself to the role of the honest broker. Throughout the international monetary negotiations, the King government was particularly conscious of the fact that whatever plan was adopted, it would have to meet with a favourable response in the United States, particularly in Congress and among the American people. At one point early in the planning process, Ottawa even suggested that "in order to avoid the appearance of competition and of differences in principles," London should abandon the Keynes plan altogether, accepting White's proposal as a basis for further talks. London, not surprisingly, rejected this suggestion out of hand.[33] Ottawa's sympathy for Washington's position was motivated in part by the knowledge that it would be the United States that would foot the bill of monetary stabilization. It was also motivated by a similarity of interest, as it became clear that Canada would also enjoy postwar creditor status.[34] At the Bretton Woods conference in July 1944, Canada secured amendments to the IMF Articles of Agreement that reflected this reality, such as provision for the appointment of the second largest creditor nation to the

Executive Board and the right of creditors to draw upon fund resources for capital account transactions.

Canada's anticipated creditor position also led it to side with the United States at Bretton Woods against British efforts to dilute the obligation of IMF members to maintain fixed exchange rates and ensure currency convertibility. Minister of Finance James Ilsley suggested that if Britain succeeded in securing for members the right to change their exchange rates without IMF approval, "it might mean that Canada would have to remain out of the Fund and ... there would be very little, if any, chance of the United States accepting the Fund."[35] Similarly, the dispute over the obligation to ensure currency convertibility grew so tense that it seemed possible that the negotiations might break down altogether.[36] During the final week of the conference, one British delegate wrote to London of the Canadian fear "that the whole object of the Fund has been destroyed, due to the success of the U.K. in turning the Fund away from the original objectives of stability of exchanges combined with convertibility."[37] On the fixity of exchange rates, the British prevailed.[38] But on the obligation to ensure convertibility, the result was less clear. The Americans and Canadians thought that they got their way, while the British believed they got theirs; the real result was months of Anglo-American correspondence on the issue.[39] Despite Ilsley's fears and the Canadian delegation's disillusionment, Rasminsky endorsed the work done at Bretton Woods as "realistic and constructive" and "a good beginning."[40] Given Canada's overriding interest in Anglo-American agreement, an imperfect IMF was better than no IMF at all.

Currency convertibility would mean nothing if Canadian exporters could not sell their goods abroad. And so when, in April 1943, London notified the dominions that it would propose a far-reaching multilateral commercial convention to Washington, Ottawa was quick to offer support. Norman Robertson, the under-secretary of state for External Affairs, commended the initiative to King as "the only really sound and comprehensive method of securing satisfactory conditions of trade and perhaps, in the long run, of political security."[41] Two months later, at a meeting of Commonwealth experts in London, Canadian officials lent the British initiative their "wholehearted support."[42]

For a country whose prosperity was so dependent upon foreign trade, and that welcomed markets wherever it could find them, support for a major multilateral trade liberalization effort appears virtually a given. One potential benefit of such a project would be the diversification of Canada's trading portfolio.[43] Ottawa was keen, for example, to retain the country's position in the markets of the other dominions. During the 1930s, Canadian exporters had increased their sales to countries such as Australia and South Africa, thanks both to imperial preferences and the relatively swift economic recovery of these nations.[44] The King government was also interested in improving Canada's access to markets outside the Commonwealth, providing postwar loans to countries such as France, the Netherlands, and China to help them rebuild their economies with the aid of Canadian exports.[45] The markets of Latin America also beckoned, prompting Ottawa to send a delegation south at the end of the war to seek out new opportunities.[46] Canada's interest in improving its access to markets outside the North Atlantic triangle was reflected in the fact that it concluded fourteen trade agreements at the first postwar round of tariff negotiations, held in Geneva in 1947. Two of these agreements, those with the United Kingdom and the United States, covered markets in which Canada had enjoyed a strong presence for decades. But the other twelve – with the Benelux nations, Brazil, Ceylon, Chile, China, Cuba, Czechoslovakia, France, India, Norway, South Africa, and Syria-Lebanon – were with countries that had traditionally taken far fewer Canadian exports.[47]

But the development of markets in Europe, Latin America, and Asia was a long run project; moreover, no single non-Anglo-American market promised to serve as a realistic substitute for either of Canada's two traditional markets. In the short run, there were – as there had ever been – two primary outlets for Canadian exports, the United States and the United Kingdom. And multilateralism promised significant gains in both markets. In his list of reasons why Ottawa should endorse London's multilateral trade initiative, Robertson did not omit the benefits it could bring in terms of U.S.-Canadian economic relations. Noting that it had gained almost all of the tariff cuts possible under the RTAA, Robertson asserted that Canada "would have very little, therefore, to gain by further negotiations on a bilateral basis and must look to a multilateral convention, on the broad lines of the British proposal, if we are to secure ready access to the United States and to world markets."[48] Several months later, William A. Mackintosh, the Queen's University economist who spent the war as a special adviser in the Department of Finance, identified several more reasons why the government should continue to throw its weight behind the British initiative:

We have a great deal to gain from U.K.-U.S. agreement and our support may become the decisive factor. We have a great deal to gain also in supporting those in the United Kingdom who are pressing for multilateral solutions and in avoiding a relapse into bilateralist proposals. We need both the U.K. and the U.S. as customers but we need them under a multilateral arrangement where neither can apply undue pressure to us. There would be no net gain in any move which would merely substitute one market for the other. A multilateral convention is also our best chance of re-entry into the European market from which we would probably be excluded under regional arrangements."[49]

Ottawa was interested in market diversification, but it was the Anglo-American angle that was uppermost in Canadian minds.

Multilateralism's potential for expanding export opportunities in the United States in particular was a recurrent theme in Ottawa's thinking in 1943 and 1944.[50] In May 1943, for example, Deputy Minister of Finance W. C. Clark suggested that Canada might be best off proposing "a ten-year agreement with the United States with progressive reduction in the tariff on all commodities to a nominal level all round by the close of the period and the formation of an 'economic club' on this basis open to participation by all countries who are willing to abide by the same rules."[51] Robertson floated a similar idea past Jack Hickerson, assistant chief of the European Affairs Division at the Department of State, suggesting that Canada would "go the whole distance as far as abolition of preferences is concerned, provided the United States and the United Kingdom are willing to make compensatory tariff reductions."[52] Robertson went further still in February 1944, proposing a bilateral sectoral free trade agreement to American officials. In December 1943, Washington, which had just hosted a series of Anglo-American talks on postwar economic issues, invited Ottawa to bilateral talks on international commercial policy. Robertson urged on King the importance of the talks in furthering the multilateral project and asserted that "there may be a chance, right now, of securing a comprehensive and thorough going trade agreement with the United States, which could be the first major instalment of the multilateral programme which nearly everybody recognizes as the desirable goal."[53] Two months later, during the second session of the talks, Robertson proposed that Canada and the United States consider bilateral free trade in various commodities, the benefits of which would be universalized through the most favoured nation principle. In presenting his proposal, Robertson argued that "some such arrangement would be necessary in order to enable Canada to adhere to [the multilateral] convention."[54] Over the next two years, Canadian officials twice more proposed sectoral bilateral free trade to the Americans, in July 1945 and January 1946.[55] Despite the fact that none of these suggestions was taken up by Washington, in April 1946 Canadian officials were still considering whether the limits imposed by the RTAA on America's tariff cutting authority made a supplementary bilateral trade deal desirable.[56]

Canada was not the only country that saw in multilateralism its best chance of cracking the American market. The other nations of the Commonwealth, including the United Kingdom, were also keen to increase their sales to the United States. And, as it turns out, the Commonwealth had something that the United States wanted. Or, more precisely, something the United States wanted to get rid of – imperial preferences. Washington was determined to dismantle the Ottawa system of preferences, on both ideological and economic grounds.[57] But no Commonwealth country, including Canada, would reduce preferences unless it received compensatory tariff cuts from the United States.[58] The fact that the Ottawa preferences were bound suggested that any trade negotiations between the United States and the Commonwealth nations would be very complicated indeed; the 1938 U.S.-U.K.-Canadian trade talks had shown that bound preferences automatically expanded a bilateral negotiation into a multilateral one. Ottawa consistently argued in favour of unbinding preferences for the purposes of negotiations with third parties, promising to consult affected Commonwealth partners on proposed reductions.[59] In part, the King government opposed the binding of preferences as an infringement of Canadian independence. But bound preferences also circumscribed its negotiating authority. And as Francine McKenzie notes in her study of imperial preferences in the 1940s, "[l]ike all the other negotiating teams" at the 1947 Geneva tariff negotiations, "the Canadians sought tariff concessions in the US above all else."[60]

Understanding why Ottawa was quick to endorse multilateralism also helps to explain why it was just as quick to consider alternatives to it. Multilateralism offered the best chance of ensuring Canadian exports to both the United States and the United Kingdom; that is, of securing Canada's place within the North Atlantic triangle. When it began to appear, by the spring of 1944, that multilateralism might not ensure Canada's access to the British market after all, senior officials began to consider alternatives. Barely a year after it had first proposed a comprehensive multilateral trade agreement, London began to back away from it. Churchill's wartime coalition cabinet was divided over the best way of ensuring British prosperity and influence in the postwar world. While some ministers continued to support multilateralism, others put their faith in preferences and the sterling bloc.[61] In March, Robertson suggested to Clark that

as the multilateral programme becomes more modest and more remote, we shall have to look more seriously and more quickly at the specific problems of Canadian-American trade relations. I had envisaged a bilateral agreement with the United States, supplementing a general multilateral tariff reduction, but if effective multilateral action is to be indefinitely deferred and, when achieved, prove modest, then I think we may have to look at the question again from the continental viewpoint.[62]

Clark agreed, replying that "for some time I have been growing increasingly sceptical of the possibilities of real achievement under the multilateral program and therefore increasingly concerned with the advisability, from our point of view, of a radical continental approach coupled with a radical Canadian-British program."[63] In April 1944, at a meeting of Commonwealth prime ministers in London, Canada was the only country that remained committed to multilateral trade liberalization; the United Kingdom was divided, while the other dominions favoured retaining imperial preferences.[64] That autumn, reports began to roll in from around the Commonwealth of discrimination against Canadian exports on the basis of dollar scarcity.[65] Britain's commitment to multilateralism, as well as its openness to Canadian exports, was slipping away.

A British retreat into economic regionalism augured ill for Canada. Economically, not only would the loss of British and Commonwealth markets represent a disaster, but officials such as Towers worried that London might convince the Europeans and perhaps other nations to join an anti-dollar economic bloc.[66] The political implications were equally undesirable. At the very least, economic regionalism would engender friction between the United Kingdom on the one hand and Canada and the United States on the other.[67] It might even lead, some feared, to the disappearance of Canada. Mackenzie King fretted over the potential political implications of British protectionism, writing in his diary in February 1945 of "the possibility of Britain to save her own position lending herself to a series of restraints in trade which might raise the most serious problems within the Empire that have come up thus far. Something that might drive Canada into a position of annexation with the States through inability to get any markets in Britain."[68] King was not the only one who feared this possibility. The previous month, Gordon Munro, an officer at the U.K. High Commission, reported "that the Canadians are really worried at the prospect that discrimination against them as being a non-sterling country will drive them into the arms of the United States and may even lead to an outcry for secession if the economic pressure becomes extreme."[69]

Ottawa's response to the deteriorating situation was to offer, in February 1945, a loan to help the United Kingdom through the postwar transitional period, with the dual goals of keeping it on the multilateral straight and narrow and keeping it buying Canadian goods.[70] Graham Towers, the intellectual force behind the initiative, tellingly entitled an early memorandum on the subject, "A Proposal for Maintaining Canada's Exports to the Sterling Area during the Post-War Transitional Period."[71] Asserting that "it is the volume of our exports to the United Kingdom which constitutes the crux of our post-war problem," Towers proposed that Ottawa provide Britain with a credit on concessionary terms, in return for which London would promise not to discriminate against Canadian exports on currency grounds and provide hard currency to sterling bloc members for purchases of Canadian goods.[72] Over the ensuing months, Ottawa and London reached two agreements geared toward protecting Canada's exports to Britain. First, London promised, in return for the continuation of wartime assistance, not to forgo essential imports of goods traditionally purchased from Canada on grounds of dollar scarcity for the remainder of the war.[73] After the war, London agreed, even before the Anglo-Canadian loan negotiations began, to continue to import a token amount – 20 percent of pre-war value – of selected goods from traditional Canadian suppliers. In agreeing to the token import scheme, London heeded the advice of officials such as Munro, who asserted that "it is what the President of the Board of Trade may be able and prepared to do rather than what the Chancellor of the Exchequer is prepared to accept which will be the deciding factor as regards the terms of any financial loan that we shall obtain from Canada."[74]

The United Kingdom was to apply both its pledge not to discriminate against essential wartime imports on grounds of currency scarcity and its token import policy on non-discriminatory grounds; that is to say, London decided to extend similar treatment in both cases to imports from the United States as well.[75] This was more or less in keeping with the spirit of multilateralism; at the very least, both policies were non-discriminatory. But Ottawa was also willing to pursue less multilateral tactics to protect Canada's access to the British market. In 1946, the two countries concluded a deal that guaranteed Canadian wheat farmers four years of sales and the British government four years of stable (and, as it happened, lower than market value) prices. The agreement was largely the work of the minister of Agriculture, Jimmy Gardiner, who simply gave the Saskatchewan farmers he represented in Parliament what they wanted.[76] Despite the warnings of officials such as Robertson that the deal "would be in direct conflict with the general policy of freer international trade,"[77] the Cabinet approved it.[78] Washington immediately protested that the arrangement "would cut right across the middle of the whole multilateral idea;"[79] it was also, of course, detrimental to America's economic interests. In deference to American sensitivities, the deal was not signed until after Congress approved a $3.75 billion reconstruction loan to the United Kingdom. Nevertheless, the deal was what it was: a distinctly bilateralist effort by Canada to hold on to its place in the British market.[80]

Canada's $1.25 billion loan to Great Britain was not enough to keep it in the black. Nor did the $3.75 billion loan from the United States do the trick. Britain's economic problems were far too big for easy resolution, as were those faced by the newly liberated nations of Europe and

Asia. For such countries, the immediate, or even imminent, relaxation of financial and commercial controls was unthinkable. Ottawa grew increasingly concerned, casting about for other means of securing access to Canada's two largest markets. Before the war was even a year over, Clark was writing to Robertson of his worry that "the thinking of most of the world outside of the United States, Canada and (perhaps) the United Kingdom – [is] that multilateralism is becoming a dream which no one really believes in any longer and for which very few are prepared to make any immediate sacrifice of their power to manoeuvre." While not ready to give up the fight, "whether because of a jaunty idealism or a realization of how much the prosperity of Canada depends upon multilateralism," Clark wondered whether Ottawa "should cease dreaming and go to work on an attempt to get from the United States an approach to a completely open door so far as Canada alone is concerned. However, the time does not seem to me to be ripe even for this and so I would continue to do as much as I can to promote the ITO objectives."[81] In the autumn of 1946, when international experts gathered in London for commercial policy talks, delegates from both war-ravaged nations and newly industrializing countries proposed so many conditions and caveats to the draft ITO charter that the Canadians feared "that the final document might well be almost useless." To Robertson, now High Commissioner to the United Kingdom, the prospect of such a treaty suggested that "it might be wise to abandon the attempt and start instead from the other end of the scale." Perhaps the United States, the United Kingdom, and Canada should form their own trade organization, which other nations could join if they so chose.[82]

But the multilateral trade liberalization effort soldiered on. In April 1947, representatives from twenty-three countries gathered in Geneva for the first postwar round of tariff negotiations, as well as to continue work on the ITO Charter. Canada's tariff negotiations went relatively smoothly; far more smoothly, at any rate, than those between the United States and the United Kingdom. By September, the dispute over imperial preferences that had bedevilled the Anglo-American relationship for years grew so tense that it threatened the breakdown of the negotiations, prompting Secretary of State for External Affairs Louis St. Laurent to suggest to his fellow cabinet members:

if the United Kingdom and the United States failed to reach agreement, there would be nothing of substance left for Canada in the tariff agreements negotiated at Geneva. The efforts to establish a multilateral system which Canada had supported strongly from the outset would have failed. In this event, urgent consideration would have to be given to the negotiation of more extensive bilateral arrangements with the United States. A careful assessment would have to be made of the comparative advantages to Canada of such new arrangements with the United States as an alternative to the maintenance and development of the Commonwealth preferential system.[83]

In the end, the Americans and the British reached a compromise and the negotiations did not break down. In October 1947, all twenty-three nations, including the United States, the United Kingdom, and Canada, signed the GATT, which, when the ITO failed to materialize, provided the framework for decades of trade liberalization. The world did not end. But St. Laurent's doomsday prediction was telling. If the United States and the United Kingdom could not come to terms, Canada would have nothing to gain from economic multilateralism and would be forced to decide where its destiny lay. Was it with the United States or with the United Kingdom? This was a choice that Ottawa did not want to make.[84] The King government had avoided this choice in early 1945 by offering Great Britain a loan. Now it sought to avoid the choice again. When London floated a Commonwealth customs union trial balloon in September 1947, Ottawa quickly shot it down.[85] Ottawa was equally unwilling to consider a customs union with the United States, but it was willing to consider a bilateral free trade deal that would leave imperial preferences intact. The negotiations, which took place during the winter of 1947–1948, also resulted in a plan for a second free trade deal, between Canada and the United Kingdom. Neither deal came to pass, as King, who really had learned the lesson of the 1911 election and who sought, above all else, national manoeuvrability, put a stop to the negotiations.[86] This suggests possibly the most important factor driving Ottawa's embrace of multilateralism. A multilateral global economy founded on Anglo-American cooperation would allow Canada not to have to choose between its two most important markets and its two most important relationships. Currency convertibility and the IMF meant that Canada would not have to choose between the dollar bloc and the sterling bloc. Multilateral trade negotiations and the GATT meant that Canada would not have to choose between reciprocity and imperial preferences. Multilateralism was Canada's best bet to achieve "continuing prosperity, and harmony with both the United States and the Commonwealth."[87] If forced to choose, the King government would more likely have chosen North America over the Commonwealth, but this was a choice it did not want to make. Multilateralism represented Canada's best hope of avoiding that choice.[88]

Ultimately, this was a choice over which Ottawa had little control.[89] Sapped of every last ounce of its economic strength, Britain's postwar transitional period lasted for several long decades, rather than the hoped-for few short years. As the years went by, the United Kingdom's relative importance as a destination for Canadian exports declined. None of the markets outside the North Atlantic triangle proved capable of picking up the slack – not elsewhere in the Commonwealth, not in Europe, not in Asia, not in Latin America – either singly or combined. Ottawa long hoped to find such a market; initiatives such as Liberal Prime Minister Pierre Trudeau's "Third Option" reflected this hope. But the pull of the robust market just over the border proved too strong, a reality recognized in bilateral agreements such as the 1965 Auto Pact and the 1989 Canada-U.S. free trade deal. In this respect, economic multilateralism failed to achieve its primary purpose of maintaining Canada's exports to both of its traditional markets, the United Kingdom and the United States. Ottawa's decades-long effort to secure national prosperity through the North Atlantic triangle, an effort as old as the country itself, had come to an end.

In a recent essay, Tom Keating observes that "John Holmes once warned against turning a good idea into a dogma. Multilateralism is not an end in itself."[90] For the Canadian policy makers who first embraced it during the 1940s, economic multilateralism was a practical response to a problem, not a principled stand. The problem was ensuring the continued flow of Canadian exports to the United States and the United Kingdom. Before the war, Ottawa had tried to secure Canada's access to its two most important markets through the bilateralism of imperial preferences and reciprocity. After 1941, it changed tactics, embracing multilateralism instead. While Ottawa certainly welcomed an expansive, universal multilateralism that included as many countries as possible, what it sought above all else was an international economic order in which Canada could continue to trade with both the United States and the United Kingdom, relieved of the necessity of choosing one country over the other. For the government of William Lyon Mackenzie King, multilateralism did not represent an alternative to achieving prosperity within the North Atlantic triangle; it was simply a new means of seeking an old end.

NOTES

[*] The views expressed here are the author's and are not necessarily those of the U.S. Department of State or the U.S. Government. Information presented here is based on publicly available declassified sources.
1 Robert Bothwell and John English, "Canadian Trade Policy in the Age of American Dominance and British Decline, 1943–1947," reprinted in J.L. Granatstein, *Canadian Foreign Policy: Historical Readings, Revised Edition* (Toronto: Copp Clark Pitman Ltd., 1993), 191.

2 Tom Keating, *Canada and World Order: The Multilateralist Tradition in Canadian Foreign Policy* (Toronto: McClelland & Stewart Inc., 1993), 48.
3 Michael Hart, *A Trading Nation: Canadian Trade Policy from Colonialism to Globalization* (Vancouver: University of British Columbia Press, 2002), 133.
4 While scholars such as Bothwell and English, Keating, and Hart certainly acknowledge the role of the North Atlantic triangle in the King government's approach to economic multilateralism, they tend to assign it less importance as a motivating factor. See, for example, Bothwell and English, "Canadian Trade Policy," 183, 186; Keating, *Canada and World Order*, 52, 59; Hart, *A Trading Nation*, 133.
5 Hector MacKenzie reaches a similar conclusion about Canadian foreign economic policy in the immediate postwar period: "With the objectives of prosperity and economic security transcending other aims, there was no sharp doctrinal schism in Ottawa between adherents of 'multilateralism' and 'bilateralism' but an opportunistic or pragmatic approach exploring both strategies. Markets for Canada's exports had to be assured by whatever means were available. Even when wholeheartedly supporting ambitious and innovative multilateral schemes for international economic cooperation, Canadian policy-makers viewed such plans and commitments for the future (the 'longer term' so revered by economists and economic planners) through the lens of Canada's past and present finance and trade arrangements with the United Kingdom and the United States." Hector MacKenzie, "The ABCs of Canada's International Economic Relations, 1945–1951." Accessed May 6, 2008 via the Department of Foreign Affairs and International Trade website, http://www.dfait.gc.ca/hist/coldwar_section08-en.asp.
6 John Gerard Ruggie, *Winning the Peace: America and the World Order in the New Era* (New York: Columbia University Press, 1996), 20–22.
7 Library and Archives Canada (LAC), Privy Council Office Records, 7C/C4654/5671, Minutes of Cabinet War Committee meetings held 22 August 1941 and 18 September 1941. See also LAC, Diaries of William Lyon Mackenzie King (WLMK), 12 August 1941.
8 Hart, *A Trading Nation*, 61–4, 75, 126.
9 Francine McKenzie, *Redefining the Bonds of Commonwealth, 1939–1948: The Politics of Preference* (Houndmills, Basingstoke, Hampshire: Palgrave, Macmillan, 2002), 19.
10 Robert Bothwell, Ian Drummond, and John English, *Canada 1900–1945* (Toronto: University of Toronto Press, 1987), 223–5; Ian Drummond and Norman Hillmer, *Negotiating Freer Trade: The United Kingdom, the United States, Canada, and the Trade Agreements of 1938* (Waterloo, Ontario: Wilfrid Laurier University Press, 1989), 15; McKenzie, *Redefining the Bonds of Commonwealth, 1939–1948*, 19.
11 Hart, *A Trading Nation*, 58, 64–5, 69–70.
12 Bothwell, Drummond, and English, *Canada 1900–1945*, 224; *New York Times*, 12 May 1923.

13 F. H. Leacy, Editor, *Historical Statistics of Canada*, Second Edition (Ottawa: Statistics Canada, 1983), Series G389-395 and F1-13. Accessed 16 May 2008 via the Statistics Canada website, http://www.statcan.ca/english/freepub/11-516-XIE/sectiona/toc.htm.
14 F. H. Leacy, Editor, *Historical Statistics of Canada*, Second Edition (Ottawa: Statistics Canada, 1983), Series G389-395 and F1-13. Accessed 16 May 2008 via the Statistics Canada website, http://www.statcan.ca/english/freepub/11-516-XIE/sectiona/toc.htm.
15 *New York Times*, 17 September 1930 and 2 June 1931.
16 Kenneth Norrie and Douglas Owram, *A History of the Canadian Economy* (Toronto: Harcourt Brace Jovanovich, 1991), 504.
17 Drummond and Hillmer, *Negotiating Freer Trade*, 15; McKenzie, *Redefining the Bonds of Commonwealth, 1939–1948*, 21–5.
18 *New York Times*, 21 February 1933 and 30 April 1933.
19 Hart notes that "strictly speaking," the 1935 Canada-U.S. trade deal "was not a reciprocity agreement. Nevertheless, it was a fitting heir to that tradition and in many ways contained broader obligations." Hart, *A Trading Nation*, 122–124. (Quotation is from page 122.)
20 Hart, *A Trading Nation*, 125–6.
21 Norrie and Owram, *A History of the Canadian Economy*, 511, 524–5.
22 F. H. Leacy, Editor, *Historical Statistics of Canada*, Second Edition (Ottawa: Statistics Canada, 1983), Series G389-395. Accessed May 16, 2008 via the Statistics Canada website, http://www.statcan.ca/english/freepub/11-516-XIE/sectiona/toc.htm.
23 Norrie and Owram, *A History of the Canadian Economy*, 525–526; Hart, *A Trading Nation*, 127, 129.
24 See, for example, LAC, Department of Finance Records, Volume 576, 152-P, Angus to Robertson, 21 September 1943.
25 LAC, Department of External Affairs Records, Volume 2869, 1843-A-40c Part 1, Macdonald to Mackintosh, 25 March 1943. Keating observes that "[e]ven if Canada failed to redesign the new order to meet the country's specific interests, the effects of whatever arrangements the Americans and British arrived at would be profound for Canada." Keating, *Canada and World Order*, 54.
26 Ann Capling, *Australia and the Global Trade System: From Havana to Seattle* (Cambridge University Press: Cambridge, England, 2001), chapter 1.
27 LAC, Privy Council Office Records, 44/D-13-5-A/1943–1945 August, Secretary of State for External Affairs (SSEA) to Canadian High Commissioner to Australia (CHCA), No.233, 11 December 1943 and SSEA to CHCA, No.4, January 5th, 1944. See also WLMK, 5 December 1943.
28 Bank of Canada Archives (BOC), Graham Towers Papers, GFT75-10, Towers to Robertson, May 28th, 1942 and Unsigned memorandum, 28 May 1942. (Quotation is from the second document.)

29 Keating reaches a similar conclusion. Keating, *Canada and World Order*, 50.
30 LAC, Department of Finance Records, Volume 3447, International Clearing Union, "United Nations Currency Stabilisation and Clearing Fund," Unsigned and undated memorandum.
31 LAC, Department of External Affairs Records, Volume 3259, 6000-D-40 Part 2, Robertson to King, 29 May 1943; LAC, Department of Finance Records, Volume 3447, International Clearing Union, Mackintosh to Ilsley, 2 June 1943; LAC, Privy Council Office Records, 7C/C4875/5679, Minutes of Cabinet War Committee meeting held 2 June 1943.
32 Bank of England Archives (BOE), OV38/5, L. P. Thompson-McCausland to C. F. Cobbold, 3 October 1943. Thompson-McCausland noted that Keynes "got the same impression" in a subsequent discussion with Rasminsky.
33 LAC, Department of Finance Records, Volume 3981, M-1-7-2, SSEA to Secretary of State for Dominion Affairs (SSDA), No.43, 9 March 1943 and SSDA to SSEA, No.58, 15 March 1943. (Quotation is from the first document.)
34 J. L. Granatstein, *The Ottawa Men: The Civil Service Mandarins, 1935–1957* (Toronto: Oxford University Press, 1982), 143–5.
35 LAC, Department of Finance Records, Volume 3448, Post-war Agreed Monetary Fund, Memorandum on "International Monetary Fund," by Clark, 7 July 1944.
36 D. E. Moggridge, Editor, *The Collected Writings of John Maynard Keynes, Volume XXVI* (London: Macmillan Publishers Ltd., 1980), 124, 160, 162, 170–172; D. E. Moggridge, *Maynard Keynes: An economist's biography* (London: Routledge, 1992), 751; L. S. Pressnell, *External Economic Policy Since the War, Volume I: The Post-War Financial Settlement* (London: Her Majesty's Stationary Office, 1986), 172–3.
37 BOE, OV38/9, Unsigned letter from Bretton Woods, 14 July 1944.
38 Pressnell, *External Economic Policy Since the War, Volume I*, 160–161.
39 Ibid., 168–182.
40 LAC, Department of Finance Records, Volume 3391, 04747P-13, "United Nations Monetary and Financial Conference, CI/RPI, Report of Commission I (International Monetary Fund) to the Executive Plenary Session, July 20, 1944, Louis Rasminsky (Canada), Reporting Delegate."
41 LAC, Privy Council Office Records, 44/W-22-3/1941–1943, Memorandum from the Department of External Affairs to King, 26 April 1943. Robertson used similar arguments in his presentation to the Cabinet War Committee on the U.K. initiative. See LAC, Privy Council Office Records, 7C/C4875/5678, Minutes of Cabinet War Committee meeting held 28 April 1943.
42 National Archives of the United Kingdom (NAUK), T230/129, Post-War Commercial Policy Discussions, P.C.P. (43) 5, "Summary of Discussions between Officials of the United Kingdom, the Dominions and India held in London in June 1943."
43 Robert Bothwell, Ian Drummond, and John English, *Canada Since 1945: Power, Politics, and Provincialism* (Toronto: University of Toronto Press, 1989), 63.

44 Drummond and Hillmer, *Negotiating Freer Trade*, 13.
45 Hector MacKenzie, "The ABCs of Canada's International Economic Relations, 1945–1951." Accessed 6 May 2008 via the Department of Foreign Affairs and International Trade website, http://www.dfait.gc.ca/hist/coldwar_section08-en.asp.
46 James Rochlin, *Discovering the Americas: The Evolution of Canadian Foreign Policy Towards Latin America* (Vancouver: University of British Columbia Press, 1994), 27.
47 Michael Hart provides a useful summary of the effects of the trade agreements Canada concluded in Geneva in 1947 in *Also Present at the Creation: Dana Wilgress and the United Nations Conference on Trade and Employment at Havana* (Ottawa: Centre for Trade Policy and Law, 1995), 40–1.
48 LAC, Privy Council Office Records, 44/W-22-3/1941-1943, Memorandum from the Department of External Affairs to King, 26 April 1943.
49 LAC, Department of Finance Records, Volume 3989, T-2-2, Memorandum on "Special Trade Agreement Possibilities," by Mackintosh, 14 December 1943.
50 Keating asserts that "a multilateral system of trade liberalization would provide the benefits of better access to American markets without the political liabilities inherent in an exclusive bilateral arrangement." Keating, *Canada and World Order*, 59.
51 LAC, Department of Finance Records, Volume 3989, T-2-9-2, Volume 1, Clark to Wrong, 8 May 1943. A Canadian official identified only as "R" suggested that when it came to commercial policy, "Agreements should be reached by the principal trading countries. U.S., U.K. + Canada would suffice. Other Domin, China, Russia + perhaps some others could be admitted. A club would thus be formed open to admission by other countries and the price of admission should be made stiff. Countries unwilling to pay the price would be deprived of benefits. Can. is prepared to denounce all her commercial treaties on this basis." See Library of Congress, Leo Pasvolsky Papers, Box 5, International Organizations, Unidentified Papers, Untitled, unsigned, and undated memorandum.
52 Robertson also suggested to Hickerson "that this would involve in many cases reductions on our part greater in extent than those authorized on the trade agreement side. In this view I believe he is correct." National Archives and Records Administration (NARA), Department of State Records, Lot Files Pertaining to Europe, Records of the Office of European Affairs, Matthews-Hickerson Files 1935–1947, M1244, Box 8, Miscellaneous Files of John Hickerson, Memos to Mr. Atherton on Canada, Hickerson to Atherton, 30 June 1943. U.K. official James Meade reported his "impression – particularly from Rasminsky and Mackintosh – that they would be willing to see the virtual abolition of preferences in return for a really good convention which also covered tariffs." See Susan Howson and Donald Moggridge, Editors, *The Wartime Diaries of Lionel Robbins and James Meade, 1943–1945* (New York: St. Martin's Press, 1991), 144.

53 LAC, Department of External Affairs Records, Volume 5798, 265(s), Robertson to King, 21 December 1943.
54 NARA, Records of International Conferences, Commissions, and Expositions, International Conference on Trade and Employment (International Trade Organization), International Trade Organization Subject File 1933–1950, Box 20, Article VII - Discussions with Canadians - General, "Minutes of Meeting held Sunday Morning, February 13th."
55 LAC, Department of External Affairs Records, Volume 5773, 200(s), "Informal Discussions on Commercial Policy Between Officials of the Canadian Government and Officers of the Department of State"; LAC, Department of External Affairs Records, Volume 3808, 8378-40C, Part 1, "Trade and Employment Proposals," Undated.
56 LAC, Privy Council Records Office, 111/U-40-3/Volume 1/1945–1946, "Memorandum for File: International Meeting on Trade and Employment", 15 April 1946; LAC, Department of External Affairs Records, Volume 3808, 8378-40C, Part 2, "Commercial Policy," 10 April 1946.
57 For more on American opposition to the Ottawa system, see Richard N. Gardner, *Sterling-Dollar Diplomacy in Current Perspective: The Origins and the Prospects of Our International Economic Order* (New York: Columbia University Press, 1980), 16–20 and Thomas W. Zeiler, *Free Trade, Free World: The Advent of GATT* (Chapel Hill: The University of North Carolina Press, 1999), 7–9, 20–6.
58 See, for example, NAUK, T230/129, "Post-War Commercial Policy Discussions, P.C.P. (43) 5, Summary of Discussions between Officials of the United Kingdom, the Dominions and India held in London in June 1943." See also McKenzie, 125 and Zeiler, 24.
59 See, for example, LAC, Department of Finance Records, Volume 3591, L-11c, Article VII Discussions with Representatives of the Dominions and India, A.S.D. (Trade) (44) 5th Meeting, Minutes of a meeting held 3 March 1944; LAC, Department of Finance Records, Volume 3607, ITO-2, Preparatory Committee on Trade and Employment, British Commonwealth Talks, T.N. (P) (B.C.) (46) 14th Meeting, Minutes of a meeting held November 9th, 1946; LAC, Department of External Affairs Records, Volume 3845, 900-L-40, Part 1, Memorandum to St. Laurent, "On the Relation of Fixed Margins of Preference to the International Tariff Negotiations Opening in Geneva on April 8, 1947," Undated; LAC, Privy Council Office Records, A5a/T2365/2639, Cabinet Conclusions of Meeting held 19 February 1947, Meeting Number 329; and LAC, Department of External Affairs Records, Volume 3845, 900-L-40, Part 1, CHCUK to SSEA, No.540, 25 March 1947.
60 McKenzie, *Redefining the Bonds of Commonwealth, 1939–1948*, 221.
61 Pressnell, *External Economic Policy Since the War, Volume I*, 131–133; Zeiler, *Free Trade, Free World*, 37–40.
62 LAC, Department of Finance Records, Volume 3989, T-2-9-2, Volume 1, Robertson to Clark, 10 March 1944.

63 LAC, Department of Finance Records, Volume 3989, T-2-9-2, Volume 1, Clark to Robertson, 11 March 1944.
64 Pressnell, *External Economic Policy Since the War, Volume I*, 135; McKenzie, *Redefining the Bonds of Commonwealth, 1939–1948*, 160–1.
65 LAC, Privy Council Office Records, 29/T-50-1/1945-Aug.7, Minutes of External Trade Advisory Committee meetings held 26 September 1944, 10 October 1944, 14 November 1944, and 28 November 1944; LAC, Department of Finance Records, Volume 576, 152-P-1, Clark to Robertson, 20 September 1944 and Department of Trade and Commerce to the External Trade Advisory Committee, 18 September 1944.
66 LAC, Department of Finance Records, Volume 4369, U-3-11, "Notes on Meeting of Ministers and Officials in Office of Minister of Finance January 18, 1945, to Discuss Immediate Post-War Commercial Policy Outlook."
67 LAC, Department of Finance Records, Volume 4369, U-3-11, "Notes on Meeting of Ministers and Officials in Office of Minister of Finance January 18, 1945, to Discuss Immediate Post-War Commercial Policy Outlook." See also LAC, William Lyon Mackenzie King Papers, Primary Series Correspondence, Reel C-9881, Volume 391, SSEA to SSDA, No.47, 23 February 1945.
68 WLMK, 13 February 1945.
69 BOE, OV58/4, "Note of a conversation with Mr. Gordon Munro on 9th January 1945," by Thompson-McCausland, 9 January 1945.
70 Hector Mackenzie's "Mutual Assistance: The finance of British requirements in Canada during the Second World War" is the classic work on the link between Canada's commercial concerns and its wartime and postwar financial assistance to the United Kingdom. (Unpublished D.Phil. thesis, University of Oxford, 1981)
71 LAC, Department of Finance Records, Volume 4369, U-3-11, "A Proposal for Maintaining Canada's Exports to the Sterling Area during the Post-War Transitional Period," by Towers, 25 November 1944.
72 This summary of Towers' memorandum is based upon LAC, Department of Finance Records, Volume 4369, U-3-11, "A Proposal for Maintaining Canada's Exports to the Sterling Area during the Post-War Transitional Period," by Towers, 25 November 1944.
73 The U.K. reserved the right to re-open the matter should the increase in imports prove too financially burdensome. LAC, Department of Finance Records, Volume 4369, U-3-11, "Canadian Exports to the Sterling Area," Unsigned and undated.
74 NAUK, T236/355, "Note on Forthcoming United Kingdom-Canada Financial Negotiations," by Munro, 15 December 1945.
75 BOE, OV58/23, "Concessions for Canadian Imports into the Sterling Area – Note on Procedure in the United States," Unsigned and undated; LAC, Department of Finance Records, Volume 3437, Trade Policy and Financial Relations with U.K. and Sterling 1945, Mackintosh to Bryce, 1 August 1945.

109   Canadian Economic Multilateralism

76 Bothwell, Drummond, and English, *Canada Since 1945*, 66–67.
77 LAC, Privy Council Office Records, 68/D-10-1/1940–1948, Robertson to King, 17 June 1946. See also Bothwell and English, "Canadian Trade Policy," 152.
78 LAC, Privy Council Office Records, A5a/T2364/2638, Cabinet Conclusions of Meeting held 19 June 1946, Meeting Number 229.
79 LAC, William Lyon Mackenzie King Papers, Primary Series Correspondence, Reel C-9175, Volume 412, Canadian Ambassador to the United States (CAUS) to SSEA, WA-2518, 19 June 1946. See also Assistant Secretary of State for Economic and Business Affairs W. L. Clayton's criticisms of the wheat deal in LAC, Privy Council Office Records, 68/D-10-1/1940-1948, Memorandum by Pearson, 27 June 1946 and the aide-memoire given by the U.S. to the U.K. on the issue in LAC, William Lyon Mackenzie King Papers, Primary Series Correspondence, Reel C-9175, Volume 412, CAUS to SSEA, WA-2692, 3 July 1946.
80 Bothwell and English call the wheat deal "a practical testimony to Canada's overriding concern for trading security; if multilateral principles could not provide it, then bilateralism would have to do." See Bothwell and English, "Canadian Trade Policy," 189.
81 LAC, Department of External Affairs Records, Volume 3808, 8378-40C, Part 2, Clark to the Acting Secretary of State for External Affairs, 3 June 1946.
82 LAC, Department of External Affairs Records, Volume 3844, 9100-A-40, "Note on a Meeting in the High Commissioner's Office on 2nd November, 1946."
83 LAC, Privy Council Office Records, A5a/T2365/2640, Cabinet Conclusions of Meeting held 30 September 1947, Meeting Number 411.
84 Bothwell and English draw the same conclusion, referring to "Canada's happy split trading personality." See Bothwell and English, "Canadian Trade Policy," 183, 186. (Quotation is from page 186.) Keating puts this idea another way, noting of the effort to rebuild the global economy along multilateral lines: "Provided that the Americans and the British were partners to the plan, Canadians believed that their immediate interests would be served. Indeed, the prospects of a multilateral system in which both its principal trading partners were fully committed members was the best of alternatives for Canada." See Keating, *Canada and World Order*, 52.
85 LAC, Privy Council Office Records, 111/U-40-3/Volume 1/1947, Acting Canadian High Commission to the United Kingdom (CHCUK) to SSEA, No.1423, 4 September 1947 and SSEA to CHCUK, No.1438, 11 September 1943; LAC, Privy Council Office Records, A5a/T2365/2640, Cabinet Conclusions of Meeting held 11 September 1947, Meeting Number 410; McKenzie, 275–7.
86 Hart, *A Trading Nation*, 141–4.
87 John F. Hilliker, Editor, *Documents on Canadian External Relations, Volume 11: 1944–1945, Volume II* (Ottawa, 1977), 78–82, quoted in Hector MacKenzie, "The ABCs of Canada's International Economic Relations,

1945–1951." Accessed 6 May 2008 via the Department of Foreign Affairs and International Trade website, http://www.dfait.gc.ca/hist/coldwar_section08-en.asp.
88 Hart reaches the same conclusion. See Hart, *A Trading Nation*, 131–3. See also Bothwell and English, "Canadian Trade Policy," 186.
89 The most convincing work on Canada's inability to control its economic destiny remains Bruce Muirhead, *The Development of Postwar Canadian Trade Policy: The Failure of the Anglo-European Option* (Montreal: McGill-Queen's University Press, 1992).
90 Tom Keating, "Multilateralism and Canadian Foreign Policy: A Reassessment." Accessed 30 April 2008 via the Canadian Defence and Foreign Affairs Institute website, http://www.cdfai.org/PDF/Multilateralism%20and%20Canadian%20Foreign%20Policy.pdf.

5 The Interplay of Defence and Foreign Policy

ROGER SARTY

Canada's emergence as a player on the international stage in the twentieth century was the result of the country's large-scale military participation in the two world wars, and as a partner in the Western military alliance that waged the Cold War. In the post-Cold War world, according to many critics, the commitment of armed forces has continued to be the starting point rather than the outcome of policy. The dictum, famously propounded by the Prussian soldier and philosopher Karl von Clausewitz, that decisions for war and the nature and extent of the effort in war should flow from policy made by responsible civilian leaders, is an ideal. Still, the relationship between Canadian foreign and defence policy during the past century offers striking examples of this logic being nearly stood on its head.

Canada, whose citizens take pride in being the "unmilitary people" of a "peaceable kingdom," had a defence department – and armed forces – forty years before the establishment of a foreign affairs department in 1909, and a minister of Defence nearly eighty years before the appointment of the first minister of External Affairs in 1946. These facts are in some respects deceptive. The primary function of the minister and Department of Defence was for several decades mainly to administer a force of part-time militia. Foreign affairs, by contrast, were conducted by the prime minister himself, with the support of his own office and other departments of government. Even so, the early establishment of armed forces and a defence administration reflect the fundamental role war and preparations for war played in the creation and growth of the country.

Canada's sprawling land mass and vast seaboards are indefensible by its tiny population without the assistance of strong allies. Improbable in geographic and demographic terms, the country's existence is explained by a violent history. Britain in the Seven Years' War sought to secure the jewel of its first empire, the thirteen American colonies, by conquering New France, and then lost the thirteen colonies to revolution by taxing the American colonists for the cost of the war. A vengeful France assured the success of the American Revolution. In a belated gesture of statesmanship, Britain did not tax its remaining colonies for the costs of defence, thus saddling British taxpayers with the enormous burden of fortifications, garrisons, and communications in remote and unprofitable territories. Only these extraordinary efforts, and the power of the Royal Navy, prevented an American victory in the War of 1812. Rebellion in the Canadas against British authority, continuing border crises with the United States, and the relentless costs of defence measures brought Britain to encourage confederation of the northern colonies – the beginning of the modern Canadian state – in 1867.

The transformation of the colonies into a new nation with looser ties to Britain was an effort to reassure the United States, and the real origin of the "undefended border" in North America that remains the foundation of Canadian foreign and defence policy to the present day. Until at least the First World War, however, defence by diplomacy was administered from London, and not universally understood or accepted even there. In Ottawa the relationship between diplomacy, which remained largely the purview of the British government, and defence, which since 1867 had become an increasingly Canadian responsibility, was grasped by instinct rather than as a matter of policy until the 1930–40s.

Even the creation of the Canadian Department of External Affairs in 1909 was, in the largest sense, part of renewed British efforts early in the twentieth century to trim defence commitments by means of diplomacy. That in turn occurred because the British had a strategic problem, revealed when the South African War of 1899–1902 escalated from a minor frontier struggle to a protracted conflict so costly that the rest of the Empire was perilously exposed. Britain rapidly retreated from its nineteenth century position of "splendid isolation" to conclude an alliance with Japan in 1902, and ententes with France and Russia, long the most likely potential enemies, in 1904 and 1907 respectively. Like Germany, the United States resisted alliance, despite generous overtures. In 1903 the British government sided with the Americans in forcing settlement of the Alaska boundary dispute with Canada on terms favourable to the United States, much to the fury of

Sir Wilfrid Laurier's Liberal government and a good part of the population. U.S. President Theodore Roosevelt had threatened the use of military force over the dispute, but nevertheless in 1904 the Royal Navy withdrew its permanent squadrons in the western Atlantic and the eastern Pacific, and closed its dockyards at Halifax, NS and Esquimalt, BC. The squadrons and the dockyards had long been the embodiment of the British commitment to support Canada against dominance by the United States.

The important new element in the military withdrawal of the early 1900s was Britain's open pleas for direct military help. The self-governing colonies had, under pressure from Colonial Secretary Joseph Chamberlain, sent substantial military contingents to the war in South Africa, a total of 7368 troops in the case of Canada, and Chamberlain wanted to build upon this precedent to create a permanent system of colonial contributions of troops, money or both to common imperial defence. The response of the Liberal government of Sir Wilfrid Laurier was to assert greater autonomy in defence.

In the 1904 Militia Act, Laurier's militia minister, Sir Frederick Borden, created a Militia Council, in which the minister had greater authority than did the secretary of war in the British Army council, and opened the new senior appointment, chief of the general staff, to Canadians for the first time. In fact, only one Canadian held that appointment, and for a period of only two years, prior to 1920, but the Canadian government now insisted on the appointment of only British soldiers who had a good track record in dealing with Canadian politicians and officials.

Equally important were specific defence measures. Britain wished to maintain its army garrison that protected Halifax. Although the permanent naval squadron was being removed, a secure port was still required to assure the mobility of the British fleet and the security of British shipping. When in December 1904 the British Army, facing a budgetary squeeze, asked Canada to supply part of the garrison, Laurier proceeded to triple the size of the 1000-man Canadian regular force to take over all responsibility for the defence of both Halifax and Esquimalt. By relieving British forces of their residual responsibilities in North America, Laurier argued, Canada was allowing their redeployment for more effective collective defence.

The essential reason for these initiatives lay in domestic politics. Laurier's agreement to send troops to South Africa, even though he carefully limited the measure to volunteers who served as members of the British army when they reached the Cape, had aroused the Liberal MP Henri Bourassa to break with Laurier and lead anti-imperial opposition to the prime minister in Quebec. Canadianization of the militia command, and of the last imperial fortresses in the country, met with Bourassa's approval.

The British did prevail on another front, facilitating a general improvement in Canadian-American relations, a process known as "cleaning the slate" of bothersome disputes, a political complement to Britain's military redeployment. There was, however, one final policy issue that frustrated both sides.

Laurier responded to the Anglo-German naval crisis of 1909 and the resulting pressures from Canadian imperialists to make a direct contribution of money or "Dreadnought" capital warships to the Royal Navy by establishing the Royal Canadian Navy in May 1910. The Laurier administration argued that the new service, designed mainly for defence of Canada's seaboards, was nothing more than the seagoing arm of the militia, but Quebec nationalists vehemently disagreed. The mobility of warships, and the Admiralty's doctrine of centralized command, ensured that Canada would be dragged into British foreign wars. Imperialists in both the Liberal and Conservative parties, by contrast, were outraged that the proposed fleet of light cruisers and destroyers, the smallest classes of seagoing warships, utterly failed to provide the large capital ships that Britain most urgently needed.

The new general staff of the militia had pressed for the creation of a naval organization. The absence of any naval authority in Canada was a major impediment to defence planning on the coasts and on the Great Lakes. Worse still, the foundation stone of security on the Great Lakes, the Rush-Bagot agreement of 1817, seemed to be under attack. Following the War of 1812, the British and American governments had agreed not to maintain naval forces on the lakes, then an area whose remoteness led to enormous costs. As expansion of the U.S. Navy stepped into high gear after 1900, however, naval reserve organizations had been established in the Great Lakes states, and gunboats were coming in from the Atlantic to serve as training vessels. The Laurier government made no difficulties, and the general staff therefore leaked the story of the U.S. naval activities on the lakes to the press. Laurier now had a political problem, which fortunately discretion on the Canadian side and understanding on the side of the American president, William Howard Taft, resolved. Taft agreed that the U.S. would not increase the number of armed vessels on the lakes, and the Laurier government reverted to quiet complicity in the entry of the training warships.

The incident touched a fundamental disconnect in Canadian defence that left the new general staff in an impossible position. The role of the militia, the British War Office advised, was still to hold the frontier against a U.S. invasion while Britain despatched reinforcements. Confirmation came from the British prime minister's Committee of Imperial Defence (CID), a new body created in the wake of the South African War to coordinate British military, foreign and colonial policy. In reality, the advice to Canada reflected the failure of the CID to resolve disputes between the British services. The Royal Navy had been quick to write off the possibility of war with the United States in the 1890s, when expansion of the U.S. fleet made it highly unlikely the British fleet could muster the local superiority along the U.S. coast that had always been the fundamental strategy for the defence of Canada. The army, however, resisted this naval dictation of strategy concerning one of the Empire's only two extended land frontiers (the other was the northern frontier of India).

In the end external relations sounded the death knell of the Laurier government. Seizing the opportunity afforded by the cooperativeness shown by the Taft administration, Laurier had in 1910 negotiated what every government since Confederation had attempted to achieve and failed: a revival of the reciprocal trade agreement with the United States that had existed in 1854–66. Anti-American sentiment, however, won support in Ontario for Conservative leader Robert Borden's nationalist opposition to reciprocity in the federal election of 1911. In Quebec, Bourassa and his supporters campaigned against Laurier's naval policy.

Among Borden's first steps as prime minister was to reassure the United States of Canadian goodwill. In fact Borden was an early proponent of Canada as the "linch-pin," to use a later term, between the United States and Great Britain. Borden's attacks on Laurier's naval legislation in 1910 had also shown the Conservative leader, possibly influenced by the strongly imperialist views of some of his key supporters, to be an advocate of something close to Joseph Chamberlain's vision of a more closely united Empire. Convinced by British ministers that the international situation was grave and the naval problem alarming, Borden urged a one-time emergency contribution of funds to the Admiralty for the construction of three battleships. In an epic political battle, Borden failed to get his contribution through Parliament, and so in 1914 Borden began to consider what might be done with the rump of the Laurier navy, but much larger events intervened.

The curious aspect of Canada's large military effort in the First World War was that it transformed the country's foreign policy, but had little impact on military policy. Insofar as policy determined the objectives, nature and levels of Canadian participation, it came directly from the prime minister. From the beginning he made it clear that although Britain's declaration of war was binding on the dominions, Canada would raise forces in her own, national right. "As to our duty," he declared in the House of Commons in August 1914, "all are agreed, we stand shoulder to shoulder with Britain and the other British Dominions in this quarrel. And that duty we shall not fail to fulfil as the honour of Canada demands. Not love for battle, not lust for conquest, not for greed of possessions, but for the cause of honour, to maintain solemn pledges, to uphold principles of liberty, to withstand forces that would convert the world into an armed camp; yea, in the very name of the peace that we sought at any cost save that of dishonour, we have entered into this war..."[1]

On 2 August 1914, shortly before the declaration of war, the cabinet had quickly agreed that in the event of hostilities the country should send a contingent of troops, as in the South African war, save this time Canada would pay all the costs. As it became clear that the war would be long and enormously costly, the government approved expansion of the Canadian Expeditionary Force (CEF), ultimately, in the fall of 1915, to a limit of 250,000 troops. Then, after consulting with three colleagues, Borden, in his New Year's message of 31 December 1915, doubled that limit in a ringing reiteration of his speech of August 1914:

More than a twelvemonth ago our Empire consecrated all its powers and its supreme endeavour in a great purpose which concerns the liberties of the world and the destinies of its nations ... The Canadian Forces at the Front have indeed fought a good fight and they have crowned the name of Canada with undying laurels. ... From tomorrow, the first day of the New Year, our authorized force will be 500,000. This announcement is made in token of Canada's unflinchable resolve to crown the justice of our cause with victory and with an abiding peace.[2]

Borden's declaration that Canada was making this extraordinary effort in her own right as a nation was by no means empty rhetoric. When offering naval aid to Britain in 1912–13, the prime minister had made it clear that for such substantial military assistance Canada must receive a voice in the making of imperial policy. During the first seventeen months of the war his fury at the British government's failure to consult mounted, and on 4 January 1916 he vented to Sir George Perley, the Canadian high commissioner in London: "It can hardly be expected that we shall put 400,000 or 500,000 men in the field and willingly accept the position of having no more voice and receiving no more consideration than if we were toy automata. Any person cherishing such an expectation harbours an unfortunate and even dangerous delusion. Is this war being waged by the United Kingdom alone or is it a war waged by the whole Empire?"[3]

At the Imperial War Conference in April 1917, it was Borden who drafted "Resolution IX," which gave "full recognition of the Dominions as autonomous nations of an Imperial Commonwealth." The resolution called for a post-war conference for the "readjustment of ... constitutional relations," a recommendation that ultimately resulted in the British Statute of Westminster of 1931 that amended British legislation to accord equality of status to the dominions.[4]

The 1917 conference had been called by the new British prime minister, David Lloyd George, who was willing to give the dominions a voice in British policy in exchange for full maintenance of their vigorous military efforts. During the conference, the dominions prime ministers sat with the British war cabinet, now constituted the "Imperial War Cabinet." Borden, for his part, made sure the Canadian effort would not flag, even though voluntary recruitment had for some months all but dried up. After visiting Canadian military hospitals in France, and seeing casualties from the iconic victory of the Canadian Corps at Vimy Ridge, Borden decided to introduce conscription, despite the long-standing opposition of French Canadians to compulsory military service for overseas wars, especially those in support of Great Britain. Shortly after, Sir Julian Byng, the superb general the British Army had assigned to lead the Canadian Corps in the absence of a qualified Canadian officer, was promoted to army command, and General Sir Arthur Currie, a Canadian militiaman who had proved himself since 1915 in brigade and divisional commands, became the corps commander. Currie, with Borden's support, increasingly functioned as a national commander directly responsible to the Canadian government with right of appeal over the heads of his British superiors, and not the commander of just another British corps, the Canadians' substantive position within the British Expeditionary Force. In turn, the Canadians' achievements, not least because of Currie's own superlative performance, gave Borden weight with Lloyd George and his colleagues.[5]

In June to early August 1918, following the near collapse of the Allied lines in the face of German spring offensive, the Imperial War Cabinet began to meet again, to make plans for operations in 1919. Days after the meetings, the Allied armies, now with two million American reinforcements, counter-attacked with immediate and mounting success. This was the beginning of the "hundred days" offensive that brought Germany to sue for peace and agree to an armistice on 11 November.

At the end of November 1918 the Imperial War Cabinet reconvened to prepare for the peace conference. At no time had the contribution of the dominions been clearer or more dramatic. The Canadian Corps and the Australian and New Zealand Corps had been prominently at the head of the British victory offensive. The fighting was unrelenting and bitter: in the "hundred days," the Canadians lost 45,000 troops killed and wounded, one quarter of the casualties suffered during the full three and a half years on the Western Front. Borden led the dominions' demands for recognition of their "national" status at the peace conference. He freely referred to the sacrifices and achievements of the dominions' forces, which was the answer to U.S. President Woodrow Wilson's suspicions that dominions' representatives would serve mainly to strengthen Britain's voice. In May 1919 each of the dominions signed the Versailles Treaty under Britain's signature on behalf of the Empire, and the dominions each became members of the new League of Nations.

The First World War and its aftermath saw pivotal changes in Canadian relations with the United States, although in many instances their greatest significance lay in setting the stage for responses to the Second World War. From August 1914 until the American declaration of war on 6 April 1917, U.S. neutrality seemed to turn the clock back to the 1790s-1800s, or the 1860s. British cruisers rushed to Halifax to guard the vast seaborne trade in the western Atlantic from South American, U.S. and Canadian ports upon which the British economy depended. The main threat came from fast German liners and merchant ships that had interned themselves in U.S. ports to escape capture. Many of the vessels were well suited to take on armament and operate as raiders themselves, and all would be useful in slipping out to sea to provision the small German cruiser forces at sea in the Atlantic and Pacific. The main duty of the British cruisers, and the two Canadian cruisers, HMCS *Niobe* and HMCS *Rainbow* acquired in 1910, was to mount patrols off U.S. ports to watch for signs of the German activity.

Attacks on shipping increased in 1915 and still more in 1917, with the German "unrestricted" submarine offensives against seaborne trade in the Atlantic approaches to Britain. Cruisers were helpless against submarines, but Britain was unable to supply anti-submarine warships to cover the waters off Newfoundland and Canada. When the United States entered the war as a direct result of U-boat attacks on American merchant ships, the Canadian government soon learned that Britain had arranged for all available American anti-submarine vessels to operate in British and French waters; there was little the USN could send to Canadian waters. With great difficulty the Royal Canadian Navy (RCN) had quickly to build up a force of over 100 small anti-submarine craft. These under-powered, under-armed craft with ill-trained crews were adequate – just barely – to protect merchant ship convoys that formed up at Halifax, and Sydney in 1917–18, but could make no effective response to three long-range U-boats that in August-September 1918 sank over twenty unprotected fishing vessels off Nova Scotia and Newfoundland, and destroyed a tanker that had foolishly sailed without escort just beyond the Halifax headlands. These events converted Borden, whose own constituency was Halifax, to the necessity for development of the RCN along much the same lines as the Laurier administration had originally intended.

Sometimes wars that were not fought are as interesting as wars that were. In 1914 Canada had plans for defence against the United States –

as the United States had plans for war with Canada. In the early years of the war Canada deployed 15,000 militia troops in border areas to protect bridges, railways, hydro-electric plants and other "vulnerable points." The deployment was fed by abundant – and abundantly fanciful – rumours of German or Irish terrorists filtering north across the border from the neutral United States. Despite resistance by the very sceptical chief of the general staff, Sir Willoughby Gwatkin, the government ruled that 50,000 members of the Canadian Expeditionary Force should be kept in training in Canada at all times to provide a reserve for the frontier garrisons. There was, moreover, no relaxation in home defence measures after the U.S. entry into the war. The government feared the rise of Bolshevik inspired radicalism in the wake of the Russian revolution, with the danger of uprisings in Canadian cities, but, more particularly, in the U.S. Memories of the cross-border incursions by political radicals in the 1830s and late 1860s were deeply ingrained, as were prejudices about the republican system of government producing a violent and lawless society.

Nevertheless, U.S. entry into the war led to far-reaching economic cooperation. The financial and industrial demands of U.S. mobilization cut off access to U.S. capital markets and industrial products and resources crucial to Canadian war production. So grave were the difficulties that in February 1918 Borden travelled to Washington. A "very cordial" Wilson agreed to all that Borden asked, including U.S. procurement in Canada of products in which the dominion had established production.[6]

Borden, in London and then at the Paris peace conference, consistently asserted the need for Anglo-American harmony.[7] Although he had publicly declared these views since the early weeks of his administration, his sustained advocacy in 1918–19 marked the first time a Canadian prime minister had taken on this role at the highest levels in international relations. It was a marked change from the time of Macdonald and Laurier when more typically the British had to press reluctant Canadian governments to make concessions in the interests of Anglo-U.S. rapprochement.[8]

The most dangerous source of discord between Britain and the United States was relations with Japan. Japan, although not required to do so under the terms of the Anglo-Japanese alliance, had entered the First World War at Britain's side, seized the German concessions in China, and, in the chaos resulting from the Russian revolution, had moved aggressively to expand its influence in Siberia. These developments had heightened longstanding American enmity towards Japan and suspicion of British collusion in Japanese imperialism. Both Japan and the United States had during the war started major expansion of their battleship fleets in programmes that, with the defeat of Germany, were obviously in competition. By 1919 Britain was entering the race with plans for a new generation of capital warships.

Canadian governments had long been sensitive to the tensions between the United States and Japan. These could lead to tensions and possibly conflict along the Pacific coast. An imperial commission headed by Lord Jellicoe, a very senior British admiral, recommended that at a minimum Canada should build something like the navy the Laurier administration had planned in 1909–10, install coastal artillery to protect the immediate approaches to Vancouver and Prince Rupert and, drawing on the new technology developed during the war, establish air bases and squadrons of maritime reconnaissance and bombing aircraft. Borden found his colleagues in cabinet bitterly opposed to the costs of even the most modest of Jellicoe's proposals.

In July 1920, an exhausted Borden retired and passed the premiership to Arthur Meighen. The leading issue at the imperial conference convened in London in June-July 1921 was renewal of the Anglo-Japanese alliance. Meighen played much the same role as Borden in 1918–19, declaring that the foundation of imperial policy had to be in accord with the United States, and vehemently opposed renewal of the alliance. Meighen also supported acceptance of an invitation from Warren Harding, the new U.S. president, for a conference of Pacific powers in Washington to address both political issues and naval disarmament. The conference met in November 1921 to February 1922, and produced multi lateral treaties that included the United States, and in effect replaced the Anglo-Japanese alliance. The conference also enacted far-reaching measures that set ceilings for the size, number and armament of capital warships – battleships. The British conceded parity in battleships to the United States, though the United States did not build up to this limit, but the agreement acknowledged what had already become abundantly apparent: the Americans had the industrial and financial resources to outbuild Britain (or any other power) at any time they chose.

During the conference, in December 1921, there was a federal election and a change of government: William Lyon Mackenzie King's Liberals came to power. King, building on bitter French Canadian opposition to the imposition of conscription in 1917–18, ran against the Borden government's excessive war effort in this and in future elections. Quickly as the Borden and Meighen administrations had demobilized the CEF and reduced defence spending, King promised to cut further, and did. As an economic measure, the government combined the militia and naval departments together with the small Canadian Air Force that had been organized in 1920, in a Department of National Defence. Funding returned to pre-1914 levels which, because of the wartime inflation, meant a substantial reduction. The navy, with only two destroyers, provided free of charge by Britain, and 500 regular personnel had virtually no operational capability; its purpose was mainly to train reservists. The militia returned to its pre-war state, reverting, like the navy, to an establishment to train reservists. The Canadian Air Force, which became the Royal Canadian Air Force (RCAF) in 1924, was a branch of the militia, another cost saving measure. Officials, learning from the dismal failure of the navy to win political support, emphasized the air force's utility as the government's civil aviation authority and air service. RCAF flying personnel became "bush pilots in uniform," carrying out such missions as aerial mapping, and anti-smuggling patrols on the coasts.

The First World War had confirmed the conviction of both French- and English-Canadians who questioned the British connection that armed forces served mainly as instruments for entanglement in British foreign wars. In this light, Canada's virtual disarmament in the 1920s reflected the country's foreign policy. King embraced Borden's campaign for national status and autonomy with respect to Great Britain, but rejected the idea of a common imperial foreign policy, in the making of which Canada would have a voice, and in the execution of which the country would bear commensurate responsibilities. As one of King's ministers told the League of Nations in Geneva in 1925, "Not only have we had a hundred years of peace on our borders, but we think in terms of peace, while Europe, and armed camp thinks in terms of war ... We live in a fire-proof house, far from inflammable materials."[9]

If Canada was to stand apart from British policy, one essential requirement was to enhance the capabilities of the Department of External Affairs. King drove out of the department Loring Christie, who had been Borden and Meighen's chief foreign policy adviser, and hired instead O.D. Skelton, a professor of political economy at Queen's University, the biographer of Sir Wilfrid Laurier. He was a nationalist no less passionate than Christie, but of a different stripe. He deeply distrusted Britain, and was convinced Canada had to take charge of her own foreign policy. In 1925 King appointed Skelton under-secretary of state for External Affairs. Skelton became the most influential civil servant in Canadian history, implicitly trusted by not only King, but as well by R.B. Bennett, the Conservative prime minister from 1930-35. Skelton recruited talented young men to strengthen the policy-making capacity of the department, and to staff Canada's first diplomatic missions outside of the Empire, Washington, Paris and Tokyo.[10]

King, despite the anti-military tenor of his first election campaign and administration, came to realize that the country also needed a capable defence establishment. During his second administration, 1926-30, he appointed a strong defence minister, J.L. Ralston, and supported him against opposition in the cabinet to increases in the defence budget. The evidence suggests that chiefs of the armed services, and particularly Commodore Walter Hose, chief of the naval staff, educated the prime minister about their longstanding worries concerning the Pacific coast. The navy's two destroyers were nearing the end of their operational life, and Hose wanted to replace them as the first step in acquiring a flotilla of six large modern destroyers. This was the minimum number that could provide a credible seaward defence of the west coast. The navy feared a breakdown in Anglo-American accord, and the possibility of an American war against Japan. This fear was reinforced by the failure of the Geneva conference of 1927, which the U.S. had called to extend warship limitations from capital ships to other classes of vessels. The British flatly refused to accept U.S. proposals for the limitations of cruisers, the basic and most important type for protection of the Empire's global network of shipping. King found that he had to tap-dance – successfully as it turned out – not to be drawn into one camp or the other, and risk alienating one of the two nations essential to Canadian security.

The navy got the warships it wanted. King approved the purchase of two British destroyers as replacements for the RCN's two worn-out vessels, and, more strikingly, also authorized orders for the construction in Britain of two of the latest fleet type destroyers.

The navy's initiative proved to be the leading edge for the restructuring of the whole of the armed forces. Early in 1929 Major-General A.G.L. McNaughton became chief of the general staff, the first officer with a commanding intellect and influence to hold the post since the retirement of Gwatkin in 1920. The full extent to which the Canadian military still looked to British strength as the anchor of Canadian security became apparent with McNaughton's horrified reaction to disclosures by British Prime Minister Ramsay MacDonald in October 1929 when he met with U.S. President Herbert Hoover and exchanged a promise not to add to British bases or fortifications in the Western Hemisphere in exchange for a parallel American promise for the eastern hemisphere.[11] A horrified McNaughton argued that Britain had not only conceded American naval dominance in the Pacific as had long been apparent, but in the whole of the western hemisphere. "British command of the North Atlantic, so essential to the defence of Canada in a war with the United States, was considered by the British Premier so impractical that it could be definitely renounced in advance of the crisis."[12] It also made impractical the basic plans of the Canadian military, to raise 15 divisions (250,000 men) to resist an American invasion pending British reinforcement. McNaughton in the early 1930s ruled out the contingency of war with the United States, and trimmed the organization of the militia to seven divisions, the maximum number, experience in the First World War suggested, that could be sustained for overseas service in the event of another major war. The major home defence priority was now the protection of the west coast, on a scale sufficiently strong to persuade the United States not to intervene on Canadian soil with unrequested assistance, a danger that would be greatest if the Empire should be neutral, even for a few days, in the event of war between the United States and Japan. McNaughton, in view of the resources the military might realistically expect to get, gave priority to the full training and equipment of two divisions, a force that could provide adequate security on the Pacific coast or, alternatively, could provide the first elements of an overseas expeditionary force. McNaughton also gave high priority to the military reorganization and re-equipment of the RCAF's largely civil organization to provide coastal defence units on the Pacific, and the air wing of an expeditionary force.

McNaughton made these proposals when in 1931 the Japanese invaded Manchuria, the first blow in the collapse of international order. But then the Great Depression in Canada forced the Conservative government of R.B. Bennett that had come to power in 1930 to impose deep cuts on the armed forces, particularly the air force. The Bennett government supported Britain in appeasement of Japan, a policy that did nothing to ease American suspicions that the spirit of the Anglo-Japanese alliance was still very much in evidence.

When King returned to power in the fall of 1935, he immediately supported British and French appeasement of Italy in the wake of that power's invasion of Ethiopia. He also carried on with the expansion of the navy's destroyer force, and accepted McNaughton's programme for the land and air force as the basis for rearmament. The resulting re-equipment and expansion of the forces in 1936–39, limited as it was, constituted the first sustained attempt in Canada to create combat capable forces in peacetime.

King's overarching policy in the face of the international crisis was one of "national unity," a conscious contrast to Borden's administration. On the matter of rearmament, he confessed in his diary, "I am now where Sir Wilfrid was, in a more dangerous time in the world's history – but still between the devil and the deep blue sea in having to steer between Imperialism and Nationalism in extreme forms."[13] C.P. Stacey, an observer unlikely to exaggerate, agreed that from the time of the Ethiopian crisis there were "violent controversies" within Canada about external policy.[14] King achieved balance with his pledge that "Parliament will decide" whether Canada would enter a future war, by avoiding specific military commitments to Great Britain that might compromise that decision. He also promised that there would be no conscription even if the country went to war, stressed that the rearmament programme was for home defence and – promptly cut the increased funding requested by the military by fifty percent, giving priority to the air force and navy, the services that bore the primary responsibility for coastal defence.

King also addressed the danger of uninvited American intervention on Canadian soil. He had little choice as word got out in the press that senior U.S. officers saw the dominion's military weakness as a potential threat, and in August 1936 President Franklin Roosevelt pledged that "we can and will defend our neighbourhood."[15] King and Roosevelt were the first Canadian and American leaders to have regular summit meetings; these led to a secret meeting between the Canadian and American chiefs of staff in January 1938, in which the Canadians reassured their colleagues with details of the new coastal defence arrangements in British Columbia. When in the summer of 1938 Roosevelt again proclaimed his country's commitment to hemisphere defence, King quickly responded: "We, too, have our obligations as a good friendly neighbour," including defence measures to ensure that "enemy forces should not be able to pursue their way, either by land, sea or air to the United States, across Canadian territory."[16]

King consulted regularly on the defence programme with his closest advisor, Skelton, but to some extent he used the latter's suspicion of Britain to balance his own more nuanced perspective. As Skelton pointed out, the defence department plan did provide the means for direct military support of Britain, an aspect of the programme that King, much as he intentionally obfuscated, accepted. The world has reviled British Prime Minister Neville Chamberlain's ultimate effort to avoid war in the Munich conference in September 1938, but King, and many Canadians, were profoundly impressed by this demonstration of Britain's commitment to peace. From then on, King realized that if war came, he would have no choice but to join the conflict.

In August 1939, the government authorized the Canadian forces to begin mobilizing in lock step with the British. Parliament did "decide," as King had promised, voting nearly unanimously in favour of the government's recommendation for war, which took effect on 10 September, but the Canadian forces had already been on a war footing since Britain and France had entered the conflict on 3 September. As Stacey has remarked, "[i]t is interesting, and thoroughly typical of the King administration" that the document on "Canadian War Policy" considered by cabinet came from the pen of Skelton and not the military. Skelton's paper prescribed a policy of "limited liability" for the war effort. Limited liability, essentially an implementation of King's emphasis on national unity, gave priority to the direct defence of Canada, and economic support to the overseas allies; if overseas military action was required then "it should, in the first instance, be in the air service rather than by military contingents." Air forces did not risk the heavy casualties of land forces, and required a large infrastructure to manufacture equipment and train personnel, activities that would keep Canadians at home and prosperous.[17] The 1st Canadian Infantry Division was sent overseas as a result of the demands of English Canadian ministers, but there was no intention of greatly augmenting this largely symbolic land force.

Canada's war effort and, arguably, the country's international stature to the present day, were transformed by the collapse of France, with her massive army and formidable navy, in May-June 1940. Suddenly Canada became Britain's strongest ally. The immediate impact of this disaster was in relations with the neutral United States. In August 1940 Roosevelt and King created the Permanent Joint Board on Defence (PJBD), comprised of senior military officers and diplomats of the two countries. The leaders chose the term "Permanent" to show that this was the beginning of a new, long-term relationship, and the board is still the umbrella for Canada-U.S. cooperation in continental defence. In 1940–41 the board's priority was to make joint plans so that in the event of a British collapse, United States forces could provide for the defence of Canada. The board from the first served to enshrine protection for Canadian sovereignty; U.S. commanders would take charge of operations in the Canadian area only if large scale attack was imminent. Britain's survival, Major-General H.D.G. Crerar, chief of the general staff, forcefully argued, was the key to Canadian security. The Axis powers could mount substantial attacks on North America only if Britain and her still dominant navy were knocked out the equation. The PJBD and the guarantee of American assistance in Canadian defence provided assurance that persuaded the government to dispatch all available forces overseas.

From Mackenzie King's perspective the pact with the United States was a master stroke in bringing the United States along the road from isolation to support for the Allied cause. After the collapse of France, only the United States had the military and economic power necessary to defeat the Axis in western Europe and on the Atlantic.

King's interpretation of the defence pact with the U.S. as an essential first step in provision of all-out North American support for Britain turned out to be the correct one. In March 1941, the Roosevelt administration responded to the exhaustion of British finances with the Lend-Lease Act, which essentially gave Britain and other Allied nations free access to war materials from the U.S. Canada, as a matter of national pride, never availed itself of Lend-Lease, but in an agreement reached by King and Roosevelt at Hyde Park in April 1941 largely integrated Canadian and U.S. war production, with U.S. purchases in Canada to offset Canadian balance of payments problems with U.S. dollars resulting from Britain's inability to pay with hard currency for its Canadian purchases.

King, despite the limited liability policies of 1936–40, hesitated little in vastly expanding the Canadian effort in direct response to British need. He was, like many Canadians, fundamentally convinced that Britain was a cornerstone of a liberal-democratic world order essential for Canadian security and prosperity. In December 1939, King had agreed to the British Commonwealth Air Training Plan (BCATP) for the training of Commonwealth air crew in Canada. Canada, in 1940, assumed responsibility for a progressively larger share of Britain's commitments to the scheme. Of the 131,553 air crew trained under the BCATP by 1945, 72,835 were Canadians, who constituted about a fifth of all of the aircrew in the Royal Air Force's combat commands. Following the fall of France, the government approved virtually open-ended expansion of the shipbuilding industry for the production of both merchant ships, to replace heavy British losses, and naval vessels for the Royal Canadian Navy. At the same time, as German submarine attacks spread across the Atlantic and threatened to cut supplies to Britain, the RCN assigned most of its ships to the defence of transatlantic merchant ship convoys and by 1942 provided fully half of the naval escorts. The most dramatic change in Canadian military policy, however, was the positive response of the government to Britain's appeals for land forces. The government approved the expansion of the expeditionary force in England into a full field army of two corps incorporating five divisions and two additional tank brigades, a force considerably larger than the Canadian Corps of the First World War. In all, 1.1 million Canadians served in uniform in 1939–45 as compared to about 640,000 in 1914–18.

The overwhelming focus of the Canadian war effort on the north Atlantic and Europe met Britain's most urgent requirements, but it was also an expression of Canadian policy. The purpose of the Canadian overseas effort was to ensure British security and liberate the European democracies. That role had really been defined by the Canadian Corps in the First World War, particularly its spearhead of the Allied Victory offensive in 1918 that had in many ways identified Canada as an international actor. The defining policy for the army in the Second World War was to follow the model of Currie in 1917–18 and resist any British suggestion that formations should be broken off for piecemeal employment under British control away from the principal European theatre. That nationalist impulse meshed well with the King government's determination that large numbers of young Canadians should not endure injury and death in operations to help Britain retain its dependent colonies, as in North Africa.

In 1939–40 the navy and the air force were really little more than minor branches of the British forces. As these services rapidly expanded in 1941–42, they had the government's strong support in following the army's example by consolidating their main combat elements as national forces.

There were elements of paradox in Canadian policy. Almost all Canadian forces operated under British high command as integral parts of larger British formations, and by 1944 the large Canadian contribution was vital in enabling an exhausted Britain to muster the strength in the crucial European theatre to claim full partnership in the Grand Alliance in face of the increasingly overwhelming predominance of U.S. (and Soviet) forces. Yet the King administration rejected, as firmly as it had in the 1920s, any suggestion that the Commonwealth should remain more closely united in the post-war world to balance American and Soviet power. King was motivated at least in part by the over-riding priority for Canadian interests of Anglo-American accord, and the Roosevelt administration made no secret of its abiding suspicion of British imperialism.

Yet the United States, from the moment it became evident in late 1940 and early 1941 that Britain would not collapse, found it convenient to treat Canada as a dependent of Britain. Drawing a sharp distinction between continental defence and international strategy, the Americans in the latter instance dealt directly with Britain as embodying the whole of the Empire and Commonwealth. The Canadian government, to avoid the sort of commitments that had resulted in conscription in 1917–18, had reversed the policy of Borden and discouraged the constitution of any sort of Commonwealth war council or cabinet. King's stature as a senior leader of the Commonwealth, the well developed habit of consultation among Commonwealth governments, and the strong presence of Canadian forces in Britain allowed for full Canadian access to British authorities on any issue of significance. It was not so in Washington. The sense that Canada had no voice in the "combined" British-American organization that came into full development after the United States' entry into the war following the Japanese attack on the U.S. fleet in Pearl Harbor in December 1941 led a new generation of activists in the Department of External Affairs to press for Canadian representation on Allied councils. Following Dr Skelton's death from overwork early in 1941, Norman Robertson had become under-secretary of state for External Affairs, and the influence of several other brilliant young foreign service officers, notably including Hume Wrong and Lester Pearson, had increased. Wrong is credited with having developed the idea of "functionalism," which King himself proclaimed in the House of Commons in 1943. The many smaller members of the Alliance should have senior representation – and influence – in specific Allied agencies that dealt with matters in which those powers made a significant contribution. Functionalism was the concept that Canada brought, with some limited success, to the organizing meetings of the United Nations in April 1945 and after.

Functionalism, which more than faintly echoed Robert Borden's campaign to win international recognition for Canada's extraordinary war effort at the Versailles Peace conference, reflected even more than Borden's efforts a new sense of Canadian power. In both world wars, Canada's military effort was extraordinarily successful in bringing the nation to prominence in the foremost campaigns. It was a stunning achievement for a country that was still in the early stages of building basic military institutions in 1914, and in 1919-35 had determinedly followed a policy of disarmament.

Canada's economic performance in 1939-45 was at least as notable as the military achievements. Canadian industry provided most of the equipment used by the Canadian forces, but, more remarkably still, did so with only about a third of its production; two-thirds of production was supplied to Allied forces under "Mutual Aid," Canada's version of American Lend-Lease. The economic effort of 1939-45 was in many respects the beginning of the modern Canadian industrial economy, whose effects in such areas a telecommunications, computers, aviation, and nuclear energy are still felt today.

Canada's international position had also been transformed by upheavals from the war that were still further reaching than those of 1918-19. Most of the traditional great powers, Britain, France, Germany, Japan and Italy, had been prostrated by the war, and the world was now dominated by two superpowers, the United States and the Soviet Union. A bankrupt Britain, inadequately sustained by emergency loans from Canada and less generous ones from the U.S., had no choice but to pull back from the Empire and its international presence, most dramatically with the withdrawal from India and from the Mediterranean in 1947-48. Canada by contrast had prospered as a result of the war, but that prosperity had been part of a signal shift from the Commonwealth to partnership with the United States. The wartime boom had been possible largely because of the integration of war production with that of the United States, and postwar economic difficulties were overcome by a revival of wartime cooperation through privileged Canadian access to the U.S. defence market, and, in 1948, eligibility on much the same terms as the U.S. for business funded by the U.S. Marshall plan for the economic recovery of Europe.[18]

Canada's new international stature did not immediately change its defence policy, even though Canadian leaders and officials were early to recognize the threat to international order posed by the Soviet Union. Among the first events signalling the collapse of the wartime's

Grand Alliance was the defection in Ottawa in September 1945 of Igor Gouzenko, a Soviet cipher clerk at the Soviet embassy, who revealed to the Royal Canadian Mounted Police (RCMP) the existence of a widespread Soviet espionage network in Canada, Britain and the U.S. Still, Soviet prostration after the enormous losses it had suffered during the war with Germany suggested there was little danger of a Soviet military offensive. In 1946 the United States approached Canada through the Permanent Joint Board on Defence about continued cooperation in continental security, particularly for the development of weather stations and airfields in the Canadian north in view of the increasing importance of transpolar flying operations. Canadian and American officials discovered they agreed that the Soviet military threat, including transpolar air attack, was potential rather than actual. The major outcome of the negotiations was an agreement, announced in February 1947, on measures to ensure that U.S. military activities on Canadian soil did not impinge on Canadian sovereignty.[19] Canada, like the United States, was still focussing on the rapid demobilization of its wartime forces. The peacetime regular forces would be considerably stronger than in the 1930s, but built on the same principle: their role was to prepare the reserves for mobilization of combat formations in the event of a major war.

The Cold War transformation of Canadian defence policy began in 1948–49 when the country took a leading part in the creation of the North Atlantic Treaty Organization (NATO). The Soviets, in defiance of wartime agreements, were installing puppet regimes in eastern European states, and maintaining strong occupation forces there; Soviet obstruction paralyzed the functioning of the United Nations as an instrument of collective security. The negotiations took place against the backdrop of the Soviet blockade of Allied access to the western portions of Berlin, which instantly belied Allied intelligence estimates that the Soviets would not for some years be in a position to risk military confrontation. It was not a coincidence that Canadian initiative in supporting the creation of a western bloc to counter the emerging eastern bloc occurred when Mackenzie King retired, and was replaced as prime minister by Louis St. Laurent. The latter, who had been Quebec's senior representative in cabinet since 1941, was less prone than King and other English-Canadian politicians to worry about treading on French-Canadian sensibilities. In 1946 St. Laurent had become secretary of state for External Affairs, and he shared the views of the activist officials who saw close parallels with the 1930s and were determined that Canada should not again support North American isolationism and appeasement of totalitarian states. Pearson, one of the leading activists, entered politics to replace St. Laurent in the External Affairs portfolio.

The negotiations that created NATO were the culmination of the Canadian impulse, evident from the time of the Borden administration, to serve as a bridge between Britain and the United States. The Canadian government stood foursquare behind British efforts to ensure that the Americans took Britain's place as a force for international stability, and in particular remained actively engaged in supporting the still devastated states of western Europe against the emerging Soviet menace. Nearly a half-century after British officials had had to pull a balky Laurier along in building Anglo-American amity, Canada was taking a leadership role in consolidating the Anglo-American alliance. Not surprisingly, Canadian officials endeavoured to build the new alliance in the image of the British Commonwealth, the military alliance that Liberal politicians had always stoutly denied was a military alliance. The Empire/Commonwealth, in which Canada had found the freedom to become a nation, had featured few military commitments, a great deal of consultation, and decision by consensus. Canada's voice had always been heard in London, much more than in Washington on matters beyond strictly continental concerns. In the final analysis, the military effectiveness of the Commonwealth had grown from shared values: an overriding commitment to democracy and the rule of law, as Laurier had declared when he reluctantly agreed to send troops to South Africa in 1899, and Canadian leaders had repeatedly proclaimed during the two world wars. From the beginning of the NATO negotiations through to the present Canada had always been a leader in promoting the cultural and political community of the North Atlantic powers.

Soon the new alliances demanded the large-scale deployment of armed forces on a permanent basis, precisely what Canada had resisted in peacetime since the late-nineteenth century. When North Korea invaded South Korea in June 1950, the American president, Harry Truman, surprised his advisers and his allies by his decision to resist, using the authority of the United Nations. Truman expected assistance from his allies, and he got it, even if Canada's skeletal armed forces could not immediately send more than three destroyers and an RCAF transport squadron – the only deployable units available as the Canadian forces struggled to rebuild after the precipitous post-war demobilization. Nevertheless, the Americans insisted, the small initial Canadian effort must be supplemented by substantial ground forces. Canada also hesitated because the real danger was of an eastern bloc offensive in Europe, strategically crucial as Korea was not. At NATO Council in December 1950, Canada agreed to the appointment of a NATO military commander, and the creation of an "Integrated Military Force." At that time, China had entered the Korean War with devastating impact on the UN forces, and the Canadian government believed there was an immediate danger of a general war in Asia and Europe. Allied pressure for Canada, then one of the few prosperous western states, to deploy forces to the full extent of its capability was as heavy as the pressure to send ground forces to Korea. Public opinion polls showed wide support for military action; French Canadians, like English Canadians, saw communism as a danger that had to be countered.[20]

By 1952–53 the defence appropriation soared to $2 billions, nearly fifty percent of the federal budget, as compared to $225 million in 1947–48, and remained at that high level. In the 1950s, now known as the "golden age" of Canadian international influence, the strength of the regular forces soared to over 110,000 personnel.[21] In 1951–53, Canada deployed a reinforced brigade group in Korea, while also building up another strong brigade group and an air division of twelve jet fighter squadrons, a total of over 10,000 military personnel, in France and Germany under NATO command. At home, there were another two brigades, committed to reinforce the brigade in Germany to a full division in the event of war. The navy had a fleet of some sixty ocean-going combat vessels, most of them for anti-submarine warfare under NATO's supreme allied Commander Atlantic against the large and expanding Soviet submarine fleet. In continental defence, the RCAF and USAF cooperated in the construction of three air defence radar and electronic detection systems, one to cover the main centres of population in southern Canada, another along the 55th parallel and the third in the Arctic, while the RCAF deployed nine squadrons of jet interceptors as the Canadian share of forces to counter the growing number of long-range Soviet bombers that could deliver atomic weapons. In 1957 RCAF and USAF air defences were fully integrated under the new North American Air Defence Command (NORAD).

Canadian forces were employed in other international roles to serve the same objective as the NORAD and NATO forces, to strengthen western security while ensuring Canadian influence in the service of Canadian interests. In 1954 a contingent of Canadian military personnel and diplomats went to Indochina as part of the International Commission of Supervision and Control created in negotiations at Geneva that arranged for the departure of French colonial forces that had been defeated by Communist nationalist forces in the northern part of Vietnam. Canada served as the western representative on the commission, with Poland from the eastern bloc, and India representing non-aligned nations. Elections planned for reunification of the country never took place, and for the next nineteen years Canadian military personnel and diplomats reported on violations, mainly by communist insurgent forces from the north, of the demilitarized zone that separated North and South Vietnam. Canadian military personnel and diplomats also served the western cause in the Suez crisis of 1956. American condemnation of British and French military intervention in Suez, following an Israeli attack on Egypt that the British and French had in fact orchestrated, confronted the Canadian government with the situation it had always most feared: a fundamental rift between Britain and the United States. It was to ease that rift, a dangerous threat to western unity that invited Soviet intervention in an international hot spot, that inspired Lester Pearson's initiative to create a United Nations peacekeeping force to monitor the cease-fire. Canadian forces formed part of the peacekeeping force, notably in communications and logistics, which were becoming an important Canadian competence because of the demands of home defence of the country's vast territories, and of sustainment of the large forces in Europe.[22]

In retrospect, the Canadian military mobilization of the 1950s bears more than a passing resemblance to the country's mobilization for the world wars. If anything, the mobilization was more confident and far-reaching than the initial responses to the earlier global conflicts. In contrast to the depressed economic conditions of 1914 and 1939 that had reinforced the self-image of a developing nation that could be expected to do little, the country had become one of the leading western economies, especially because of the economic prostration of several of the traditional great powers. In contrast to 1939, there was agreement among the diplomats, the military and the political leadership about the imperative need to counter potential aggression; no one spoke of "limited liability." The consensus extended to the general population.

The conditions that had created the "golden age" of Canadian foreign policy and defence began to change in 1959–60. The downturn in the Canadian economy that forced the first substantial cuts to the defence budget occurred against the backdrop of the recovery of Britain and Europe and the formation of a strong trading bloc, the European Economic Community. At the same time the arms race between the eastern and western blocs was rapidly transforming military technology. Budget cuts forced difficult decisions on the Canadian military, which faced the obsolescence of much of the equipment procured earlier in the decade or recycled from Second World War stocks. Most famously, in 1959 cost overruns compelled the Conservative government of John Diefenbaker to cancel development of the CF 105 Avro Arrow, a supersonic interceptor intended for continental air defence.

The very nature of warfare was being transformed, or so it seemed, and with it Canada's role. It was somewhat ironic that the NORAD command was established in 1957 to coordinate the extensive defences against manned bombers in the same year that the Soviet launch of the first space satellite demonstrated the capability to produce a terrifying new weapon, a nuclear armed inter-continental ballistic missile (ICBM) against which there could be no effective defence. The warning time of a bomber attack would be in the order of two or three hours; the entire time of flight of an ICBM was in the order of thirty minutes.

The experience in the world wars was that Canadian forces, even if small in numbers relative to the great powers, could with the right organization, training and equipment carry out high profile missions and earn international recognition. So it was in the late 1950s, when Canada led the way among the NATO powers in accepting the small nuclear weapons the United States was now willing to deploy with its non-nuclear partners under dual control with the receiving nation. Within NORAD, Canada purchased American fighters to take the place of the Arrow, and US BOMARC air to ground missiles procured to cover the approaches to southern Ontario and Quebec were to be armed with nuclear munitions. In Europe the air division was to re-equip with supersonic U.S.-designed, Canadian built CF 104 Lockheed Starfighters for strike reconnaissance, the delivery of small nuclear bombs behind Soviet front lines to overcome the vast Soviet preponderance in conventional forces. In the age of thermo-nuclear munitions, missiles and supersonic aircraft, a major war might well be decided in a matter of hours, not the weeks or months required fully to mobilize reinforcements in Canada, despite a much higher level of readiness than ever before in Canadian history. The forces at home and abroad had to be ready for instant effectiveness and only nuclear munitions could assure that effectiveness. Because of the impossibility of defence against ballistic missiles, western security increasingly depended upon the "survivability" of enough of the American strategic nuclear forces so that a Soviet first strike would trigger a devastating western counterstrike. The essential role of NORAD and NATO thus was to protect U.S. strategic nuclear forces.[23]

In the face of fully developed nuclear deterrence – neither side dared strike for fear of "Mutually Assured Destruction," in reality the end of human civilization – the consensus that had supported Canadian rearmament in the 1950s broke apart. These events, which unfolded through the whole of the 1960s, are the aspects of post-1945 Canadian defence most thoroughly treated in both popular and scholarly literature.[24] The growing international nuclear disarmament movement had for some years won the sympathy of officials in the Canadian government, particularly in the Department of External Affairs. These views gained weight when in 1959 Howard Green, a convinced advocate, became Diefenbaker's secretary of state for External Affairs. Partly out of conviction and partly for political advantage, Diefenbaker delayed acceptance of the U.S.-controlled nuclear munitions even as the military acquired the new weapons systems designed to carry them. The climax of the growing controversy and a widening rift between the Diefenbaker government and the new administration of John F. Kennedy in the United States came with the Cuban missile crisis of October 1962, the brink of nuclear war. When Kennedy ordered a naval blockade of Cuba to stop shipments of Soviet nuclear missiles, and placed continental defences on heightened alert, Diefenbaker delayed authorization for the Canadian forces to follow suit. Without the government's approval, the navy's east coast commander nevertheless authorized the RCN's Atlantic fleet to put to sea, for the essential duty of replacing U.S. warships that had to be deployed to Cuba; Soviet submarines were known to be operating off the Canadian and northern U.S. seaboard. Meanwhile, the defence minister, Douglas Harkness, authorized the RCAF to act under NORAD arrangements. Although Pearson, now leader of the Liberals, had grave doubts about the nuclear role for the Canadian forces, early in 1963 he declared that his party supported the acquisition of the weapons in view of the commitments the country had made to its alliance partners. Nevertheless, Diefenbaker's now strident anti-Americanism proved popular enough that the Liberals achieved only minority government status in the election of 1963.

The Pearson administration was also intensely nationalist, with some of its leading members proclaiming the dangers of U.S. hegemony. It was thus ironic that the defence minister, Paul Hellyer, was profoundly influenced in his programme by the business-style management reforms of the U.S. forces by Kennedy's secretary of defence, Robert McNamara, former CEO of Ford Motors. McNamara asserted stronger civilian control to help implement a strategic policy of "flexible response" to the Soviet threat. The main instrument was stronger and more mobile conventional forces that would allow a wider range of counter-action than the "massive [nuclear] retaliation" that had been the hallmark of the Eisenhower administration in the 1950s.

The Pearson government unveiled its defence programme in a 1964 White Paper, largely the work of Hellyer.[25] To give the minister and the government more direct control over the forces and department, there would be a single chief of the defence staff, served by a single integrated staff in place of the air, navy and army staffs; the deputy minister's branch, the civilian part of the headquarters that had carried out mainly financial administration would also be integrated into the single staff, with civilian officials playing a much greater part in all aspects of the defence programme. The army in Canada would be reconstituted as a "Mobile Force," with the air and sea transport and fire support elements needed for rapid deployment anywhere within Canada or overseas at the government's direction. Possible missions included reinforcement of the NATO brigade on the central front in Europe (in the past the primary role of the army in Canada), new roles on the less well protected flanks of NATO, or missions under other international auspices, such as the UN, or the Geneva accords on Indo-China. A speedy response might well prove to be the key to controlling escalating violence, but an effective response would likely involve combat roles in ongoing conflicts, and not just observation of compliance in agreed cease-fires. Although not remarked at the time, the effort to consolidate a more identifiably national force in the face of specific alliance commitments that pulled the Canadian effort in different directions strongly echoed policies for the overseas military forces of both world wars.

The White Paper upheld Canada's existing alliance commitments, but let the forces committed to NORAD and deployed in Europe under NATO shrink over time. The European states would be able to carry an increasing share of the burden for their own defence, and there were promising signs that progress of arms limitations and other developments in detente between the superpowers would ease nuclear confrontation further back from the brink. In the meantime, savings from the integration of the service staffs and other support services would allow the re-equipment of the new "Mobile Force." In the event, shrinkage became Canada's *de facto* defence policy for both forces at home and abroad for the next four decades.

In 1968 Hellyer carried through full unification of the armed forces in a revision of the National Defence Act that combined the former Canadian Army, Royal Canadian Navy and Royal Canadian Air Force into a new legal entity, the Canadian Armed Forces (CAF). The unified force was organized into functional commands, the most important of which was the new "Mobile Command," but there was no money for the new equipment promised in the 1964 White Paper. The Pearson government's priority was funding for expanded national social welfare programmes, and particularly the implementation of universal medical care in 1965, which soon became the defining element of Canadian public policy, and indeed the nation's identity.

Pearson's successor as Liberal leader, Pierre Trudeau, who won a strong mandate in the election of 1968, pressed his predecessor's defence programme to extremes that Pearson's government had contemplated but rejected. Trudeau believed that "golden age" internationalism was unnecessary and unhelpful meddling in great power interests, and actually ignored or undermined Canadian interests. In 1969 Trudeau proposed the withdrawal from Europe of the costly brigade and air group. Strong resistance from both External Affairs and National Defence led him to cut the commitment in half, 5,000 personnel, an understrength brigade and two air squadrons. These forces abandoned the nuclear role in 1972. A new White Paper in 1971, although not pulling back further on alliance commitments, made Canadian sovereignty the top defence priority. By 1976 the strength of the regular forces had fallen to just under 78,000 personnel, as compared to 98,000 in 1968 and 114,000 in 1965. In the 1970s the defence budget fell to about 2.2 percent of GDP, from 3.8 percent under the Pearson administration, and an average of over six percent in the 1950s.

The Conservative administration of Brian Mulroney of 1984 to 1993 endeavoured to revive the country's international presence, not least with a commitment to expand the armed forces and procure desperately needed new equipment. The context was the "new" Cold War, an increase in tensions resulting from the Soviet invasion of Afghanistan in 1979, and large military programmes by U.S. President Ronald Reagan. The Mulroney government's military ambitions were overtaken by an economic downturn in 1989 and steep social programme costs that drove up the national debt. Canada particularly welcomed the destruction of the Berlin wall in 1989 and the disintegration of the eastern bloc that it signalled as a chance to reap a "peace dividend" through reduced defence expenditures. The Iraqi seizure of Kuwait in 1990, however, evoked an international response reminiscent of western solidarity when North Korea invaded South Korea in 1950, and, as in the earlier crisis, the U.S. led coalition to liberate Kuwait had the sanction of the United Nations. Through desperate measures, the Canadian Forces cobbled together two warships and a naval replenishment vessel, and a squadron of fighter-bombers that carried out mainly supporting roles in Desert Storm, the swift and successful offensive against the Iraqi forces in Kuwait early in 1991. In 1992, for purely budgetary reasons, Mulroney suddenly announced the entire withdrawal of the Canadian NATO force in Europe. At this very time Yugoslavia descended into civil war, and Canada, in part to demonstrate its continued interest in European security, contributed to a UN intervention force, a commitment that continued all through the 1990s and at its peak saw more than 2000 Canadian military personnel in the theatre. There were many factions, open warfare and no accords, resulting in the Canadians' embroilment in combat to secure areas under their responsibility.

The leading challenge to Jean Chrétien's Liberals who came to office in 1993 was the government fiscal crisis that had beleaguered the latter part of the Conservative administration. Cuts in the defence estimates under Mulroney had reduced expenditure to just over two percent of GNP, but the armed forces were still the largest single item of discretionary spending, and the Liberals further slashed spending to just over one percent of GNP. The regular force had already fallen to fewer than 73,000 personnel by 1994 and the Liberal budgets set a target of only 60,000. Yet more than 4000 personnel were deployed overseas, many in operations like those in Yugoslavia that bore no relation to the cease-fire observation role of classic peacekeeping. Hopes for a peace dividend in the post-Cold War world turned out to be wildly exaggerated. Early in 1993 the government had, in the absence of any other units, deployed the ill-prepared Canadian Airborne Regiment into Somalia where central authority had collapsed into violence among many armed factions. A failure of discipline in the regiment resulted in the torture and murder of a Somali teenager and efforts by the unit to cover up the incident. As a result of the strain on Canadian forces and those of other nations in a position to support distant deployments, when in 1994 Canadian General Roméo Dallaire received command of the UN contingent in Rwanda, he had exceedingly meagre resources. The small force proved powerless when the country disintegrated into genocidal attacks on Tutsis.

As the Chrétien government endeavoured to maintain international military commitments with dwindling resources, in 1996–2000 foreign minister Lloyd Axworthy aggressively exercised the other traditional thread of Canadian policy, moral suasion. In sharp contrast to the "golden age" principle of quiet diplomacy designed to promote allied unity and moderate confrontation between the eastern and western blocs, Axworthy did not hesitate openly to challenge the great powers in service of the greater cause of universal human rights. He carried through a signal achievement, the international agreement on the banning of land mines, in defiance of American and Russian insistence on the necessity for land mines for effective military operations.

Such was the appeal of moral suasion, and so daunting the costs of rebuilding the forces after three decades of shrinkage and "rust-out" that during the 1990s the need for the forces to maintain – more properly, reacquire – a "general combat capability" became a contentious issue. The context of discussion changed with another seismic event, the terrorist attacks on New York's World Trade Center and, the Pentagon in Washington, DC, on the morning of 11 September 2001. The links between security and prosperity were instantly thrown into sharp relief by disruption of communications for New York's financial exchanges, in many respects the centre of the new global economy, and the threat of severe disruption of the Canadian economy by increased security checks at the U.S. border. Although continental defence had always been directed towards external attack, the well developed command structure and facilities allowed Canada immediately to support U.S. security efforts, a crucial element in preserving the Canadian economy.

As in other such turning points in international relations, the deployment of substantial forces overseas has also become an essential element in upholding Canadian interests. When in 2004 the new Liberal administration under Paul Martin assembled an *International Policy Statement* to define a course for the country in the "post 9–11" world, for the first time since the 1950s the most compelling vision came from the armed forces. Chief of Defence Staff General Rick Hillier highlighted the menace of failed and failing states as breeding grounds for terrorism, and called for a coordinated military, diplomatic and economic development effort to counter the threat.[26] The specific challenge lay in Afghanistan, where the Martin government accepted a mission in Kandahar province, the centre of terrorist insurgency. The Canadian battle group operated under NATO which, broadening and redefining its role from that of a Cold War western alliance, had accepted a large role in Afghanistan. Canada was thus again taking a leadership position in the alliance it had helped to shape. That mission was not only continued by the Conservative government of Stephen Harper that came to power in 2006, but became the focus for substantial increases in the defence budget to rebuild the armed forces. The priority objectives, which include upgraded weaponry for the army, acquisition of major strategic and tactical air transport and sea transport, in no small measure carry out plans for Mobile Command for something very like the roles envisioned in the 1960s to enhance Canada's influence in support of international stability, the essential basis for the interests of a nation so dependent on external trade, and whose population growth has been sustained primarily by immigration of diverse peoples.

Unusual international circumstances – the two greatest wars in the planet's history – had as one result the rise of Canada as a significant military power. The aftershocks of those wars also conferred on Canada during the 1950s the status of a near major power, only if temporarily and by default because of the war-exhaustion of the traditional great powers. The country, moreover, willingly undertook mobilization in peacetime during the early Cold War to ensure the survival of the western bloc, and more particularly to promote the values of democracy and rule of law that allowed Canada to prosper. Canadians questioned the large military effort only in the early 1960s when the recovery of the European powers, and the stabilization of Soviet-U.S. relations in mutual deterrence by massive nuclear forces, suggested that Canada's participation in the nuclear standoff was not essential to western strength, and the very scale of the competing nuclear forces left little room for Canadian influence. Yet Canada, because of its Cold War mobilization and diplomatic influence that flowed from it, had been able to play a salient role in lower-level conflicts that threatened to destabilize superpower relations. The Canadian part in lower level conflicts depended upon highly capable, well-equipped armed forces. Those armed forces were available because of the Cold War mobilization, and the shrinking remnants of those forces provided the basis for Canadian military action in the 1970s-80s when stability in super-power relations allowed Canada to slash the defence budget to meet domestic priorities. Still further cuts in the 1990s, the "peace dividend" at the end of the Cold War, ran hard up against regional conflict that resulted in part from the dissolution of the eastern bloc. Once again, Canada has been called upon by its alliance partners, and by the United Nations, to commit armed forces, but now in circumstances where the collapse of authority within states has resulted in open combat. It is perhaps a part of the anti-Americanism that arose strongly in the 1960s that Canadians have latched onto "classic" observation missions of reasonably well-established cease-fires during the Cold War to make "peacekeeping" a part of the national identity. Yet even in those cases, Canada was able to play a role because of its military capability, and the influence the country possessed because of its participation in the western alliance.

Current debates about Canada's continuing role in continental defence and the commitment of a battle group to combat in Afghanistan bear more than a passing resemblance to controversies in the early 1900s and 1920s and 1930s about Canadian military participation in its first great alliance, the British Empire and Commonwealth. It was the military strength of that alliance that had warded off American aggression, built the foundations of the "undefended border" and, in the two world wars, became the vehicle by which the country emerged as an international actor.

NOTES

1 *Robert Laird Borden: His Memoirs*, Henry Borden, ed. (Toronto: Macmillan, 1938), I, 461, in House of Commons, 18 August 1914.
2 Borden, *Memoirs*, I, 527–8.
3 Quote in C.P. Stacey, *Canada in the Age of Conflict* (Toronto: University of Toronto Press, 1977), I, 192.
4 R. Craig Brown and Robert Bothwell, "The Canadian Resolution," in *Policy by Other Means: Essays in Honour of C.P. Stacey* (Toronto: Clarke, Irwin, 1972), 165–78.
5 Stephen Harris, "From Subordinate to Ally: the Canadian Corps and National Autonomy, 1914–1918," *Revue Internationale d'histoire Militaire* No. 51 (1982): 109–30.
6 Robert Craig Brown, *Robert Laird Borden: A Biography* (Toronto: Macmillan, 1980), II, 126–7.

7 For a recent and cogent statement see Margaret MacMillan, *Paris 1919: Six Months That Changed the World* (New York: Random House, 2002), 47–8.
8 Brown, *Borden* II, 149.
9 Quoted in Stacey, *Canada in the Age of Conflict* (Toronto: University of Toronto Press, 1981), II, 61.
10 J.L. Granatstein, *The Ottawa Men: The Civil Service Mandarins 1935–1957* (Toronto: Oxford University Press, 1982); see also Granatstein, *A Man of Influence: Norman A. Robertson and Canadian Statecraft 1929–68* (Ottawa: Deneau, 1981).
11 General Staff, nd, "Memorandum. Details concerning Naval Stations which were the subject of conversation between Mr. MacDonald and Mr. Hoover...,' Library and Archives Canada (LAC), MG 30E133, A.G.L. McNaughton papers, box 103, file "Disarmament Book B."
12 General Staff, "Memorandum on the Reorganization of the NPAM of Canada," 29 January 1931, LAC, RG 24, vol. 2740, HQS 5902 pt 1.
13 King diary, 11 February 1937, LAC, MG 26 J, William Lyon Mackenzie Papers.
14 *The Military Problems of Canada: A Survey of Defence Policies and Strategic Conditions Past and Present* (Toronto: CIIA and Ryerson, 1940), 102.
15 Quoted by Ernest Lapointe, House of Commons, *Debates*, 4 February 1937, 549.
16 Quoted in Stacey, *Military Problems of Canada*, 35.
17 Stacey, *Arms, Men and Governments: The War Policies of Canada 1939–1945* (Ottawa: Queen's Printer, 1970), 9; see also John Hilliker, *Canada's Department of External Affairs*, I: *The Early Years, 1909–1946* (Montreal and Kingston: McGill-Queen's University Press, 1990), 210–11.
18 Robert Bothwell, *Alliance and Illusion: Canada and the World, 1945–1984* (Vancouver: UBC Press, 2007) is particularly strong on economic policy and the economic aspects of defence through the whole period discussed in the book.
19 On continental air defence see Joseph T. Jockel, *No Boundaries Upstairs: Canada, the United States and the Origins of North American Air Defence, 1945–1958* (Vancouver: UBC Press, 1987) and the same author's *Canada in NORAD 1957–2007: A History* (Montreal and Kingston: McGill-Queen's University Press, Queen's Centre for International Relations and The Queen's Defence Management Program, 2007).
20 David Jay Bercuson, *The Life of Brooke Claxton 1898–1960* (Toronto: University of Toronto Press, 1993), chapters 9–11.
21 Douglas L. Bland, ed., *Canada Without Armed Forces?* (Kingston and Montreal: McGill-Queen's University Press and the School of Policy Studies, Queen's University, 2004), 122–127 is a valuable digest of information about defence spending and the general organization of the armed forces.
22 Denis Stairs, "The Military as an Instrument of Canadian Foreign Policy," in Hector Massey, ed., *The Canadian Military: A Profile* (Toronto: Copp Clark, 1972), is still one of the best overviews.

23 Sean M. Maloney, *Learning to Love the Bomb: Canada's Nuclear Weapons During the Cold War* (Washington: Potomac Books, 2007).
24 Jon B. McLin, *Canada's Changing Defense Policy, 1957–1963: The Problems of a Middle Power in Alliance* (Baltimore: Johns Hopkins Press, 1967) is still valuable. For more recent accounts based on newly opened archival sources see, in addition to Maloney, *Learning to Love the Bomb*, Andrew Richter, *Avoiding Armageddon: Canadian Military Strategy and Nuclear Weapons 1950–63* (Vancouver: UBC Press, 2002); broader is scope is Erika Simpson, *NATO and the Bomb* (Montreal and Kingston: McGill-Queen's University Press, 2001).
25 Brian W. Tomlin, Norman Hillmer and Fen Osler Hampson, *Canada's International Policies: Agendas, Alternatives, and Politics* (Toronto: Oxford University Press, 2008), chapters 6–7, is excellent on defence white papers and other key government policy statements for the whole period from 1945 to 2008.
26 Janice Gross Stein and Eugene Lang, *The Unexpected War: Canada in Kandahar* (Toronto: Viking, 2007), 152–9.

6 Canada's Contribution to International Law

WILLIAM A. SCHABAS

One of Canada's great international legal scholars, Maxwell Cohen, once described the country as "sired in warfare, mothered in treaties, and nurtured in the dedicated crèche of both imperial constitutional relations and international law as they were in the latter eighteenth century."[1] Obligations set out in international legal instruments of the time, notably the Treaty of Paris of 1763, and in the earlier Treaty of Utrecht, define not only the country's territorial existence but also such matters as obligations to minorities, something that is reflected in constitutional provisions applicable to the present day. Canada's identity was forged in the complex dynamic of a struggle for autonomy within the British Empire and the establishment of sovereignty alongside an emerging superpower. It was in this context that a Canadian perspective on international law emerged, and with it a Canadian contribution.

An early dispute on the Niagara River set an international law precedent that is still cited. In 1837, William Lyon Mackenzie's rebel group fled across the border, but were reinforced by sympathizers in the United States. Camping on Navy Island, they launched attacks on Canada with the benign tolerance of the American authorities. British forces reacted with a bit of "preemptive self defence," seizing a ship called *The Caroline*, setting it on fire, and sending it down the river and over the falls and killing two American citizens.[2] The *Caroline* precedent holds that the doctrine of "anticipatory self-defence" applies when its necessity is "instant, overwhelming, and leaving no choice of means, and no moment for deliberation."[3] *The Caroline* was referred to in the Nuremberg judgment of the International Military Tribunal.[4] As recently as 2003, *The Caroline* was being cited in the debate on the invasion of Iraq, which was allegedly intended to neutralise threatening weapons of mass destruction in much the same way as the British sought to prevent a rebel threat to Canada's borders.[5]

Even in the late nineteenth century, Canada had assumed a modest presence internationally, establishing offices abroad and participating in the Universal Postal Union. A Department of External Affairs was created in 1909, but it remained under the wing of the prime minister until the late 1920s. The position of *jurisconsult* or legal advisor within the Department of External Affairs was established in 1913. The *Canada Treaty Series*, an annual volume containing important treaties ratified by Canada, began publication in 1928, following recognition of an independent treaty-making authority at the Imperial Conference of 1926.

Because Canadian foreign policy was in the hands of the British government for the first several decades of the country's existence, only gradually did a truly Canadian position and a Canadian contribution begin to emerge. Professor Cohen noted that even if "the Commonwealth was the 'original' school for Canadian nationhood and for evolving international personality, it was the United States that gave Canada its first taste of learning to live in the severe world of *realpolitik* where bilateral dealings with an immensely powerful neighbour were the basic geopolitical facts of life for Canada."[6] Indeed, Canada was one of the first countries that had to co-exist with the United States, and this involved international legal solutions to a range of problems, from tariffs, reciprocity, boundaries including boundary waters and fisheries to immigration and aboriginal peoples.

The International Joint Commission was created in 1909 by the Boundary Waters Treaty. A century later, it remains an institution of great significance. The Treaty sets out general principles concerning navigation and free use of all boundary waters, including Lake Michigan, and makes more specific provision for exploitation of the Niagara River for hydroelectric purposes. The treaty "provided Canadians with a feel for a bi-national regulatory mechanism dealing with perhaps the most complex and lengthy water boundary system in the world."[7]

Regulation of the relationship where the two countries meet also features in the famous *Trail Smelter Arbitration*, where a dispute about pollution originating in Canada was adjudicated in accordance with principles of public international law. The award made an important finding, widely accepted as authoritative, that "under the principles of international law ... no State has the right to use or permit the use of its territory in such a manner as to cause injury by fumes in or to the territory of another or the properties therein, when the case is of serious consequence and the injury is established by clear and convincing evidence."[8]

Proximity also contributed to famous skirmishes as entrepreneurs sought to service frustrated Americans from abroad during the prohibition period. Boatswain Leon Mainguy drowned when the schooner *I'm Alone*, registered in Lunenburg, Nova Scotia, was sunk by the United States Coast Guard on 22 March 1929. Along with the boat, more than $100,000 worth of beverages were lost. A 1924 agreement between the United Kingdom and the United States provided that claims concerning incidents of this sort would be adjudicated by a two-person panel, one member appointed by each side. The Canadians chose Lyman Duff, then a justice of the Supreme Court of Canada. When it became clear that the ship was actually owned and operated by Americans, the panel decided it would be improper to order the United States to compensate its own nationals. But the commissioners also decided that the sinking could not be justified under international law, and that as a result the United States owed Canada an obligation, which it assessed as $25,000, an amount comparable to what Ottawa had spent on the litigation.[9]

Canada famously participated in its own right at the Paris Peace Conference. It was a founding member of the League of Nations, managing to extract from Clemenceau, Wilson and Lloyd George recognition that Canada might actually sit on the League Council.[10] Canada signed the Treaty of Versailles on 28 June 1919, but in a manner indicating it was attached to the British signature, so as to appease the Americans. In September, resolutions in the House of Commons and the Senate confirmed Canada's acceptance of the treaty, and implementing legislation was subsequently adopted.[11]

At the Paris Peace Conference, Sir Robert Borden circulated a memorandum, dated 13 March 1919, with a number of criticisms and comments on proposed provisions of the Covenant of the League of Nations.[12] He was particularly troubled by article 10 – then known as the Monroe Doctrine clause – by which League members undertook "to respect and preserve as against external aggression the territorial integrity and existing political independence of all Members of the League." Borden later wrote: "My observations with respect to article 10 were not intended to affect the recognition of the Monroe Doctrine as an International Convention. Hitherto it has been simply an article of foreign policy on the part of the United States Government; but even with that limitation it has been of great service in maintaining the peace of the world. Probably if it received recognition as suggested, the responsibilities which it entails would be more definitely understood, not only in the United States but among all the nations."[13] Borden's reservations about article 10 had more to do with his fear that it would freeze the forms of international relations – boundaries, treaties, whatever. Put another way, he was not confident that the "retired burglars," the great powers of 1919, would always have the strength to prevail over those states that wished to continue burgling. Thus, Canada was being asked to give its support to a system whose stability was seriously at risk, and in Borden's view this was not in Canada's interest.

Canada proposed an amendment at the first Assembly of the League aimed at eliminating article 10. Later, at the 1922 session of the Assembly, Canada unsuccessfully attempted to weaken the text with two amendments.[14] The debate provided Canada with the pretext to participate in meetings of the Council itself.[15] For countries like Canada, article 10 seemed the imposition of an excessive duty, given their remoteness from zones where there was a history of armed conflict. Eighty years later, with the enthusiastic support of its dynamic foreign minister Lloyd Axworthy, Canada promoted the concept of a "responsibility to protect" vulnerable groups from persecution. But in its debut on the stage of international lawmaking, Canada appeared isolationist. Maxwell Cohen wrote that "Canadian internationalism in the interwar years was skin deep," his example being Canada's repudiation of its own League representative for having voted in favour of strengthened sanctions against Italy following the invasion of Ethiopia.[16]

Canada also participated in the International Labour Organization, which was established by Part XIII of the Treaty of Versailles. When the institution sought a temporary non-European home during the Second World War, it moved to Montreal, at McGill University. The Constitution of the International Labour Organization was adopted in Montreal on 9 October 1946.[17] During the 1930s, Prime Minister Bennett used the ratification of several International Labour Organisation conventions to justify the constitutionality of federal legislation in what had hitherto been clearly a matter of provincial jurisdiction.[18] The federal government defended the legislation successfully before the Supreme Court of Canada, but the statutes were eventually declared *ultra vires* by the Judicial Committee of the Privy Council, which was still the court of last resort for Canada.[19] Lord Atkin famously declared that Ottawa could not invoke international legal obligations in order to change the constitutional division of powers, an enduring precedent[20] although one that is oft criticised.[21]

After the Second World War, Canada's independent contribution to international relations, and to international law, became more robust. Lester B. Pearson's award of the Nobel Peace Prize in 1957, honouring the role of United Nations peacekeeping in the resolution of conflicts, gave the country much recognition as a middle power that could promote multilateral initiatives when the "great powers," now known more modestly as the "permanent five," were unwilling or unable to act. But for the first few decades following the Second World War, the attention of international lawyers in the Canadian foreign ministry and in the academy was generally fixed on issues that were more directly associated with the national interest, such as law of the sea, protection of the environment and arctic sovereignty. These were areas in which the law was not clear, or rather where it was in the process of definition. Canadian lawmaking took two complementary forms: active engagement negotiating multilateral instruments, and unilateral action to set down markers concerning the Canadian view of the country's rights and obligations under international law. During the debates that foreshadowed adoption of the United Nations Convention on the Law of the Sea, this two-pronged approach was explained to the First Committee of the United Nations General Assembly in 1970 by J. Alan Beesley, speaking of Canada's views on the extent of its territorial sea:

Mr. Chairman, there have been a number of references during our debate to the relative merits of unilateralism as compared to multilateralism as methods of developing the Law of the Sea. The Canadian position on this issue is well-known. In brief, we do not consider multilateral action and unilateral action as mutually exclusive courses; they should not, in our view, be looked on as clear-cut alternatives. The contemporary international law of the sea comprises both conventional and customary law. Convention or multilateral treaty law must, of course, be developed primarily by multilateral action, drawing as necessary upon principles of international law and progressive development of new principles. Customary international law is, of course, derived primarily from state practice, that is to say, unilateral action by various states, although it frequently draws in turn upon the principles embodied in bilateral and limited multilateral treaties. Lawmaking treaties often become accepted as such not by virtue of their status as treaties, but through a gradual acceptance by states of the principles they lay down. The complex process of the development of customary international law is still relevant and indeed, in our view, essential to the building of a world order. For these reasons we find it very difficult to be doctrinaire on such questions.[22]

Canada manifested its attachment to multilateralism by its active participation in the evolving norms concerning oceans. It had inherited the United Kingdom position, with its three-mile territorial sea limit and historic attachment to freedom of the seas, given its history as a naval power. By the 1950s, Canada was becoming supportive of expanding jurisdiction over the sea. It was hardly alone, and Canadian initiatives were probably provoked by unilateral actions of other states, including the United States. The 1952 *Customs Act* established a Canadian customs zone that added nine miles to the existing three.[23] In

1956, Canada argued for a much larger contiguous fishing zone, something that became known in international legal circles as the "Canadian proposal." Failing consensus, and faced with a growing number of States that were extending their territorial sea, Canada again took unilateral action.[24] The twelve mile territorial sea was eventually codified in the United Nations Convention on the Law of the Sea.[25]

During the 1970s, Canada was a very active participant in the negotiations and adoption of the United Nations Convention on the Law of the Sea. Pierre Elliott Trudeau himself wrote about the importance of the treaty for its protection of Canadian interests as well as being a vehicle for international cooperation.[26] Strangely, after promoting the Convention, which was adopted in 1982 and which entered into force in 1994, Canada waited until 2003 before ratification, possibly out of concern it might find itself isolated from other industrialised states, who were unhappy with the provisions concerning mineral resources.

Another example of pro-active lawmaking in the international sphere is the Arctic Waters Pollution Prevention Act.[27] It constituted an exercise of jurisdiction over a swathe of ice and ocean defined by the controversial "sector theory," by which Canada claimed sovereignty based upon "straight baselines" drawn from the extremities of its land territory to the North Pole. In recent years, Canada has not tended to invoke the "sector theory" however, preferring to base its arctic jurisdiction over claims to the islands in the archipelago, and to the maritime rights that go with them. Climate change has given issues of sovereignty over the arctic new acuity, and may result in future nuances as creative Canadian lawmakers respond to melting ice.

Canada could bare its unilateral teeth on occasion. Faced with a dramatic decline in fish stocks in the North Atlantic,[28] in March 1995 the Canadian government adopted regulations authorising the use of force by fishery protection officers against foreign fishing boats, specifically those with Spanish and Portuguese flags. A few days later, shots were fired by a Canadian patrol boat, the *Leonard J. Cowley*, at a Spanish flagged ship. The *Estai* was stopped on the high seas, its catch was seized and the vessel then escorted to St. John's where it was impounded. Spain charged that Canada had infringed the 1978 Convention on Future Multilateral Co-operation in the Northwest Atlantic Fisheries. Canada's justification was the need to protect "straddling stocks" of turbot that meandered back and forth across the nose and tail of the Grand Banks, over which Canadian sovereignty was undisputed. The Canadian government understood it was on the fringes (or, perhaps, the cutting edge) of the law, because shortly before seizing the *Estai* it had placed a reservation on its acceptance of the jurisdiction of the International Court of Justice so as to shelter Canadian behaviour from issues relating to implementation of the 1978 Convention. As a result, when Spain sued Canada before the International Court of Justice, its application was rejected for want of jurisdiction.[29] Shortly after seizing the *Estai*, agreement was reached on straddling stocks and migratory fish stocks that was satisfactory to Canada.

International human rights law emerged in the late 1940s as an important new dimension of public international law, and its significance has continued to grow. Today, Canada's huge contribution to the development of norms and instruments would be widely accepted, but Ottawa's enthusiasm for human rights is a relatively recent phenomenon. The website of the Department of Foreign Affairs boasts that "Canada has been a consistently strong voice for the protection of human rights and the advancement of democratic values, from our central role in the drafting of the Universal Declaration of Human Rights in 1947–8 to our work at the United Nations today,"[30] a statement that is quite simply false. Canada's participation in the drafting of the Universal Declaration of Human Rights, which is the seminal statement of international human rights law, was at best indifferent and at times quite destructive, shocking traditional allies like the United States and the United Kingdom. When the negotiated text came to a vote in the Third Committee of the General Assembly, Canada abstained, along with the Soviet Union and its five allies. According to historian Robert Spencer, Canada's abstention was an "embarrassing association with the Soviet group" that "caused a mild sensation."[31] John Humphrey, a former dean of the McGill Law School who became the senior United Nations official in the human rights field, and who, as an international civil servant, is widely credited with authoring the first draft of the declaration, wrote:

It was the Canadian abstention which shocked everyone, including me. The Canadians had given me no warning, and I was quite unprepared for what happened. Although I knew that the international promotion of human rights had no priority in Canadian foreign policy, it had never occurred to me that the government would carry its indifference to the point of abstaining in such an important vote. I could hardly have prevented the scandal even if the delegation had taken me into their confidence, but I could at least have warned them of the company in which they would probably find themselves.[32]

Lester B. Pearson, who headed the Canadian delegation at the General Assembly in 1948, had always intended to vote in favour of the Universal Declaration in the plenary session. He explained that the abstention was meant to show deference to the division of powers between provincial and federal jurisdiction in Canadian constitution law. But this was unconvincing, and the Canadian archives reveal that the real factor was the influence of lobbies that were hostile to fundamental rights whose tentacles reached to the federal cabinet.[33] Pearson himself was far more interested in the establishment of the North Atlantic Treaty Organization (NATO) than in laying the foundations of the modern international legal protection of human rights.

Referring to a foreign policy review in the early 1970s characterizing Canadian policy in the area of human rights as "cautious," John Humphrey described this as an "understatement of the first order. The truth is that until quite recently Canada's approach to human rights issues in the United Nations was almost completely negative."[34] It was really not until the 1980s that Canadian policy in the area of human rights matured, and Canadian leadership began to be recognised. The turning point was probably the so-called "Winegard Report," *Sharing Our Future*, issued in May 1987 by the Standing Committee of the House of Commons on External Affairs and International Trade, and chaired by William Winegard, a Progressive Conservative MP.[35] Human rights became one of the pillars of Canadian foreign policy, and this strategic focus inexorably took on a law-making direction.

Canadian diplomats honed their skills in helping to craft intricate new treaties like the Convention on the Rights of the Child, adopted by the United Nations General Assembly in 1989. It was also a time of great change within Canadian law, driven to some extent by evolving norms at the international level. For example, the Canadian Charter of Rights and Freedoms, which entered into force in April 1982, was drafted with an eye to compliance with human rights treaties accepted by Canada, as the Supreme Court of Canada has acknowledged. Human rights commissions, present in all provincial and territorial jurisdictions as well as at the federal level, generated a sensitivity to a range of important issues, and this began to be reflected in foreign policy.[36]

An early manifestation of Canadian commitment to international human rights was participation in negotiations within the so-called Helsinki process. These were really a series of conferences, held periodically since the early 1970s, that had gradually raised the temperature for the Soviet Union and its allies in Central and Eastern Europe. When the Berlin Wall fell in November 1989, the Conference on Security and Co-operation in Europe was at the zenith of its normative activity. This was "soft law," expressed through declarations rather than treaties, but of great legal significance nevertheless. Canadian diplomats played a central role in drafting the human rights clauses of the Copenhagen Document, adopted in 1990.[37] The instrument was later described by Theodor Meron as going "far beyond any existing human rights instruments."[38] Provisions in the Copenhagen Document concerning minority rights were especially edifying, and they subsequently influenced the development of treaty norms, such as the Framework Convention for the Protection of National Minorities of the Council of Europe.[39]

During the 1990s, Canadian international lawyers were exceedingly influential in such bodies as the United Nations Commission on Human Rights. They often piloted several important resolutions at the annual sessions of the commission. But although Canada was frequently in the lead on important thematic issues, it could also hold back on occasion when national issues appeared to be in conflict. For example, in 1999 Canada resisted the inclusion of language concerning extradition in an annual death penalty resolution of the Commission because of discomfort about pending litigation in the Supreme Court of Canada concerning an extradition request from the United States.[40] The Supreme Court subsequently held that extradition to the United States was unconstitutional, to the extent that the suspect might be subject to capital punishment. Noting that "principles of fundamental justice" were drawn from "basic tenets of our legal system," the court concluded in this context that the abolition of the death penalty had emerged as a major Canadian initiative at the international level, and that it reflected a concern increasingly shared by most of the world's democracies. The court referred to resolutions adopted by the United Nations Commission on Human Rights calling not only for the abolition of the death penalty but also "request[ing] States that have received a request for extradition on a capital charge to reserve explicitly the right to refuse extradition in the absence of effective assurances from relevant authorities of the requesting State that capital punishment will not be carried out."[41] What the court described as "Canada's international advocacy of the abolition of the death penalty" might have been seen by some European States, who were more unequivocal on the subject, as a bit of an overstatement.

One of the most significant recent Canadian contributions to the development of international law has undoubtedly been in the field of international criminal law, an area closely related to both human rights law and the law of armed conflict or, as it is called today, international humanitarian law. Canada was not a very keen supporter of war crimes prosecutions following the Second World War. Unlike most of its allies, it did not even bother to participate actively in the United Nations War Crimes Commission,[42] nor did it accede to the Charter of the Nuremberg Tribunal,[43] although a Canadian judge sat on the Tokyo Tribunal. Post-war war crimes prosecutions were unconvincing and they were accompanied, as it later became clear, by a relaxed immigration policy that allowed large numbers of Nazis to settle in Canada.[44] Their shameful presence eventually provoked a Royal Commission, chaired by Jules Deschênes, that recommended the Criminal Code be amended to facilitate prosecution.[45]

The amendments were duly adopted, enabling Canada to exercise what is known as "universal jurisdiction" over war crimes and crimes against humanity.[46] There had been much talk of universal jurisdiction in academic circles, but apart from Israel's celebrated trial of Adolf Eichmann, Canada was really the only country to take this aspect of international law seriously. Initial prosecutions showed the difficulty of such an undertaking,[47] but Canada had positioned itself as a pioneer in this area, one who could field a growing cohort of home-grown experts. Judgments of the Supreme Court of Canada pursuant to the legislation have addressed complex issues concerning the application of the international law of war crimes and crimes against humanity.[48] This case law has had considerable international influence.[49] When the United Nations Security Council decided to establish the International Criminal Tribunal for the former Yugoslavia, in 1993,[50] several Canadian international lawyers joined its staff. Justice Jules Deschênes was elected a judge of the Tribunal by the United Nations General Assembly. Assigned to the Appeals Chamber, he was one of the authors of the most important international criminal law judgment since Nuremberg.[51] In 1996, Justice Louise Arbour of the Ontario Court of Appeal took leave to become the Prosecutor of the International Criminal Tribunal and of its sister institution for Rwanda.

Against this backdrop, momentum was growing for the establishment of a permanent international criminal court. There is no sign of Canadian engagement or interest in the project during its early stages, when it lingered on the agenda of the International Law Commission. But when the United Nations General Assembly took ownership of the process in 1994, Canada quickly moved to the leadership. Canada chaired the most influential caucus throughout the negotiations, known as the "like-minded." Composed of a diverse group of small and middle powers, such as South Africa, Argentina, Germany and Singapore, it united around a policy whose overarching theme involved weakening the grip of the United Nations Security Council on the proposed court. Canada relinquished its position shortly before the Rome Diplomatic Conference of 1998, not because its leadership of the "like minded" was questioned, rather the contrary. Canadian *jurisconsult* Philippe Kirsch had been selected to chair the entire process. A team of skilled Canadian international lawyers was at the core of the negotiations, and takes great responsibility for the eventual result.[52] In particular, Kirsch's diplomatic instincts combined with his skill as an international lawyer helped produce a package that achieved very broad support, if not consensus. When the Rome Statute of the International Criminal Court entered in to force in 2002, Kirsch was elected a judge and became the institution's first president.

Issues of human rights and international criminal law fit within a broader rubric that Canadian policy makers like to call "human security." Significant engagement with the cognate field of international humanitarian law, or the law of armed conflict, dates to the late 1960s, when Canada was largely responsible for initiatives aimed at extending the reach of existing rules and standards to that they would contemplate non-international armed conflict as well as international armed conflict. A resolution drafted by Canada and Switzerland at the 1969 International Conference of the Red Cross and Red Crescent, held in Istanbul, entitled "La reaffirmation et la mise au point des lois et des coutumes applicables en cas de conflict armé," proposed the enlargement of the single provision in the four Geneva Conventions applicable to civil wars.[53] Canada made similar submissions to the United Nations Secretary General.[54] At the first Government Experts Conference, convened in 1971 by the International Committee of the Red Cross, Canadians tabled a draft text for a protocol dealing with non-international armed conflicts.[55] These initiatives resulted in the adoption of a new treaty, in 1977.[56] Other manifestations of Canadian leadership include the Convention on the Prohibition of the Use, Stockpiling, Production and Transfer of Anti-Personnel Mines and on Their Destruction, better known as the "Ottawa treaty" for the city of its adoption in 1997,[57] and the Report of the Panel of Experts on the Situation in Angola, chaired by Canadian Ambassador Robert Fowler, something that led to the establishment of the Kimberley Process and the suppression of "conflict diamonds."[58]

These strands all came together in the emerging doctrine of the "responsibility to protect," a concept imposing upon states not only a duty to assist their own citizens but also to act as part of a broader community when vulnerable groups suffer persecution in another country. In 2000, the Government of Canada established the International Commission on Intervention and State Sovereignty. Its report, issued a year later, was entitled *The Responsibility to Protect*. The twelve-member commission included three prominent Canadians, Gisèle Côté-Harper, Michael Ignatieff and Ramesh Thakur, and its Advisory Board was chaired by Lloyd Axworthy, who is widely acknowledged as the author of the "responsibility to protect" concept. The recommendations of the commission were eventually incorporated in the document adopted by the summit of heads of state and government held on the occasion of the sixtieth anniversary of the adoption of the Charter of the United Nations.[59] They constitute an emerging doctrine of public international law that has been endorsed, albeit in a somewhat different form, by a judgment of the International Court of Justice.[60]

Surely one of the most significant contributions of Canada to international law has taken place within the country rather than on an international plane, in the innovative case law of Canadian courts. Though the Canadian legal system ostensibly discourages a close relationship between international law and national law, since the early 1980s judges have shown great willingness to use international norms and authorities, especially in the area of human rights law. Canadian judges regularly refer to international authorities to bolster and support interpretations of the Canadian Charter of Rights and Freedoms, ensuring, in effect, that Canadian law coincides with international law.[61] The phenomenon has been variously described as "transjudicial pluralism,"[62] "transnational judicial dialogue,"[63] "transnational legal process,"[64] and "judicial globalization."[65] Canadian approaches have been emulated in many countries, including South Africa. In its very first decision, the post-apartheid South African Constitutional Court borrowed from the constitutional analysis of the Supreme Court of Canada dealing with limitations on fundamental rights.[66]

Canadian courts must themselves interpret international law, on occasion, and here they have also made significant contributions. The paradigm is the 1998 *Secession Reference* of the Supreme Court of Canada. Did international law authorize or prohibit unilateral secession in the case of Quebec?, the Court was asked. Few tribunals, be they national or international, have ever faced such a difficult but fundamental issue. Self-determination of peoples has an internal and an external dimension, the Court explained.[67] Its external dimension, that is, secession, only becomes operative in special cases. The two circumstances clearly recognized in such positive law statements as the 1970 Declaration on Friendly Relations[68] are decolonisation and severe national oppression,[69] neither of them applicable to contemporary Quebec. A possible third exception, said the Court, was denial of the right to meaningful internal self-determination. These conclusions, consistent with most academic writing, nevertheless constitute the most important judicial determination on the matter. The Supreme Court ruling also contained important statements about democracy, constitutionalism and the rule of law.

In 1974, three leading Canadian scholars conceded that one could not speak of a "Canadian school" of international law. Other countries can claim specific visions of international law, usually harmonised with strategic national policy and objectives.[70] But "[i]n Canada it is not yet possible to hail the emergence of a major Canadian legal theorist who is likely to attract a national following of Canadian students on the strength of his distinctive style in international law. There is no Canadian 'school' with an identifiable leader."[71] More than thirty years later, that statement is probably still true. Perhaps the explanation lies in multilateralism, an approach that inherently discourages the emergence of a national perspective. Among scholars, Professor Thomas Franck would be looked to for great intellectual leadership, but though raised and educated in Canada, he joined the New York University School of Law in 1960 and has been associated with it ever since. Most of his admirers are probably not even aware of his Canadian roots.

Nor were the same three writers inclined to indicate a "national philosophy" of international law. Indeed, "[i]t might be said that the *absence* of a tradition that could sustain such a philosophy is characteristically Canadian."[72] They tended to attribute this to cultural diversity, and they said they expected that Canadians would excel in areas where technology and technical expertise would be featured. Here, such an appreciation was probably less perceptive. Canadian leadership, and influence, in international law has probably been greatest in the cluster of issues that includes human rights, international criminal prosecution, international humanitarian law and the "responsibility to protect." Such a result is ironic, given Canada's rather pathetic profile in these areas in the early days of the United Nations. Perhaps it was a niche waiting to be filled, and Canadians offered the right combination of expertise, objectivity and enthusiasm. They are not alone in this field, but nor do they have many serious competitors. Engagement has benefited from the dynamic support of ministers like Lloyd Axworthy and Bill Graham, and suffered when others, less inspired by such an agenda, held office. The philosophy of human security may not appeal in the same way to all of Canada's political constituencies, but it is probably the area in which Canada has been most successful and that, arguably, coincides most closely with the shared values of its people.

NOTES

1 M. Cohen, "Canada and the International legal Order: An Inside Perspective," in R. St. J. Macdonald, G.L. Morris and D.M. Johnston, eds., *Canadian perspectives on International Law and Organisation* (Toronto: University of Toronto Press), 3–32, at 3.
2 *The Caroline, United Kingdom v. United States*, (1837) 2 Moore 409.
3 "Letter from Daniel Webster to Lord Ashburton, 6 August 1842," in David J. Harris, *Cases and Materials on International Law* (London: Sweet and Maxwell, 1998), 1049.
4 *France* et al. v. *Göring* et al., (1947) 22 IMT 448.
5 Abraham D. Sofaer, "On the Necessity of Pre-emption," *European Journal of International Law* 14 (2003): 209; Michael Wood, « Necessité et légitime défense dans la lutte contre le terrorisme: quelle est la pertinence de l'affaire de

la *Caroline* aujourd'hui, » in *La Nécessité en droit international* (Paris: Pédone, 2007), 281–6.
6 M. Cohen, "Canada and the International Legal Order: An Inside Perspective," 6.
7 *Ibid.*, 9.
8 *Trail Smelter Arbitration* (US/Can), (1938/1941) 3 RIAA 1905 (Arbitral Trib.). See: John E. Read, "The Trial Smelter Dispute," *Canadian Yearbook of International Law* 1 (1963), 213.
9 *I'm Alone* Arbitration, United States and Canada, Joint Final Report of Commissioners, 5 January 1935, *American Journal of International Law* 29 (1935): 326. Also: Charles Cheney Hyde, "The Adjustment of the I'm Alone Case," *American Journal of International Law* 29 (1935): 296.
10 "Notes of a Meeting Held at President Wilson's House, May 6, 1919," in D.H. Miller, *The Drafting of the Covenant* (New York/London: G.B. Putnam's Sons, 1928), at 489.
11 *Treaties of Peace Act*, 1919, SC 1919 (2nd sess.) v. 30.
12 D.H. Miller, *The Drafting of the Covenant*, at 358.
13 *Ibid.*, 363.
14 Jean Ray, *Commentaire du Pacte de la Société des Nations selon la politique et la jjurisprudence des organes de la Société* (Paris: Recueil Sirey, 1930), at 350–5.
15 *Ibid.*, 215.
16 M. Cohen, "Canada and the International legal Order: An Inside Perspective," 9.
17 *Constitution of the International Labour Organization*, [1946] CTS 48.
18 John Mainwaring, *The International Labour Organization, A Canadian View* (Ottawa: Supply and Services Canada, 1986). Bryce M. Stewart, *Canadian Labour Laws and the Treaty* (New York: Columbia University Press, 1926), 36 and ff.
19 *AG Canada v. AG Ontario (Labour Conventions Case)*, [1937] AC 326, [1937] 1 DLR 73, [1937] 1 WWR 299 (JCPC).
20 Stéphane Beaulac, "The Canadian Federal Constitutional Framework and the Implementation of the Kyoto Protocol," *Revue juridique polynésienne (hors série)* 5 (2005): 125.
21 Maxwell Cohen & Anne F. Bayefsky, "The Canadian Charter of Rights and Freedoms and International Law," *Canadian Bar Review* 61 (1983): at 292–3.
22 Cited in *Canadian Yearbook of International Law* 9 (1971): 276.
23 *Customs Act*, 1 Edw. VIII, c. 30, RSC 1952, c. 58.
24 *An Act Respecting the Territorial Sea and Fishing Zones* of Canada, SC 1964, 13 Eliz. II, c. 22. See: A.E. Gotlieb, "The Canadian Contribution to the Concept of a Fishing Zone in International Law," *Canadian Yearbook of International Law* 2 (1964): 55; Jacques-Yvan Morin, « La zone de pêche exclusive du Canada, » *Annuaire canadien de droit international* 2 (1964): 77.
25 *United Nations Convention on the Law of the Sea*, [1994] 1833 UNTS 3, art. 3.

26 Ivan Head and Pierre Trudeau, *The Canadian Way: Shaping Canadian Foreign Policy, 1968–1984* (Toronto: McClelland & Stewart, 1985), at 61–3, 208.
27 *Arctic Waters Pollution Prevention Act*, SC 1970, c. 67. See: J. Alan Beesley, "The Canadian Approach to International Environmental Law," *Canadian Yearbook of International Law* 11 (1973), 3; Donat Pharand, *Canada's Arctic Waters in International Law* (New York: Cambridge University Press, 1988); Robert S. Reid, "The Canadian Claim to Sovereignty over the Waters of the Arctic," *Canadian Yearbook of International Law* 12 (1974): 111; Ivan L. Head, "Canadian Claims to Territorial Sovereignty in the Arctic Regions," *McGill Law Journal* 9 (1962–63): 200.
28 Paul Fauteux, « L'initiative juridique canadienne sur la pêche en haute mer, » *Canadian Yearbook of International Law* 31 (1993): 33.
29 *Fisheries Jurisdiction (Spain v. Canada)*, Jurisdiction of the Court, Judgment, [1998] ICJ Reports 432.
30 http://www.international.gc.ca/foreign_policy/human-rights/hr1-rights-en.asp (consulted 16 June 2008).
31 Robert A. Spencer, *Canada in World Affairs, 1946–1949* (Toronto: Oxford University Press, 1959), 162–163. The phrase "mild sensation" was used in the Canadian Press wire story: *The Globe and Mail*, 8 December 1948, 1.
32 John Humphrey, *Human Rights and the United Nations: A Great Adventure* (Dobbs Ferry, New York: Transnational, 1984).
33 William A. Schabas, "Canada and the Adoption of the *Universal Declaration of Human Rights*," *McGill Law Journal* 43 (1998): 403.
34 John Humphrey, "The Role of Canada in the United Nations Program for the Promotion of Human Rights," in R. St.J. Macdonald, G.L. Morris and D.M. Johnston, eds., *Canadian Perspectives on International Law and Organisation* (Toronto: University of Toronto Press, 1974), 612–19, at 613.
35 Irving Brecher, "New Directions in Canada's Foreign Aid, The Winegard Report and Beyond," in Donald Savoie and Irving Brecher, *Equity and Efficiency in Economic Development* (Montreal/Kingson: McGill-Queens University Press, 1992), 247–88.
36 William A. Schabas and Stéphane Beaulac, *International Human Rights Law and Canadian Law: Legal Commitment, Implementation and the Charter*, 3rd ed. (Toronto: Carswell, 2007).
37 Document of the Copenhagen Meeting of the Conference on the Human Dimension, 29 June 1990, *International Legal Materials* 29 (1909): 1305.
38 Theodor Meron, "Democracy and the Rule of Law," *World Affairs* 153 (1990): 23–4, at 24.
39 [1998] ETS 157.
40 Daniel LeBlanc, "Canada wants UN to soften extradition proposal," *The Globe and Mail*, 19 April 1999, A3; Daniel LeBlanc, "EU firm on extradition proposal," *The Globe and Mail*, 20 April 1999, A2.

41 *United States v. Burns and Rafay*, [2001] 1 SCR 283, paras. 84, 85.
42 United Nations War Crimes Commission, History of the United Nations War Crimes Commission and the Development of the Laws of War (London: His Majesty's Stationery Office, 1948).
43 Agreement for the Prosecution and Punishment of Major War Criminals of the European Axis, and Establishing the Charter of the International Military Tribunal (IMT), (1951) 82 UNTS 279.
44 Howard Margolian, *Conduct Unbecoming: The Story of the Murder of Canadian Prisoners of War in Normandy* (Toronto: University of Toronto Press, 1998); Howard Margolian, *Unauthorized Entry: The Truth about Nazi War Criminals in Canada, 1946–1956* (Toronto: University of Toronto Press, 2000).
45 Jules Deschênes, *Commission of Inquiry on War Criminals Report* (Ottawa: Minister of Supply and Services, 1986).
46 RSC, 1985, c. 30 (3rd Supp.), ss. 3.71–3.76.
47 *R. v. Finta*, [1994] 1 SCR 701.
48 Ibid.; *Mugesera v. Canada (Minister of Citizenship and Immigration)*, [2005] 2 SCR 100.
49 *Prosecutor v. Karamera* (Case No. ICTR-98-44-AR73(C)), Decision on Prosecutor's Interlocutory Appeal of Decision on Judicial Notice, para. 35.
50 UN Doc. S/RES/827 (1993).
51 *Prosecutor v. Tadić* (Case No. IT-94-1-AR72), Decision on the Defence Motion for Interlocutory Appeal on Jurisdiction, 2 October 1995.
52 Philippe Kirsch and John T. Holmes, "The Rome Conference on an International Criminal Court: The Negotiating Process," *American Journal of International Law* 93 (1999): 2; Philippe Kirsch, "The Development of the Rome Statute," in Roy Lee, *The International Criminal Court: Elements of Crimes and Rules of Procedure and Evidence* (Ardsley, New York: Transnational Publishers, 2001), 451–61.
53 "Canadian Practice in International Law, 1969," *Canadian Yearbook of International Law* 8 (1970): 370–373.
54 UN Doc. A/7720; UN Doc. A/8052
55 "Canadian Practice in International Law, 1973," *Canadian Yearbook of International Law* 12 (1974): 298.
56 *Protocol Additional II to the 1949 Geneva Conventions and Relating to The Protection of Victims of Non-International Armed Conflicts*, (1979) 1125 UNTS 609, [1991] CTS 2.
57 L. Wexler, "The International Deployment of Shame, Second-Best Responses, and Norm Entrepreneurship: The Campaign to Ban Landmines and the Landmine Ban Treaty," *Arizona Journal of International & Comparative Law* 20 (2003): 561.
58 "Report of the Panel of Experts on Violations of Security Council Sanctions Against UNITA," UN Doc. S/2000/23, annex.

59 "Outcome Document of the 2005 World Summit," UN Doc. A/RES/60/1, paras. 138–139. Also: UN Doc. S/RES/1674 (2006), para. 4.
60 *Case Concerning the Application of the Convention on the Prevention and Punishment of the Crime of Genocide (Bosnia and Herzegovina v. Serbia and Montenegro)*, Judgment, 26 February 2007, para. 426.
61 For example, *Reference Re Public Service Employee Relations Act*, [1987] 1 SCR 313, at 348–50.
62 Anne-Marie Slaughter, "A Typology of Transjudicial Communiçation," *University of Richmond Law Review* 29 (1994): 99.
63 Melissa A. Waters, "Mediating Norms and Identity: The Role of Transnational Judicial Dialogue in Creating and Enforcing International Law," *Georgetown Law Journal* 93 (2005): 487.
64 Harold Hongju Koh, "Transnational Legal Process," *Nebraska Law Review* 75 (1996): 181; Mary Ellen O'Connell, "New International Legal Process," *American Journal of International Law* 93 (1999): 334.
65 Claire L'Heureux-Dubé, "The Importance of Dialogue: Globalization and the International Impact of the Rehnquist Court," *Tulsa Law Journal* 34 (1998): 15; Anne-Marie Slaughter, "Judicial Globalization," *Virginia Journal of International Law* 40 (2000): 1103; Karen Knop, "Here and There: International Law in Domestic Courts," *New York University Journal of International Law & Policy* 32 (2000): 501; Paul Schiff Berman, "The Globalization of Jurisdiction," *University of Pennsylvania Law Review* 151 (2002): 311.
66 *State v. Zuma and Two Others*, Constitutional Court Case No. CCT/5/94 (5 April 1995), para. 15, citing *R. v. Big M Drug Mart*, [1985] 1 SCR 295.
67 *Reference re Secession of Quebec*, [1998] 2 SCR 217, at para. 126.
68 *Declaration on Principles of International Law concerning Friendly Relations and Co-operation among States in accordance with the Charter of the United Nations*, G.A. Res. 2625(XXV).
69 *Reference re Secession of Quebec*, [1998] 2 SCR 217, at paras. 133, 135, 138.
70 See, e.g., E. McWhinney, "The 'New Thinking' in Soviet International Law: Soviet Doctrines and Practice in the Post-Tunkin Era," *Canadian Yearbook of International Law* 28 (1990): 309; John F. Murphy, *The United States and the Rule of Law in International Affairs* (Cambridge: Cambridge University Press, 2004).
71 R. St.J. Macdonald, G.L. Morris and D.M. Johnston, "Canadian Approaches to International Law," in R. St.J. Macdonald, G.L. Morris and D.M. Johnston, eds., *Canadian Perspectives on International Law and Organisation* (Toronto: University of Toronto Press, 1974), 940–54, at 945.
72 *Ibid.*, 947 (emphasis in the original).

7 "And who is my neighbour?" Refugees, Public Opinion, and Policy in Canada since 1900*

JULIE GILMOUR

In June 2006, the Canadian government announced a plan to accept an initial group of 800 Karen refugees from Myanmar (Burma). As a *Globe and Mail* editorial noted, compared with the anxiety Canadians displayed over refugee debates in 1915 or 1938, the arrival of the Karens was "greeted with a big yawn."[1] The *Globe* had its history right. The decision to allow the settlement of Armenian orphans in 1915 or a handful of Jewish refugees from Germany in 1938 had roused Canadians to feverish debate. A century had made a difference in how Canadians perceived the world, and their place in it. Our understanding of who we are had changed.

It has become commonplace for Canadians to assume that Canada is a good international citizen with respect to allowing for the entry of refugees endangered because of their religion, politics, gender, race, or sexual orientation. Issues of race and discrimination are not absent from the Canadian discourse on immigration today, but the lack of dissent in Parliament and in the media on refugee issues such as the arrival of the Karens is nevertheless noteworthy. In the minds of Canadians, policies providing refugee assistance are relatively unremarkable and are, in fact, now part of how we see our nation and our place in the world.

In 1977, Gerald Dirks convincingly argued in *Canada's Refugee Policy* that we have been open to refugees only when it suited us.[2] Gallup poll data between 1949 and 2001 show that Canadians have rarely ranked immigration, or indeed refugee acceptance, as a national priority over the last sixty years. Not surprisingly, this has been particularly true in times of economic downturn.[3] That this was the case during the Great Depression of the 1930s – admittedly before polls but with plenty of evidence – is especially unsurprising. Canadian historians have frequently remarked over the past thirty or forty years on the fact that mixed with economic fears was racial or ethnic prejudice. Even the prosperous Canada that came into existence after 1945 shows that there remains a correlation between prosperity, or the lack of it, and the nation's receptivity to strangers.

So why is the idea that we are *by nature* a haven for the persecuted so strongly rooted? What experiences as a nation have convinced us that this is so? I would argue that despite moments when public fears of high costs, social disruption, and economic strain might have stalled refugee assistance, the influence of key individuals has kept the issue of refugee's needs on the table. More bluntly, officials and politicians, backed by Canada's foreign policy public, and sustained by a disciplined and centralized political system in some cases succeeded in opening Canada's doors to large numbers of people seeking a new start. These moments of refugee acceptance have made a huge impact on Canadian society and how we view ourselves.

While there have been many waves of migration to these shores, none were officially "refugees" by immigration status until Canada ratified the 1951 Geneva Convention Relating to the Status of Refugees in 1969. If we adopt a general rather than legal definition of "refugees," persons seeking political as well as economic security have been coming to these shores since the United Empire Loyalists in 1783. In the nineteenth and early twentieth century, there were Doukhobors and Mennonites from tsarist Russia and the new Soviet Union, seeking a life farther from political turmoil. There were some unofficial refugees; especially Jews, from Europe in the 1930s. However, the first mass refugee wave to Canada in the twentieth century was arguably the movement of Displaced Persons (DPs) after World War Two.

Immigration histories point to the arrival of the DPs as crucial to two changes in Canadian society. First, it contributed to the development of a multi-ethnic Canada through sheer numbers. Shifts in the religious and ethnic make up of Canada's cities were considerable. Further, the arrival of this wave and the ones that followed created a growing awareness of ethnic difference.[4] Few historians, with the exception of Gerald Dirks and Milda Danys, have looked in depth at the decision to allow for their entry and the conditions under which the Canadian government made this commitment. An examination of the documents related to this decision reveals that although domestic economic issues were critical to making this movement of DPs possible, the role of individuals working within a larger international community of interests is critical to understanding the tidal change under way.

Michael Marrus' work, *The Unwanted*, convincingly argues that although people had been displaced by war or persecution for centuries, the European refugee crisis of the 1930s and 1940s was a largely new phenomenon, as great numbers of refugees were unable to return to their place of origin and found themselves permanent outsiders in the receiving societies. As a result, for the first time, argues Marrus, there was a need for an internationally coordinated response to a refugee crisis.[5] In the case of Canada, we have in this crisis a pivotal moment when national and international interests came together and transformative policy making was the result.[6] The case of the decision to accept DPs from Europe after the war will demonstrate how Canada's approach to refugees was shifting and provided a basis for developments in policy in the years after 1950.

Put simply, between 1906 and 1943 Canada's response to immigration, including the entry of those displaced by politics, war, or disasters, was increasingly restricted. The years after World War Two saw the rise of a new generation of officials and an immense growth in Canadian willingness to consider the entry of refugees in a process independent of existing immigration requirements. This culminated in Canada's recognition of the 1951 Geneva Convention Relating to the Status of Refugees in 1969. Subsequently, in the late 1970s and 1980s Canada was widely considered an exemplary international citizen, allowing for the entry of more than 60,000 refugees from Indochina. Most recently, while Canadians generally consider refugee relief to be an important part of our national culture, the post-11 September world of economic crisis, increased security, and scrutiny, has created a context in which some groups have ceased to be considered worthy 'neighbours' and the process of inclusion seems to face resistance.[7]

This paper will argue that an important policy transition occurred in the years between 1937 and 1951 that continues to shape the Canadian sense of nation today. During the wartime and post-war years Canada struggled with the issue of European refugees and began to devise a strategy for non-discriminatory immigrant selection process for the movement of DPs after the war. Canada began to consider the implementation of a refugee strategy based on humanitarian need outside of the standard immigration regulations, and it began to consider selection criteria based on factors other than race. This paper will explore this time of transition and the role that officers of the External Affairs Department played in bringing their international perspective to the issue.

Over the last one hundred years we have seen considerable changes in Canadian assumptions about the nation's role in the international community; the "preferred" immigrant; and how the government should maximize any benefits accruing to Canada from immigration. What has remained, however, is the underlying assumption that immigration is only positive when it does not reduce the standard of living of established Canadians.

In 1909, Methodist minister and future leader of the Co-operative Commonwealth Federation (CCF) party in Canada, J.S. Woodsworth, published an eclectic collection of materials under the title *Strangers Within Our Gates or Coming Canadians*. He was writing at a time when Canadians were reacting to the perceived difficulties arising from the relatively open immigration policies of Sir Wilfrid Laurier and Clifford Sifton (1896-1905). The rising numbers of southern and eastern European immigrants were shocking to a society that defined itself largely as Anglo and Protestant (with the obvious exception of Quebec). Winnipeg, where Woodsworth worked, had become the epicentre of the movement of these migrating people. He was therefore at the centre of debate about how best to reduce the negative impact of the arrival of so many struggling settlers.

While sympathetic to the plight of the poor immigrants starting a new life in Canada, the tone of this work is largely fearful. The author feared a wave of immigrants who were unable to integrate into Canadian society. From his perspective those who would preserve different habits of behaviour and thought were not only "non-ideal" but should be excluded entirely if possible. "We, in Canada, have certain more or less clearly defined ideals of national well-being; These ideals must never be lost sight of. Non-ideal elements there must be, but they should be capable of assimilation. Essentially non-assimilable elements are clearly detrimental to our highest national development, and hence should be vigorously excluded."[8]

His fears of difference, disease, poverty, and political disruption reflect those of Canadian society in general at this time towards those fleeing European unrest. Not only did the Canadian government not recognize these people as refugees with a just humanitarian claim for entry into the country, but after 1906 when Canada gained a new immigration minister, Frank Oliver, they were faced with an increasingly restrictive immigration policy altogether.[9] The 1906 Immigration Act began what became known as a "White Canada Immigration Policy"[10] and a process of exclusion by legislation culminating in March 1931 with an Order-in-Council, P.C. 695. This cabinet order restricted immigration to individuals in four categories. "1. British subjects from the United Kingdom, Ireland, Newfoundland, New Zealand, Australia or the Union of South Africa, who possessed sufficient means to maintain themselves until employment was secured. 2. United States citizens, similarly possessed of means and maintenance. 3. Wives, unmarried children under 18, or fiancées (sic) of men resident in Canada. 4. Agriculturists with sufficient means to farm in Canada."[11]

This isolationist approach reached its nadir in 1938–39 when, despite vigorous lobbying efforts, the Government of Canada disallowed the entry of Jewish refugees.[12] In 1938–39 Canada turned down request after request for the entry of Jewish refugees. These refusals were justified under the existing immigration regulations and strongly influenced by Canadian assumptions about Jewish immigrants. In addition, attempts to liberalize the regulations were further constrained by fears of economic hardship and unemployment. Canada was still in the throes of the Great Depression; these refugees were not agriculturists and they had no means to support themselves because of the confiscation of their property by the German government. It was therefore an unfortunately simple thing for the Immigration Branch to deny these refugees entry.

During 1942, at the height of World War II, only 7,576 immigrants of any type were admitted to the country.[13] Many emigrants found themselves without proper documentation and even those who had transit visas and passports found that it had become virtually impossible for civilians to find passage on trans-Atlantic crossings. This exclusionary approach to immigration continued until the pressures of wartime dislocation in the 1940s became acute, Canada re-examined its commitment to international action, and a growing discourse on human rights made refugee claims on humanitarian grounds an increasingly important category for consideration.

If we examine the Canadian responses to refugees before and after the Second World War we can see at least two significant shifts. The first is the use of humanitarian criteria in consideration for entry to Canada. Prior to World War Two, while allowing for the settlement of individuals and groups facing persecution in their homelands, applicants were required to meet the standards set by Canada's general immigration policy. There was no separate category of refugees based on humanitarian need. Groups like the Mennonites and Doukhobors negotiated with the government on the specifics of entry, bloc settlement, and wartime exemptions; however, they first had to convince officials that they would be "desirable" as settlers under the accepted immigration legislation.

The second shift occurring during this time was the opening of debate on the benefits of and the means to find an end to discriminatory policies based on race and religion. Existing assumptions and prejudices held by Canadian society in general, and government officers specifically about the talents, skills and potential of particular groups were significant factors in immigration decisions before the war.[14] Ethnic portraits as presented by Woodsworth reflect widely held prejudices that could affect the outcome for many applicants. This was most obvious in policies such as the Chinese head tax and the government's refusal to allow for the entry of Jewish refugees in the 1930s. However, these assumptions about who Canada's settlers should be were under growing pressure. Individuals working in new arenas of international politics; anti-Nazi and anti-communist ideology; and domestic calls for humanitarian aid and economic development combined to force an expansion in the pool of potential "new Canadians."

Despite Canada's failure to recognize the claims of Jewish refugees in 1938, and world wide failure to assist them, efforts to allow the emigration of European Jews were *beginning* to change the attitudes of at least some policy makers towards a humanitarian category for immigration; Ottawa reluctantly but steadily followed this trend. Despite Mackenzie King's reluctance to have Canada participate in the 1938 Evian Conference, Canada's new membership in international bodies concerned with the plight of refugees had significant impact for the nation in the post-war period.[15] Participation on international committees gave an emerging generation of Canadian bureaucrats like R.G. Riddell an international perspective on the crisis and made it more difficult to ignore in Ottawa. It was complicated for the Canadian government, as signatories, to refuse to participate in efforts to solve the crisis by opening its doors to European refugees during and after the war. As early as 1943, after the Bermuda Conference on Refugees, Great Britain expressed concern about Canada's restrictive immigration policies. Britain claimed that since Canada had such a vast territory, it should agree to accommodate more refugees than the already heavily burdened nations of Europe.[16]

On 29 July 1943, the British secretary of state for dominion affairs, Clement Attlee, sent Mackenzie King a proposed draft from the United States government on the question of refugees. It praised those states that had accepted refugees whose "lives and liberty are in danger on account of their race, religion or their political beliefs." It also highlighted the urgency of the problem and significantly it noted that:

It cannot be expected that these [neutral] countries [of Europe], some of which are already overcrowded, should maintain these people for an indefinite period. The above mentioned Governments [Belgium, Czechoslovakia, Greece, Luxembourg, Netherlands, Norway, Poland, USSR, United Kingdom, United States and Yugoslavia] hereby declare that they will, at the termination of this war, admit to their territories all their nationals who may have been displaced by the war into other countries.[17]

Canada's allies recognized both the immediate crisis and the necessity for countries like the United States and Canada, which had space and resources, to become receiving countries after the war in light of the burden already carried by European powers.

There was no doubt in the minds of any observers that this was a crisis on an unprecedented scale. Reports from the "Allied agencies" and United Nations Relief and Rehabilitation Administration (UNRRA) in September 1945 put the number of refugees and displaced persons under their care at more than 6,795,000 people.[18] When added to the number of refugees in the Soviet zone and the displaced Germans the number is staggering. It was an international priority, and, as good citizens in the post-war international community, Canadians were expected to take part in creating solutions.

R.G. Riddell, a Canadian diplomat and his country's representative to the UN International Refugee Commission, concluded publicly in August 1946 that it was an "international responsibility, not only to find new homes for them but to provide at least some of the rights granted ordinary citizens."[19] As Canada was one of the twenty-member commission on refugees which had met in London in April, it would be embarrassing for the nation, and especially for Canadian diplomats like Riddell, if Canada continued to support the UN's efforts without providing immigration opportunities.

Although difficult to measure, one cannot help but conclude that this generation of officials, having spent more time abroad than their predecessors and having worked extensively with their foreign counterparts during the war and immediately after, might have brought a new, more international, perspective to decision making in Canada.

Canadians abroad represented a variety of bodies; External Affairs, the Preparatory Commission of the International Refugee Organization (PCIRO) and the Canadian Military Mission in Berlin. All of these organizations faced the increasingly obvious need for a solution to the crisis. 1.4 million European refugees who had refused repatriation sat in DP camps administered by UNRRA and the allied occupation forces. Each required housing, feeding and permanent homes.

John Holmes, the first secretary at Canada House in London between 1944 and 1947 and chargé d'affaires in Moscow in 1947–8, was a vocal witness to events in Europe. In the summer before he was stationed in Moscow he travelled with C.D. Howe,[20] who among his other responsibilities was acting minister of Mines and Resources (and therefore immigration), to inspect several DP camps in Germany. Holmes remarked on both the difficult conditions in Germany and his impressions of the DPs. He seemed both concerned for their continued wellbeing and impressed by the quality of the lives DPs had managed to build up until this point under trying circumstances. "It was astonishing how the D.P.'s (sic), many of them obviously persons of distinction, managed to preserve their dignity, even when their handiwork was being shown off by our American guide as if it were the surprising product of a kindergarten."[21]

He later set out his retrospective concerns about the refugee crisis in *The Shaping of Peace*. This account from his viewpoint in External Affairs is unambiguously critical of the resistance from the Immigration Branch to opening Canada's doors to refugees immediately after the war.

Within the civil service the facts of life, including the conservatism of the cabinet on population policies, were recognized as setting limits to policy proposals, even though External Affairs officials in particular were aware of the handicap placed on their vision of the country by Canada's insensitivity to the plight of refugees, its archaic immigration regulations, and the racism clearly evident in practice. External Affairs battered vigorously against what they regarded as the defensive mentality entrenched in the Immigration Branch, sought to warn the cabinet of the desperate realities they saw in Europe, and to encourage an imaginative approach to population policy for Canada.[22]

There is a great deal of correspondence between the Department of Labour, External Affairs and the Immigration Branch that backs up Holmes' observations. Officers of the Department of Labour were frequently equally critical of the limited approach of the immigration branch.[23] Holmes, officers of the Department of Labour in Germany, and other Canadians stationed abroad after the war were perhaps more aware of the humanitarian issues at stake than those manning the offices of the Immigration Branch in Ottawa. It is possible that discussions with other international diplomats and trips through Germany such as Holmes made with C.D. Howe in 1947 brought a special urgency to the crisis and a certain embarrassment about Canada's old-fashioned parochialism. It is clear that the trip made a lasting impression on Holmes and that he and other officers of the departments of External Affairs brought this perspective to discussions of policy.[24]

Responding to what must have been becoming a more common accusation of discrimination in the immigration branch's policy, a confidential memo to the Department of Labour candidly defends the Immigration Branch's approach.

The claim is sometimes made that Canada's immigration laws reflect class and race discrimination: they do, and necessarily so. Some form of discrimination cannot be avoided if immigration is to be effectively controlled. In order to prevent the creation in Canada of expanding non-assimilable (sic) racial groups, the prohibiting of entry to immigrants of non-assimilable races is necessary. Many organizations have passed resolutions urging "selective immigration." The term is so general that it can be applied to mean almost anything from near exclusion to an extremely wide range of immigrant classes. Certainly it is not possible to have selective immigration on the one hand and no discrimination on the other. The very act of selection results in discrimination.[25]

This tension between branches of the Canadian government seems to be, in part, a function of a changing sense of what the term "discrimination" meant. There was a growing sense (especially among Canadians in External Affairs like Riddell and Holmes, and in ethnic and religious organizations) that a rejection based solely on race or, in the case of Jewish applicants, religion, was not acceptable in a world that had just defeated Nazism.[26] And yet the maintenance of deeply rooted ethnic and religious stereotypes in Canada (and elsewhere) provided rationalizations for either rejecting applications for immigration outright, or restricting members of particular groups to specific occupations. The Immigration Branch official who penned this memo was unable (or unwilling) to consider the more difficult question of how to formulate a policy that would both benefit Canadians and would evaluate potential immigrants according to a set of criteria that, as much as possible, could be said to avoid arbitrary decisions based on ethnic origin.

He was not alone. In this transitional period race and ethnic origins remained a critical element in discussions of suitability despite attempts to move away from "discrimination." In May 1947, H.L. Keenleyside, the Deputy Minister of Mines and Resources, wrote to Laurent Beaudry, the acting under-secretary of state for External Affairs, with some recommendations for the treatment of DPs. This memo, more than any other document, shows the convergence in 1947 of Canada's domestic needs and an opening for action abroad. Delays in the establishment of the International Refugee Organization (IRO) and in Congress in the passing of legislation required to allow for the passage of DPs to the United States opened up the possibility for Canada to appear as a leader on this issue and gain an opportunity to "select the D.P.'s (sic) in accordance with our own ideas as to who would be likely to make the best Canadian citizens."[27]

This expression of Canadian intentions included a concern for the refugees "who continue to suffer" and the hope that Canada's actions would encourage "other countries to make an early contribution to the problem." There was also the very opportunistic hope to "have the satisfaction of being able to say that Canada was the first country to make any serious effort to contribute to a solution to this problem ..." and that it "would enhance the reputation of Canadians as a humanitarian and practical people." In addition, Keenleyside expressed the hope that it would improve the optics domestically for Canadian immigration policy showing that "the Government is seriously interested in immigration and is acting effectively to obtain a good type of immigrant."[28]

While the former Allies sought solutions to the unprecedented refugee crisis, Canadians were considering ways to maintain and increase the nation's new international stature. The assumption that wealthy, under-populated nations like Canada should contribute and Canada's desire to lead on this issue came together in the DP scheme of 1947–1951.

Keeping the above context in mind it is easy to understand how a directed labour immigration project such as the movement of DPs could be relatively easy to defend politically in the late 1940s. Canadians could respond in keeping with their perceived "Christian duty," while at the same time receiving assurances that the privations of the 1930s could be avoided. Canada could bend to internal and external pressure without accusations that the economy would not "absorb" refugee labour since employment was guaranteed. It was a win-win situation from the perspective of the Department of Labour, woods operators and most refugees;[29] Canada's resource industries could be expanded, Canada could hold its head up in international circles, and those displaced persons seeking to get as far away from the Soviet Union as possible found work in the Canadian bush.

Forest industry representatives had been actively working with the department of labour during the war in the movement of prisoners of war (POWs) to the bush, and the same organizations began to press the federal government to allow for the immigration of DPs in a scheme based on the model used for the settlement of Polish Veterans during 1946. If they could not have Germans because of the continued restriction on the immigration of "enemy aliens" (this restriction on Germans was removed in 1950), they would press for woods workers from among the Baltic DPs, who had been sending requests to the Ontario Forest Industries Association and others.

This plan was all the more attractive because of the *surprisingly* low level of general unemployment in 1945 and the high demand for woods labour. Department of Labour officials were pleasantly surprised to find that the anticipated level of unemployment did not occur. In their estimation this was because women were leaving the workplace to "return to their homes"; a significant number of retirees had left the workplace; and an unexpected number of plants were successfully converted to civilian production.[30]

International context coincided with perceived domestic needs: a humanitarian impulse; labour requirements; resource development; and a relatively sparse population over a large area. Railway and resource industry representatives, ethnic lobby groups, and religious organizations, were already pressing for changes in Canada's "non-immigration" policy in 1946.[31]

In April 1946 immigration was front and centre in the House of Commons. W. Ross Thatcher, the CCF MP for Moose Jaw (and future

Liberal Premier of Saskatchewan), proposed a bill to the House on "Immigration Planned in Relation to Absorptive Capacity, Economic Need and Development Possibilities."[32] Although Thatcher's bill naturally did not pass, immigration was on the table. Around the same time the previously dormant Senate Standing Committee on Immigration and Labour (1946–1949) was revived with a mandate to inquire into the possibility of amendments to the Immigration Act, its administration and "a) the desirability of admitting immigrants to Canada, b) the type of immigrant which should be preferred, including origin, training and other characteristics, c) the availability of such immigrants for admission, d) the facilities, resources and capacity of Canada to absorb, employ and maintain such immigrants, and e) the appropriate terms and conditions of such admission."[33]

Many groups were invited to present their opinions to the Senate Standing Committee on Immigration and Labour after it was reconvened in 1946. In the first year these included representatives of Ukrainian, Polish, Finnish and Jewish organizations as well as speakers from the Department of Mines and Resources, Canada's railways, labour unions, Canadian National Committee on Refugees and the Cunard White Star Line.[34]

Initially authorities could point to shipping shortages as the reason Canada could not open its doors wide to refugee immigrants, but once Canada's armed forces had largely returned and shipping was freed up for civilian transport, the question could not be avoided any longer. The Cabinet Committee on Immigration Policy, chaired by J.A. Glen, the minister of Mines and Resources, saw "it was a matter of some urgency" to formulate a new immigration policy by March 1946.[35]

Although R.G. Riddell was aware of the humanitarian need for assisted immigration to Canada, he presented the Cabinet Committee on Immigration Policy with a limited proposal. He started small, asking only that the alien husbands of Canadian women and European orphans be considered since they "would make good immigrants."[36] The Committee agreed to this. A subsequent memo to Arthur MacNamara, the deputy minister of Labour, acknowledged that the Committee's decision to begin with relatives was a way of avoiding the increasingly thorny issue of race.[37]

Despite awareness of the problems in Europe, immigration and ethnicity were significant and potentially volatile issues for Canadians at home. While British and American immigrants were welcome neighbours, being "our own," there was more antagonism towards other groups.[38] In April 1946 the *Ottawa Evening Citizen* published data from a Gallup poll. In response to the question "Would you like to see a large number of people from the European continent migrate to Canada or not?" 61% chose "no." Only 21% were in favour of increased

European immigration and 10% gave a "qualified" yes. Furthermore, the article reported that among the qualifications presented by responders was "that the immigration should be carefully selected" and that no immigration should occur until "unemployment is overcome and our veterans are settled."[39] In answer to the question "From what countries would you particularly like to see these people come?" the *Ottawa Evening Citizen* reported that "Scandinavian countries headed the list by quite a margin. Holland and France were second and third respectively, with Belgium, Czechoslovakia, Poland, 'the Balkans', Russia and Ukraine finishing in that order."[40]

Canadian opinions about immigration and ethnic "preferences" were taken into consideration by the Department of Labour and the cabinet committee on immigration policy in their deliberations about a DP labour scheme. Industry representatives were consulted specifically as to their preferences and reports from Europe included extensive discussions about the relative merits of various groups.

There was ongoing debate in the cabinet and in the House about the means of maintaining selectivity without resorting to discrimination. J.A. Glen, the minister of Mines and Resources (and therefore immigration minister), told the House that "When it is suggested in an editorial that there should be selective immigration, and in the next breath that there should be no discrimination, then I venture to say to those who are making the suggestions that I do not see how we can have selective immigration without discrimination."[41]

Eventually the international context intervened in the domestic debate and Canada's participation in the UN General Assembly and Economic and Social Council (ECOSOC) forced the Cabinet Committee on Immigration Policy to take action to ensure the formulation of a clear, defensible position. It could not be put off any longer since as Hume Wrong reminded the committee that in a matter of weeks "Canadian delegations ... would be called upon to discuss the question of Canada's attitude to the refugee problem" and the UN organization was not going to look kindly on policies based on racial or other discriminatory categories.[42]

On 14 August 1946, after months of investigation, the Senate Standing Committee on Immigration and Labour submitted its report and recommendations. In addition to general agreement that "as a humane and Christian nation" it was important for Canada to "do her share towards the relief of refugees and displaced persons," the situation was also considered "urgent" in order for Canada "to hold [its] place abroad and maintain and improve [its] standard of living at home."[43] The committee concluded that it was generally agreed "that immigrants should be admitted, subject to the qualification that immigrants should be carefully selected and that admissions should not exceed the number which [could] be absorbed from time to time without creating conditions of unemployment, reducing the standard of living or otherwise endangering the Canadian economy."[44]

Significantly, despite the committee's agreement that immigrants should be "carefully selected," it also added the warning that "any suggestion of discrimination based upon either race or religion should be scrupulously avoided both in the Act and in its administration ..." Yet even here, discrimination against Asian immigration seems to remain acceptable "being based, of course, on problems of absorption."[45]

Action on immigration in the cabinet and support from Canadians in general was therefore possible in 1946–47, even on humanitarian grounds, only with the promise that it would be stopped if Canada faced an economic crisis as it had in the years after World War One and during the Great Depression of the 1930s. Thus "absorptive capacity" and "selective immigration" were catch-all terms which could represent a range of approaches to immigration. Those who perceived certain groups as "unassimilable" (sic) could argue for their exclusion using these concepts, and those who imagined mass immigration as a benefit to Canada could argue that its enormous size and natural wealth could allow for the "absorption" of a nearly limitless number of immigrants each year.[46] Canadians were interested in aiding the humanitarian crisis, but not at the cost of reducing Canadians' standard of living. So while the international context is critical to understanding the course of events, domestic pressures created limits on the policy options selected.

In the space of five years, Canada allowed for the entry of more than 160,000 DPs from ethnic groups that had previously been "non-preferred";[47] a significant change to a Canadian population of approximately twelve and a half million people in 1947. The arrival and successful integration (although significantly not always assimilation) of such a significant number of people from areas outside Britain and the United States shifted Canadian identity in profound ways, not the least of which was a new sense of Canada as refugee receiving nation. Canada and its government generally received positive press for its role in finding solutions to the European refugee crisis. And despite the short duration (the project came to an end in 1952) and some local resistance from labour organizations and some veterans groups to the idea of living and working with "New Canadians," the project was generally considered a grand success. The DPs became the latest chapter in the narrative of Canada's development and the face of Canada was changed.[48] Most significantly, the increasing importance of a human rights discourse in the post-war years created an atmosphere in which the concept of discrimination and its implications was seriously debated and the humanitarian refugee was recognized in practice. Although antisemitism and racial discrimination continued, this opening of a debate in the area of immigration and refugee policy was significant.

By 1948 when the United States got into the business of moving DPs to North America the Canadian program began to slow down. There were still workers to arrive and family members to join them, but the greatest force behind the movement (a chance for Canada to choose the "best" workers and to be a recognized leader) was gone. Those "hard core" DPs remaining in Europe were generally aged, infirm or ill, considered poor choices for a program looking to fill Ontario's bush camps. We see here the limits to the humanitarian logic of the movement and the importance of the domestic pressures. Only those who needed help *and* were perceived to be potential contributors to the development of the economy (or were immediate family of a worker) were allowed to come to Canada in this program. Others would have to either remain in Europe or find assistance elsewhere from a variety of religious and ethnic organizations.[49]

In 1949 this strategy seemed to be paying off. Industrial development was keeping up with demand, particularly in the pulp and paper and timber industry, and Canadians did not seem to be overly concerned by the changes. A CIPO poll from May 1949 asking about Canadians' priorities for the "post-election [June 1949] government" found that the issue front and centre for Canadians was housing; 20% of Canadians (both French and English speaking) who answered this question suggested housing, while only 1.3% listed immigration.[50] In 1951 the same question resulted in 38.8% suggesting that the "cost of living" was the most important issue of the day. Only 1.0% listed immigration.[51]

Nevertheless, the Canadian government was giving serious thought to its stand on immigration in 1951. Fearing a loss of its sovereign right to select whomever it deemed desirable and under what conditions, Canada declined to sign the United Nations Convention Relating to the Status of Refugees. Similarly, the 1952 Immigration Act maintained the *status quo* on immigration protecting the Canadian government's right to decline applications "by reason of such factors as nationality, ethnic group, occupation, lifestyle, unsuitability with regard to Canada's climate, and perceived inability to become readily assimilated into Canadian society."[52]

These stipulations seem to have had some resonance with the Canadian public based on the results of a February 1955 CIPO poll. Although quite a large number of Canadians polled declined to state a preference based on ethnicity, these two questions demonstrate that a significant number of Canadians were seeking to stop mass immigration and had preferences about the ethnicity of settlers. The first section of this question asked about whether the respondent wanted to see the population of Canada rise or stay about the same. 48.0% preferred a "smaller population"; 42.9% chose larger and 6.2% thought it was "about right."[53]

The second, for those who sought growth, was open ended (respondents could choose more than one answer and had to come up with the categories themselves) about the preferred origins of settlers. 53.3% did not answer the question; 20.4% chose "North East Europe"; 18.8% chose the United Kingdom; 7.4% had "no preference"; 4.2% wrote in some other European group; 2.9% Mediterranean; 2.7% did not know; 2.3% suggested the United States; 1.3% Central Europe; 3.1% other; 0.4% Asia; 0.2% USSR and Ukraine.[54]

Canada continued the debate on discrimination into the 1950s. Under pressure from its Commonwealth ties and under the influence of Lester Pearson, Canada signed agreements in 1951 with India, Pakistan and Ceylon to raise the annual quota of immigrants above those of other Asian groups.[55] But as we saw in the 1955 CIPO survey, Canadians continued to demonstrate a very low preference for "Asian" immigration.

Valerie Knowles is correct that Canada's response to the 1956 Hungarian crisis "paved the way for immigration authorities to respond more quickly and with more flexibility to later refugee and ordinary immigration movements..."[56] However it would be a mistake to ignore the importance of the experience of the DP movement, the importance of the Cold War conflict, and the continued strength of the economy (the downturn was not until 1957) which made the Hungarian movement itself a viable plan. In the context of the now familiar Cold War struggle with the Soviet Union, providing aid to this group of refugees was both obvious (Canada was now a nation concerned with humanitarian issues abroad and these refugees were the victims of communism) and utilitarian, since adding anti-communist voters and workers to the Canadian population was perceived to be politically and economically beneficial to the nation as a whole. In January 1957, 41.5% of Canadians polled approved "Canada's immigration policy;" 35.5% did not.[57] In July 1959 after the economic slowdown, 29.9% of Canadians polled thought the country needed immigrants "at the present time" and 63.9% disagreed.[58] And yet, in January 1960 when Canadians were polled about allowing 100 refugees with tuberculosis into the country in honour of World Refugee Year, 53% approved.[59] At a time when most were against immigration in general, there was still strong support for this limited humanitarian act.

It was not long before some Canadians called for changes to this approach and Canada's immigration law. John Diefenbaker included revisions to Canada's immigration law and an end to discrimination in his 1957 election platform and in his call for a bill of rights.

In 1958 Ellen Fairclough became Diefenbaker's minister of Citizenship and Immigration and initiated a period of high activity in the department.[60] 19 January 1962 Canada's new immigration regulations officially ended the use of racial categories as criteria for selection, although restrictions on Asian immigration remained until the 1967 "points system." This system aimed to remove race and ethnicity from the calculations altogether, replacing them with educational and occupational criteria.

In her analysis of the process of producing the 1962 regulations, Freda Hawkins placed responsibility for change firmly in the hands of Canada's bureaucracy rather than with popular agitation or parliamentary fiat. "This very important policy change was made not as a result of parliamentary or popular demand but because some senior officials in Canada, including [Dr. George Davidson the deputy minister of Citizenship and Immigration], rightly saw that Canada could not operate effectively within the United Nations, or in the multiracial Commonwealth, with the millstone of a racially discriminatory immigration policy round her neck."[61] Polling data from 1961 supports Hawkins conclusions, as 53.1% of Canadians polled supported continued restrictions on the "admission of non-whites;" although 35.7% called for fewer.[62] In the end, change occurred despite any resistance. Comparable changes occurred in Australia in 1973 and the United States in 1975. Clearly, then, the role of individuals within Canada's bureaucracy continued to have a significant impact on policy making in this period.

It took Canada until 1969 to finally ratify the 1951 Convention and the 1967 Protocol on Refugees. After this date, the government of Canada became a *cautious* supporter of humanitarian settlement. In 1972 Canada, along with other Commonwealth members was asked to assist refugees (of South Asian descent) carrying British passports to leave Uganda. 45.3% of Canadians polled approved of this action and 43.5% did not. 11.2% remained undecided.[63] Eventually 4,420 individuals[64] came to Canada as the situation in Uganda became untenable. While limited in scope and courage, the government did manage to act on this matter despite a divided and possibly resistant public.

As a result of the work of Robert Andras, the minister of the newly created Canada Manpower and Immigration Department, and Allan Gotlieb, his deputy, the 1967 regulations were reviewed, interested parties consulted, and findings published in the 1975 *Green Paper on Immigration*. Summing up the report, Andras wrote; "Canadians will want, I believe, an immigration policy that meets our social, economic and cultural needs, that respects the family, that is free from discrimination, and that keeps the door open to refugees."[65] The recommendations made by this report and the practices developed under the "points system" formed the basis for the subsequent 1976 Immigration Act.

While Canada's relationship with the Commonwealth obviously had a significant impact on its drive to end racial discrimination in immigration, the debate was begun in those crucial years around World War Two. By 1976, not only had the humanitarian impulse to help the world's refugees become more common in Canada, it had become one of the 1976 Act's "fundamental principles," which included "the promotion of Canada's demographic, economic, cultural and social goals; family reunion; the fulfilment of Canada's international obligations in relation to the United Nations Convention (1951) and the 1967 Protocol relating to refugees, which Canada signed in 1969; non-discrimination in immigration policy; and cooperation between all levels of government and the voluntary sector in the settlement of immigrants in Canadian society."[66] Nevertheless, because of high unemployment and uncertainty in the economy, only 10.2% of Canadians polled in 1975 preferred to increase immigration.[67]

The pressures on Canada's immigration and refugee apparatus in this period and in the following decades have been documented elsewhere,[68] but it is important to note the scale and variety of the movements organized after 1979. In this year Canada created designated refugee classes that included refugees of the crisis in Indochina, Latin America, and the Communist bloc. By 1981, Canada had opened its doors to 77,000 Indochinese refugees.[69] This occurred despite the fact that in 1979, when polled, 51.4% of Canadians considered the 5,000 scheduled for 1979 "too high" and 36.6 thought 5,000 was "about right."[70] Public opinion changed dramatically between February and November when the "Boat People" had become a cause supported by Canadian churches and therefore more prominently discussed in the press. By July 1979, 48.4% supported allowing "more of these refugees to re-locate to Canada."[71] By November 1979, 33.6% of Canadians thought that 50,000 refugees from Vietnam, 3,000 per *month*, was "just about right."[72]

This era was perhaps the high water mark for Canada's refugee activities. In 1986, the nation as a whole was recognized by the United Nations High Commissioner for Refugees with a Nansen Medal in recognition of these sponsored refugee programs of the 1970s and 1980s.[73] By the early 1990s, highly publicized examples of illegal arrivals and another economic downturn had reduced Canadians' interest in refugee assistance and immigration although support for immigration rose again to a limited extent in the late 1990s.[74] In 1997 Canada expanded its categories of possible refugees to ensure that some of those in need who failed to meet relatively specific convention criteria could still be assisted.[75]

It is perhaps too soon to judge the long term effects of the "War on Terror" on Canadian attitudes and policies on refugees. Recent changes to Canada's immigration regulations passed by the Harper Government in May 2008 suggest that there has been a revived emphasis on economic rather than humanitarian priorities and on ministerial discretion rather than bureaucratic regulation. Among the critiques made by the Canadian Bar Association aimed at this package was the claim that it would mean a return to a time when ministerial discretion was absolute and ungoverned by bureaucratically imposed selection criteria.[76]

For the time being, examples such as the Karen settlement suggest that Canadians will continue to accept some groups of refugees as the need arises. The post war positive experience of being widely known as a receiver nation is now deeply embedded in Canadian views of themselves in the world. Despite the return to ministerial discretion this may ensure that if any minister became negligent in applying the principles of the 1982 Charter of Rights and Freedoms, which prohibits discrimination in general, or reduced perceptions of Canada's willingness to welcome refugees in recognized crises, they would face significant public censure. This is neither "natural" to Canada, nor is it something we have always done.

As we have seen, between 1906 and 1943 a balance of Canadians and Canadian policy makers were in agreement that immigration should be restricted to the "preferred" groups; settlers from Britain, the United States, family members and farmers able to support themselves upon arrival. The wartime crisis changed the context in which immigration and refugee policies were being made. A new generation of bureaucrats with wartime experience abroad and with extensive contact with foreign peers were returning to Ottawa concerned about the refugee crisis and frustrated by the limits of old approaches to immigration. Canada's continuing participation in international bodies like the United Nations and concern with the question of discrimination meant that there was a significant amount of pressure on policy makers to assist in refugee settlement. Furthermore, this pressure opened up a significant debate about ways to balance national interests and non-discrimination. In this process individuals like Riddell, Holmes and Wrong led the nation past the limitations of its own public opinion. Rather than a regular march in one direction in this area, Canadians have often expressed the desire to limit settlement. Nevertheless, some significant moments of refugee migration have occurred when individuals responsible were committed to change.

The movements of DPs and Hungarians occurred at convenient intersections of national economic interest and new international perspectives. In the 1960s faced with changes to the Commonwealth, the boundaries were stretched again to include mass movements of "non-white" groups. By 1976, open refugee and immigration policies were "principles" borne out in practice during the height of the sponsored refugee movement of the 1970s and 1980s and expanded in 1997. In each case policy elites rather than elected governments or public pressure led the way.

The debates, disagreements, foot dragging and compromises initiated by individuals between 1937 and 1951 resulted in a shift among policy makers towards a sense of responsibility towards refugees. Continued waves of refugee settlement have re-enforced this notion in the broader Canadian public.

NOTES

* Thanks to the members of the Trinity College SCR, particularly to Stephen Waddams and Bruce Bowden, for the discussion which led to the choice of this title. This quotation comes from *The Bible*, King James Version, Luke 10: 25–30. It precedes the story of the Good Samaritan and demonstrates the difficulty people sometimes have accepting responsibility for giving aid to those who are different or distant. Thanks also to Robert Bothwell, Jean Daudelin, Jeff Kilpatrick, Janine Rivière, Carla Hustak, Cara Spittal and the other authors who attended the writers' workshop for their comments on early versions of the draft.

1 "How Canada recovers from past discrimination," in *Globe and Mail*, 23 June 2006, A20.
2 Gerald E. Dirks, *Canada's Refugee Policy: Indifference or Opportunism?* (Montreal: McGill-Queen's University Press, 1977).
3 I surveyed the CIPO Gallup materials between 1949 and 2001 available online at Carleton University, paying particular attention to data on immigration and refugee programs. See below for more detail. http://www.library.carleton.ca/ss-data/surveys/pop_gallup.html
4 See Franca Iacovetta, *Gatekeepers: Reshaping Immigrant Lives in Cold War Canada*, (Toronto: Between the Lines, 2006) as a recent example.
5 Michael R. Marrus, *The Unwanted: European Refugees in the Twentieth Century*, (New York: Oxford University Press, 1985), 3–13.
6 I am grateful to Greg Donaghy for his comments during the Authors' Meeting on the importance of these intersections of national and international policy.
7 For more on the changes in immigration policy after 11 September 2001, see Erin Kruger, Marlene Mulder, and Bojan Korenic, "Canada after 11 September: Security Measures and "Preferred" Immigrants," in *Mediterranean Quarterly* 15, no. 4 (Fall 2007): 72–87.
8 J.S. Woodsworth, *Strangers Within Our Gates, or, Coming Canadians* (Toronto: University of Toronto Press, 1972), 232. Also cited in Valerie Knowles, *Strangers at Our Gates: Canadian Immigration Policy, 1540–1997* (Toronto: Dundurn Press, 1997), 97.

9 For more on Frank Oliver and immigration policy, see Knowles, *Strangers at Our Gates*, 79–89.
10 For more on the White Canada Immigration Policy and the comparable policy in Australia, see Freda Hawkins, *Critical Years in Immigration: Canada and Australia Compared* (Kingston and Montreal: McGill-Queen's University Press, 1989), 3–41.
11 Cited by Prime Minister King in his 1947 immigration policy statement to the House of Commons on 1 May 1947. Canada, House of Commons, *Official Report of Debates*, 1947, 2644.
12 Irving Abella and Harold Troper, "'The Line Must be Drawn Somewhere': Canada and Jewish Refugees, 1933–1939," in *Canadian Historical Review* 60, no. 2 (June 1979): 178–209.
13 Dirks, *Canada's Refugee Policy*, Appendix A, 260.
14 One might even characterize the post-war changes as a movement away from ministerial and bureaucratic discretion towards standardized immigration criteria and review processes.
15 Dirks, *Canada's Refugee Policy*, 57.
16 Dirks, *Canada's Refugee Policy*, 93. Dirks quotes the British Foreign Office on the issue; "The absorptive capacity accessible to neutral countries in Europe seems to be approaching its limit. Allied countries cannot very well go on exhorting these countries not to turn back any refugees without offering cooperation in accommodating a portion of them."
17 Library and Archives Canada (LAC), Mackenzie King Correspondence, mfm C-7044, p.303523-4, 29 July 1943, Secretary of State for Dominion Affairs to Secretary of State for External Affairs, Canada.
18 Tony Judt, *Postwar: A History of Europe since 1945* (New York: Penguin Books, 2005), 29.
19 Canada, Labour, Department of, *The Labour Gazette* xlvi (1946): 1205.
20 For more on C.D. Howe see Robert Bothwell and William Kilbourn, *C.D. Howe: a biography* (Toronto: McClelland and Stewart, 1979).
21 Trinity College Archives, John Holmes – Memoirs (General), Box 74 E/II/7, August 21, 1947. Thanks must go to Adam Chapnick for providing me with this reference.
22 John W. Holmes, *The Shaping of Peace: Canada and the search for world order, 1943–1957*, vol. 1 (Toronto: University of Toronto Press, 1979), 94.
23 For some examples of the tension between departments, see LAC, RG2, box 18, vol. 166 Privy Council Office – Immigration, I-50-5 – Immigration – Immigration-Labour questions (interdepartmental committee) 1947–1951 and RG 26, vol. 101 3-18-3, Immigration –Labour Committee – General File.
24 See also LAC, RG2, box 83, Privy Council Office – Immigration, I-50-2, 5 December 1946, Norman Robertson forwards correspondence from a Latvian logger interested in employment in Canadian industry to the Canadian Government. Robertson endorses his request based on the

"favourable impressions of the Balts formed by Canadian officials who have had the opportunity of visiting Displaced Persons camps ... "

25 LAC, RG27, v. 895, 8–9-63–1, pt. 1, Department of Labour – Cabinet Committee on Immigration - Confidential Memorandum re Immigration – Department of Mines and Resources, 5 September 1945. The Cabinet Committee on Immigration Policy included representatives from the departments of Mines and Resources, Agriculture, Labour and the Secretary of State. A.L. Joliffe was the Director of Immigration and functioned under the Department of Mines and Resources.

26 For an extended discussion of the impact of UNRRA service abroad on individuals' desire for change in Canada's immigration laws and the lengths they went to to communicate these ideas to policy makers, see Susan Armstrong-Reid and David Murray, *Armies of Peace: Canada and the UNRRA Years* (Toronto: University of Toronto Press, 2008), 331–50. For Hume Wrong's concerns about discrimination see LAC, RG27, v. 895, 8–9-63-1, pt. 1, Department of Labour - Cabinet Committee on Immigration – 8 August 1946 – Cabinet Committee on Immigration Policy (Chair-J.A. GLEN) "Policy with respect to Refugees." For Mackenzie King's fear on the UN reaction to "discrimination" in Canadian immigration policy see LAC, *William Lyon Mackenzie King Diaries, 1893–1950*, MJ26-J13, 13 February 1947.

27 LAC, W.L. Mackenzie King Correspondence, mfm c-11038, p. 386210-1. H.L. Keenleyside to Laurent Beaudry, Acting Under-Secretary for External Affairs, 15 May 1947, Ottawa.

28 Ibid.

29 This is not to say that this scheme was seen to be universally positive by Canadians. The department of labour received a significant number of official complaints from a variety of unions about this practice and from individual Canadians who felt that the federal government was taking jobs away from "our boys" by assisting in the immigration of displaced persons. In addition, although most cases were declared "successful," reports of immigrants who faced significant social, physical or mental health challenges do exist in the administrative files of the Immigration Labour Committee of the Department of Mines and Resources, Immigration Branch. LAC, RG26, v. 72. More on the contemporary criticisms of the program will follow in future research.

30 Canada, Labour, Department of, *The Labour Gazette* xlvi (1946): 511. "Review of Canadian Manpower Situation During 1945."

31 This idea of a "non-immigration Act" comes from the report of the Senate standing committee on immigration and labour. Canada, *Journals of the Senate of Canada*, Wednesday, 14 August 1946, 497. For discussions of the various groups putting pressure on the federal government in this period see Dirks, *Canada's Refugee Policy*, 60–71 and Howard Margolian, *Unauthorized Entry: The Truth about Nazi War Criminals in Canada, 1946–1956* (Toronto: University of Toronto Press, 2000), 70–82.

32 Canada, House of Commons, *Official Report of Debates*, 3 April 1946, 524.
33 Canada, *Journals of the Senate of Canada*, Wednesday, 14 August 1946, 492.
34 Canada, *Journals of the Senate of Canada*, Wednesday, 14 August 1946, 492–3.
35 Also present were other members of the cabinet committee on immigration policy; J.G. Gardiner, the minister of Agriculture, H. Mitchell the minister of Labour, P. Martin the secretary of state and A.L. Joliffe, who ran the immigration branch of the ministry of mines and resources.
36 LAC, RG27, v. 895, 8–9–63–1, pt. 1, Department of Labour - Cabinet Committee on Immigration – 26 March 1946, 4.
37 LAC, RG27, v. 895, 8–9–63–1, pt. 1, Department of Labour - Cabinet Committee on Immigration – 27 March 1946, Harry Hereford forwards the minutes of the 26 March 1946 meeting to A. MacNamara with a memo stating that "This method of handling the matter keeps away from dealing with racial groups and also will not necessarily increase the shelter problem."
38 Ninette Kelley and Michael Trebilcock, *The Making of the Mosaic: A History of Canadian Immigration Policy* (Toronto: University of Toronto Press, 1998), 308.
39 LAC, RG27, v. 895, 8–9–63–1, pt. 1, Department of Labour - Cabinet Committee on Immigration – clipping from the Ottawa Evening Citizen, 24 April 1946, "Plurality Vote Against British Immigration."
40 Ibid. It should be noted that at the time it was a relatively common error to mistake 'the Balkans' for the Baltics. There are even cases of government officials in the Department of Labour making this mistake. Therefore we might assume that when some Canadians reported they supported immigration from 'the Balkans' they may in fact have supported immigration from the Baltic nations of Latvia, Lithuania and Estonia.
41 Canada, House of Commons, *Official Report of Debates*, 27 August 1946, 5496.
42 LAC, RG27, v. 895, 8–9–63–1, pt. 1, Department of Labour - Cabinet Committee on Immigration – 8 August 1946 – Cabinet Committee on Immigration Policy (Chair-J.A. Glen) "Policy with respect to Refugees." For Mackenzie King's fear on the UN reaction to "discrimination" in Canadian immigration policy see LAC, *William Lyon Mackenzie King Diaries, 1893–1950*, MJ26-J13, 13 February 1947.
43 Canada, *Journals of the Senate of Canada*, Wednesday, 14 August 1946, 494.
44 Canada, *Journals of the Senate of Canada*, Wednesday, 14 August 1946, 493–4.
45 Canada, *Journals of the Senate of Canada*, Wednesday, 14 August 1946, 497.
46 Canada, House of Commons, *Official Report of Debates*, 3 April 1946, 524–34 and 27 August 1946, 5493.
47 Statistics compiled from annual reports by Alan G. Green, *Immigration and the Postwar Canadian Economy* (Toronto: Macmillan of Canada, 1976), 28.

48 Freda Hawkins, *Critical Years in Immigration*, 60. Point 9 of the 1975 Green Paper includes the following statement; "The settlement of post-war immigrants alongside our founding cultures had been one of the most positive chapters in Canada's post-war history, and the Committee looked to immigration to continue to contribute to the economic, cultural and social well-being of the country ..."
49 For the account of one family's search for means to get to Canada outside of the department of labour program, see Modris Eksteins, *Walking since daybreak: a story of Eastern Europe, World War II, and the heart of our century* (Boston: Houghton Mifflin, 1999).
50 http://www.library.carleton.ca/ssdata/surveys/doc/gllp-49-may187-doc. Accessed 10 June 2008.
51 http://www.library.carleton.ca/ssdata/surveys/doc/gllp-51-aug212-doc. Accessed 10 June 2008.
52 Quoted in Knowles, *Strangers at Our Gates*, 138.
53 http://www.library.carleton.ca/ssdata/surveys/doc/gllp-55-feb241-cbk. Accessed 10 June 2008.
54 http://www.library.carleton.ca/ssdata/surveys/doc/gllp-55-feb241-cbk. Accessed 10 June 2008.
55 Knowles, *Strangers at Our Gates*, 137.
56 Knowles, *Strangers at Our Gates*, 142.
57 http://www.library.carleton.ca/ssdata/surveys/doc/gllp-57-jan255-doc. Accessed 10 June 2008.
58 http://www.library.carleton.ca/ssdata/surveys/doc/gllp-59-jul276-doc. Accessed 10 June 2008.
59 http://www.library.carleton.ca/ssdata/surveys/doc/gllp-60-jan280-doc. Accessed 10 June 2008.
60 Knowles, *Strangers at Our Gates*, 146.
61 Hawkins, *Critical Years in Immigration*, 39.
62 http://www.library.carleton.ca/ssdata/surveys/doc/gllp-61-jul290-doc. Accessed 10 June 2008.
63 http://www.library.carleton.ca/ssdata/surveys/doc/gllp-72-sep355-doc. Accessed 10 June 2008.
64 Citizenship and Immigration Canada http://www.cic.gc.ca/ENGLISH/resources/publications/legacy/chap-6a.asp
65 Knowles, *Strangers at Our Gates*, 167.
66 Cited in Knowles, *Strangers at Our Gates*, 169. See also Hawkins, *Critical Years in Immigration*, 57–72.
67 http://www.library.carleton.ca/ssdata/surveys/doc/gllp-75-jun377-doc. Accessed 10 June 2008.
68 See particularly Knowles, *Strangers at Our Gates*; Dirks, *Canada's Refugee Policy*; Hawkins, *Critical Years in Immigration*.
69 Knowles, *Strangers at Our Gates*, 174–5.

70 http://www.library.carleton.ca/ssdata/surveys/doc/gllp-79-feb421a-doc. Accessed 10 June 2008.
71 http://www.library.carleton.ca/ssdata/surveys/doc/gllp-79-jul427b-doc. Accessed 10 June 2008.
72 http://www.library.carleton.ca/ssdata/surveys/doc/gllp-79-nov431a-doc. Accessed 10 June 2008.
73 Amnesty International http://www.amnesty.ca/Refugee/history.php. Accessed 24 June 2008.
74 Donna Dasko, Senior Vice President, Environics Research Group Limited, "Portraits of Canada 2001 Paper: Immigration" http://www.library.carleton.ca/ssdata/surveys/documents/cric-poc-01-not_000.doc. Accessed 10 June 2008.
75 A helpful quick reference resource on refugee policy is available at the Canadian Council for Refugees website. http://www.ccrweb.ca/history.html
76 The Canadian Press, "Proposed immigration changes 'major step backwards,' says bar association." *The Canadian Press*. Accessed 13 May 2008. http://canadianpress.google.com/article/ALeqM5iYduvHLWyTgnj2ts9eBwU7qg76AA

8 Foreign Aid and Canadian Purpose: Influence and Policy in Canada's International Development Assistance

IAN SMILLIE

Canada's official foreign aid program dates from the start of the Colombo Plan in 1950, although Canadian missionaries and non-governmental organizations had been working in Africa, Asia and Latin America for many decades before that. In 1960 the growing number of projects and programs operating under Colombo Plan aegis were consolidated into an "External Aid Office" within the Department of Foreign Affairs, and by the late 1960s, Canada was starting to become a serious donor country, spreading beyond its initial half-dozen Asian programs to Africa and the Commonwealth Caribbean.

The twin architects of Canada's early aid program were Lester Pearson and Maurice Strong. Pearson is widely hailed as the father of UN Peacekeeping and he was a signatory to the original Colombo Plan. Foreign aid grew and was consolidated under his government, which also drew up plans for the creation of the International Development Research Centre (IDRC). The idea for an IDRC was vigorously promoted by Pearson's second External Aid Office (EAO) Director, Maurice Strong, who also promoted an expansion of the operation and its conversion into a more autonomous body with a "president" at the helm. The re-branding of the EAO was one of Pierre Trudeau's first announcements after becoming prime minister in the spring of 1968, and during his leadership, the Canadian International Development Agency (CIDA) would grow rapidly, both in size and sophistication.

The late 1960s were years of great ferment in the world of international development assistance. The Cold War was in full spate, and other wars were testing Canadian resolve in a variety of ways. The Biafran War

(1967–70) was forcing difficult tradeoffs between humanitarianism and political pragmatism, and what were sometimes called "race wars" in Southern Africa were forcing tradeoffs among ideas about security, ideology and democracy. After his retirement from public office, Lester Pearson chaired a World Bank Commission on International Development, submitting a report in 1969 – often referred to as *The Pearson Report* – that became something of a benchmark for international development assistance worldwide.

This chapter deals mainly with the period after the creation of CIDA in 1968, and it discusses the difficulties in keeping an aid program – advertised to taxpayers on the basis of its development, poverty alleviation and humanitarian mandates – balanced in a complex world of political, commercial and security-related concerns.

ORGANIZATION

Historically, between 75 percent and 80 percent of Canada's Official Development Assistance (ODA) has been managed by CIDA, which is a government department for the purposes of the *Financial Administration Act*, represented in cabinet by a minister for International Cooperation. In the years when CIDA did not have its own minister (1968–79, 1980–84, 1993–6), the agency reported to the minister of External Affairs. The Department of Finance manages Canada's contribution to international financial institutions, and funding for IDRC has been independent of both. A variety of additional organizations have been funded independently as well, although the list has changed over the years: the International Centre for Human Rights and International Development (later changed to Rights and Democracy), the International Centre for Ocean Development, and the Petro-Canada International Assistance Corporation are examples. Other government departments such as Public Works and Health Canada have from time to time administered small portions of the International Assistance Envelope (IAE).

The Department of Foreign Affairs and International Trade's (DFAIT's) role has fluctuated over the years, from the days when its minister had full responsibility for ODA, to periods where its direct responsibility was minor. In 2000, for example, DFAIT had direct responsibility for only 4 percent of the IAE. Currently, the IAE is organized into five programming and funding pools. The development pool, with 68 percent of the IAE in 2007–8 (a record low) is managed by CIDA. Funding for international financial institutions remains with the department of finance. A Peace and Security pool, representing 8.6 percent of the IAE is managed by DFAIT, with input from the department of national defence; and a crisis pool is co-managed by CIDA and DFAIT, with input from the

Privy Council Office, Finance and Treasury Board. The fifth pool, Research and Development, represents funding for IDRC.

WHY AID?

The *Pearson Report* was clear on the basic purpose of international development assistance: "It is to reduce disparities and remove inequities. It is to help the poorer countries to move forward, in their own way, into the industrial and technological age so that the world will not become more starkly divided between the haves and the have-nots, the privileged and the less privileged." Pearson understood that the moral incentive for aid was "valid and compelling in itself," but that the appeal of "enlightened and constructive self-interest" – while not invalidating the fundamental purpose – might be more persuasive.[1] But in chairing the Pearson Commission, the former prime minister no longer spoke for Canada or Canadian development assistance policy.

Against a backdrop of growing international debate about the quality, volume and purpose of foreign aid, CIDA tried in 1969 to clarify the aims and objectives of Canadian development assistance. An *aide mémoire* at the time listed a number of problems in reaching clear objectives:

- "Our aid program until now has been intellectually incoherent;
- All governments state the wrong motives for their international aid;
- We should give underdeveloped nations enough aid to keep them quiet;
- A principal foreign policy objective is to find a policy which will help the best possible relationship with the United States."[2]

This list itself may seem intellectually incoherent and not a little disingenuous, but a subsequent background paper was more revealing of views at the time. It suggested that Canada's motives for providing development assistance should fulfill three objectives, in the following order:

- "First would be the political objective to establish within the recipient countries those political attitudes or commitments, military alliances or military bases that would assist Canada or Canada's western allies to maintain a reasonably stable and secure international political system;
- A second objective might be the establishment of markets for Canadian products and services;
- A third objective might be the relief of famine and personal misery."[3]

Security and political concerns were unambiguously first, commercial interests second, and the "relief of famine and personal misery" third. CIDA's 40-year inability to satisfy its many supporters and critics stems inevitably from this continuing and conflictive trinity of objectives. A perceived need to address all of them at the same time has been confused by the changing weight given to each by the government of the day, CIDA's ever-changing senior management, and pressures applied in favour of one objective or another by Parliament, the non-governmental community, the private sector, the media, the military, academia and others.

Poverty

Despite the fact that "relief of famine and personal misery" placed only third in the 1969 internal ranking, poverty reduction has usually been the primary publicly stated objective of Canadian foreign aid. In 1987, for example, CIDA produced a "Development Charter" that for a time could be found on the walls of almost every office in the building. The first line in the charter was: "The primary purpose of our development effort is to help the world's poorest countries and people." Statements like this have been made by every prime minister, CIDA minister and president, and they have appeared in every parliamentary report on the subject since the agency began. CIDA's mandate today, according to its website, is "to support sustainable development in developing countries, in order to reduce poverty and to contribute to a more secure, equitable, and prosperous world."[4] This is elaborated in further statements that all contain the word *poverty*, plus one general statement which says that CIDA will "advance Canadian values of global citizenship, equity, and environmental sustainability, as well as Canadian interests regarding security, prosperity, and governance." This is the heading under which today's vaguely articulated political, security and commercial objectives fall.

Political

External Affairs Minister Paul Martin Sr., defending Canadian aid to Tanzania in 1967, said, "Had Canada not extended aid, China and perhaps one or two other communist countries would have."[5] Things change. He might have foreseen that China would provide aid to Tanzania anyway, but not that China would someday become Canada's own largest aid recipient, or that 40 years hence, calculations would again be made about how Western, if not Canadian aid to countries like Tanzania might offset a new Chinese incursion. Never far from the fore, the political agenda can be seen in CIDA's (temporary) rush to the Philippines as the Marcos regime fell; its catch-up game in Southern Africa in the dying days of apartheid; the dash to Eastern Europe after 1989; and the current (apparent) growing emphasis on South America.

There is another aspect to the political motivation behind foreign aid: prestige. The quality and size of the aid program determines Canada's place at the table in a variety of fora, not least within United Nations agencies, at the Organisation for Economic Co-operation and Development (OECD) and among international financial institutions. Prestige must be at least a partial driving force in the agency's current desire to be among the top five donors in its core program countries. And foreign aid has much to do with the prestige Canada seeks in its posture as a middle power and trusted broker at difficult times, and in difficult parts of the world.

Security

Anti-communism was a clear factor in early Canadian aid, but other security-related themes can be traced through the years as well, ebbing and flowing with circumstance. "Peace and security" in the Cold War years referred largely to arms control, disarmament and peacekeeping issues. But within that framework, Canada's aid to developing countries on "the cutting edge" of security issues played an important role. Canada's position on proxy wars in Southern Africa, its understanding and articulation of human rights policies in the Middle East, in Central America during the Sandinista period, or through its aid program to Cuba (which was cancelled in the wake of the U.S. invasion of Grenada), all had security-related considerations.

In today's post-9/11 world, there is a tendency to forget or to downplay earlier concerns, but terrorism has been with us now for decades. A 1986 parliamentary report, *Independence and Internationalism*, said that "Terrorism in recent years has become a scourge that no civilized nation can ignore in its foreign relations."[6] Today, of course, the security agenda is most evident in Canadian aid to Afghanistan and Iraq. The 2007 Development Assistance Committee (DAC) Review said that "this approach, outlined in the Speech from the Throne on 4 April 2006, is in line with the *National Security Policy* (2004), which considers development assistance to be an element of counter terrorism."[7] The security agenda extends farther, however, into discussions about, and project funding related to, population movements, global pandemics, global warming and other aspects of the "global war on terror."

Commercial

CIDA's commercial mandate was most clearly articulated 40 years ago in the creation of what was then called the Business and Industry Program. This aimed to assist "Canadian business and industrial firms in the establishment of enterprises which could make an important contribution to the development of the countries concerned."[8] Renamed the Industrial Cooperation Program (INC), it was evaluated in 1992, and was found to be making an important contribution to the development of the *companies* concerned, having generated three or four dollars worth of contracts for Canadian suppliers for every dollar invested by CIDA.[9]

A more recent evaluation in December 2007 reached very different conclusions.[10] It sampled 721 projects carried out between 1997 and 2002, and found that only 15.5 percent were successful, leading to actual investments or contracts. The report found that INC operations had "not become more cost effective over the years" since then, that INC does not operate on a "results" basis, and that there has been little feedback, lesson-sharing or follow-up to the investments made. While not a major part of CIDA's work, the expenditures add up. Between 1978 and 2007, more than $1.1 billion dollars was spent on the program and the top twenty recipient firms received more that $100 million.[11]

A larger commercial benefit has flowed from CIDA's bilateral projects and the simple provision of Canadian goods and services. Between 1986 and 1998, for example, a $38.8 million CIDA project that aimed to upgrade the Senegalese railway resulted in contracts worth a total of $37.9 million to Canadian General Motors, Hawker Siddley, Sydney Steel and others. After-sales service and parts contracts were worth as much again.[12] Similar returns were undoubtedly seen on CIDA-financed railway projects in Mali, Tanzania and elsewhere. Between 1972 and 1981, CIDA spent over $90 million on the Bangladesh railway, and that was only the start. In fact the Bangladesh Railways project is probably CIDA's biggest single project of all time. Much of it was focused on the supply of Canadian-built rolling stock, even though a shortage of motive power was never the railway's biggest problem. The commercial leveraging power of CIDA money, however, had its limits. In 1980, when Bangladesh requested funding for a further 50 locomotives, CIDA said it would provide 25 if Bangladesh would pay for the rest itself and buy all of them in Canada. When the funders of the additional 25 refused to limit procurement to Canada alone, the Canadian offer was withdrawn.[13]

CIDA was undoubtedly a Canadian stalking horse for commercial interests in China. In the immediate aftermath of the Chinese government's suppression of the pro-democracy movement in June 1989, Foreign Minister Joe Clark announced the suspension of five aid projects budgeted at $61 million. Although Canada would not jeopardize longstanding links between Canadian and Chinese institutions, it halted any support that might strengthen the Chinese government's repressive capacities, and three projects were eventually cancelled.

Two years later, in October 1991, Prime Minister Mulroney, speaking at a Commonwealth Heads of Government Meeting, said that nothing was more important in international relations than respect for individual freedoms and human rights:

For Canada, the future course is clear: we shall be increasingly channelling our development assistance to those countries that show respect for the fundamental rights and individual freedoms of their people. Canada will not subsidize repression and the stifling of democracy.[14]

A month later, when Indonesian troops opened fire on independence demonstrators in East Timor, the Mulroney government was true to its word – sort of. New aid projects to Indonesia were frozen, although ongoing aid programs were not affected. At about $35 million a year, Indonesia remained one of Canada's largest aid recipients through the 1990s, but that figure was dwarfed by two-way trade of $1.6 billion in 1997, and by Canadian arms sales to Indonesia of $420 million between 1993 and 1997. Meanwhile, despite the cutbacks in China, that country actually remained the second largest recipient of Canadian government assistance, courtesy of CIDA and Export Development Canada (EDC) concessional loans.[15]

Human Rights and democratic development had by the mid-1990s risen significantly in importance on the foreign aid agenda. But when Foreign Minister André Ouellet spoke at a meeting of Association of Southeast Asian Nations (ASEAN) foreign ministers in 1996, he ignored the growing international clamour against the barbarity of Indonesian rule in East Timor. Trade, he said, was the best way to promote democratic development: "Canada has expressed, through this new government, our desire to vigorously pursue a series of [trade] initiatives in a number of countries *irrespective of their human rights records*"[16] (emphasis added).

So, Why Aid?

The internal CIDA document of 1969 said that "our aid program until now has been intellectually incoherent." Policy coherence has continued to bedevil CIDA ever since, and comments about the absence of coherence are a regular feature in DAC Peer Reviews, including the most recent one in 2007: "The lack of a clear framework to promote policy coherence for development hinders CIDA's leadership on development issues in government discussions and negotiations."[17]

FADS, FOOD AND FADE

International development assistance falls prey with surprising frequency to fads that flash like comets across the aid system, consuming huge amounts of intellectual and financial attention, often disappearing soon afterwards without a trace. CIDA has been heavily influenced by many of them. "Integrated Rural Development" (IRD) for example, swept the world of bilateral and multilateral aid agencies in the 1970s, along with ideas about "basic human needs" and "redistribution with growth." The idea of integrated rural development grew out of Ford Foundation projects in India and East Pakistan. According to a 1984 CIDA study on the subject, "All donors now agree that the targeted rural peoples must be both the principal actors and favoured beneficiaries of a process of development that involves, in practice, the carrying out of diversified and coordinated activities."[18] The report spoke of the organization of markets, credit and social services, investment in infrastructure and land reform and a host of other activities to complement the stimulation of agricultural production. "Indeed," the authors said, "it is increasingly recognized that *rural development must be integrated*" (emphasis in the original).

In theory it sounded good, and growing numbers of integrated rural development projects were initiated by the World Bank, the United States Agency for International Development (USAID), Sweden, Germany and other donors across Asia, Africa and Latin America. CIDA would apply the approach with varying degrees of intensity in Ghana, Tanzania, and elsewhere, but never with as much vigour as it did in Haiti. There, in 1974, CIDA initiated the hugely ambitious *Développement Régional Intégré du Petit-Goâve à Petit-Trou-de-Nippes*, a project with the infelicitous acronym, DRIPP. "DRIPP was to be a showpiece," according to a North-South Institute report. "Here was a project which would epitomize the new basic needs approach in one of the neediest countries, proving that CIDA was abreast of the latest development wisdom and able to reach the truly poor."[19]

CIDA took up the challenge in an area of 1,700 km² with 300,000 people, tackling education, health, transportation and agricultural production simultaneously. CIDA's initial investment was $21 million, an extremely large sum at the time.

It would take ten years or more for the generic flaws in the IRD approach to emerge, or at least to be acknowledged. Plans were usually too rigid and failed to take into consideration local views and experience. Human and social factors were often neglected, and many of the inputs were simply inappropriate. In 1983 Robert Chambers wrote scathingly of "the ritual call for integration and coordination, and even maximum integration and coordination," and of the bad choices made by ill-informed outsiders in how funds would or would not be used.[20]

The fact that Canada had little expertise in the field of integrated rural development was almost beside the point. The overall approach was, by the early 1980s, being abandoned by most donors as a costly and ineffective way of dealing with the development challenge. At best, if it worked, IRD created expensive enclave operations that were not replicable, taught few lessons and fell quickly into disarray when the integrated rural developers withdrew. The DRIPP project in Haiti was abruptly cancelled in 1981 when it became the subject of investigative Canadian media reporting which showed how little had been accomplished. The North-South Institute report concluded that "DRIPP was too ambitious and grew too quickly, in terms of CIDA's knowledge and capabilities and Haiti's absorptive capacities at local levels and in government."[21] The report might also have concluded that while it had not been alone in joining the donor rush into integrated rural development, CIDA had certainly fallen prey to an expensive fad that eventually vanished without a trace.

Structural Adjustment

As integrated rural development passed from the ODA agenda, a new beacon appeared. The World Bank's 1981 *Accelerated Development in Sub-Saharan Africa: An Agenda for Action* offered a new recipe for effective administrative reform: smaller government; improved cost-effectiveness of the civil service, particularly near the top; better definitions of accountability and incentives; "novel approaches to community involvement"; and finally, high-quality analysis and prescription tailored to a country's specific needs.

The report emerged at a time that was, for many developing countries, as bad, economically speaking, as the depression of the 1930s. The oil crisis of the 1970s, global recession, famine and drought, commodity and debt crises led one country after another into difficult IMF stabilization agreements. During the 1970s, the IMF had engaged in about ten stabilization programs a year. In 1980 the number rose to 28 and by 1985 there had been 129 more. Typically, adjustment programs had three components: expenditure reduction; expenditure switching; and institutional and policy reforms (trade liberalization, privatization, fiscal reform, and less state involvement in the economy). This approach reflected a new orthodoxy that would soon become known as the "Washington Consensus," a consensus that Canada actively endorsed. The Canadian lead on structural adjustment was provided at first by the departments of Foreign Affairs and Finance rather than CIDA, although by the middle of the decade that was changing.

By the late 1980s, the side effects of the adjustment cure were proving worse in many cases than the disease. In 1987, UNICEF produced an influential review of the experience thus far and concluded that "overall, prevailing adjustment programs tend to increase aggregate poverty, or in other words the number of people – and of children – living below the poverty line."[22]

Nevertheless, CIDA's 1985–86 *Annual Report* stated that "economic stabilization programs negotiated with the IMF are beginning to bear fruit,"[23] and in 1987, *Sharing our Future* said that 45 percent of bilateral funding would be devoted to Africa and that it would use "a significant part of the increase for assistance to structural adjustment."[24] To its credit, CIDA sought to have greater social considerations built into adjustment programs, but Canadian enthusiasm for the general principles of adjustment remained strong. That year the minister for CIDA reported on a United Nations Special Session on Africa at which "Africans pledged reform, and the international community promised more support."[25] While ODA was in reality poised on the edge of a decade-long decline, "reform" – in the shape of more structural adjustment – was not. In its 1989–90 *Annual Report*, CIDA still had economic reform and structural adjustment at the top of its list of priorities.[26]

Although structural adjustment would continue, the accompanying dogmatism of the past became more muted. "Adjustment programs should continue to evolve," said a somewhat chastened Bank in a new publication on Africa in 1989. And programs would "take fuller account of the social impact of reforms."[27] Much was changing in the world of development spending, not least the challenges emerging in Eastern Europe as the Soviet Union fell apart. CIDA remained faithful to the old ideal longer than most. In its 1989–90 *Annual Report*, it acknowledged that "The wave of democracy sweeping Eastern European countries is shaking some African nations, whose people are calling for more democracy." But this did not yet appear to have a place in CIDA's programming, where macro-economic rectitude remained the number one priority. "In 1989–90, Canada was steadfast in its support for structural adjustment programs," the report stated, without qualification.[28]

Sustainability

The concept of sustainability is inherent in the idea of development, but the term itself was virtually absent from development writing until the mid-1980s. The word "sustainability" was used just five times in CIDA's expansive 1987 policy statement, *Sharing our Future*, and then only in the context of environmental development. Within three years, the vocabulary had changed and the expression "sustainable development" was used nine times alone in the president's one-page preface to CIDA's 1990–91 *Annual Report*. By then, CIDA had become focused on "five pillars of sustainability":

- environmental sustainability [the environment was an emerging issue at the time; Canada would play an active part in the June 1992 United Nations Conference on Environment and Development (UNCED) "Earth Summit" in Rio. Maurice Strong, CIDA's first president, served as secretary general of the conference.];
- economic sustainability [including "appropriate policies" – structural adjustment by another name];
- cultural sustainability;
- political sustainability [human rights, democracy, good governance – the latter a fast-emerging idea in aid discourse];
- social sustainability [income distribution; gender equity, basic needs, participation].

Food

Starting in the 1950s, food aid became a significant component of Canada's development assistance, aimed largely at disposing of large agricultural surpluses. Because food aid was supply driven, Canada's food aid policy was for many years one of the most restrictive, requiring that 90 percent of the budget be spent on buying and shipping Canadian commodities. Writing fifteen years ago, Mark Charlton enumerated the familiar critique of food aid: "Food aid discourages local agricultural production; it creates a taste for expensive imported foods; it enables governments to forestall necessary agricultural policy reforms; and it fosters a dependency that makes recipient governments vulnerable to political manipulation."[29]

CIDA struggled with these challenges for more than three decades, until recently, when Canada's food aid policy began to change dramatically. Canadian commodity surpluses are no longer large, and most of what Canada produces it can sell, so the motivation for food aid has changed. The volume of food as a percentage of ODA has dropped from 20 percent in the 1960s and 1970s, to less than 5 percent today. There have been other factors in the change, including the inefficiencies in tying food aid. The 90 percent tying rule meant that huge volumes of funding were devoted not to food, but to shipping costs. A 2005 study found that of the $165m budgeted for food aid that year, $66m or 40 percent would be spent on shipping. "In August 2004, for example, the price of local wheat in Nazaret, Ethiopia, was C$248 per tonne. The price in Montreal was virtually the same: C$253 per tonne. But to deliver Canadian wheat to Nazaret cost an additional C$172 for each tonne."[30]

In 2005 CIDA loosened the tied aid restriction, announcing that up to 50 percent of Canada's food aid could be purchased in developing countries. In 2008 it increased the untying to 100 percent, with an emphasis on procurement in developing countries or in countries with similar policies on untying.[31]

The days of large Canadian grain shipments as part of the aid program have seemingly drawn to a close. If titles are any indication, the conversion of the Food Aid Centre to the Program against Hunger, Malnutrition and Disease (PAHMD) would suggest this to be the case. As CIDA's website explains it, "On the one hand, PAHMD continues to fund food aid programs and projects by working with the WFP [World Food Programme] and Canadian organizations like the Canadian Foodgrains Bank, and participating in bilateral food aid projects. On the other, PAHMD now funds Micronutrient Initiative activities, aimed primarily at fighting malnutrition, as well as health initiatives."[32] The approach to food, no longer supply driven, has become more strategic and more developmental. With 2008 wheat prices at an all-time high, and global reserves at an all-time low, the approach to food shortages in developing countries is set to become a lot more "strategic" than ever before.

Governance

In the government's 2005 *International Policy Statement*, and in this chapter, "good governance" is used as a proxy for several things: democratization, human rights, the rule of law, and public sector capacity building. Historically these have emerged as different streams in Canadian policy and programming, with different emphases at different times. Human rights has the longest record, perhaps because as a discipline it is well articulated internationally, although the application has been both variable and situational. Concerns about Indonesian human rights violations in East Timor, for example, were not allowed to interfere with the sale of weapons and other commodities. But Canada's Progressive Conservative government took a principled position on South African apartheid in the mid 1980s, in contrast with its conservative counterparts in the United States and Britain.

As an explicit tool in the ODA arsenal, "governance" has a more recent provenance, emerging largely from economic structural adjustment programs in the 1980s and the "Washington Consensus." Canada was an eager member of this consensus, which emphasized cutbacks to the state in some areas without much thought about state strengthening where it was badly needed. It is only in the past decade that the need to *build* state capacities has been seen as an important part of governance, a position that Canada now strongly endorses.

The promotion of democracy and democratic processes emerged as the most recent part of the Canadian agenda in the mid-1990s, spurred in part by concerns about corruption among governments whose probity and poor management had been little questioned during the Cold War years. Canada's promotion of good governance too has been somewhat situational. Critics lament the absence of coherent policies tying all aspects of the agenda together. A patchy, project-by-project approach with no obvious central policy and no central management, they say, is unlikely to yield coherent results. This may be true, but given the overwhelming size of the governance agenda and the limited track record in its promotion by any donor, healthy doses of humility and caution are warranted. Given the complexity of the challenge, a case can be made for selective interventions, made in concert with other donors, aimed at learning what works and what does not.

Gender

A chapter covering the entire gamut of influences on Canadian ODA policy cannot do great justice to any of them. One area worthy of a chapter of its own is the evolution of Canadian thinking on gender and development. Here is an area where CIDA was among the first bilateral aid agencies to recognize an issue, appointing a Special Advisor on Women and Development in 1975 and creating an "Integration of Women in Development Responsibility Centre." For ten years, as the Women in Development (WID) approach became more sophisticated and focused increasingly on gender, CIDA was a leader on the subject in ODA circles. By the 1990s, gender had been "mainstreamed" throughout the agency.

Unlike CIDA's approach to many development issues, its approach to gender has not faded. Gender programming remains important in Canadian ODA, and "gender equality" remains high as a cross-cutting issue in government and CIDA policy declarations. In 2005, CIDA published a thoughtful and comprehensive *Framework for Assessing Gender Equality Results*, and the subject received as much attention in the 2005 *International Policy Statement* as health or education, in which gender issues were additionally infused. Perhaps, given the arrival and departure of so many fads in Canadian ODA, one might conclude that gender is a success story, both for its sticking power and for its depth.

Themes, Sectors, Policies, Strategies and Results

By the early 1990s, the list of priorities, themes, sectors, policies, strategies and cross-cutting issues was becoming more complicated, and the complexity increased with the 1993 Auditor General's report, which said that one of CIDA's major challenges was its accountability in managing for results: "CIDA has not focused on the results that are to be achieved or that have been achieved."33 "Results" had so far not been mentioned in any CIDA documents (the terminology in use until the advent of *results* had been "impact," although evaluation for impact in CIDA was at best patchy), and it was a new area for the auditor general as well. But when the auditor general sneezes, government departments run for the Kleenex. By the following year, *results* had risen to sudden prominence in a "CIDA Renewal Plan."34 In the fifteen years since then, results-based management has dominated the agency's systems and behaviour, although not always with great clarity or consistency.

In fact it can be argued that the drive to ensure results has led CIDA in a perverse direction. In order to ensure that results will be achieved, projects and programs now undergo much more rigorous planning. More consultants are used, more rigid blueprints are drawn up, spending limits have been lowered and centralized, implementing agencies cannot easily deviate from the plans and contracts they win, and there is greater monitoring to ensure that everyone does precisely what they said they would do. Over-planning and micromanagement were the big weaknesses in "integrated rural development." (And, it might be added, rigid central planning was the downfall of the soviet economic system.) Results are certainly essential, but in business as in most other walks of life, emergent strategies are also essential, along with the ability of managers on the shop floor to manage.

By 1995 it looked as though a clear set of sectoral priorities had at last emerged. *Canada in the World* set out "a clear mandate for Canadian ODA":

- basic human needs [25 percent of the total];
- women in development;
- infrastructure services [rumoured to have been added at the last minute on instructions from then Foreign Minister André Ouellet];
- human rights, democracy, good governance;
- private sector development [something completely new];
- the environment [last on the list, now that UNCED was receding from memory].35

A 2002 policy document, *Strengthening Aid Effectiveness*,36 applied some revisionism to this "clear mandate," downgrading it to a "broad menu of thematic options" rather than a "focused agenda." Today, with agriculture having come and gone as a priority in the interim, CIDA's website hedges the bets by saying "In the broadest sense, programming is concentrated in five sectors which directly relate to achieving the Millennium Development Goals (MDGs) – a unique approach to achieving sustainable development built around a partnership of the global community. These sectors, along with a cross-cutting theme of gender equality or equality between women and men are:

- Governance
- Health
- Basic Education
- Private Sector Development
- Environmental Sustainability[37]

The list is, in fact, very much like the 1995 list, with a clearer articulation of "basic human needs" (health and basic education), the complete disappearance of infrastructure development, and the integration of women in development into all programs as a "crosscutting theme."

WHERE AID?

Canadian aid programs started in Asia and spread through Africa, Latin America and the Caribbean during the 1960s and 1970s. A 1980 Parliamentary Task Force on North-South Relations said that the distribution of Canadian aid had not changed since 1975, and that 27 countries accounted for 79 percent of the program. "Nevertheless," is stated, "we remain concerned about the widespread geographic dispersion."[38] It called for a reduction in the geographic spread, a refrain that would follow in every parliamentary and OECD report over the next 27 years. In 1987, *Sharing Our Future* said that bilateral aid would become "more focused," that "tough decisions" were needed and that "choices must be made." The 1990 DAC peer review said "the current dispersion of the Canadian aid effort appears to be a major problem," But by 1992 there had been some tightening, with 73 percent of bilateral aid going to 17 countries. The OECD still questioned the dispersion, however, and did so again in its reports of 1998 and 2002.

"Canada's International Policy Statement" of 2005 painted a grim picture of aid gone geographically amok, spread over "155 countries, a number which exceeds that of any other donor,"[39] and it promised to "focus bilateral spending in fewer sectors and countries." Not satisfied with the progress in two years, the DAC Peer review of 2007 "strongly" encouraged Canada to "accelerate the concentration of bilateral aid on fewer countries."[40] CIDA has said repeatedly in recent years that "fewer countries" is the plan, but as of this writing, it still lists 25 "development partner programs," not including three of the largest aid recipients – Iraq, Afghanistan and Haiti.

In fact CIDA itself has never operated in 155 countries. That number can only be reached if every dollar going to every NGO and community college and partnership project is tracked to its conclusion. And no matter what kind of focusing is done at the centre, that number is unlikely to change appreciably. CIDA's real geographic spread in 2004–5 was reflected in 64.7 percent of bilateral spending going to 30 countries,[41] a level of dispersion that was nevertheless higher than the OECD average, and as high as it had ever been since the formation of CIDA.

There are obviously political reasons for the dispersion of CIDA spending and the inability over the years to "focus." Canada is a member of the Commonwealth, *la Francophonie* and the Organization of American States, all of which exert pressures. Political imperatives draw Canada to Iraq, Afghanistan and Haiti; commercial imperatives are at least a part of the draw to Indonesia and China; humanitarian as well as development needs take Canadian aid to Ethiopia, Sudan and the Democratic Republic of the Congo. Prestige is an important part of the spread as well: Canada, a member of the G8, wants to be seen as a *player*, and to do this it must be active in UN agencies, OECD gatherings, international financial institutions and others. The question rarely asked in the 30-year drive for "focus" (and never answered with any assurance) is whether the quality of aid would improve in a given country by spending more, and whether spending only $20 million in, say, Burkina Faso, means *ipso facto* that the quality will be poor.

At the international level, the OECD's advice that Canada should focus on fewer countries might make more sense if the OECD itself had any grand plan, but this appears not to be the case. The same recommendation about greater geographic focus was made in the 2004 DAC Review of France, the 2005 Review of Germany, the 2006 Review of Netherlands and a host of others. Nowhere in all of these recommendations is there a suggestion that this should be in some way coordinated to avoid crowding – as is the case in Mozambique, a priority country for at least eleven donors (including Canada) – or the abandonment of especially needy countries like Sierra Leone.

HOW AID?

Channels

In addition to direct government-to-government programs, a significant proportion of Canadian ODA has been channelled over the years through United Nations and other multilateral bodies, and since 1990 there has been a large increase in spending on humanitarian emergencies, through NGOs, the Red Cross and UN agencies. Multilateral agencies provide both relief and development assistance that member governments often cannot – professionally, sectorally and geographically. And they can level off the peaks and valleys resulting from the political priorities of donors working on their own. As well, during the 1960s, Canada began to provide funding to Canadian non-governmental organizations working overseas. There were various reasons for this. NGOs could also go places that government could not, and could often move more quickly. And the government also wanted to encourage – through "matching grants" – the private donations that taxpayers were making to international assistance, over and above their tax dollars.

In 2005, 26 percent of Canadian ODA was delivered through multilateral channels, a figure somewhat higher than the DAC average of 21 percent.[42] This represented a significant decline in Canada's multilateral assistance from earlier years (1979: 44 percent; 1993: 36 percent[43]), although the overall DAC average has also declined. As noted earlier, responsibilities for the management of Canadian multilateral assistance are diffuse. The Department of Finance manages the relationship with international financial institutions in consultation with CIDA and DFAIT. CIDA handles the bulk of the funding relationship with UN agencies, but DFAIT is responsible for the political relationship with the UN. The departments of Health, Agriculture and Environment are also involved in the management of funds channelled through specialized UN agencies.

CIDA was one of the first bilateral agencies to establish a special mechanism for funding NGOs. Funding began on a project-by-project basis, using a matching grant formula. This gradually expanded to include multi-year program support, and special "windows" in sectoral and geographic areas, with increasingly generous matching ratios. During the 1980s, bilateral programs began to fund NGO-initiated projects as well, and for a time the array of funding opportunities was both wide and confusing. In 1991–92, CIDA estimated that 8 percent of total ODA and 13 percent of bilateral ODA was being channelled through NGOs.[44] By 2000 the percentage had risen to 17 percent, although the volume has declined somewhat since then. By 2005, almost 20 percent of the support to NGOs – or more correctly to a broad collection of civil society organizations – was being channelled through organizations based outside of Canada, many of them in developing countries.[45]

Hole of Government?

It is easy to forget, given Maurice Strong's long career, that he started as a mere director general at CIDA's outset, with a smallish program responsible to the minister of External Affairs. Today CIDA is an autonomous body with a president who holds deputy ministerial rank, answerable to CIDA's own minister. Of course many other departments contribute to Canada's international development effort, and CIDA's relationship with them has at times been difficult. Natural Resources Canada, for example, has an interest in promoting Canadian mining interests abroad, while extractive industries have never been high on CIDA's list of priorities. There are similar pressures from other departments for CIDA to fund their international outreach programs, and this is resisted, often with good reason. The result is that CIDA has sometimes been regarded as an outlier in government circles. Criticism of CIDA in Parliament today, and in documents like the 2007 Senate Report on Africa – which went so far as suggesting that CIDA should be closed down or taken over by DFAIT – speak to a legacy of mistrust, misunderstanding and in some cases, deliberate disinformation.

The issue of coherence in Canada's international assistance policies is not new. In 1968, Foreign Affairs Minister Mitchell Sharp deprecated "giveaway" programs, saying that Canadian aid had "increasingly to be supplemented by a much more complex and sophisticated set of arrangements in the fields of trade, investment, education, science and technology, designed to support and strengthen the self-help efforts and initiatives of the less-developed nations."[46] This is not a million miles removed from the "whole of government" and "3-D" approaches espoused by Prime Minister Martin in 2004, and by many governments in between.

Countries cannot work, Martin said, unless they have institutions that work. "In Canada we refer to the three Ds – defence, diplomacy and development. This means we are integrating our traditional foreign policy instruments more tightly – especially when responding to the needs of vulnerable states to build up their own capacity to govern themselves." Referring to Afghanistan, he said that security and political stability go hand in hand, and that the effort requires more than "some police training and a prison or two." He could have been referring as much to Canadian ODA as to Afghanistan when he said, "The three Ds means building public institutions that work and are accountable to the public for their actions. Not just policing, but also government ministries, a system of laws, courts, human rights commissions, schools, hospitals, energy and water and transportation systems." The prime minister admitted the difficulty of the task – perhaps in Canada as much as in recipient countries.[47] Being part of a whole-of-government approach while at the same time resisting cash grabs from budget-starved departments with their own international priorities has been, and remains, a delicate CIDA balancing act.

Decentralization

Where decisions are made has a lot to do with their content, quality and the time required to make them. The OECD and others have long argued for greater decentralization in ODA planning and decision making, and decentralization has been a central thrust in the advice given by donors to many developing countries. The idea of greater decentralization in CIDA was taken to heart by the Mulroney government, responding perhaps in part to recommendations made in a 1986 Report of the Standing Committee on External Affairs and International Trade, *For Whose Benefit?* The response, spelled out in *Sharing our Future* (1987), was dramatic. At that time, CIDA had 100 field positions against 1,100 at headquarters. The new policy was clear: "The Auditor General, the Public Accounts Committee and the North-South Institute have all commented at length on the need for improved, closer-to-the-action design, monitoring and technical support. Moreover, almost all of the new initiatives now taking place in Canada's development assistance program can be done well only if there are more aid staff in the field, and if they have more decision-making authority and administrative flexibility."[48]

The plan said that "a large measure of authority over bilateral programming and approval will be decentralized away from CIDA headquarters" and that up to one quarter of CIDA's staff would be relocated to field offices. Project approval authority of up to $5 million would also be decentralized to the field in order to speed up what by then had become one of the slowest bilateral decision-making processes in the OECD.

It didn't happen. The reasons given for reversing the policy not long after it was enunciated were largely financial in nature, although there had been considerable discomfort on the part of senior managers, concerned about being held accountable for decisions over which they might exercise little control. By 1994, the situation was much as it had been before *Sharing our Future*: 124 CIDA officers overseas out of a total complement of 1,307, with plans to cut the overseas numbers by a further 10 percent.[49] Spending delegation, at only $500,000, was one tenth of what had been proposed seven years earlier.

By 2007, little had changed, except that the HQ-field imbalance had become worse. There were only 132 Canada-based staff serving overseas, against 1,852 at headquarters – 7.1 percent in the field, versus 8.3 percent 20 years earlier. Although the value of the dollar had declined by 44 percent, delegated spending levels in the field remained as they were twenty years earlier. A 2007 Senate report said "CIDA as a top-heavy agency is inflexible and unresponsive, negating the two key advantages that bilateral aid agencies have over multilateral agencies... As one CIDA official working in Africa told the Committee: "My authority is $50,000, but my colleague in DFID [U.K. Department for International Development] has authority for 7.5 million pounds." This, combined with delays in our funding, "makes it seem like we're not a player." The Senate report noted that "Denmark has decentralized decision-making considerably to its embassies, which operate with five year spending plans. Similarly, the Netherlands' embassies receive forecasting for three years."[50] The OECD too criticized the top-heavy centralized nature of the organization and its decision making, but it did so in a political climate where controls were tightening rather than the opposite, and where few changes could be foreseen.[51]

Who's On First?

CIDA has had an incredible array of ministers and presidents. Since the establishment of the agency in 1968, there have been twelve presidents – thirteen counting Marcel Massé's two terms. On average these appointments have lasted about three years, although the average is skewed by the six-year presidencies of Marcel Massé and Maggie Catley-Carlson, and by the seven-year tenure of Paul Gérin-Lajoie. More recent presidencies have been of much shorter duration. There has always been a minister responsible for CIDA, whether it was the minister of Foreign Affairs or a minister dedicated to international cooperation. Of the latter, there have been 11, covering a period of slightly under 22 years. The average life expectancy of a CIDA minister has therefore been in the neighbourhood of two years, but this has declined considerably since 1996. The 2007 DAC Peer Review noted that, "In Canada, issues relating to development co-operation in general and policy coherence for development in particular, have suffered from a lack of policy continuity and consistency. Since 2003 there have been four different governments and four different Ministers for International Cooperation."[52]

Despite the great talent that some ministers and presidents have brought to their positions, the revolving door on the top floor of 200 Promenade du Portage, especially over the past decade, has had two policy-related results. The first is tremendous uncertainty as each new manager, minister or government takes office, often causing hard-won and far-reaching programs to be delayed, transformed or cancelled, and new ones to be introduced suddenly. The second is constant change, as new managers, ministers or governments seek to impose their own priorities on Canada's aid program, dismissing much of what went before as irrelevant.

Maria Minna (August 1999 – January 2002), for example, set an important new thematic focus for CIDA. Her successor, Susan Whelan (January 2002 – December 2003) added agriculture to the list. No sooner was she gone than agriculture slipped from the agenda. Aileen Carroll (December 2003 – February 2006) accepted the OECD recommendation that Canada reduce its geographic spread, and various lists began to appear. "Partner countries" were to be reduced to fifteen in number, or perhaps even fewer, but with the election of the Conservative government in 2006, focusing appeared to stall, and in 2008 CIDA's web site listed 25 "Development Partner" countries, not including the three countries where CIDA spending dwarfs all others, accounting for more than 20 percent of the total: Afghanistan, Haiti and Iraq.

The massive CIDA reorganization of 2007 is one in a long string of "massive reorganizations" instituted by president after president. In many cases, as with the 2007 reorganization, the changes take place shortly before the departure of the instigator, leaving the incoming president to sort out the glitches, or to set in motion yet another reorganization. The 1994 DAC Peer Review observed that "Few donors have questioned, re-oriented and revitalized their aid programs as intensively or as repeatedly as Canada."[53] It is questionable whether these reorganizations and the musical chairs at the top have ever actually "revitalized" the organization. They do create uncertainty and impermanence, and they exact a high cost in staff morale.

WHOSE AID?

CIDA's Public Profile

Opinion poll after opinion poll has shown high public support for Canada's international aid program, averaging 75 percent positive ratings or higher in recent years. The truth is, however, that few Canadians know much about the subject. Most think the federal government spends five times more on aid than it actually does.[54]

CIDA is not a household name, and neither is its minister. A measure of CIDA's position in the perceived pecking order could be seen when CIDA minister Josée Verner switched jobs with Heritage Minister Bev Oda in 2007. The switch was widely reported as a promotion for Verner and a demotion for Oda, even though CIDA's budget is almost triple that of the Department of Canadian Heritage.

CIDA and the overall ODA package represent one of the largest spending envelopes – more than two percent of overall government expenditure – but the agency's profile remains low unless there is a scandal. Federal budget announcements barely mention foreign assistance, and despite its size, CIDA is rarely mentioned in media coverage of the budget speech. The February 2008 budget was a case in point: the minister of Finance mentioned ODA only in passing, and there was no mention of it at all in the *Globe and Mail*, the *National Post* or the *Ottawa Citizen*. CIDA itself keeps a very low profile. The agency's entire communications budget in

2007–08 was $12.5 million, less than 30 percent of what World Vision Canada spent on advertising that year. It is not surprising, therefore, that public opinion plays a very small part in CIDA policy development.

Parliament too plays a limited role in Canada's ODA policy making. That is not to say that parliamentary committees have not studied CIDA and Canada's aid policies extensively. There have been many reviews over the years, but their recommendations all too often fall on completely deaf ears. For example in May 1987, the Standing Committee on External Affairs and International Trade produced a large report on Canadian ODA which recommended, *inter alia*, "that CIDA substantially increase assistance for education at the primary level and, in particular for literacy programs." CIDA's response in 1987 said that this recommendation was "accepted in principle," stating that it would "express its willingness to provide developing countries with assistance in this area." It said that it would help to promote adult literacy, making no mention at all of primary education.[55] When *Sharing Our Future* appeared not long afterwards, it stated that "primary education has always been a priority in development. *But adults need education too.*"[56] This was apparently shorthand for a policy statement: in 1994–95, out of total bilateral spending of $1.47 billion, CIDA spent only $1 million on basic education.[57] Meanwhile, scholarships for tertiary education rose from 6,000 in 1987 to more than 20,000 four years later.

A measure of parliamentary frustration can be found in a 2007 Senate report which raised the spectre of closing CIDA down entirely. "Canada should conduct an immediate review of the future of the Canadian International Development Agency (CIDA)," it said, "to determine whether the agency should be abolished or whether it should be improved with a statutory mandate."[58]

CONCLUSION:
THE OVERLOADED RICKSHAW

Abolishing CIDA would hardly make sense unless Canada was planning to abandon official development assistance altogether, an unlikely prospect. A new CIDA, standing on its own or under DFAIT, would simply have to be re-invented. But without fundamental changes in the pressures and policies that have made CIDA so ineffective in the eyes of its frustrated critics, little would change.

In essence, this brings the discussion about international development full circle, back to the 1969 concern that Canada's aid program was "intellectually incoherent." Canada's aid program was, and has remained, intellectually incoherent because its masters made it so. It was advertised almost exclusively on its development promise, but it was at the same time forced to act as a milch cow for commercial interests, and as a hearts and minds operation for Canada's changeable political and security agendas. And it was consistently destabilized by a fickle and ever-changing leadership, too eagerly served by middle managers prone to fads and the Next Big Thing.

The Senate report was onto something more fundamental in the idea of a statutory mandate for CIDA, something long recommended by those who advocate a clearer developmental role for the agency. In fact a private member's bill aiming to do precisely this, strongly supported by Canadian NGOs, was slowly making its way through the tortuous parliamentary process when the Senate report discussed a statutory mandate. In May 2008, Bill C-293, known to its promoters as "the Better Aid Bill," received final approval and became the law of the land. The Act requires that Canadian development assistance "be provided with a central focus on poverty reduction, as well as in a manner that is consistent with Canadian values, Canada's foreign policy, sustainable development and democracy promotion and in a manner that promotes international human rights standards."[59] And the act requires the minister to report more quickly and more transparently to Parliament on aid spending against these criteria.

The extent to which the Better Aid Bill can improve on the organization's intellectual and programmatic coherence remains to be seen, but to many CIDA watchers, it was a landmark, a first clear statement of developmental principle against which government can be held accountable.

A department of health, provincial or federal, has the health of Canadians as its primary mandate. It has many functions that are not immediately related to hospitals or nurses or doctors, however: research, education, communications, environmental scans. But all are related to *health*. That clarity of purpose, while fulsomely and frequently proclaimed, has, historically, been almost entirely absent in practice from Canada's international development assistance. If the confusion continues, Canadian ODA will never make satisfactory headway in what Lester Pearson said it was supposed to be all about: "to reduce disparities and remove inequities...so that the world will not become more starkly divided between the haves and the have-nots, the privileged and the less privileged."

In Bangladesh, three wheeled bicycle rickshaws are commonly used for public transportation. It is not unusual for a passenger to demand that a rickshaw driver carry more than the vehicle can support, loading it with too many people, too many boxes, or too many bags of cement. The result is predictable. If the rickshaw is able to move at all, it will do so slowly and with caution. It will creak under the strain, and the overworked driver will soon tire. More often than not, however, the overloaded rickshaw simply collapses under the weight, the goods spill into the street and the rickshaw driver is blamed by the customer who caused the distress in the first place.

NOTES

1 Lester Pearson (Chair), *Partners in Development: Report of the Commission on International Development* (New York: Praeger 1969), 7–9.
2 CIDA, "Aide-Mémoire: Panel Discussion on the purpose of Development Assistance," 23 January 1969; quoted in David R. Morrison, *Aid and Ebb Tide: A History of CIDA and Canadian International Development Assistance* (Waterloo: Wilfrid Laurier University Press 1998), 87.
3 CIDA, "Background Paper for Development Assistance Policy Review Conference, 16–18 May, 1969", cited in Morrison, *Aid and Ebb Tide*, 88.
4 http://www.acdi-cida.gc.ca/CIDAWEB/acdicida.nsf/En/NIC-5493749-HZK
5 Clyde Sanger, *Half a Loaf: Canada's Semi-Role Among Developing Countries* (Toronto: Ryerson Press 1969), 222.
6 Canada, *Independence and Internationalism, Report of the Special Joint Committee on Canada's International Relations* (Ottawa: June, 1986), 61.
7 Development Assistance Committee, *Review of Canada 2007* (Paris: OECD 2007), 30.
8 CIDA, *Annual Review 1968–69* (Ottawa: 1969), 51.
9 Consulting and Audit Canada, "Evaluation report: Industrial Cooperation Program – CIDA," (Ottawa, December 1992), 68–71.
10 CIDA, "Executive Report on the Evaluation of the CIDA Industrial Cooperation Program," (Ottawa: December 2007)
11 Ibid. 13.
12 CIDA, "Investments in the Rail Sector in Senegal," undated, http://www.acdi-cida.gc.ca/INET/IMAGES.NSF/vLUImages/Performancereview4/$file/SenegalEXECUTIVSum.pdf
13 Roger Ehrhardt, *Canadian Development Assistance to Bangladesh* (Ottawa: North South Institute 1983), 61.
14 Brian Mulroney, "Notes for a Speech by Prime Minister Brian Mulroney," Commonwealth Heads of Government Meeting (Harare Oct. 16, 1991).
15 Total Canadian aid and EDC loans to China in 1991–2: $66.02 million; in 1991–2: $54.9 million. Source: Morrison, *Aid and Ebb Tide*, 349.
16 Sharon Scharfe, *Complicity: Human Rights and Canadian Foreign Policy*, (Montreal: Black Rose Books, 1996), 29.
17 Development Assistance Committee, *Review of Canada 2007*, 31.
18 M.A. Crener, G. Léal, R. LeBlanc, B. Thébaud, *Integrated Rural Development: State of the Art Review – 1982–83* (Ottawa: CIDA, 1984). 10.
19 Philip English, *Canadian Development Assistance to Haiti* (Ottawa: North-South Institute, 1983) 125.
20 Robert Chambers, *Rural Development, Putting the Last First* (Burnt Mill, Essex: Longmans, 1983), 154.
21 English, *Canadian Development Assistance to Haiti*, 156.

22 A. Cornia, R. Jolly and F. Stewart, *Adjustment with a Human Face: Protecting the Vulnerable and Promoting Growth* (Oxford: Oxford University Press, 1987), 66.
23 CIDA, *Annual Review 1986* (Ottawa: 1986), 11.
24 CIDA, *Sharing Our Future: Canada's International development Assistance* (Ottawa, 1987), 58.
25 CIDA, *Annual Review 1988* (Ottawa: 1988), 5.
26 CIDA, *Annual Review 1990* (Ottawa: 1990), 15.
27 World Bank, *Sub-Saharan Africa: From Crisis to Sustainable Growth* (Washington 1989), 14.
28 CIDA, "Probing the 1990s: Topics for Discussions on CIDA's Environment in the 1990s," (Ottawa: February 1990), 21.
29 Mark Charlton, *The Making of Canadian Food Aid Policy* (Montreal and Kingston: McGill-Queens University Press, 1992), 3.
30 Oxfam, "Food aid or hidden dumping?" (Oxford: March 2005), 13.
31 On Sept. 5, 2008, CIDA Minister Bev Oda announced that CIDA would untie all of its ODA "by 20-12-13"; http://www.acdi-cida.gc.ca/CIDAWEB/acdicida.nsf/En/NAT-9583229-GQC.
32 http://www.acdi-cida.gc.ca/CIDAWEB/acdicida.nsf/En/REN-218132022-PHV, "last updated 2007.06.08."
33 Auditor General of Canada, *1993 Report of the Auditor General of Canada, Chapter 12, CIDA* (Ottawa: 1993), para. 12.58.
34 CIDA, "CIDA Renewal Plan 1994–1995," (Ottawa: 1994).
35 Department of Foreign Affairs and International Trade, *Canada in The World: Government Statement* (Ottawa: 1995), 42.
36 http://www.acdi-cida.gc.ca/aideffectiveness.
37 http://www.acdi-cida.gc.ca/cidaweb/acdicida.nsf/En/NIC-53131840-NB8.
38 Canada, *Parliamentary Task Force on North-South Relations* (House of Commons: 1980), 40.
39 Canada, *Canada's International Policy Statement: Development* (Ottawa: 2005), 6.
40 Development Assistance Committee, *Review of Canada 2007* (Paris: OECD, 2007). 36.
41 CIDA, "Statistical Report on ODA 2004–5," (Ottawa: 2006).
42 Development Assistance Committee, *Review of Canada 2007* (Paris: OECD, 2007) 40.
43 Development Assistance Committee, *Review of Canada 2007* (Paris: OECD, 1994), 35.
44 *Ibid.*, 42.
45 Development Assistance Committee, *Review of Canada 2007* (Paris: OECD, 2007), 39.
46 Morrison, *Aid and Ebb Tide*, 62.
47 Martin, Paul, "Speech by the Prime Minister", Washington, April 29, 2004, URL: http://pm.gc.ca/eng/news.asp?id=192.

48 CIDA, *Sharing Our Future: Canada's International development Assistance* (Ottawa: 1987), 33.
49 Development Assistance Committee, *Review of Canada 2007* (Paris: OECD, 1994), 30.
50 Canada, *Overcoming 40 Years Of Failure: A New Road Map For Sub-Saharan Africa* (Ottawa: The Standing Senate Committee on Foreign Affairs and International Trade, February 2007), 92.
51 Development Assistance Committee, *Review of Canada 2007* (Paris: OECD, 2007), 46–7.
52 Development Assistance Committee, *Review of Canada 2007* (Paris: OECD, 2007), 30.
53 Development Assistance Committee, *Review of Canada 2007* (Paris: OECD, 1994), 25.
54 CIDA, "Canadian Attitudes Towards Development Assistance" (Ottawa: 2004), 4.
55 CIDA, *Canadian International Development Assistance, To Benefit a Better World: Response of the Government of Canada to the Report by the Standing Committee on External Affairs and International Trade*, Minister of Supply and Services Canada (Ottawa: September 1987).
56 CIDA, *Sharing Our Future: Canada's International development Assistance* (Ottawa: 1987), 38.
57 Development Assistance Committee, *Review of Canada 2007* (Paris: OECD, 2007), 78.
58 Canada, *Overcoming 40 Years Of Failure: A New Road Map For Sub-Saharan Africa* (Ottawa: The Standing Senate Committee on Foreign Affairs and International Trade, February 2007), x.
59 Library of Parliament, "Notes on Bill C-293," http://www.parl.gc.ca/information/library/PRBpubs/prb0631-e.htm.

9 Tools and Levers: Energy as an Instrument of Canadian Foreign Policy

DUANE BRATT[*]

In the lead up to the 2006 G8 Summit in St. Petersburg, Prime Minister Stephen Harper began touting Canada as an "emerging energy superpower." At a speech in London, Harper told his audience that "We are currently the fifth largest energy producer in the world. We rank 3rd and 7th in global gas and oil production respectively. We generate more hydro-electric power than any other country on earth. And we are the world's largest supplier of uranium."[1] By deliberately invoking the term superpower, Harper meant that Canada was more than just a major exporter of energy, but was interested in using the "energy lever for political power" like Russia and Saudi Arabia.[2]

If Harper is planning on using Canada's energy resources as a tool or lever to support Canadian foreign policy, it would be useful to examine how this has been done in the past. The purpose of this chapter is to analyze the historical role that energy has played in advancing Canada's foreign policy. Canada has abundant energy resources in many different forms, but space limitations means focusing on only oil & gas and nuclear and excluding other sources like hydroelectricity and coal. Oil & gas and nuclear were chosen above the others for a number of reasons. First, they were explicitly recognized in Harper's "Energy Superpower" speech. Second, in addition to generating large amounts of export dollars, they have been used to advance larger, and divergent, foreign policy goals. For example, oil & gas has been used as a lever in a number of macroeconomic policies including, especially, the protection/liberalization of international trade and foreign direct investment. In the case of nuclear power, Canada has used the sale of uranium and CANDU nuclear reactors to pursue non-economic goals such as the non-proliferation of nuclear weapons, fight communism, advance relations with developing countries, and mitigate climate change. Third, there is a further contrast in that oil & gas highlights the bilateral relationship between Canada and the United States, and nuclear power highlights Canada's relations with the rest of the world.

This chapter argues that it may be possible for the Harper government to use energy to promote larger foreign policy goals, but an examination of the historical record is mixed. Nuclear was used as an effective lever, but the high water mark was in the mid-1970s. Since that time, Canada's international nuclear presence has shrunk, and with it, its ability to act as a lever in the pursuit of its larger foreign policy goals. In the case of oil & gas, it has tended to reflect Canada's macroeconomic policy shifts rather than as a tool to change them. Moreover, while there were moments when the oil & gas tool was wielded *by* Ottawa, more often than not it was wielded by either the Alberta government or the oil & gas sector *against* Ottawa.

THE FOREIGN POLICY ASPECTS OF CANADIAN OIL & GAS POLICY

Centred in Calgary, which houses the headquarters of the major firms and their industry representatives, the Canadian oil & gas sector includes all aspects of the industry: upstream (exploration and production), midstream (processing, storage, transportation) and downstream (refining, marketing, distribution). Historically, the sector was dominated by large foreign-owned multinationals (Imperial Oil/Exxon, Shell, Gulf, Texaco), but over the last several decades large Canadian-owned firms have also emerged (Petro-Canada, TransCanada, ATCO, EnCana, Nexen, etc). In addition to these large multinationals, there are a vast number of mid-sized and small oil & gas companies. The oil & gas industry's collective voice is split into several different organizations. The Canadian Association of Petroleum Producers (CAPP) represents the 140 largest upstream foreign and Canadian-owned companies. It is joined by other organizations like the Small Explorers and Producers Association (SEPA), the Canadian Energy Pipeline Association (CEPA), the Canadian Independent Petroleum Marketers Association (CIPMA), and the Canadian Gas Association (CGA).

Jurisdiction over Canada's oil & gas sector is split between the federal and provincial governments. Section 109 of the Constitution Act 1867 grants jurisdiction over natural resources to the provinces.[3] Other constitutional provisions grant the federal government jurisdiction over trade and commerce and international treaties. As the introduction of the

National Energy Program (NEP) and ratification of the Kyoto Protocol showed, there are often constitutional battles in the governance of the oil & gas sector.[4]

Canada is one of the world's largest producers of oil & gas and the sector is one of the country's most economically important sectors. In 2006, the sector generated revenues of $106.5 billion and paid $27 billion in royalties and taxes to Ottawa and the provinces. It directly and indirectly employs 350, 000 Canadians. Every day, Canada exports 1.77 million barrels of oil and 9.9 million cubic feet of natural gas.[5] Canada is the second largest supplier of oil to the United States (behind Mexico) and the number one supplier of natural gas. Canada's conventional oil and natural gas supplies are dwindling, but this is made up for by the existence of the oil sands in Alberta which has proven reserves of 178.8 billion barrels of oil. In the future, the oil sands will be an important source of energy for both domestic uses and exports.[6] Its economic size, the presence of large American multinationals, and the extensive north/south linkages (infrastructure, supply patterns, etc.) have all combined to make the oil & gas sector a major influence on Canada-U.S. macroeconomic relations.

OIL & GAS: THE EARLY YEARS (1858–1968)

The early days of the oil & gas industry in Canada have been characterized as the colonial period, 1858–1930.[7] Development was concentrated in southwestern Ontario, but by the 1920s, Turner Valley, Alberta, had become Canada's oil capital.[8] However, "the high cost and engineering difficulties of bringing oil and natural gas from the Canadian west and north to market, encouraged Canadian petroleum companies to rely on imports."[9] The colonial period ends in 1930 with the transfer of natural resources from the federal government to the prairie provinces.

The 1947 Leduc oil discovery in Alberta marks the beginning of the modern oil industry in Canada. The Leduc strike was critical because it finally ended Canada's huge dependency upon oil imports from the United States. For instance, by the end of the 1920s, Canada was "importing almost thirty times as much crude oil as it produced."[10] Prior to Leduc, Canada produced less than one percent of the amount of oil as that of the United States.[11] During World War II there was an acute danger of oil shortages within Canada.[12]

To ensure that the Leduc strike was fully exploited, the Alberta government "actively encouraged the development of Alberta's oil and gas reserves through U.S. multinationals at the expense of smaller Canadian firms."[13] This was consistent with Canadian investment policy during this era. Attracting foreign investment had been a cornerstone of Canadian economic policy since prior to confederation. The pre-confederation period saw British investment in the Canadian economy. John A. Macdonald's National Policy (1878) invited U.S. capital to invest in Canada to promote Canadian economic development. By the early 1920s, the Americans had supplanted the British as the major source of foreign capital. The entry of American FDI in Canada intensified after World War II. A small number of sectors were protected (media, banks, etc), but Ottawa's policies were designed to provide incentives for attracting U.S. capital.[14] These incentives applied equally to national and international capital, but since there was a lack of domestic capital, the end result was an increase in American FDI.

To protect the emerging oil & gas sector in Western Canada from cheaper foreign imports, the Diefenbaker government in 1961 introduced the national oil policy. This policy restricted oil imports to east of the Ottawa River, which meant that Western Canada, and more especially the large market of Ontario, were required to use domestic oil. This policy supported both the expansion of the Canadian industry and aided Ottawa's balance of payments by importing "cheap oil" east of the Ottawa Valley and exporting "expensive oil" west of it.[15] The U.S. multinationals were also pleased with the national oil policy because it reflected their desire to entrench its North-South linkages. As Brownsey has noted, the Canadian subsidiaries of Shell, Imperial/ Exxon, Gulf and Texaco "had little interest in shipping Alberta crude to central and eastern Canada. Through their multi-national parents, the big four provided their refineries in the Montreal area with cheap imported oil."[16] James Laxer adds that "the pipeline that delivered crude to American markets before entering Ontario physically linked the two countries. The price of oil in Canada west of the Ottawa Valley was set to conform to the price set in Chicago."[17]

ECONOMIC NATIONALISM (1968–1984)

Canada made a policy shift towards economic nationalism in the early 1970s. Three creatures of that period were to be particularly relevant to the oil & gas sector: the Foreign Investment Review Agency (FIRA), Petro-Canada, and the NEP.

Starting in the late 1950s, there were a series of reports that warned about the high level of U.S. ownership of the Canadian economy. The Gordon Report (1958) stated that the extent of U.S. foreign direct investment (FDI) was not in the best interests of Canada. A decade later, the Watkins Report (1968) demonstrated the inefficiencies of Canada's branch plant economy due to transfer pricing and a lack of research and development by U.S. multinationals. The Gray Report (1972) was the most comprehensive of these reports, showing that U.S. investors controlled 45 percent of all manufacturing, 99 percent of oil & gas, 56 percent of mining and smelting, 84 percent of tobacco, 99 percent of rubber, 39 percent of paper products, and 81 percent of chemicals. It conducted a cost/benefit analysis of the impact of U.S. FDI and recommended a Canadian screening agency to monitor the performance of FDI and force US investors to increase their benefits to Canada.[18]

The Foreign Investment Review Agency was created in 1973 as a permanent mechanism that would determine that all foreign-controlled takeovers and expansion of existing branch plants into new fields were of "significant benefit" to Canada. It established a screening threshold of $5 million. However, in practice, FIRA rarely denied takeovers; for example, by 1979, 90 percent of all applications had been approved. Therefore, in 1980 the Liberal government decided to enhance FIRA's powers by allowing it to conduct periodic reviews of all "established foreign-controlled industries." In addition, it would "publicize foreign takeover applications" allowing "Canadian firms to make counteroffers using government loans to bolster their bids."[19] Finally, Herb Gray, the author of the Gray Report, was put in charge of FIRA as minister of Industry, Trade, and Commerce.

The oil & gas sector was not singled out by FIRA. It was simply one, out of many, critical area of U.S. foreign ownership that FIRA was designed to reduce. The agency's activities, however, did foreshadow the two major initiatives to Canadianize the oil & gas sector: the creation of Petro-Canada and the establishment of the NEP.

The first oil shocks of 1973, which saw a quadrupling of world oil prices, forced Ottawa to reconsider its oil & gas policy. A number of initiatives were taken; the most important was the creation of a special crown corporation in 1975. Petro-Canada was formed by consolidating the federal government's ownership shares in Syncrude and PanArctic. Petro-Canada would expand through additional takeovers of Atlantic Richfield and Pacific Petroleum in 1976 and Petrofina in 1981. The purpose of Petro-Canada was not only Canadianization, but also to provide a "window" that would increase Canadian knowledge about the domestic and international oil industry.[20]

The Iranian Revolution in 1979 led to the second oil shock as prices doubled from $20 to $40 a barrel with fears that oil prices would go even higher. In response, the Liberal government introduced the National Energy Program in 1980. The NEP was a series of regulations that included changes in tax structure, drilling incentives, and conservation measures.

There were three objectives behind the NEP. First, it would restructure the oil & gas industry to achieve energy self-sufficiency for Canada. This would include a "made in Canada" price policy that would reduce prices below world levels. Eastern Canada – meaning east of Ontario – would especially benefit because it relied on expensive oil imports. Second, it would channel fiscal revenues towards the federal government and away from oil-producing provinces (i.e., Alberta). Third, it would increase Canadian ownership levels in the oil & gas sector, with a target of 50 percent.

Canada's oil & gas sector was historically foreign-controlled. In 1980, 74 percent of all oil companies were foreign-owned and they controlled 81.5 percent of the market. Nineteen of the twenty-five largest companies were more than 50 percent owned by non-Canadians and these nineteen firms accounted for 75 percent of the market.[21] The NEP set a goal of 50 percent Canadianization by 1990. The principal instrument to Canadianize the industry was a 25 percent "back in" equity to the Crown, or a Crown corporation like Petro-Canada, for every oil & gas development in Canada. This would also be applied retroactively to existing projects.

The NEP sparked outrage in Alberta and Premier Peter Lougheed retaliated by instituting a reduction in oil production. Lougheed, and most people in the province, saw the NEP as a unilateral, unwarranted, and illegitimate intrusion, only made worse by the federal government's lack of representation in Western Canada: the 1980 election that returned the Liberals to power gave them only two seats in the West and none in Alberta. Although Ottawa and Alberta reached a pact in September 1981 on pricing and tax levels, when world oil prices subsequently collapsed, creating a major recession in Alberta, the NEP was blamed. Twenty-eight years later, resentment towards the NEP remains so strong that "Liberal" (when applied either to the federal or provincial party) remains a dirty word throughout much of the province.

The NEP also sparked outrage in the United States. The newly elected Reagan administration, for ideological reasons, believed that the market should determine oil prices. In addition, the NEP violated several international trade commitments through the General Agreement on Tariffs and Trade (GATT). Beyond ideological convictions and international trade law, there were other reasons for the U.S. to oppose the NEP. As Stephen Clarkson has written, "its price strategy raised real questions affecting America's *national* interest. Its Canadianization provisions impinged on American *corporate* interests."[22]

FIRA, Petro-Canada, and the NEP were all initiatives designed to Canadianize the oil & gas sector. The sector, especially the U.S. multinationals and their Canadian subsidiaries tried to resist these efforts by appealing to both the Alberta government (their host state) and the United States government (their home state).[23] In the short-term, the Canadianization project failed. The Mulroney government would quickly dismantle FIRA and the NEP and took steps to privatize parts of Petro-Canada. Moreover, when you look at the history of Canadian trade and investment policy, the 1970s-1984 period was only a small blip of economic nationalism. In the long-term, however, this short period of economic nationalism created the environment that led to a significant degree of Canadianization within the oil patch. During the brief life of the NEP, Canadian ownership of the industry rose from 6.7 percent to 34.7 percent.[24] While over the longer-term, in combination with some of the policies of the Lougheed government in the 1970s,[25] there has been the emergence of several large Canadian-owned champions like EnCana, Canadian Natural Resources Limited (CNRL), and Talisman. The fact that there has been massive growth in the oil & gas sector over the last couple of decades also means that the percentage of Canadianization is much more valuable than it used to be.

ECONOMIC LIBERALISM (1984–1993)

During the 1984 election campaign, Brian Mulroney and the Conservatives explicitly rejected the economic nationalism of the Liberals by promising to "open Canada for business." After winning the election, the Mulroney government transformed FIRA into Investment Canada. Instead of trying to block FDI, Investment Canada would encourage it. The screening threshold was raised to $150 million meaning that only the largest foreign takeovers would be examined. Takeovers would be approved if they could show a "net benefit" as opposed to FIRA's "significant benefit." Since the establishment of Investment Canada, no foreign takeover has been rejected, although, in some cases, conditions were applied.

Next on the hit list was the NEP. The Mulroney government's caucus included a large contingent of Westerners who, along with their supporters in the oil & gas sector, had the death of the NEP at the top of their agenda. Thus, soon after taking power, the Mulroney government killed the controversial "back-in" provision for oil & gas investment. The NEP was formally abolished when the Western Accord, signed in March 1985, introduced significant deregulation of the oil and gas industry.

Now that the oil & gas sector's major irritants with the previous government had been removed, the Mulroney government saw a chance to give them something that they had longed for: a comprehensive free trade agreement with the United States that would cover oil & gas exports. Obviously there was more to the decision to initiate free trade negotiations than just the wishes of one sector (no matter how economically important), but it is clear that the sector's support was important. So was the advocacy role of Alberta Premier Peter Lougheed who "shore[d] up Mulroney's resolve" on free trade with the United States.[26] Lougheed's successor, Don Getty, also played a role in the negotiation and passage of the Canada-U.S. Free Trade Agreement (CUSFTA).

There were two overwhelming reasons why the oil & gas sector desired a free trade agreement with the United States. The first reason was to prevent any future NEPs. A free trade agreement would bind the hands of future federal governments and allow market forces to prevail in the Canadian oil patch. A second reason was to ensure secure access to the American market. The United States in the early 1980s, in retaliation for the NEP and other Liberal economic nationalist policies, had deployed trade protection instruments like anti-dumping and countervailing duties to Canadian exports. The oil & gas sector wanted a rules-based agreement that would facilitate the flow of energy products across the border.[27]

The Canada-United States Free Trade Agreement included a number of energy provisions: a prohibition on the use of minimum export or import price measures; national treatment on the application of taxes; a recognition of the use of incentives for oil and gas exploration and development; a recognition of existing Canadian ownership requirements; and an exemption for the oil and gas sector in the investment chapter. The most controversial measure was the proportionality clause, whereby any reductions in the amount of energy exports had to be proportional to reductions in domestic consumption. In other words, the United States was given secure access to Canadian oil & gas exports because they could not be arbitrarily cut off.

The Mulroney years saw a significant restructuring of Canada's international economic relations. Not only did they turn back the clock on the Liberals' efforts at economic nationalism, but they went even further by negotiating the CUSFTA and later the North American Free Trade Agreement (NAFTA). Over a hundred years of trade protection with the U.S., dating back to John A. Macdonald's National Policy in the 1870s, ended as Canada took its "leap of faith." It is clear that the oil & gas sector was a major influence in this transition to economic liberalism.

THE FOREIGN POLICY ASPECTS OF CANADIAN NUCLEAR POLICY

The Canadian nuclear sector is made up of crown corporations, private firms, industry organizations, and federal and provincial government departments. Atomic Energy of Canada Limited (AECL), a crown corporation established in 1952, is the leader of the Canadian nuclear industry.

AECL, with around 4,800 employees, is the designer, engineer, distributor, patent holder, and marketer of the CANDU nuclear reactor. The provincial utilities – Ontario Power Generation (previously called Ontario Hydro), Hydro-Québec, and New Brunswick Power – are the owners of the CANDUs operating in Canada. The private sector is also heavily involved in the nuclear industry with over 150 companies including reactor operators (Bruce Power), component suppliers (Babcock and Wilcox, Sulzer Bingham Pumps, Velan Valves), engineering firms (SNC Lavalin and Canatom), uranium mining (Cameco), and medical radioisotope technology (MDS Nordion). The Canadian Nuclear Association is the industry's collective voice, and it is joined by other organizations like the CANDU Owners Group and the Organization of CANDU Industries.

Canada has eighteen operational nuclear reactors that provide about 15 percent of Canada's electricity (and over 50 percent of Ontario's).[28] Most years, the Canadian nuclear industry exports over $1 billion worth of reactor components and technology. This may be a very small percentage of Canada's overall trade, but it is important because the Canadian nuclear industry is in the high tech sector. As former International Trade Minister Michael Wilson once maintained, CANDU exports were a positive influence on Canada's trade balance in "high value-added goods and services" – an area in which Canada continually possesses a trade deficit.[29]

Canada has historically claimed only a small share of the world's nuclear reactor export market at between 10–15 percent.[30] Between 1956 and 1996, Canada has exported nuclear reactors (CANDUs and research reactors) to India, Pakistan, Taiwan, South Korea, Argentina, Romania, and China. Today it has to compete against a handful of giant nuclear firms: Areva (France), Westinghouse (United States-United Kingdom), General Electric-Hitachi (United States-Japan), and Atom-EnergopProm (Russia).

In addition to CANDU exports, Canada is also the world's largest uranium producer, supplying 30 percent of the global demand. However, in terms of proven reserves, Canada is third behind Australia and Kazakhstan. Uranium mining (largely in northern Saskatchewan), refining, and conversion are all done in Canada, but enrichment and reprocessing, required for non-CANDU light water reactors, are done outside of Canada. Like other commodities, there are great fluctuations in the value of Canada's annual uranium exports due to both demand and price. For example, in the 1997–2002 period uranium exports were in the $700–900 million range, but in 2005–2007 they had climbed to between $4–5 billion.[31] Caveats about predicting commodity prices aside, uranium exports are expected to remain high for the foreseeable future for two reasons. First, there is an ongoing global nuclear revival which is leading to more reactors requiring fuel. Second, since the end of the Cold War, there was a surplus of highly enriched uranium from decommissioned American and Soviet nuclear weapons, but it can only meet 13 percent of the global reactor demand.[32]

The international presence of its nuclear industry has given Canada a tool with which to pursue other foreign policy goals. For example, in the absence of nuclear exports, it would have been very difficult for Canada to play an influential role in creating/enhancing the nuclear non-proliferation regime.[33] For example, Canada would not have been one of the permanent members of the IAEA's Board of Governors or one of the seven charter members of the Nuclear Suppliers Group (NSG) if it was not a player in the international nuclear sales game. Not only that, but Canada has used its position as a nuclear exporter within multilateral institutions to pursue its national interests (supporting the indefinite extension of the Nuclear Non-Proliferation Treaty (NPT) in 1995) as well as using it as leverage in bilateral relations (threatening to terminate nuclear cooperation if Argentina and South Korea did not strengthen their nuclear safeguards agreements).

NON-PROLIFERATION OF NUCLEAR WEAPONS

Canada's initiation into the world of the atom was forged in the Manhattan project that developed the atomic bombs that were ultimately used on Hiroshima and Nagasaki. While Canada has never pursued an independent nuclear weapons capability it has, at times, supported the weapons program of its allies. In the late 1940s and early 1950s, Canada's research reactors at Chalk River, Ontario, were used to produce plutonium for American bombs. Uranium exports were also initially used to fuel the nuclear weapons programs of the United States and later Britain. Canada allowed the United States, beginning in 1948, to make over flights of Canadian territory with bombers equipped with nuclear weapons and to store nuclear weapons at its bases in Newfoundland and the Canadian Arctic from 1950 until 1971.[34] Finally, Canada actually took the step of acquiring U.S. nuclear weapons in 1963 and did not fully divest itself until 1984.[35]

Very soon Canada reversed course and began, in 1968, to remove all nuclear weapons from its territory. The process of nuclear weapons removal allowed Pierre Trudeau to give his famous nuclear suffocation speech at the United Nations General Assembly in 1978. On that occasion, Trudeau bragged that Canada was "not only the first country with the capability to produce nuclear weapons that chose not to do so, we are also the first nuclear-armed country to have chosen to divest itself of nuclear weapons."[36] However, Trudeau failed to mention that there were still nuclear weapons in Canada and it would not be until 1984 that Canada was completely free of nuclear weapons. Despite removing U.S. nuclear weapons from its forces and territory, Canada remains firmly under the protection of the American nuclear umbrella and it participates in the nuclear defence of North America through its membership in NATO and NORAD.

Despite the above realities, it is clear that over the years there was a consistent message by Canadian policy makers that nuclear power should be for peaceful purposes only. Despite its experience and expertise with nuclear technology obtained during World War Two, Canada decided that it would not build or acquire its own nuclear weapons. The earliest and most famous public renunciation of nuclear weapons was delivered by the relevant minister, C.D. Howe, in the House of Commons on 5 December 1945: "we have not manufactured atomic bombs, we have no intention of manufacturing atomic bombs."[37] Over time, Canada's official policy came to include two fundamental aspects: 1) promote the evolution of a more effective and comprehensive international non-proliferation regime; and 2) ensure that Canada's nuclear exports did not contribute to nuclear weapons proliferation.

An illustration of Canada's commitment to the non-proliferation of nuclear weapons has been its role in creating and strengthening the international nuclear non-proliferation regime. It did this by participating in the development of the key international organizations that make up the regime: the International Atomic Energy Agency (IAEA), the NPT, and the NSG. It also needs to be said that Canada used its presence in the non-proliferation regime to protect and advance its economic interests in exporting uranium and CANDUs.

The IAEA was formed in 1957 with the twin objective of promoting "the contribution of atomic energy to peace, health and prosperity throughout the world," while, at the same time, ensuring "that assistance provided by it or at its request or under its supervision or control is not used in such a way as to further any military purpose." The first objective would be achieved by fostering "the exchange of scientific and technical information on peaceful uses of atomic energy." The second objective would be achieved through the establishment of a nuclear safeguards system that would ensure that nuclear materials are not diverted from peaceful uses to build nuclear weapons. This safeguard system would include nuclear material accounting reports, containment and surveillance measures, and on-site inspections of individual nuclear facilities.[38] Canada's major role in establishing the IAEA was recognized with a seat on the Board of Governors and W.B. Lewis, a senior nuclear scientist, was appointed to its scientific advisory committee. "Canada has achieved this position," as Bill Bennett, the head of AECL, explained, "largely because of the emphasis which has been placed on fundamental research since the inception of the Chalk River project."[39]

The second pillar of the international nuclear non-proliferation regime was the Nuclear Non-Proliferation Treaty. The NPT, opened for signature in 1968 and ratified in 1970, established two classes of countries: nuclear-weapons states (Britain, China, France, Soviet Union, and the United States: the only countries which had already tested nuclear weapons) and non-nuclear-weapons states (everybody else). The essential bargain contained in the NPT was the inalienable right of the world's non-nuclear-weapons states to develop nuclear energy for peaceful purposes and to have access to the full range of peaceful nuclear technologies. The IAEA was also charged with administering the NPT safeguards regime. NPT safeguards are commonly referred to as full-scope safeguards because they comprehensively covered the entire fuel cycle and all of a country's known nuclear facilities.

Canada, befitting its role in the international nuclear community, played a significant role in the negotiation of the NPT and was an original signatory of the Treaty. Ottawa believed that the NPT was an important step in preventing nuclear war. "The treaty" would "be an important factor in maintaining stability in areas of tension, in creating an atmosphere conducive to nuclear-arms control and generally enhancing international stability."[40] External Affairs Minister Mitchell Sharp, in announcing Canada's ratification of the NPT, stated that "as a leading proponent of the treaty and one of the major 'near-nuclear' signatories, Canada has an opportunity to provide leadership by demonstrating our faith in the non-proliferation treaty."[41] The basis for Canada's support of the NPT was more than just a desire to stop the spread of nuclear weapons. Canada also believed that its commercial interests were being met by the NPT because the treaty would enhance the "development of the nuclear programmes of signatories for legitimate peaceful purposes" and the "international trade in nuclear material and equipment."[42] Thus Canada was linking the NPT to two overarching foreign policy goals: international peace and security and economic prosperity.

In the aftermath of the 1974 Indian nuclear test the third pillar of the international non-proliferation was created: the Nuclear Suppliers Group. The purpose of the NSG was to establish a uniform standard on export controls of nuclear materials. In 1975, the world's major nuclear suppliers (U.S., UK, USSR, France, West Germany, Japan, and Canada) met in London to begin establishing a list of nuclear materials, equipment, and technology whose trade it would restrict. These guidelines were based on the Zangger Committee's (the IAEA's Nuclear Exports Committee) 1974 trigger list that included six major components: complete nuclear reactors, pressure vessels, reactor control rods, fuel reprocessing plants, fuel fabrication plants, and isotope separation equipment.[43] The NSG guidelines also adopted a requirement for physical protection measures, agreement to exercise caution in the transfer of sensitive facilities, technology and weapons-useable materials, and strengthened re-transfer provisions.[44]

Canada's role in shaping the international non-proliferation regime was one way of demonstrating its commitment, the other way was through its own bilateral relations. For example, in 1965 Canada reversed its policy on uranium exports by announcing that, henceforth, "export permits will be granted, or commitments to issue permits will be given, with respect to sales of uranium covered by contracts entered into from now on, only if the uranium is to be used for peaceful purposes."[45] A more important indicator would be Canada's response to blatant violations of the norm against horizontal nuclear proliferation. In particular, how would Canada respond to India's 1974 nuclear weapons test?

On 18 May 1974, India joined the nuclear weapons club with a nuclear test in the Rajasthan desert. Canada felt partially responsible for India's action because the plutonium used in the device had been diverted from a Canadian-built research reactor. In addition, Canada had provided extensive technical transfers and assistance to India's nuclear program during the 1950s and 1960s, assistance that helped to create India's self-sufficiency in nuclear technology. In response, Canada immediately suspended, and then terminated, all nuclear cooperation with India. In announcing the suspension of Canada's nuclear cooperation, External Affairs Minister Mitchell Sharp stated that India's explosion was a direct violation of Canada's policy of nuclear power for peaceful uses only. Sharp maintained that Canada could not be expected to "assist and subsidize, directly or indirectly, a nuclear program which, in a key respect, undermines the position which Canada has for a long time been firmly convinced is best for world peace and security."[46] Canada further implemented its non-proliferation policy by also terminating nuclear cooperation with Pakistan who it feared, correctly, was pursuing the same weapons path as the Indians. The nuclear safeguards agreements for CANDUs in South Korea and Argentina were also renegotiated. Finally, Canada temporarily suspended uranium exports to Japan and the European Community while it renegotiated its safeguards arrangements.[47]

On 22 December 1976, Canada announced a new comprehensive nuclear non-proliferation policy. External Affairs Minister Don Jamieson stated that "shipments to non-nuclear weapon states under future contracts will be restricted to those which ratify the Non-Proliferation

Treaty or otherwise accept international safeguards on their entire nuclear program. It follows from this policy that Canada will terminate nuclear shipments to any non-nuclear weapon state(s) which explode a nuclear device."[48] This was the most stringent policy of any of the nuclear suppliers until the United States matched Canada in 1978. It was not until 1995, at the NPT extension conference, that the rest of the world finally agreed that nuclear exports "should require, as a necessary precondition, acceptance of full-scope Agency safeguards."[49]

There were some immediate benefits to the nuclear non-proliferation regime through Canada's unilateral action. India's civilian nuclear program paid a price for its actions because its two CANDUS "suffered repeated breakdowns due to deficient engineering quality control, a shortage of heavy water that has prevented the units from reaching their design capacity and inefficient operations."[50] India's six MADRAS reactors (often referred to as CANDU-clones) also performed very poorly because of Canadian sanctions. Dhirendra Shama has written that "the Pokharan explosion...led to India's nuclear technological debacle when all external cooperation was withdrawn. The post-Pakharan fall out delayed India's nuclear projects by 10 to 15 years."[51] In the case of Pakistan, its Canadian-built KANUPP power reactor "has been operating at a sharply reduced level due to [the] cutoff in Canadian fuel supplies."[52] The Pakistan Atomic Energy Commission has concluded that KANUPP has been a failure due to factors directly related to the termination of Canadian nuclear cooperation namely "inadequate training of operators" and frequent "equipment failures."[53] Pakistan's nuclear weapons program was also set back. South Korea ratified the NPT in 1976, halted its efforts to acquire a French nuclear reprocessing plant, and had enhanced safeguards placed on its nuclear reactors. Similarly, Argentina was forced to accept enhanced safeguards on its Canadian-made Embalse nuclear reactor.[54]

These successes in the non-proliferation realm involved costs in the commercial realm. The possibility of economic consequences of its nuclear non-proliferation policy had been acknowledged by Ottawa when it announced its tougher policy in 1976. Jamieson had emphasized that Canada was "prepared to accept the commercial consequences of being clearly ahead of other suppliers." This was the price Canada had "to pay to curb the threat to mankind of nuclear proliferation."[55] In fact, Canada did suffer for its heightened concern over nuclear proliferation. Outside of a very problematic sale to Romania, Canada was shut out of the reactor export business until a 1990 sale to South Korea. In several instances, most notably a 1979 effort to sell a second reactor to Argentina, countries refused to purchase a CANDU because of Canada's reputation as an unreliable supplier.[56] Thus, using nuclear exports as a lever for larger foreign policy objectives succeeded, but at the expense of nuclear exports themselves. It is also interesting to note that Canada had significantly less leverage to respond to the 1998 nuclear tests by India and Pakistan because they had no nuclear cooperation with either of them.

ANTI-COMMUNISM

During the height of the Cold War, Canada used its nuclear exports as a tool in the fight against communism. Obviously, Canada would not sell uranium or reactors to a communist state. It would not be until the mid-1970s, during the era of détente, that Canada finally negotiated a nuclear co-operation agreement with a communist country (Romania). However, the larger goal was to prevent non-aligned countries from working with the Soviet Union on nuclear projects. A reactor sale meant a long-term partnership between supplier and recipient, and Canada did not want to see stronger economic or political relations emerge between the Soviet Union and other states, especially vulnerable developing countries. Canadian officials firmly believed that it was better if India acquired "nuclear expertise and facilities through cooperation with countries like Canada than as a result of assistance from the Soviet Union."[57]

During the Cold War, Canada would rather weaken its nuclear safeguards demands than allow the Soviets to use a nuclear reactor to establish closer ties with a developing country. This was most evident in Canada's nuclear cooperation with India in the 1950s and 1960s. For example, during the negotiations over the CIRUS, Canada dropped its demands on the repatriation of irradiated fuel rods despite the fears over the plutonium produced by the reactor. This was because, as Jules Léger, the under-secretary of state for External Affairs, rationalized, "India will acquire a reactor from some source (friendly or otherwise) and will be producing this material."[58] In other words, India was determined that it would acquire nuclear technology without safeguards, so it was better that Canada be the supplier than the Soviet Union.

RELATIONS WITH THE DEVELOPING WORLD

In the post-World War Two period, an important foreign policy goal for Canada was to assist in the economic and political development of the developing world. There are many arguments for Canada to pursue development assistance: reducing global poverty, enhancing Canadian prosperity and security, or advancing global human security.[59] Canada indicated its willingness to assist the developing world by creating the Canadian International Development Agency (CIDA) and participating in a number of multilateral organizations like the World Bank, the United

Nations Development Programme, and the Development Assistance Committee of the Organization of Economic Co-operation Development.

Nuclear technology transfers were viewed as a specific mechanism through which Canada could help assist the developing world. Canada believed that the peaceful benefits of nuclear power should be at the disposal of all states. Many of Canada's early nuclear pioneers accepted that nuclear energy could bring enormous benefits to underdeveloped countries. For instance, W.B. Lewis had long advocated the sharing of nuclear knowledge between the developed and underdeveloped world.[60] Decades later, Prime Minister Pierre Trudeau would reiterate the obligations that Canada had in trying to assist developing countries. In a 1975 speech to the Canadian Nuclear Association entitled *Canada's Obligations as a Nuclear Power,* Trudeau asserted that "it would be unconscionable under any circumstances to deny to the developing countries ... the advantages of the nuclear age ... Technological transfer is one of the few, and one of the most effective, means available to us of helping others to contribute to their own development....Nuclear technology is one of the most certain means of doing so ... The decision taken by Prime Minister St. Laurent to enter a nuclear-assistance program with India was a far-sighted and generous act of statesmanship."[61]

Since the original locus of Canada's foreign assistance was the Commonwealth, India and Pakistan were viewed as logical recipients of Canadian nuclear assistance. J.G. Hadwen, a former Ambassador to Pakistan and High Commissioner to India, noted that the common belief in External Affairs during the 1950s and 1960s was that "Canada, during the war period, had developed considerable expertise in the generation of electricity by nuclear processes. We believed that Canadian technology was the most efficient of the nuclear technologies available. We thought of it as the safest of alternatives and as the one best suited to peaceful generation of electricity."[62]

CLIMATE CHANGE POLICY

Canadian officials have historically been concerned about the possible environmental dangers of nuclear power. This has included radiation, nuclear waste, and reactor safety. Since the 1950s Canada has been a charter member of the United Nations Scientific Committee on the Effects of Atomic Radiation. The earliest high-profile statement on the environmental implications of nuclear power came from Prime Minister Pierre Trudeau. In a 1975 speech to the Canadian Nuclear Association, Trudeau reminded the industry that it had an obligation to provide "safe sources of energy" and to "preserv[e] the environment." This must be done through all of the stages of nuclear power "exploration, mining, processing, fabrication, design, and sales."[63]

The issue of environmental protection has traditionally been viewed as a constraining factor against nuclear exports. However, it is now being argued that nuclear power has some environmental benefits. In particular, the issue of climate change has suddenly made nuclear power appear more environmentally friendly. This is because nuclear power, unlike other conventional energy sources, does not contribute to the major cause of climate change: the emission of greenhouse gases. This fact has naturally led the international and domestic nuclear industry to proclaim that nuclear power is the solution to the problem of climate change. A joint International Atomic Energy Agency-World Nuclear Association study showed that "the planet avoided approximately 600 million tones of carbon emissions in 2000 thanks to the 438 nuclear reactors operating that year."[64] Robert Van Adel, former President of AECL, writes that "in terms of emissions – the key for clean air and climate change – it is worth noting that a typical CANDU plant in a single year avoids the discharge of about five million tonnes of carbon dioxide (greenhouse gas), sulphur dioxide (acid rain) and other key by-products such as particulates, that lead to the creation of smog....Without present-day nuclear capacity, Canada's greenhouse gas levels would be some 15–20% higher."[65]

The Canadian government has also argued that maintaining and enhancing the use of nuclear energy is the best way of achieving the emission targets contained in the Kyoto Protocol. For example, Ralph Goodale, a former minister of Natural Resources, asked rhetorically, "without those zero-emission CANDUs, how would we hope to meet the climate change commitments Canada made in Kyoto?"[66] This is because "a typical nuclear plant of 1 000 Megawatts capacity operating at 80 per cent capacity factor will offset the emission of over 5 million tonnes of CO_2 annually."[67]

Ottawa, based on the fact that Canada is an exporter of uranium and nuclear reactors, has attempted to get the international community to recognize nuclear energy as part of the solution to the problem of climate change. At the Climate Change Conference in Berlin in the fall of 1999, Canada campaigned to have nuclear energy included as part of Kyoto's Clean Development Mechanism (CDM). The CDM allows firms in developed countries to receive emission credits for investing in projects in developing countries that reduce or avoid greenhouse gases. Since countries that plant forests can use this to offset their other emissions, it was believed that building more nuclear plants could be utilized for the same purpose. This led Canada to argue, along with other nuclear proponents like France and Japan, that selling reactors to developing countries should result in emission credits. Nevertheless, this initiative was opposed by a number of European states including Britain, Norway, and Germany, who claimed that it would simply replace the environmental hazard of greenhouse gases with that of nuclear waste. The British Environment Minister argued that "nuclear is not a creator of carbon dioxide but it's not a renewable source of energy in quite the same category as wind or water power."[68]

CONCLUSION

It is apparent from this survey that Canada has attempted to use energy policy as a lever in trying to achieve other foreign policy goals. In the nuclear case, Canada used the existence of its uranium resources and the CANDU to influence the creation/maintenance of the non-nuclear weapons proliferation regime, anti-communism, relations with the developing world, and climate change policy. This case is also useful because it reveals a number of foreign policy tensions residing within Canadian nuclear policy. For example: economic motivations versus proliferation concerns, proliferation concerns versus fears of communism, environmental costs (nuclear safety) versus environmental benefits (addressing climate change).

The oil & gas case is a bit more complex. It has reflected, but at some crucial times influenced, Canada's macroeconomic policies with the United States. In tracing the chronology, we can see that the development of the Canadian oil & gas sector coincided with Canada's macroeconomic policies concerning investment and trade. The first hundred years of Canada saw a desire to attract American investment generally, and the result was the dominance of the Big Four (Shell, Imperial/Exxon, Gulf, Texaco) in the oil & gas sector. The period of economic nationalism in the 1970s and early 1980s had the Canadianization of the oil & gas sector as an explicit goal though FIRA, the creation of Petro-Canada, and the NEP. The third period, during the Mulroney years, saw the rolling back of economic nationalism, with the full encouragement of the oil & gas sector, and its replacement with trade and investment liberalization. The successful completion of the CUSFTA was due, in part, to the strong support of the oil & gas sector (both foreign-owned and Canadian-owned). The oil & gas sector was only one of many groups that supported free trade, but ask yourself this question: if the sector had opposed free trade would oil & gas have been given an exemption from the treaty (as it was in Mexico with NAFTA) or would it have completely derailed the negotiations because the Americans would not have obtained secure access to oil and gas resources? By viewing the influence of the oil & gas sector in this fashion, it is easier to appreciate their impact on free trade.

A bigger question is how effective has the energy tool been? In the nuclear case, Canada was influential. For example, its response to the first Indian nuclear test made it a leader in the non-proliferation realm. However, what is striking is that the 1970s were the high water mark in the influence of the Canadian nuclear level. Since the 1970s, Canadian influence in the non-proliferation regime has been in steady decline.[69] This was also seen in the climate change issue where, despite its lobbying, Canada was unable to get nuclear power accepted as part of Kyoto's CDM.

The oil & gas tool was also quite effective in the 1970s and 1980s. The Trudeau government used Petro-Canada and the NEP to Canadianize the oil & gas sector. The Mulroney government also used the oil & gas tool, by promising secure access to Canadian energy resources, as part of its strategy to get the United States to agree to continental free trade. The United States, as Michael Hart has noted, "had long sought assurances that Canada would be a reliable supplier and not cut supplies arbitrarily."[70] What makes the oil & gas case more unusual than nuclear is that in several other important instances, the oil & gas tool was used by the sector *against* the Canadian government to promote macroeconomic policies that they favoured. For example, the sector greatly influenced both the repeal of the NEP and the decision to negotiate free trade with the United States. This has meant that it is now difficult for Ottawa to use the oil & gas tool because the free trade agreements mandate "national treatment."

What unites the two case studies, and what clearly puts into question Harper's vision of Canada as an energy superpower, is that the capacity to use oil & gas and nuclear as levers in Canadian foreign policy has declined. In the nuclear case it is due to the emergence of new uranium and reactor suppliers, the inability of Canada to stay at the cutting edge of technology, and the lack of human and financial resources dedicated to international organizations. In the oil & gas case, it is due to international agreements which allow market forces to dominant against state intervention.

NOTES

* I would like to thank Annette Hester and Keith Brownsey for their comments on an earlier draft of this chapter.
1 Stephen Harper, "Address by the Prime Minister at the Canada-UK Chamber of Commerce," London, United Kingdom, 14 July 2006. Available at: <http://pm.gc.ca/eng/media.asp?id=1247>
2 Annette Hester, "Canada as an 'Emerging Energy Superpower:' Testing the Case" (Canadian Defence and & Foreign Affairs Institute, 15 October 2007). Available at <http://www.cdfai.org/PDF/CDFAIconference2007.pdf>

3 As a consequence of the delayed entry into confederation of Alberta, Saskatchewan, and Manitoba, the federal government, after significant political lobbying, only transferred control to the prairie provinces in 1930.
4 Christopher J. Kukucha, "Expanded Legitimacy: The Provinces as International Actors," in *Readings in Canadian Foreign Policy: Classic Debates & New Ideas*, Duane Bratt and Christopher J. Kukucha (eds.) (Toronto: Oxford, 2007), 214–30.
5 Canadian Association of Petroleum Producers, *Industry Facts and Figures: Canada*, 2008. Available at <http://www.capp.ca>
6 Keith Brownsey, "The New Oil Order: The Post Staples Paradigm and the Canadian Upstream Oil and Gas Industry," in *Canada's Resource Economy in Transition: The Past, Present, and Future of Canadian Staples Industries*, Michael Howlett and Keith Brownsey (eds.) (Vancouver: Emond Montgomery Publications Limited, 2008), 234–5.
7 Ibid., 237–8.
8 There was also an important discovery in Norman Wells, Northwest Territories.
9 Brownsey, "The New Oil Order," 238.
10 Robert Bothwell, Ian Drummond, and John English, *Canada, 1900–1945* (Toronto: University of Toronto Press, 1987), 218.
11 Earle Gray, *Impact of Oil: The Development of Canada's Oil Resources* (Toronto: McGraw-Hill Ryerson, 1969), 8.
12 Bothwell, Drummand and English, *Canada, 1900–1945*, 353–60.
13 Brownsey, "The New Oil Order," 239; John Richards and Larry Pratt, *Prairie Capitalism: Power and Influence in the New West* (Toronto: McClelland and Stewart, 1979).
14 John N. McDougall, *Drifting Together: The Political Economy of Canada-US Integration* (Peterborough: Broadview, 2006), 103–29.
15 G. Bruce Doern and Glen Toner, *The Politics of Energy: The Development and Implementation of the NEP* (Toronto: Methuen, 1985), 82.
16 Brownsey, "The New Oil Order," 239.
17 James Laxer, *Oil and Gas: Ottawa, the Provinces and the Petroleum Industry* (Toronto: Lorimer, 1983), 8–9.
18 Canada, *Foreign Direct Investment in Canada* (Gray Report) (Ottawa: Information of Canada, 1972).
19 Stephen Clarkson, *Canada and the Reagan Challenge: Crisis and Adjustment 1981–85* (Toronto: Lorimer, 1985), 83.
20 Doern and Toner, *The Politics of Energy*, 91; Laxer, *Oil and Gas*, 52; Brownsey, "The New Oil Order," 242.
21 Clarkson, *Canada and the Reagan Challenge*, 68.
22 Ibid., 68–69.
23 J.L. Granatstein and Robert Bothwell, *Pirouette: Pierre Trudeau and Canadian Foreign Policy* (Toronto: University of Toronto Press, 1990), 320.

24 Steven Kendall Holloway, *Canadian Foreign Policy: Defining the National Interest*, (Peterborough: Broadview, 2006), 165–66.
25 Some of these initiatives included: offering incentives to smaller Canadian companies and created Alberta-owned corporations like Alberta Energy Company (which would later become EnCana).
26 Brian W. Tomlin, "Leaving the Past Behind: The Free Trade Initiative Assessed," in *Readings in Canadian Foreign Policy: Classic Debates & New Ideas*, Duane Bratt and Christopher J. Kukucha (eds.) (Toronto: Oxford, 2007), 293.
27 G. Bruce Doern and Brian W. Tomlin, *Faith and Fear: The Free Trade Story* (Toronto: Stoddart, 1991), 120–5.
28 Sixteen of these reactors are in Ontario and one each in Quebec and New Brunswick. Ontario also has two reactors that are being refurbished. There are proposals for additional reactors in New Brunswick, Ontario, Saskatchewan and Alberta.
29 Michael Wilson, "Address to the Canadian Nuclear Association," *Statement* 92/04, 11 February 1992.
30 This percentage excludes reactors built by domestic firms, ie., Canadian reactors by AECL, French reactors by Areva, etc.
31 Statistics Canada, "Snapshot on uranium: Revival as a viable resource," *The Daily* (14 August 2007). Available at <http://www.statcan.ca/Daily/English/070814/d070814a.htm>
32 World Nuclear Association, *Military Warheads as a Source of Nuclear Fuel*, March 2008. Available at <http://www.world-nuclear.org/info/inf13.html>
33 Duane Bratt, *The Politics of CANDU Exports*, (Toronto: University of Toronto Press, 2006), 170–71; Trevor Findlay, "Canada and the Nuclear Club," in *Canada Among Nations 2007: What Room for Manoeuvre?* Jean Daudelin and Daniel Schwanen (eds.) (Montreal and Kingston: McGill-Queen's University Press, 2008), 216.
34 John Clearwater, *U.S. Nuclear Weapons in Canada* (Toronto: Dundurn, 1999), 12.
35 John Clearwater, *Canadian Nuclear Weapons: The Untold Story of Canada's Cold War Arsenal* (Toronto: Dundurn, 1998), 15.
36 Pierre Elliott Trudeau, "Disarmament: the problem of organizing the world community." Address to the UN Special Session on Disarmament, New York, 16 May 1978, in *Canadian Foreign Policy 1977–1992: Selected Speeches and Documents*, Arthur E. Blanchard (ed.) (Ottawa: Carleton Library Series #183, 1994).
37 Canada, Parliament, House of Commons, *Debates*, 5 December 1945.
38 The IAEA's safeguard system has been extended twice to cover large reactor facilities, reprocessing plants, conversion plants, and fabrication plants. See: IAEA doc. INFCIRC/66/Rev.2.
39 Robert Bothwell, *Nucleus: The History of Atomic Energy of Canada Limited* (Toronto: University of Toronto Press, 1988), 214.

40 Canada, "Nuclear Non-Proliferation Treaty: The Canadian Position," in Arthur E. Blanchette (ed.) *Canadian Foreign Policy 1966–1976: Selected Speeches and Documents* (Ottawa: Carleton University Press, 1968), 18.
41 Canada, Parliament, House of Commons, *Debates*, 19 December 1969.
42 Canada, "Nuclear Non-Proliferation Treaty," 19.
43 IAEA doc. INFCIRC/209, Communication Received from Members Regarding the Export of Nuclear Material and of Certain Categories of Equipment and Other Material (3 September 1974).
44 See: IAEA doc. INFCIRC/254, *Nuclear Suppliers' Group Guidelines for Nuclear Transfers* (21 September 1977). The NSG's guidelines were revised in 1993, see IAEA doc. INFCIRC/254/Rev.1 (July 1993). The revised guidelines included restrictions on dual-use equipment, material and related technology whose transfer its members would restrict through national export legislation. They also agreed to export such items only to states that had either ratified the NPT or had accepted comprehensive IAEA safeguards.
45 Canada, Parliament, House of Commons, *Debates*, 3 June 1965.
46 Barrie Morrison and Donald M. Page, "India's Nuclear Option: the nuclear route to achieve goal as world power," *International Perspectives*, July/August 1974.
47 Bratt, *The Politics of CANDU Exports*, 117–49.
48 Canada, Parliament, House of Commons, *Debates*, 22 December 1976, 2255.
49 Berhanykun Andemicael, Merle Opelz, and Jan Priest, "Measure for measure: The NPT and the road ahead," *IAEA Bulletin*, 37/3 1995.
50 Richard P. Cronin, "Prospects for Nuclear Proliferation in South Asia," *Middle East Journal* (1983), 598.
51 Rodney W. Jones, "India." In *Non-Proliferation: The why and the wherefore*, Jozef Goldblat (ed.) (Stockholm: SIPRI, 1985).
52 Cronin, "Prospects," 600.
53 Zia Mian and A.H. Nayyar, *Pakistan's Chashma Nuclear Power Plant: A Preliminary Study of Some Safety Issues and Estimates of the Consequences of a Severe Accident*, Report No. 321 (Princeton, NJ: Princeton University, Center for Energy and Environmental Studies 1999), 24–5.
54 Bratt, *The Politics of CANDU Exports*, 131–7.
55 Canada, Parliament, House of Commons, *Debates*, 22 December 1976, 2256.
56 Bratt, *The Politics of CANDU Exports*, 155–64.
57 Iris Heidrun Lonergan, *The Negotiations Between Canada and India for the Supply of the N.R.X Nuclear Research Reactor 1955–56: A Case Study in Participatory Internationalism*, Unpublished MA Thesis (Ottawa: Carleton University 1989), 132.
58 Bothwell, *Nucleus*, 353.
59 See Ian Smillie's article in this volume.
60 Ruth Fawcett, *Nuclear Pursuit: The Scientific Biography of Wilfrid Bennett Lewis* (Montreal and Kingston: McGill-Queens University Press 1994), 74.

61 Pierre Trudeau "Canada's Obligations as a Nuclear Power," *Statements and Speeches*, 75/22, 17 June 1975.
62 J.G. Hadwen, "A Foreign Service Officer and Canada's Nuclear Policies." In *Special Trust and Confidence: Envoy Essays in Canadian Diplomacy*, David Reece (ed.) (Ottawa: Carleton University Press 1996), 160.
63 Trudeau, "Canada's Obligations as a Nuclear Power."
64 Hans-Holger Rogner, *Nuclear Power and Climate Change* (Vienna: International Atomic Energy Agency, 2003).
65 Robert Van Adel, *Smog season calls for fresh look at nuclear energy* (Mississauga: Atomic Energy of Canadia Limited, August 2002). Available at <http://www.aecl.ca/images/up-RVA_0208.pdf>
66 Canada, Natural Resources Canada, *Statements and Speeches*, 2001/29, 26 March 2001.
67 Robert Morrison, *Nuclear Energy and Sustainable Development* (Toronto: Canadian Nuclear Association, 2000).
68 Andrew Duffy, "Europeans won't buy CANDU green credit," *The Calgary Herald*, 10 October 1999, A6.
69 Trevor Findlay, "Canada and the Nuclear Club," 215–18.
70 Michael Hart, Bill Dymond and Colin Robertson, *Decision at Midnight: Inside the Canada-US Free-Trade Negotiations* (Vancouver: UBC Press, 1994), 378.

PART THREE
"Geographic" Files

10 A Special Relationship? The Importance of France in Canadian Foreign Policy

JUSTIN MASSIE

Canada surely shares a "special relationship" with both the United States and the United Kingdom. The former rests on the exceptional character of the North American security community, especially given the structural imbalance of power on the continent. The latter, of course, follows from Canada's longstanding constitutional, institutional, demographic, military and commercial ties to the British Empire. The purpose of this chapter is to examine whether Canada shares a similar relationship with its other "mother country," France.

France has often been relegated to Canada's second-tier allies, well behind the pre-eminent place occupied by the United States and Britain. This is certainly justifiable from historical, military, and economic perspectives. The "British connection" as well as Canada's geographic proximity with the U.S. profoundly marked and were indeed central to the development of Canada's foreign and defence policies.[1]

Given these limits, the question addressed in this chapter may seem gratuitously provocative, if not completely unwarranted. After all, the fact is that Gaullist France directly undermined Canada's political integrity by supporting, on several occasions, the separatist movement in Quebec. And France often considered and treated Canada as a mere puppet of the United States. President Giscard d'Estaing opposed, for example, Canada's membership in the Group of Seven industrialized countries (G7) in Rambouillet in 1975, notably on the grounds that Canada was an economic appendage of the United States and that, consequently, a separate representation was unnecessary.[2] Thus, is it reasonable to even consider the possibility that France and Canada share a "special relationship?"

While it is certainly erroneous to assert that the two countries share a close and harmonious relationship, I will argue that, for Ottawa, France indeed represents a truly "special" political and military ally, despite France's episodic hostility towards Canada. The analysis is thus an attempt to move beyond the traditional focus on the Ottawa-Quebec-Paris axis and its well-documented impact on Canadian diplomacy vis-à-vis la Francophonie and foreign aid policy towards French African states.[3] The chapter is divided in three parts. First, the concept of special relationship is briefly discussed to put forth some criteria of specialness. Given the fact that the concept has been used to describe Canada's relations with both the United States and Great Britain, it is assumed that it provides useful analytical tools to assess the importance of other countries in Canadian foreign policy. Second, the logic and determinants underlining the Franco-Canadian relationship are discussed. Two schools of thoughts are identified: the national interest perspective and the European identity perspective. Third, historical empirical evidence is provided to assess France's importance in Canadian strategic thinking. It is argued that if France represents for Canada a "special" ally, it is not because of a shared transatlantic European identity, but rather because of the distinctive interests stemming from Canada's bicultural national identity.

THE SPECIALNESS OF SPECIAL RELATIONSHIPS

The notion of special relationship is under-conceptualized and over-utilized. It generally refers to a uniquely intimate relationship between two states. Thus at different times in history, Germany has been argued to share a special relationship with the United States, Russia, Israel, and France.[4] For its part the U.S. is said to have developed special relationships with Israel, Canada, Germany, China, Mexico, and Japan, in addition, of course, to Britain.[5]

The commonality of the usage of the term "special relationship" may weaken its analytical usefulness to assess the "specialness" of bilateral relationships. But the notion has the advantage of having been examined in great detail by scholars studying, in particular, the Anglo-American relationship. Chief among them is political scientist Alex Danchev. In his *On Specialness*, he identifies ten criteria to help specify specialness.[6] Most of them relate to the *quality* of a bilateral relationship. They are: transparency, informality, generality, reciprocity, exclusivity, clandestinity, reliability, durability, potentiality, and mythicisability. Danchev's list is not only an attempt to "do better" in specifying specialness than historian David Reynolds' two broad categories, quality and importance.[7] Danchev is also keen on stressing the value of quality over importance. "Clearly one can be important – or be considered important – but not special."[8] To be deemed special in Danchev's eyes, bilateral relations should be characterized by exceptional and distinguishing processes of interaction, including exclusive consultation and sensitive information exchange between state leaders.[9]

Yet Danchev's conclusion – the end of the Anglo-American special relationship – is not so much informed by empirical evidence regarding the quality of the relationship as it is by arguments pertaining to its importance, or lack thereof, for each country. Indeed, he argues that "the relationship has been governed by two basic requirements: in the first place, the British ability to deliver; in the second place, the American willingness to defer."[10] In what may be a dated reference (Danchev was writing in the late 1990s), he argued that Britain does not benefit anymore from exclusive consultations with its U.S. ally on international security issues given the absence of common enemies and the decline of Great Britain.[11] In the post-9/11 era, it could be, and has been, argued that the U.S. is willing again to defer, and the U.K. to deliver, viz. the popularity of the "Anglosphere" in the immediate aftermath of the war in Iraq.[12]

To identify specialness, one must thus necessarily assess the importance of a relationship in terms of degree and extent. This explains Danchev's keenness in distinguishing friendship based on utility, pleasure, or goodness. When friendship is founded on mutual usefulness or pleasure, it is impermanent, for it changes according to circumstances.[13] When a state is preoccupied with the welfare of another state, on the other hand, genuine specialness may be argued to exist. This distinction is also made by Abraham Ben-Zvi, who develops a "special relationship paradigm" contrasting with a "national interest paradigm." Contrary to the "cold-eyed geostrategic calculations" implied by the latter, the former is characterized by "goodwill" towards another state, as expressed by "strong and persistent commitment to [in his case, Israel's] continued existence, integrity, and security."[14]

A first measure of specialness is thus the distinction between the "thick" or "thin" variants of specialness. The "thick" variant pertains to affinity and affection, relationships being founded upon shared values, common ethnicity (religion, language), and/or sentimentalities deriving from common ancestry or a sense of collective identity. Canada's relations with Britain and the U.S. are sometimes depicted using such arguments. For example, historian Edward Kohn claims that "Canadians and Americans referred to each other as 'cousins' or 'brothers' who shared the common 'mother' of Great Britain" in the late nineteenth and early twentieth century.[15] There are indeed, according to Martin Wright, "associations between powers that seem to be deeper than formal alliances, to be based on affinity and tradition as much as interest, to be not so much utilitarian as natural."[16]

The "thin" variant of specialness rests upon such utilitarian, interest-driven relations. U.S. Secretary of State Dean Acheson pointed out to this form of special relationship when he asserted to a British-American parliamentary group in June 1952: "I shall not bother you by doing what is done so often on occasions like this, of talking about all that we have in common: language, history, and all that. We know all that. What I wish to stress is one thing we have in common, one desperately important thing, and that is we have a common fate." A common fate entails common security interests in defeating or containing a mutual enemy. It does not arise naturally from a sense of collective identity, but requires constant nurturing and renegotiation.[17] Eschewing the collective-identity thesis, Danchev hence proposes that the Anglo-American connection was largely the product of the Second World War, forging what some have called the "pax anti-Germanica," and later the "pax anti-Sovietica." No sentimental attachments were involved or any existential sense of community.

Reinterpreting Danchev's criteria in light of this discussion, I propose five criteria to assess specialness between states. First is the depth of the relationship, that is, the identity- or interest-based motivations underlying the foreign policy of a state towards another. Whereas interest-based relations tend to be impermanent, identity-based ones tend to persist in the absence of material benefits. Second is exceptionality. To be deemed special, a relationship must embody properties which are not replicated with another state. In other words, the relationship must be exceptional in character. A third measure is the scope of the links between the two states, e.g. economic, military, cultural, etc. The greater the interdependence, the more special a relationship may be argued to be. Fourth is durability. The longer the relationship endures – across generations and various political alignments – the stronger it is. Fifth is reciprocity, that is, the extent and degree of the mutuality of the specialness of the relationship. This measurement will not be fully examined, for it would necessitate an analysis of the Franco-Canadian relationship from a French perspective as well. What follows is rather an historical examination of France's importance in Canadian foreign policy according to the first four criteria – depth, exceptionality, scope, and durability.

THE DETERMINANTS OF THE RELATIONSHIP

The scholarly literature on Franco-Canadian relations is mostly silent on the criteria discussed above. This is partly the product of the popularity of two related themes. On the one hand, many have examined Quebec-France relations, usually described as "direct and privileged," and hence have argued that the latter are more genuine or natural than Canada-France relations.[18] Some have even asserted that "Québec entretient de meilleures relations avec la France en tant qu'entité subétatique que le

Canada n'en a avec la Grande-Bretagne en tant que pays!"[19] On the other hand, Canada-Europe rather than Canada-France relations have received most of Canadian foreign policy analysts' attention, especially in the post-Cold War era.[20]

Notwithstanding the periodic bitterness of the bilateral relationship, the complexity of Franco-Canadian relations suggests it is worthwhile to assess the importance of France in Canadian foreign policy. Both Louis St. Laurent and Brian Mulroney, at very different times in history, referred to France as one of Canada's traditional allies.[21] Scholars have, for their part, developed two contending schools of thought regarding the nature of France's (or more accurately Europe's) importance in Canadian foreign policy. These two approaches broadly reflect the differences between the "thick" and "thin" variants of special relationships.

The National Interest Perspective

The first viewpoint may be called the national interest perspective. In his attempt to delineate Canada's national interests, political scientist Steven Kendall Holloway put forth five defining elements: national security, political autonomy, national unity, economic prosperity, and the projection of identity.[22] In each of these domains, France is seen as having some significance for Canadian foreign policy. In other words, it is held that France has been an important Canadian ally because of its *utility* in achieving Canada's core national objectives.

In terms of national security, France and Canada have shared common enemies for more than a century. To use Danchev's expression, both countries were part of the "Pax anti-Germanica," and later defended common security interests notably against Communism and radical Islamic militants through the UN, NATO or coalitions of states. Therefore, in some sense France and Canada have shared a "common fate," to use Acheson's expression, since at least the Great War. However, it does not follow that Canada "used" France's power and status to further its own national security objectives. In fact, regarding the defence against external threats, Canada has contributed more to the security of France than vice-versa, as the thousands of Canadian soldiers' graves in France solemnly attest. Furthermore, some hoped that NATO would lead to the creation of a transatlantic institutional framework which would prevent further U.S. infringement of Canadian sovereignty and help "multilateralize" the (imbalanced) Canada-U.S. bilateral defence of North America. As is well known today, such attempts never materialized and were, most importantly, never actively sought by Canadian authorities.[23]

Proponents of the national interest (or utilitarian) perspective have thus focused less on security-related arguments and more on two other dimensions: independence and national unity. Regarding the former, it has become almost commonsensical in Canadian foreign policy analysis to use the concept of counterweight to account for a policy Canada has pursued to gain greater political independence. Speaking in 1957 on Canadian-American relations, Frank Underhill asserted that Canada's "survival" as a "distinct individual Canadian entity" was secured mainly thanks to its "balancing" strategy "in a triangle of forces in which Britain is at one corner and the United States at the other corner of the triangle. (…) We had to make sure that we were included [in the triangle], that is, that the relationship was in the nature of a triangle. Otherwise we should have remained an insignificant dependent colony of Britain or become an insignificant dependent satellite of the United States." But in 1940, according to Underhill, with the growing cultural, economic, and military dependence on the United States, "the British corner of the [North Atlantic] triangle is no longer weighty enough. We must do something to add weight in that corner." The balancing of "our historic connection with Britain against" the United States became insufficient to the survival of Canada as an independent political entity.[24]

The best place to look, thought Underhill, was Western Europe, where Canada could find the "new balance which will be needed to make the North Atlantic triangle work … well for us in this new American century." According to many, Ottawa did so by joining the North Atlantic Alliance, which "served to satisfy an instinctive Canadian desire to secure a balancing mechanism against her preponderant U.S. neighbour."[25] Now, it is worth recalling that, for Canadian officials in 1948, "Western Europe" meant primarily France and Great Britain. Indeed the then newly-appointed secretary of state for external affairs, Lester Pearson, believed that to "be associated with our two mother countries, Britain and France, with our neighbour, the United States … and with Germany … seemed to me to be both a Canadian and an international objective worthy of every effort." It would help Canada "escape the dangers of too exclusively continental relationship with our neighbour without forfeiting the political and economic advantages of that inevitable and vitally important association."[26] This belief in France and Great Britain as the two primary European pillars of Canada's counterweight strategy through NATO was shared by Escott Reid, for whom "the farther the North Atlantic Community moved towards political and economic unification the more protection it would give Canada from the power of the United States. We believed that the more developed the constitutional structure of the Community became the more the power of the United States would be restrained by the influence of its allies, especially Britain and France."[27]

From a utilitarian perspective, Canada's relationship with France (and Great Britain) in the late 1940s was thus vital for two primary international security goals. The first was to "contain" or "restrain" the U.S., that is, to prevent it from adopting too aggressive policies towards the Soviet Union. Second, France and Britain were hoped to help "securing recognition of Canadian independence, identity, and influence, all of which have been regarded as being in peril if Canadian defence policy were to rest exclusively on a North American pillar."[28] It is thus not surprising that Canada's diplomatic efforts during the negotiations leading up to the creation of NATO concentrated on trying to prevent it from becoming a solely military alliance (by trying to make it, instead, a *community* strengthened by economic, political, as well as cultural bonds) and emphasized the shared obligations and control over policy. Only an institutionalized, rule-governed, and cohesive West would allow Canada to exert some influence, or at least participate in, matters of high politics.

The counterweight metaphor is also used to characterize Canada's economic relations with France. Commercial relations with Europe more generally are indeed often argued to be in the service of Ottawa's political ends. Pierre Trudeau's Third Option policy, which notably led to the 1976 Canada-Europe Framework Agreement, was followed decades later by Jean Chrétien and Stephen Harper's interest in the establishment of transatlantic free trade (TAFTA), despite (or perhaps because of) the federal government's incapacity to turn around the long-term relative decline of transatlantic economic relations (see below). Regardless of the continentalist orientation of their respective national economies, Canada and France share a common interest in shaping an international order conducive to free(er) trade.[29] For Ottawa, the utility of TAFTA is mainly political: "L'objectif réel du Canada en proposant des négociations commerciales transatlantiques était de rappeler aux autres, et à nous-mêmes, que nous avons un rôle à jouer, que nous ne vivons pas complètement dans l'ombre des États-Unis."[30] The appearance of political independence, in other words, was and remains the primary objective of Canada's economic diversification policy.

Advocates of the national interest perspective have also argued that Canada's inclination towards fostering closer ties with France rests on the imperative of maintaining national unity – that is, harmony between Québécois and English Canadians within the federation. This is not to say that they are oblivious to the fact that General de Gaulle and some of his successors have deliberately attacked Canadian integrity by supporting Quebec's sovereignist movement. On the contrary, the underlying motivation behind de Gaulle's actions represents the chief incentive for the Canadian government to cultivate greater cooperation with France. The late diplomat Eldon Black described the Canadian government's basic assumptions regarding its relationship with France as follows:

[T]he federal government and certain provinces would be continuing their long-range policy of ensuring that French-speaking Canadians would have the same opportunity as their English-speaking compatriots to participate actively in the life of the country. The French policy of support for French-speaking Canada was likely to continue, though in a more restrained and reasonable fashion, accepting normal international practice, after De Gaulle had left the scene. Therefore Canada would, for many years, have a *special relationship* with France. No matter how cordial or frigid diplomatic relations might be at any given time, this particular relationship was likely to remain a constant in Canadian policy.[31]

These are the terms of what Black calls Canada's "business as usual" policy towards France. The enduring specialness of the relationship is thus founded upon an exceptional fact: Canada is the only non-European country where a population of French origin has preserved its language and culture. Therefore, because of the country's bicultural character, both Québécois and English Canadians must believe that the federal government is a legitimate representative and defender of their culture at home as well as abroad. Accordingly, Ottawa has to promote Franco-Canadian cooperation on the basis of a shared interest in advancing Francophone culture and interests on the international scene. This logic led to the triangular rivalry between Paris, Ottawa, and Quebec regarding diplomatic relations with and foreign assistance to French-speaking African states.[32] This externalization of Canada's bicultural character was, in turn, expected to thwart the province's sovereignist aspirations as well as its ambition towards establishing a distinct international personality.

Because the province of Quebec has not sought greater powers in matters of exclusive federal jurisdictions such as national defence, the externalization of Canada's bicultural character might not be excepted in this domain. To argue that it has, as some have, one must depart from a purely utilitarian perspective and invoke the effects of national identity on the conception of Canadian national interests.

The Collective Identity Perspective

Holloway's fifth dimension of the national interest, the projection of identity, suggests the existence of a "thicker" transatlantic connection than that entailed by utilitarian self-interests. Indeed, the projection of a self-image implies the externalization of national attributes abroad.[33] This is precisely what some have argued to be at the foundation of Canada's relationship with Europe and hence with France: the Europeaness of Canada's national identity.

Transnational collective identity refers to the cognitive identification of at least two sociopolitical entities to a common Self; that is, the merger of the Self and the Other into a single, overarching collective Self.[34] The factors accounting for this process are several: collective identities may be founded upon perceptions of geographic proximity, familiarity, similarity (e.g. ethnicity), collective memory (shared historical narratives), social recognition (by members of the in-group), common threats, and/or idea convergence (such as shared values and attitudes).[35] Because none of these factors automatically generate collective identities, the latter tend to vary in degree of profundity.[36] Language or culture is different from, yet may form the basis of, the necessarily affective character of collective identity, the latter being discernible when actors "define the welfare of the Other as part of the Self."[37]

The case of Canada is particularly interesting for it is composed of (at least) two potentially contending national languages, cultures, and historical narratives. To explain Canada's peculiar attachment to Europe, scholars and political elites have invoked ethnicity, political values and culture, as well as history as the primary foundations of Canada's "Europeaness." As Kim Richard Nossal put it:

Certainly the idea of Canada as a European nation did not suddenly originate with the acceleration of Anglo-American cooperation after the fall of Western Europe in May 1940; it had been deeply rooted in Canadian self-perception and political practice from the country's initial settlement and the defining decision of the 1770s not to follow the United States into independence. The vast majority of those living in the northern half of North America had always felt the transatlantic ties of birth, family, national origin, politico-cultural inspiration, commercial intercourse, and even, it has been argued, psychological dependence.[38]

Yet what Nossal and many others invoking the transatlantic connection usually have in mind is the ethnic or emotional link between English Canada and Great Britain.[39] This leads Nossal to assert that, with fewer blood ties and the decline of the British Empire, the transatlantic connection faded during the interwar period and was only revived and expanded in the 1940s based on a "hard-headed" redefinition of the national interest: the security of North America was henceforth tightly bound to that of Western Europe.[40] Indeed, common threats – Nazi Germany and later the Soviet Union – led to the expansion of the "realm" needing to be defended and induced Canadians to identify with the "West" rather than with the British Empire.[41]

Nonetheless, France enjoyed then and arguably still enjoys a special status among West European states for Canada, precisely because of ethnic and emotional ties. To be sure, the transatlantic French connection was never perceived as powerful as that linking English Canadians to Britain until the Second World War; most English Canadians were of British origin and indeed shared a collective identity with their mother country.[42] The French connection, mainly confined to French-speaking Quebec and based on fewer blood ties (see below), was certainly not as "thick" as the British connection, but still mattered to French Canadians' "collective psychology."[43] Historian Armand Yvon distinguished between the era of "sentiment" (1830–1880) and that of "critique" (1880–1914), the latter emerging with the strong negative reactions to an increasingly anti-clerical France under the Third Republic.[44] Thus on the eve of war in 1939, poet Robert Chouette described as follows the sentiment of solidarity towards France amongst French Canadians:

Mais fidélité à qui? À la France? Et fidélité voulue, consciente, éclairée? Fidélité de l'esprit? Non. Mes éducateurs ont cru sage de construire des brises-larmes; la pensée française contemporaine s'éteint sur mes rives en molle écume. Fidélité à la vieille France? À la France idéalisée dont parlent mes chansons, mes contes et mes légendes? Oui. Donc, fidélité aveugle, fidélité du sang.[45]

In this perspective of transatlantic solidarity towards Catholic Old France, the following declaration made in Ottawa by General de Gaulle in July 1944 may have been intended to revive the French connection between Francophones across the Atlantic:

[L]a France est – à mon avis et à l'avis de la France – dans un état d'esprit vis-à-vis du Vatican, vis-à-vis du Saint-Père et vis-à-vis de la religion, qui implique le plus tôt possible des relations normales entre le Vatican et mon pays. (...) La France a une très grande position de puissance catholique, elle la gardera et elle désire naturellement entretenir avec le Saint-Père les relations.[46]

The emphasis on Catholicism was also present in the reformulation of Canadian foreign policy in the immediate postwar era. Three years after De Gaulle's declaration, in his articulation of the basic principles of Canadian foreign policy, Secretary of State for External Affairs Louis St. Laurent mentioned the need to "protect and nurture" the values of the Christian civilization. He added that Canada had "always believed in the greatness of France" and that the two countries undoubtedly had "similar objects in world affairs."[47] French Prime Minister René Pleven argued the same during his visit to Ottawa in February 1951, noting "the remarkable extent to which French and Canadian views coincided on the most important world problems."[48]

Liberal-democratic values were also central to Franco-Canadian cultural commonalities. The visit of French President Vincent Auriol to Ottawa in April 1951 is a telling example. Auriol remarked to Prime Minister St. Laurent that he had kept "le souvenir de vos origines [françaises]" and that he perpetuated "cette civilisation chrétienne et humaine que la France fut la première à vous apporter." St. Laurent replied the next day that while Canada and France shared deep ethnocultural and historical ties, and were indeed "hereditary friends," the links uniting them were not exclusive: "le Canada, comme la France et la Grande-Bretagne, a aussi des idéaux héréditaires, la tradition de la liberté, de la démocratie, du respect du droit et de la raison dans les rapports internationaux."[49]

Proponents of Canada's Europeaness have similarly argued that Canada's "underlying political and social values are ultimately European-derived ones: peace, order, and good government, constituted authority, political community, individual liberty, and citizen equality."[50] Diplomat Jeremy Kinsman adds that Canada's "value system is the legacy of the Enlightenment which spread from France in the 18th century to become our bedrock faith, a global asset, and our best protection."[51] This has, according to political scientist Philip Resnick, concrete influence on Canadian foreign policy: "... the result has been to align Canada more closely with Europeans. The fact that we are now dealing with a post-imperial Europe makes it considerably easier for Canadians than it might have been true at the time of the Algerian War or the Suez Crisis."[52] Canada's inclination to support the promotion of democracy and human rights abroad represents, in other words, the concrete manifestation of a community of liberal values with France, "post-imperial" France that is.[53]

Others have suggested, along the lines of the Self/Other duality, that anti-Americanism, particularly salient amongst French Quebecers since 9/11, may constitute the basis for a Franco-Canadian common identity.[54] For example, commenting on Canada's refusal to take part in the war against Iraq, political scientist Louis Bélanger claimed that two main factors were decisive: the Liberal Party's anti-American nationalism, as well as Quebec's access to and consumption of French media (via the Agence France-Presse for example). Both of these factors do not amount to a "thick" collective identity however. While French-speaking Quebecers may have been influenced by French interpretations of U.S. motives, Bélanger acknowledges that opponents to the war in Quebec never invoked the French position to justify their own opposition.[55] Indeed, political mobilization in the wake of Quebec's provincial election may better explain Quebecers' historic opposition to the war than the existence of a Franco-Quebec epistemic community.[56]

Nevertheless, anti-Americanism remains for some a feature of Canada's political culture and thus may shed some light on the apparent similarity of their international interests. According to Resnick, "... both English Canadians and Québécois have reasons to look to Europe as a source of civilizational support in their attempt to shore up their continued existence. (...) Europe represents ... a cultural and political counter-model for both Canada and Quebec in the age of the American Empire."[57] Former ambassador Marie Bernard-Meunier agrees and notes some of the values which are said to distinguish Canadians/Europeans from Americans. These include "American culture of individualism versus that of European solidarity ... accumulation of wealth versus quality of life, unconstrained economic growth versus sustainable development, property rights versus human rights and nature rights, and unilateral exercise of power versus global cooperation." She claims that these diverging values partly explain the similarity of Canadian and European foreign policy views on such issues as the International Criminal Court, the Responsibility to Protect and, more generally, the "shared commitment to an effective multilateral system."[58]

FRANCE'S IMPORTANCE IN CANADIAN FOREIGN POLICY

While the alleged existence of a transatlantic identity founded on common values is not restricted to Canada and France, as it includes other West European states, the primary determinants of the relationship are nevertheless argued to be stronger than what advocates of the utilitarian perspective are ready to acknowledge. These determinants include shared historical narratives, common threats to the values and culture both states cherish, as well as a common identity referent: (imperial) America. The national interest perspective, on the other hand, claims that it is Canada's search for an international status as an independent and influential state which, together with the need to maintain national unity, best explains its relationship with France. One way to determine which of these interpretations best describes the importance of France for Canada is to assess them in respect of four criteria of specialness: the exceptionality, depth, scope, and durability of the relationship.

The Economic Dimension

The scope of the Franco-Canadian relationship is undoubtedly narrow. Table 1 illustrates the slight importance France has for the Canadian economy since the end of the Cold War. Even before then, although a major trading nation, Canada's exports to France never reached one per cent of its total value of exports, while its imports from France never accounted for two percent of its total imports. Historically speaking, this trend is as old as modern Canada. Jacques Prévost and Jean Vinant reported the same one and two percent barriers in their survey of Franco-Canadian trade between, respectively, 1875–1930 and 1955–1983. The former noted that Wilfrid Laurier's enthusiasm for a commercial entente with France in 1893 was merely an electoral strategy aimed at acquiring French-Canadian votes. Vinant, for his part, attributes the weakness of commercial relations to the non-complementarity of the two countries' economies as well as to the concentration of French trade and investments in Quebec and, more modestly, in Ontario.[59]

Table 1
Canadian International Trade[60]

	Canadian Exports (%)			Canadian Imports (%)		
	US	France	UK	US	France	UK
1992	77,18	0,89	1,92	65,17	1,82	2,77
1993	80,34	0,70	1,59	66,99	1,34	2,63
1994	81,22	0,62	1,48	67,75	1,24	2,48
1995	79,21	0,75	1,48	66,81	1,39	2,43
1996	80,91	0,64	1,46	67,49	1,46	2,54
1997	81,82	0,56	1,30	67,56	1,88	2,38
1998	84,76	0,53	1,39	68,23	1,64	2,12
1999	86,68	0,53	1,36	67,28	1,66	2,53
2000	86,95	0,46	1,39	64,33	1,17	3,65
2001	87,05	0,54	1,25	63,62	1,61	3,42
2002	87,13	0,51	1,12	62,61	1,68	2,79
2003	85,73	0,57	1,60	60,64	1,51	2,74
2004	84,44	0,58	1,88	58,72	1,50	2,71
2005	83,85	0,58	1,89	56,50	1,31	2,74
2006	81,60	0,65	2,30	54,87	1,31	2,74
2007	79,04	0,69	2,84	54,21	1,25	2,82
Average	82,99	0,61	1,64	63,30	1,49	2,72

The Canadian government has nevertheless shown an almost invariable concern over maintaining or improving economic relations with France. For instance, between 1944 and 1947, nearly half of Canadian credits to postwar recovery under the *Export Credit Insurance Act* were allocated to France ($242.2 millions), Canada's greatest aid recipient after Britain. Canadian postwar prosperity rested on the restoration of a multilateral trading system, and hence on the economic recovery of Great Britain and France. But in the immediate aftermath of the war, humanitarian concerns were also involved in this special interest towards France.[61]

Some decades later, confronted by President Nixon's unilateral import surcharges and in response to Britain's new economic relationship with the European Community, the Trudeau government opted for the "Third Option" and began a series of visits to European capitals starting with France, the most reluctant to agree to Canadian objectives. With the support of Germany (which feared Canadian military disengagement in Europe), the Canada-Europe Framework Agreement was signed in 1976. One would expect disenchantment in Ottawa following the limited success of the agreement (as compared with the 1989 Free Trade Agreement for example, see Table 1). This failure was notably due to Europe's inability to sign a preferential trade agreement with Canada under GATT, its preference for a U.S.-Europe accord, as well as from the fact that many in France considered Canada's economy as merely an economic appendage of the U.S. (viz. President Giscard d'Estaing's opposition to Canada's membership at the G-7). Nonetheless, the Mulroney, Chrétien, and Harper governments all maintained some efforts to improve the Canada-France commercial relationship, which notably led to the 1990 Transatlantic Declaration, the establishment of the Canada-France Joint Economic Commission in 1994, the 1996 Declaration of Enhanced Partnership, and to the 2006 France-Canada Joint Action Plan. Minister of Foreign Affairs and International Trade David Emerson agreed in June 2008 to another Joint Action Plan aimed at "deepening" and "broadening" Franco-Canadian commercial relations, with the medium-term objective of establishing a "closer economic partnership between Canada and the European Union."[62]

The greatest successes of Franco-Canadian economic relations are in terms of direct investments. Table 2 illustrates the relatively little but still significant French investments in Canada and Canadian investments in France since 1987. These numbers demonstrate the qualified success of sustained Franco-Canadian efforts aimed at increasing investments in each other's country. French investments in Canada more than sextupled in 2000, from $6.6 to $36.9 billions, whereas Canadian investments in France nearly tripled in 2003, from $4.5 to $11.7 billions. This is, of course, much less than the Canada-U.S. investment relation, as Table 2 shows. Yet France represented in 2006 Canada's third largest foreign investor, contributing to 6.5% of all foreign direct investment in Canada. In turn, 3.2% of all Canadian foreign direct investment went to France, placing it fifth worldwide.[63] And interestingly, between 2000 and 2004, France invested more than the United Kingdom in Canada. While we cannot infer that these recent successes are the direct result of the new bilateral agreements between the two countries, we can certainly conclude from the statistical record that the importance of Franco-Canadian investments is growing significantly. We may also suggest that genuine economic interests motivate continued Canadian efforts to foster greater trade and investments in both countries, rather than the longstanding identity-related interest in economic diversification.

National economic prosperity should constitute Canada's primary motivation towards developing better economic relations with any prosperous country. Yet the scholarly literature suggests that it is

Table 2
Direct Investment Stock (in millions)[64]

	Foreign Direct Investment in Canada			Canadian Direct Investment Abroad		
	US	France	UK	US	France	UK
1987	74 022	1 860	12 401	48 876	585	7 341
1988	76 049	2 213	15 696	51 025	1 770	11 085
1989	80 427	3 521	15 556	56 578	1 770	11 085
1990	84 089	3 836	17 185	60 049	1 745	13 527
1991	86 396	4 167	16 224	63 379	1 719	15 262
1992	88 161	4 151	16 799	64 502	1 900	12 271
1993	90 600	4 365	15 872	67 677	1 801	12 907
1994	102 629	5 326	14 693	77 987	1 753	15 038
1995	112 948	5 710	14 097	84 562	2 516	16 412
1996	121 943	5 861	14 292	93 939	3 542	17 825
1997	128 978	6 087	15 748	110 707	3 760	22 722
1998	146 893	6 411	17 042	133 267	3 854	24 956
1999	176 045	6 624	15 279	–	–	–
2000	193 651	36 997	23 955	177 943	4 642	35 170
2001	219 927	31 477	26 913	188 481	3 834	39 682
2002	231 566	31 631	27 552	199 992	4 552	40 749
2003	238 057	36 200	26 002	169 605	11 772	43 902
2004	246 792	33 419	26 298	198 877	14 623	44 330
2005	258 997	28 355	30 026	204 604	14 509	48 893
2006	273 705	29 505	39 012	223 623	16 939	58 992

mostly political objectives that motivate Ottawa's sustained efforts towards economic diversification. Indeed the counterweight argument is commonly put forward to explain Canada's interest in establishing a transatlantic free trade area.[65] What is mostly unacknowledged, however, is that the counterweight argument implies that the quality of the Canada-France or Canada-Europe economic relationship is determined by the state of Canada's economic relation with the United States. It also implies that the Canadian government should seek to establish a Canada-EU counterpoise to the U.S. Neither of these implications is supported by the evidence of a longstanding Canadian desire towards diversification, despite the meager and very recent positive results (at least in the case of France).[66] Furthermore, it stretches credibility to think that the Harper government seeks a European "balance" to Washington by promoting free trade between Canada and Europe.

Nevertheless, the persisting fear of being left in limbo between the U.S. and Europe and the consequent enduring interest in establishing and being (independently and noticeably) part of an Atlantic community suggest that there is more to the transatlantic project for Canada than only material benefits. Three identity-based interests seem in fact to characterize France-Canada relations: (1) promoting transatlantic unity (versus balancing the U.S.), (2) avoiding political marginalization by Washington and Brussels, and (3) "federalizing" the French connection between Francophones on both sides of the Atlantic. The sociopolitical and military dimensions of the Franco-Canadian relationship tend to support this interpretation.

The Sociopolitical and Military Dimensions

Although Canada "was born in French," to use Prime Minister Harper's words,[67] it was undoubtedly British until the first half of the 20th century. In terms of ethnic origin, on every census from 1871 to 1931 a majority (between 61 and 51 percent) of Canadians reported their ancestors being from Britain, contrasting to approximately 30 percent who stated having French ethnic roots.[68] Both perceived transatlantic ethnic belongings have sustained slow but constant erosion. In 2006 for example, only 35 percent of Canadians linked their origin to Great Britain, compared with 16 percent to France, 10 percent to Germany, and 32 percent to Canada, the latter category having finally been incorporated to the list of choices in 1996.[69] Immigration did not compensate for this fading sense of shared ethnicity. Table 2 illustrates the comparatively little importance French immigrants represent for Canada's multicultural society. Between 1955 and 2005, the proportion of French immigrants has never reached three percent of Canada's total immigration.

These figures notwithstanding, Canada's sense of national identity remains strikingly European, at least according to Bernard-Meunier:

Within a generation, a majority of Canadians may well come from all other regions of the world, yet this is not to say that our European roots will become irrelevant. Our institutions, our political culture, and both of our official languages have come from Europe, helping to forge our national character. The big break-away from Europe that the American Revolution represents in the United States never happened here and accordingly our

Table 37°
Immigrants to Canada by country of last permanent residence, 1955–2005

	Total immigrants	Europe		Great Britain		France		United States		Asia	
1955	109 946	90 771	82,56%	30 420	27,67%	2 869	2,61%	10 395	9,45%	3 662	3,33%
1960	104 111	82 706	79,44%	20 384	19,58%	2 944	2,83%	11 247	10,80%	4 218	4,05%
1965	146 758	107 816	73,47%	40 718	27,74%	5 225	3,56%	15 143	10,32%	11 684	7,96%
1970	147 713	75 328	51,00%	27 620	18,70%	4 410	2,99%	24 424	16,53%	21 451	14,52%
1975	187 881	72 898	38,80%	36 076	19,20%	3 891	2,07%	20 155	10,73%	47 382	25,22%
1980	143 498	41 277	28,76%	18 976	13,22%	1 905	1,33%	9 953	6,94%	71 793	50,03%
1985	84 339	18 868	22,37%	4 721	5,60%	1 401	1,66%	6 672	7,91%	38 614	45,78%
1990	216 424	52 457	24,24%	9 092	4,20%	2 615	1,21%	6 147	2,84%	112 902	52,17%
1995	212 875	41 300	19,40%	6 393	3,00%	3 890	1,83%	5 173	2,43%	129 435	60,80%
2000	227 429	42 963	18,89%	4 825	2,12%	4 349	1,91%	5 833	2,56%	140 178	61,64%
2005	262 239	40 909	15,60%	6 109	2,33%	5 430	2,07%	9 262	3,53%	159 968	61,00%

views on domestic as well as on foreign policy issues remain quite close to those of Europeans to this day.[71]

However, this European character was essentially British in origin. Despite the French Fact – amounting to about one third of the population's perceived ethnic origin – most English Canadians conceived their country in the first half of the 20th century as a homogenously English-speaking nation part of the great British Empire. Their sense of "we" excluded "those not bred and raised in its [British] culture." Many French Canadians, on the other hand, viewed their culture as French and Catholic, and conceived their country as a bilingual association of two distinct nations, hence the prevailing idea of two founding nations in Quebec.[72] From this assumption, French Canadians insisted that the federal government acknowledge the country's bicultural character, favoured greater political autonomy vis-à-vis London, but refrained from similar emotional attachment to their own "mother country" – France having long "abandoned" the 65,000 French Canadians in North America to their own lot. In short, "French Canadians tended to define their foreign policy interests primarily as unhyphenated Canadians,"[73] that is, in contrast to English Canadians who perceived theirs as essentially British. As French-Canadian nationalist Henri Bourassa asserted: "Nous Canadiens-Français, nous n'appartenons qu'à un pays, le Canada."[74]

From this lack of "Europeaness" amongst French Canadians followed the existence of two uniculturalist conceptions of Canadian foreign policy interests, one being essentially British, the other Catholic.[75] Three hundred more French Canadians fought for the pope against Garibaldian forces in Italy than the two hundred who took part in Canada's military intervention in South Africa in 1899–1902.[76] During the First World War, few French Canadians were moved by the peril of their mother land. "Indeed," observes historian Charles Stacey, "the Third Republic's action in 1905, when it abrogated the concordat with the Papacy made by Napoleon I, had considerably widened the [transatlantic] gap. Many admirable Roman Catholic priests in Quebec saw the war of 1914 as a divine chastisement visited upon godless France."[77]

As a result of the Conscription crisis of 1917, the interwar period saw greater consideration of French Canadian views in the formulation of Canada's foreign policy, viz. "national unity Prime Minister" Mackenzie King's so-called "isolationist" policy.[78] Yet for French Canadian nationalist Lionel Groulx, this was far from enough. Quebecers had little influence on foreign policy decision making for, he complained, the Canadian government pledged allegiance to Britain in September 1939 in spite of French Canadians' reluctance, having no other "patrie" than Canada.[79] However, John MacFarlane's well documented analysis of Ernest Lapointe's influence on Canadian foreign policy decision making unwittingly casts doubt on the alleged lack of collective identification between Quebec and France during the interwar period. He makes the case that through Lapointe – the pre-eminent French-Canadian political leader at the time – French Canadians' ambivalent feelings towards France were significantly taken into consideration in King's foreign policy decisions.[80]

Prime minister King echoed most English Canadians' sentiment that if Britain was at war Canada had to stand at its side, although he sought to avoid any unnecessary confrontation.[81] In francophone Quebec, however, the threat to North America seemed remote, and there was thus limited support for what was seen as a British imperialist war. As the leader of the short-lived *Bloc populaire canadien* during the war, André Laurendeau, later put it: "Pourquoi le Canada était-il en guerre? Parce que l'Angleterre était en guerre, et uniquement pour cela. [...] Imaginez une guerre franco-russe ou franco-polonaise contre la même Allemagne et le même Hitler: il est sûr que le Canada restait neutre; peut-être le serait-il demeuré même si les Américains s'étaient joints aux Français."[82]

Ottawa reacted similarly to the fall of France in June 1940 as it did in 1927 regarding the League of Nations. At that time, Ernest Lapointe believed Canada should adopt a more internationalist and independent foreign policy by seeking a seat at the League's Council. French Canadian newspapers in Quebec were also in favour of a representation, which would, they contended, help preserve peace and avoid entanglements in European affairs, as well as assert Canada's autonomy vis-à-vis London. Interestingly, however, Prime Minister King rejected the idea on the grounds that having a Canadian representative on the Council might generate divisions in the country because of French Canadians' "pro-French leanings."[83] Similarly, in 1940, King opposed the notion that London should use force against French ships or territory controlled by Maréchal Pétain. It would be "folly," he believed, "for any ships of Canada starting firing on a French ship." Both King and Lapointe agreed that "a declaration of war against France would have serious repercussions in Canada ... [since the] Vichy government was still the government of France," and was so recognized by Ottawa. The Canadian government thus opposed any action that might impair relations with France, including the (failed) attempt to install de Gaulle in Dakar. Ottawa's position eased only when it became clear that Pétain was collaborating with Nazi Germany beyond the terms of the armistice treaty.[84] Again, French Canada's pro- (Vichy) France leanings had a decisive impact on Canadian foreign policy as a result of national unity considerations.

The immediate after-war period witnessed an increased "bi-culturalization" of Canadian foreign policy as a result of a gradual process of

"Canadianization" of Canada's national identity. Issues such as the adoption of a national flag, a Canadian citizenship, and a national anthem were driven by a resurgent bicultural nationalism aimed at ensuring harmony between the two solitudes. As future Liberal cabinet minister Fernand Rinfret stated in 1946: "We must teach to all Canadians that their country as a matter of fact and reality is a bicultural and bilingual one."[85] This process of "education" led to a redefinition of Canada's national interests, including the need, St. Laurent asserted in 1949, for "complete recognition of Canada's nationhood and the development of all aspects of the country's national life."[86] Ottawa felt the need to build a national spirit legitimate in the eyes of both French and English Canadians.

As a result, France enjoyed great consideration in the formulation of Canadian foreign policy. For instance, the Canadian government hoped that, by supporting France's accession to a permanent position at the UN Security Council, it would in return benefit from Paris' support for Canada's bid for greater influence via the functional principle and its recognition as a middle power. After all, de Gaulle had signalled his approval of the idea during his visit to Ottawa in July 1944.[87] Ottawa thus repeated its attachment to France, pushed for, particularly in London and against U.S. opposition, the official recognition at the UN of the *Comité français de la Libération nationale* and later the *Gouvernement provisoire de la République française* (GPRF), as well as defended Canada's "intérêt particulier au rétablissement rapide de la France dans son rang de grande puissance au sein du concert des nations."[88]

France's importance was also discernible in Canadian foreign policy concerns during the creation of NATO. As mentioned above, Lester Pearson's Atlantic vision involved the establishment of transatlantic community to meet the ideological and military threat posed by the Soviet Union. This meant avoiding both twin-pillared and purely English-speaking alliance formulas, Ottawa rejecting the idea of reducing its status to either a North American or Anglo-Saxon country. Prime Minister St. Laurent explained in these words his decision to withdraw Canada's objection to the inclusion of Algeria (adamantly sought by Paris) in the alliance: "Algeria was not a matter of great importance, in relation to the main purpose of the Treaty, but France was essential."[89] Indeed, "s'il nous fallait entrer dans une association de tireur avec le géant," explained former diplomat John W. Holmes, "nous voulions que nos deux mères, la Grande-Bretagne et la France, en fassent partie aussi."[90] But despite this generally favourable position towards France, no signs of close cooperation between the two countries emanated from the transatlantic negotiations. In other words, while there is evidence of France having significant importance for Canadian foreign policy interests, the quality or extent of the relationship remained relatively thin.

Canada's second main preoccupation, the establishment of "more than a military alliance" – meaning political and economic unification through the development of an Atlantic community – was only partially shared by Paris. But Ottawa's insistence was, Pearson admitted, mainly "political. We did not think that the Canadian people, especially in Quebec, would whole-heartedly take on far-reaching external commitments if they were exclusively military in character."[91] In other words, it seems that the Canadian government sought greater transatlantic union in part because of Quebecers' anti-militarism, not because of the latter's rediscovered attachment to Europe. The other determining factor was the widespread belief in Ottawa that the best strategy to preserve peace resided in adding "moral strength" to the combined economic and military power of the North Atlantic allies. In Prime Minister St. Laurent's words:

The best guarantee of peace today is the creation and preservation by the nations of the free world, under the leadership of Great Britain, the United States, and France, of an overwhelming preponderance of force over any adversary or possible combination of adversaries. This force must not be only military; it must be moral. [...] This treaty is to be far more than an old-fashioned military alliance. It is based on the common belief of the north Atlantic nations in the value and virtues of our democratic Christian civilization."[92]

In light of this, the anti-American counterweight argument loses pertinence in accounting for Franco-Canadian relations. As Harald von Riekhoff notes: "From a strictly Canadian point of view, the alliance had the advantage of combining within one single framework the power on which she depended most strongly with the two European nations with whom she maintained special historical, cultural, and in the case of Britain, also economic ties."[93] NATO was thus not conceived as a mechanism directed *against* the preponderance of the United States (as a balancing strategy implies), but as an organization aimed at securing and institutionalizing America's security guarantee to Europe (an objective shared with Paris) under a single power structure. The importance of France seems to have rested primarily on the domestic and international legitimacy it conferred to the military alliance.

In other words, the best determinant of Canada's relations with France does not seem to rest in the state of its relationship with the United States, nor in a sense of common European identity, but in the identity-based foundations of Canada's national interests, as Sokolsky argued (see above). One may see in St. Laurent's speeches on the creation of the "democratic alliance" the germ of a transnational collective identity based on shared "democratic Christian" values and beliefs.[94] There are, however, two problems with this collective identity argument. First, Canada did not conceive itself as more or less European than North American—based on which of the two continents mostly shared its values and beliefs—but as a truly Atlantic nation. Second, it is hard not to see in the speeches made by St. Laurent and Pearson a compromise between two uniculturalist visions of foreign policy interests in the form of a bicultural, pan-Canadian national interest. If this is the case, one should expect Canada's relations with France to be conditioned by the significance of the French Fact in the definition of Canada's national identity (explaining the continued importance of the relationship), as well as being subject to the influence of political developments in Quebec (explaining the fluctuations in the quality of the relationship). National unity considerations would thus primarily explain the persisting importance of France in Canadian foreign policy, the concept being defined broadly as to mean a general tendency to maintain domestic legitimacy, albeit combined with episodic reactions to Gaullist France's attacks on Canada's territorial integrity.

This is in effect what appears to characterize Franco-Canadian political and military relations since the 1940s. On the one hand, the periodic tensions in the Ottawa-Paris-Quebec triangular relations have been well documented. Suffice it to recall some major ups and downs in the Franco-Canadian diplomatic and political relationship. As late as April 1960, before the burst of the Quiet Revolution in Quebec, de Gaulle expressed his country's highest "interest, sympathy, and trust" in Canada, as well as his conviction that "les Français se sentent d'accord avec les Canadiens quant à la manière de voir et de traiter les problèmes de notre temps."[95] Seven years later, de Gaulle was to compare Canada to Nazi Germany and support the independence of Quebec, which he now believed was inevitable.[96] After the political resignation and death of the General, the normalization of Franco-Canadians relations followed, with France's emblematic and ambivalent "ni-ni" policy (*non ingérence, non indifférence*) regarding Quebec's international aspirations. But it took the departure of Pierre Trudeau and Valéry Giscard d'Estaing to refurbish the relationship. Prime Minister Brian Mulroney enthusiastically stated during President Mitterrand's historical visit to Canada in May 1987: "Today we turn a new page in the history of the relationship between France and Canada. We cannot change the past, but we can shape our future. What matters is the chapter we write together." The French President's reply concluded with a politically loaded "Vive le Canada!"[97] These words marked the formalization of the Franco-Canadian political rapprochement.

Yet with the possible secession of Quebec looming again following the failed Meech Lake Accord, France's relationship with Quebec took precedence over that with Ottawa. It was evident for French decision makers that if the Yes camp won a majority of votes in the 1995 referendum, France would have to support the independence of Quebec following Premier Jacques Parizeau's expected declaration of independence. "I will recognize a fact," President Chirac asserted on CNN on 23 October 1995.[98] A decade later, commentators attributed President Sarkozy's intent to "re-equilibrate" the triangular relationship to the weakness of the support for sovereignty in Quebec. Speaking on a day honouring the 63rd anniversary of the end of the Second World War in Europe, the French President affirmed: "You know, we are very close to Quebec, but I want to tell you, we also love Canada very much. Our two friendships, our two loyalties don't oppose each other. We will take them and turn towards the future so the future of Canada and France becomes the future of two countries that are not only allies, but two friends."[99] A few days later, he clarified his position by saying that Quebecers were France's "brothers" while Canadians were its "friends."[100]

On the other hand, despite these different qualifiers and the variations in intensity of the Franco-Canadian relationship, Ottawa pursued a foreign policy attempting to reflect the country's bicultural character. The implication of this has been that France enjoyed great importance in the formulation of Canadian foreign policy. This was the case years before the Quiet Revolution and the development of Quebec's "relations particulières" with France. Yet these two situations gave rise to Trudeau's special interest to la Francophonie, with increased foreign aid allocated to French-speaking African states.[101] Chrétien, for his part, responded to the threat of Quebec separatism in the mid-1990s by making more diplomatic visits to France than to any other country (including the U.S.) during his 1993–97 mandate, an unprecedented event in Canadian history.[102]

There have been major divergences between the two countries before Quebec's quest for an international personality. This was particularly the case vis-à-vis France's colonial wars in Algeria and its attack on Egypt in 1956, when France sought to protect its stockholders and suspected Nasser of arming Algerian insurgents. Accused of betrayal (of Britain, not of France), Prime Minister Pearson took pains to defend his position: he clarified that Canada had never criticized the purposes and motives behind the Anglo-French military intervention, that it had sought to find a face-saving exit strategy for its two mother countries, and that it believed that reuniting the alliance between the United States, the United Kingdom and France was "essential for peace and security of the free world."[103] As Peter Lyon aptly put it, Canada "helped to get Britain and France off their self-impaled hooks."[104]

Thus there is more to Canada's relationship with France than reactions to France's meddling in domestic affairs and attempts to thwart Quebec's paradiplomacy. Preserving transatlantic unity was not only essential to international peace, it was vital for national unity. After France's withdrawal from NATO's integrated military command structure in 1966, former diplomat John Holmes expressed the fear that it might trigger divergences amongst Canadians.

> Ce qui est vrai, toutefois, c'est que nous serions toujours mal à l'aise si nous nous confondions avec un camp qui serait hostile à l'une ou l'autre de ces trois puissances [les États-Unis, la Grande-Bretagne et la France]. Il y a eu, au Canada, peu de divergences d'opinion [depuis la Seconde Guerre mondiale] sur la politique étrangère où les francophones et les anglophones se soient affrontés. [...] Il ne sera pas facile, toutefois, de maintenir l'accord sur la politique étrangère parmi les deux cultures canadiennes s'il y a faille dans le monde entre les États francophones et Anglo-Saxons.[105]

National unity and transatlantic solidarity were thus perceived as being inextricably linked in Canada's conception of the country's national interest. A few examples are worth mentioning briefly. Lester Pearson refused to publicly criticize France's colonial policy vis-à-vis Tunisia, Morocco and Algeria fearing it might contribute to a greater withdrawal from NATO. Despite anti-colonial rhetoric, Ottawa quietly supported militarily the French colonial war in Indochina by diverting some of its mutual aid assistance to South Asia.[106] Because of domestic politics, Prime Minister Diefenbaker and President de Gaulle shared a similar vision of NATO in the later 1950s and early 1960s: both men sought to "s'affranchir de la tutelle américaine, à avoir les coudées plus franches au sein de l'alliance occidentale," while continuing to rely on it for the defence of their country.[107]

In the years following the collapse of the Soviet Union and the end of the Cold War's strategic imperatives, the trend continued. At first, analysts worried that Canada had "succumbed to the dumbbell" by withdrawing its forces from Europe, a fear akin to that felt when the Trudeau government cut in half Canada's military contingent stationed in Europe.[108] Many feared the continentalization of defence in Europe and in North America, as well as the consequent undesirable prospect of "an exclusive dialogue with the giant neighbour."[109] As it turns out, Canada pursued its Atlanticist international security policy by sending troops alongside its European and American allies to help maintain peace at Europe's doorstep in Croatia, Bosnia, and Kosovo. The ethnic conflicts in the Balkans (and in Africa) unexpectedly proved the continued necessity of close transatlantic cooperation for the maintenance of international peace and security.

France and Canada also refused, in part because of major domestic hostility, to take part in the U.S.-led military intervention against Iraq

(2003). Ottawa and Paris shared the view that Washington ought to avoid a *logique de guerre* and achieve its goals peacefully. But the Canadian government was prepared, admitted Prime Minister Chrétien's senior policy advisor, Eddie Goldenberg, to act similarly as it did during the first Gulf War and in Kosovo; that is, had President Chirac supported (or abstained from threatening to veto) the use of force against Saddam Hussein in March 2003, Ottawa would most likely have backed the intervention.[110] As David Haglund put it, "Canada adopted a position more in keeping with longstanding tradition, one boiling down to 'intervention if necessary, but not necessarily intervention.'" This position was "so closely aligned with France's as to become virtually identical with it."[111]

Today, Canada's two "parent countries," the United States and other allies are fighting an insurgency in Afghanistan. Canada's presence is the product of resolute diplomatic efforts to first take part to the conflict and second to "NATOize" the mission. Indeed, Canada succeeded in securing a military role in the International Security Assistance Force (ISAF) in February 2002 (in addition to its 2001 naval, air force, and special forces' contribution) despite opposition from European states, including France. Ottawa would indeed have preferred to contribute to the European-led ISAF in Kabul, but in face of European resistance, the Chrétien government ended up almost "begging" Washington to take part to the U.S.-led Operation Enduring Freedom.[112] Canada thus managed to avoid political and strategic marginalization and became the fourth largest military contributor to OEF after the U.S., the U.K., and France.[113] A year later, Canada had to convince a reluctant French ally to allow NATO to take over the ISAF mission.[114] Furthermore, the Harper government made significant efforts to convince Paris to increase its military contingent in Afghanistan and to redeploy its forces in Kandahar. This would indeed have helped Ottawa in its attempt to "sell" the mission in Quebec according to some. "Obtenir l'appui de la France, un pays réputé pour ses missions de paix, aurait permis au gouvernement conservateur de briser la perception tenace chez plusieurs Canadiens que la guerre en Afghanistan est avant tout une opération américaine."[115]

This interpretation, echoing a shared sense of anti-Americanism across the Atlantic, was shared by editorialist Bernard Descôteaux: "L'enjeu pour Stephen Harper portait sur une question d'image. Que le Canada et les États-Unis se retrouvent côte à côte sur le même champ de bataille ne pourra que renforcer la perception d'une trop grande proximité avec le président George W. Bush, que les Canadiens reprochent à leur premier ministre. Dans le climat préélectoral qui prévaut à Ottawa, travailler avec les Français aurait été préférable."[116]

France's decision to send an additional battle group to eastern Afghanistan (rather than Kandahar, as some Canadians would have preferred) was interpreted by the French press either as a sign of welcomed rapprochement between France and the U.S. (and only marginally with Canada), or negatively depicted as the result of Nicolas Sarkozy's "*obsession atlantiste.*"[117] Nonetheless, the French President's decision was considered by former Canadian ambassador to France, Jacques Roy, as another sign of the ever closer relationship between the two countries.[118] The perceived domestic and international legitimacy conferred by greater (yet not closer) Franco-Canadian cooperation in matters of international security tends to support the claim that France continues to be of significant importance to the conduct of Canadian foreign policy, despite the very asymmetrical nature of this importance.

CONCLUSION

Does Canada share a special relationship with France? While we can only provide a tentative answer to this question, having not examined the relationship from a French perspective, we can confidently conclude that France represents a special ally for Ottawa. The reciprocity of the specialness of the relationship may be seriously questioned, as the G7 incident and French support of sovereignist movement in Quebec tend to illustrate. It nevertheless seems that, regarding the four criteria examined here, there is evidence of specialness from the Canadian point of view.

In terms of exceptionality, the presence of the French Fact in North America is unquestionably a unique phenomenon. It seems doubtful that in the absence of a French-speaking national minority in Canada, the latter would have entertained similar relations with France. However, regarding the depth of the relationship, the existence of a transatlantic collective identity between Francophones across the Atlantic is only marginally supported by the evidence examined in this chapter. It rather seems plausible to conclude that the French Fact contributes to the definition of Canadian national interests, and hence helps explain the importance of France in Canadian foreign policy. These interests are, however, greater than mere utilitarian or material benefits. In involuntarily contributing to Canada's quest towards international legitimacy – a status of independent and influential ally within a cohesive Atlantic alliance, as well as a need of domestic legitimacy, that is, representation of Quebec's (and English Canada's) strategic interests (despite the ambivalence of Quebec-France relations in matters of high politics) – France has been perceived by Canadian political authorities as a special ally and friend.

The specialness is certainly narrow in scope. Interestingly, it is in matters of international security that the two countries seem to share most common interests. It must be noted however that despite being a trading partner of slight importance to Canada's economy, France has become in the last years a significant investor in the country. Identity-based (in contrast to material-based) interests nonetheless seem to better explain the persistence of France's importance to Canada's foreign policy. This is so because of a deep conviction in Ottawa that transatlantic unity is directly linked to national unity. More specifically, in the early 1940s, a redefinition of Canadian foreign policy interests has occurred which has led to the idea that maintaining solidarity between France, the United States and Great Britain – what may be termed Canada's Atlanticist international security – was essential to achieving international security, Canada's international status as an independent and influential state, as well as domestic harmony, decades before the Quiet Revolution and the threat of secessionism in Quebec. This situation seems to explain why France has been conceived as a strategically important ally to Canada, but has not benefited from close, intimate relations of the kind usually characterized by the notion of special relationship. We can therefore conclude by quoting Eldon Black, according to whom "Canada will continue to have a close and special relationship with France and the Francophone world," for this is "without doubt in Canada's national interest."[119]

NOTES

1 The dominance of the geopolitical metaphor of the North Atlantic Triangle illustrates this point. See John Bartlet Brebner, *North Atlantic Triangle: The Interplay of Canada, the United States, and Great Britain* (Toronto: McClelland & Stewart, 1958 [1945]); Charles P. Stacey, *Mackenzie King and the Atlantic Triangle* (Toronto: Macmillan, 1976); David G. Haglund, *The North Atlantic Triangle Revisited: Canadian Grand Strategy at Century's End* (Toronto: Canadian Institute of International Affairs and Irwin Publishing, 2000); and Hector Mackenzie, "Delineating the North Atlantic Triangle: The Second World War and its Aftermath," *The Round Table* 95:383 (January 2006): 101–12.
2 Kim Richard Nossal, *The Politics of Canadian Foreign Policy*, 3rd ed. (Scarborough: Prentice Hall [1985] 1997), 197.
3 See for example Jean-Philippe Thérien, "Le Canada et la coopération multilatérale francophone," in Claude Basset (ed.), *La politique étrangère canadienne dans un ordre international en mutation: Une volonté de se démarquer?* (Québec: CQRI, 1992): 99–130; and Robin S. Gendron, *Canada's Relations with and French Africa* (Montreal & Kingston: McGill-Queen's University Press, 2006).

4 See Hans W. Gatzke, *Germany and the United States: A Special Relationship?* (Cambridge: Harvard University Press, 1980); Alexander Rahr, "Germany and Russia: A Special Relationship," *The Washington Quarterly* 30:2 (Spring 2007: 137–45); Lily Gardner Feldman, *The Special Relationship between West-Germany and Israel* (Boston, 1984); and Peter Schmidt, "The Special Franco-German Security Relationship in the 1990s," EU-ISS *Chaillot Paper 8* (June 1993).

5 See for example Michael H. Hunt, *The Making of a Special Relationship: The United States and China to 1914* (New York: Columbia University Press, 1983); and Yaacov Bar-Siman-Tov, "The United States and Israel since 1948: A 'Special Relationship'?," *Diplomatic History* 22:2 (Spring 1998): 231–62.

6 Alex Danchev, *On Specialness: Essays in Anglo-American Relations* (New York: St. Martin's Press, 1998).

7 David Reynolds, "A 'Special Relationship'? America, Britain and the International Order Since the Second World War," *International Affairs* 62, no. 1 (Winter 1985–1986): 1–20.

8 Danchev, *On Specialness*, 7–8.

9 Ibid., 12 and 28.

10 Ibid., 162.

11 Ibid., 160–3.

12 See David G. Haglund, "Relating to the Anglosphere: Canada, 'Culture,' and the Question of Military Intervention," *Journal of Transatlantic Studies* 3 (Autumn 2005): 179–98; Lawrence M. Mead, "Why Anglos Lead," *The National Interest* 82 (Winter 2005–6): 124–31; Douglas Stuart, "NATO's Anglosphere Option: Closing the Distance between Mars and Venus," *International Journal* 60 (Winter 2004–5): 171–87.

13 Danchev, *On Specialness*, 157.

14 Abraham Ben-Zvi, *The United States and Israel: The Limits of the Special Relationship* (New York: Columbia University Press, 1993), 24.

15 Edward P. Kohn, *The Kindred People: Canadian-American Relations and the Anglo-Saxon Idea, 1895–1903* (Montréal & Kingston: McGill-Queen's University Press, 2004), 7.

16 Cited in Ben-Zvi, *The United States and Israel*, 24.

17 Danchev, *On Specialness*, 2–3.

18 In addition to the works cited in this chapter, see Éric Amyot, *Le Québec entre Pétain et de Gaulle: Vichy, la France et les Canadiens français, 1940–1945* (Montréal: Fides, 1999); Louis Bélanger, "The Domestic Politics of Quebec's Quest for External Distinctiveness," *The American Review of Canadian Studies* 32 (Summer 2002): 195–214; Frédéric Bastien, *Le poids de la coopération: le rapport France-Québec* (Montréal : Québec Amérique, 2006).

19 Kim Richard Nossal, Stéphane Roussel and Stéphane Paquin, *Politique internationale et défense au Canada et au Québec* (Montréal : Presses de l'Université de Montréal, 2007).

20 See Karen Wittman (ed.), "Canada and the New Europe: Political, Economic and Security Dimensions," *CDSS Occasional Paper* 21 (Winnipeg: University of Manitoba, Centre for Defence and Security Studies, 1993); Leon Brittan, "Relations Between the European Union and Canada in a Transatlantic Context," *Canadian Foreign Policy* 3 (Winter 1995): 113–8; Jocelyn Coulon, "L'option multilatérale affichée," *International Journal* 50 (Fall 1995): 738–42; Paul Buteux, "The Common Foreign and Security Policy of the European Union: Implications for Canada," *Canadian Foreign Policy* 5 (Fall 1997): 129–41; John G. H. Halstead, "Trudeau and Europe: Reflections of a Foreign Policy Adviser," *Journal of European Integration* 12, no. 1 (Fall 1998): 37–50; Evan H. Potter, *Transatlantic Partners: Canadian Approaches to the European Union* (Montréal & Kingston: McGill-Queen's University Press, 1999); Michel Fortmann and Hélène Viau, "Le Canada et la Politique européenne de sécurité et de défense (PESD): une politique à la croisée des chemins," *Revue internationale et stratégique* 44 (2001): 41–52; Frédéric Mérand, "Les nouvelles relations transatlantiques en matière de défense : Quel rôle pour le Canada?," *Canadian Foreign Policy* 12 (2005): 33–45.

21 Louis St. Laurent, "The Foundations of Canadian Foreign Policy in World Affairs," 13 January 1947, in R.A. Mackay (ed.), *Canadian Foreign Policy 1945–1954, Selected Speeches and Documents* (Toronto: McClelland & Stewart, 1971), 296; John Kirton, "Managing Canadian Foreign Policy," in Brian W. Tomlin et Maureen Molot (eds), *Canada Among Nations, 1984: A Time of Transition* (Toronto: Oxford University Press, 1985), 22–3.

22 Steven Kendall Holloway, *Canadian Foreign Policy: Defining the National Interest* (Toronto: Broadview Press, 2006).

23 John W. Holmes, *Canada: A Middle-Aged Power* (Toronto: McClelland & Stewart, 1976): 128–9; David G. Haglund and Stéphane Roussel, "Escott Reid, the North Atlantic Treaty, and Canadian Strategic Culture," in Greg Donaghy and Stéphane Roussel (eds), *Escott Reid: Diplomat and Scholar* (Montréal: McGill-Queen's University Press, 2004), 44–66.

24 Frank H. Underhill, *In Search of Canadian Liberalism* (Toronto: Macmillan, 1960), 256–60.

25 Harald von Riekhoff, "To Stay or Not to Stay," in Stephen Clarkson (ed.), *An Independent Foreign Policy for Canada?* (Toronto: McClelland & Stewart, 1968), 167. See also Peter Lyon, "The Quest for Counterweight: Canada, Britain, and the EEC," *International Perspectives* (March/April 1972): 26–31; Tom Keating, *Canada and World Order: The Multilateralist Tradition in Canadian Foreign Policy*, 2nd ed. (Don Mills: Oxford University Press, 2002): 13; Paul Létourneau, "Les motivations originales du Canada lors de la création de l'OTAN (1948–1950)," in Paul Létourneau (ed.), *Le Canada et l'OTAN après 40 ans, 1949–1989* (Québec: CQRI, 1992), 49; and Roy Rempel, *Counterweights: The Failure of Canada's German and European Policy, 1955–1995* (Montreal: McGill-Queen's University Press, 1996), 3–4.

26 John A. Munro and Alex I. Inglis (eds.), *Mike: The Memoirs of the Right Honourable Lester B. Pearson, vol. 2, 1948–1957* (New York: Quadrangle, 1973), 32 and 52.
27 Escott Reid, "The Creation of North Atlantic Alliance, 1948–1949," in J.L. Granatstein (ed.), *Canadian Foreign Policy: Historical Readings*, Revised Edition (Toronto: Copp Clark Pitman, 1993), 210.
28 Joel J. Sokolsky, "Canada, the United States and NATO: A Tale of Two Pillars," in Michael K. Hawes and Joel J. Sokolsky (eds.), *North American Perspectives on European Security* (Lewiston: Edwin Mellen Press, 1990), 213–15.
29 It should be noted however that France's commitment to free trade – especially in agriculture – is less than total.
30 Robert Wolfe, "Vers l'ALETA? Le libre-échange transatlantique et la politique étrangère canadienne," *Études internationales* 27, no. 2 (Juin 1996): 380.
31 Eldon Black, *Direct Intervention: Canada-France Relations, 1967–1974* (Ottawa: Carleton University Press, 1996), 59. Emphasis added.
32 See Gendron, *Canada's Relations with France and French Africa*.
33 Holloway under-conceptualizes the notion of national interest. He claims that the projection of identity covers everything from domestic legitimacy to principled behaviour based on ideology or religion, in addition to international legitimacy, recognition, prestige, and influence. However, seeking an international status or greater influence through middlepowermanship, for example, is quite different from externalizing the bicultural (or multicultural) character of the country. See Holloway, *Canadian Foreign Policy*, 15.
34 The most obvious example is the existence of an overarching collective European identity (a common Self) encompassing (previously very antagonistic) French and German national identities among others.
35 On the concept of collective/social identity, see John C. Turner, *Rediscovering the Social Group: A Self-Categorization Theory* (New York: Basil Blackwell, 1987); Dominic Abrams and Michael Hogg (eds.), *Social Identity Theory: Constructive and Critical Advances* (New York: Springer-Verlag, 1990); and Iver B. Neumann, *Uses of the Other: "The East" in European Identity Formation* (Minneapolis: University of Minnesota Press, 1999).
36 As they are social constructs, collective identities require human agency to exist; that is, they need to be articulated, nurtured, and institutionalized, and may thus vary according to each of these processes.
37 Alexander Wendt, *Social Theory of International Politics* (Cambridge: Cambridge University Press, 1999), 228.
38 Kim Richard Nossal, "A European Nation? The Life and Times of Atlanticism in Canada," in John English and Norman Hillmer (eds.), *Making a Difference? Canada's Foreign Policy in a Changing World Order* (Toronto: Lester Publishing, 1992), 81.
39 See for example John Bartlet Brebner, *North Atlantic Triangle: The Interplay of Canada, the United States and Great Britain* (New York: Columbia University Press, 1945 [1966]), 325.

40 Nossal, "A European Nation," 82–3.
41 Kim Richard Nossal, "Defending the 'Realm': Canadian Strategic Culture Revisited," *International Journal* 59 (Summer 2004): 503–20.
42 Anthony D. Smith, *Nationalism: Theory, Ideology, History* (Cambridge: Polity Press, 2001), 13.
43 Claude Galarneau, *La France devant l'opinion canadienne, 1760–1815* (Québec: Presses de l'Université Laval, 1970), 348.
44 Armand Yvon, *Le Canada français vu de France (1830–1914)* (Québec: Presses de l'Université Laval, 1975). See also Yvan Lamonde, *Allégeances et dépendances: l'histoire d'une ambivalence identitaire* (Québec: Nota Bene, 2001), 149.
45 Quoted in Pierre Savard, "Les Canadiens français et la France de la 'cession' à la 'révolution tranquille'," in Paul Painchaud (ed.), *Le Canada et le Québec sur la scène internationale* (Montréal : Presses de l'Université du Québec, 1977), 481.
46 Quoted in Prévost, 378.
47 St. Laurent, "The Foundations of Canadian Foreign Policy in World Affairs," 392 and 396.
48 Documents on Canadian External Relations (DCER), vol. 18 (6 February 1951), 890.
49 As quoted in Thomas J. Watson, *Liberté, égalité, fraternité: Une narration de la visite de M. Vincent Auriol, président de la République française, aux États-Unis d'Amérique et au Dominion du Canada* (New York : IBM, 1951).
50 Philip Resnick, *The European Roots of Canadian Identity* (Peterborough: Broadview Press, 2005), 61.
51 Jeremy Kinsman, "Transatlanticism: Is Europe 'Old Hat'?" *Behind the Headlines* 55:3 (May 1998): 13.
52 Resnick, *The European Roots of Canadian Identity*, 70.
53 France's post-imperialism is highly debatable. See for example Bruno Charbonneau, *France and the New Imperialism: Security Policy in Sub-Saharan Africa* (Aldershot: Ashgate, 2008). Also, Canada's liberalism could be argued to reflect that of Anglo-America as well.
54 For a critical discussion, see David G. Haglund, "French connection? Québec and anti-Americanism in the transatlantic community," *Journal of Transatlantic Studies* 6, no.1 (April 2008): 79–99.
55 Savinien de Rivet, « Entretien avec Louis Bélanger: Le Canada et les États-Unis, » *Outre-terre* 5 (2003–4) : 117–20.
56 Donald Barry, "Chrétien, Bush, and the War in Iraq," *American Review of Canadian Studies* 35 (Summer 2005): 225.
57 Resnick, *The European Roots of Canadian Identity*, 87–8.
58 Marie Bernard-Meunier, "Did You Say Europe? How Canada Ignores Europe and Why That Is Wrong," in Andrew F. Cooper and Dane Rowlands (eds.), *Canada Among Nations 2006: Minorities and Priorities* (Montreal & Kingston: McGill-Queen's University Press, 2006), 111–12.

59 Jean Vinant, *De Jacques Cartier à Péchiney: histoire de la coopération économique franco-canadienne* (Paris: Chotard & Associés, 1985).
60 Canada, *Trade Data Online* (Ottawa: Industry Canada, consulted 15 May 2008).
61 Robert A. Spencer, *Canada in World Affairs: From UN to NATO, 1946–1949* (Toronto: Oxford University Press, 1959), 197–8.
62 Foreign Affairs and International Trade Canada, "Canada and France Sign Joint Action Plan to Enhance Commercial Relations," *News Release* no. 137 (Ottawa: Department of Foreign Affairs and International Trade, 11 June 2008).
63 Foreign Affairs and International Trade Canada, "Economic Relations between France and Canada" (The Canadian Trade Commissioner Service, Canadian Embassy in France, 1 October 2007).
64 Statistics Canada, "International investment position, Canadian direct investment abroad and foreign direct investment in Canada, by country, annual," *Balance of International Payments*, Table 376–0051 (accessed through E-Stat).
65 See Wolfe, « Vers l'ALETA ? »; Black, *Direct Intervention*, 168 and 182; Maurice Torrelli et Kimon Valaskakis, "Le Canada et la Communauté économique européenne," in Paul Painchaud (ed.), *Le Canada et le Québec sur la scène internationale* (Montréal: Presses de l'Université du Québec, 1977), 355. Jens-U. Hettmann, "La politique extérieure canadienne vue de l'Europe: Fin de siècle pour les rapports canado-européens ? » *Études internationales* 27, no. 2 (Juin 1996): 303–23.
66 For a good discussion of Canada's "mythical" desire to establish an Atlantic economic community despite its improbability, see Evan H. Potter, "Transatlantic Free Trade: Myth or Reality?" in George A. Maclean (ed.), *Between Actor and Presence: The European Union and the Future for the Transatlantic Relationship* (Ottawa: University of Ottawa Press, 2001), 193–222.
67 Canada, *House of Commons Debates* 142/90 (Ottawa: Parliament of Canada, 7 May 2008), 5546.
68 Statistics Canada, "Historical Statistics, Origins of the Population, Every 10 years," *Census of Population*, Table 075–0015 (accessed through E-Stat).
69 Statistics Canada, "Ethnic Origin," *2006 Census: Data Products* (accessed online at www12.statcan.ca). While the inclusion of "Canada" as a category may distort any comparison with pre-1996 figures, the erosion of ethnic *appartenance* is a discernable trend since 1871. A hundred years later, 45 percent (compared to 61) of Canadians reported having British origins, and 28 percent (compared to 31) French ancestors.
70 Statistics Canada, "Immigrants to Canada, by Country of Last Permanent Residence, Quarterly," *Estimates of Total Population*, Table 051–0006 (accessed through E-Stat).
71 Bernard-Meunier, "Did You Say Europe?" 111.

72 José E. Igartua, *The Other Quiet Revolution: National Identities in English Canada, 1945–1971* (Vancouver: UBC Press, 2006), 1 and 5.
73 Nossal, *The Politics of Canadian Foreign Policy*, 100.
74 Quoted in Carman Miller, *Painting the Map Red: Canada and the South African War, 1899–1902* (Montreal & Kingston: McGill-Queen's University Press, 1993), 27.
75 Robert Borden and Henri Bourassa were, respectively, the emblematic representatives of these conceptions. Wilfrid Laurier and, to a lesser extent John A. Macdonald, attempted to find a balance between these two visions and formulate a compromised foreign policy. See Mason Wade, *The French Canadians, 1760–1967, vol. 1, 1760–1911* (Toronto: MacMillan, 1968 [1955]), esp. 464 and 475.
76 Five hundred volunteers joined the Catholic Pontifical Zouaves between 1867 and 1870, in contrast to about 200 who fought for the British Crown in 1899–1902. See C.-E. Rouleau, *Les Zouaves pontificaux: Quelques pages d'histoire* (Québec: Le Soleil, 1905): 90; and Jean Pariseau and Serge Bernier, *French Canadians and Bilingualism in the Canadian Armed Forces, vol. 1, 1763–1969: The Fear of a Parallel Army* (Ottawa: Directorate of History, Dept. of National Defence, 1988), 61.
77 Only 2.4 percent of Quebec's population enlisted voluntarily, in contrast to, among others, 7.5 percent in Ontario, 9.8 percent in Manitoba, and 9.5 percent in British Columbia. Charles P. Stacey, *Canada and the Age of Conflict, vol. 1: 1867–1921* (Toronto: University of Toronto Press, 1989 [1984]), 170 and 235.
78 Cf. David G. Haglund, "Le Canada dans l'entre-deux-guerres," *Études internationales* 31:4 (December 2000): 727–43; James Eayrs, "'A Low, Dishonest Decade': Aspects of Canadian External Policy, 1931–39," in Hugh L. Keenleyside et al. (eds), *The Growth of Canadian External Policies in External Affairs* (Durham: Duke University Press, 1960), 59–80.
79 Lionel Groulx, *Histoire du Canada français depuis la découverte, vol. 2*, 4th ed. (Montreal: Fides, 1976 [1960]), 329.
80 John MacFarlane, *Ernest Lapointe and Quebec's Influence on Canadian Foreign Policy* (Toronto: University of Toronto Press, 1999).
81 Ibid., 28 and 124.
82 André Laurendeau, *La crise de la conscription, 1942* (Montréal: Éditions du jour, 1962), 37.
83 MacFarlane, *Ernest Lapointe and Quebec's Influence on Canadian Foreign Policy*, 70.
84 Ibid., 160–168; Olivier Courteaux, *Les relations franco-canadiennes entre 1940 et 1946: Les relations oubliées* (Paris: Atelier national de reproduction des thèses, 2000), 128–44.
85 Quoted in Donald Creighton, *The Forked Road: Canada, 1939–1957* (Toronto: McClelland and Stewart, 1976), 130.

86 Quoted in James M. Beck, *Pendulum of Power: Canada's Federal Elections* (Scarborough: Prentice Hall, 1968), 264.
87 DCER, vol. 10 (18 July 1944), 160–1.
88 DCER, vol. 9 (26 August 1943), 1756–7.
89 Munro and Inglis, 55.
90 John W. Holmes, "Le Canada dans le monde," *Politique étrangère* 33, no. 4 (1968): 300–1.
91 Idem.
92 Louis St. Laurent, statement in the House of Commons, 28 March 1949, in Mackay, 190–1.
93 Riekhoff, "To Stay or Not to Stay," 167.
94 Thomas Risse is one of the leading proponents of this "democratic alliance" thesis. See his *Cooperation Among Democracies: The European Influence on U.S. Foreign Policy* (Princeton: Princeton University Press, 1995).
95 Quoted in Dale C. Thomson, *De Gaulle et le Québec* (Saint-Laurent: Éditions du Trécarré, 1990), 106.
96 In de Gaulle's own words: "Nous pouvons développer nos rapports avec le Canada tel qu'il est encore. Mais nous devons, avant tout, établir une coopération particulière avec le Canada français et ne pas laisser noyer ce que nous faisons pour lui et avec lui dans une affaire concernant l'ensemble des deux Canada. D'ailleurs, le Canada français deviendra nécessairement un État et c'est dans cette perspective que nous devons agir." Quoted in Frédéric Bastien, *Relations Particulières : La France face au Québec après de Gaulle* (Montréal : Boréal, 1999), 336.
97 Brian Mulroney, *Memoirs, 1939–1993* (Toronto: McClelland & Stewart, 2007), 546–7.
98 Bastien, *Le poids de la coopération*, 328.
99 Peter O'Neil, "Sarkozy stresses support for united Canada," *The Gazette* (8 May 2008); Rhéal Séguin, "Sarkozy takes strong stand on Canadian unity," *The Globe and Mail* (9 May 2008).
100 Christian Rioux, "Sarkozy corrige le tir sur le Québec," *Le Devoir* (23 May 2008).
101 Gendron, *Canada's Relations with France and French Africa*, 140.
102 Based on diplomatic visits compiled by John Kirton, *Canadian Foreign Policy in a Changing World* (Toronto: Thomson Nelson, 2007), 474–8.
103 Prime Minister Lester Pearson, quoted in Robert W. Reford, "Peacekeeping at Suez," in Don Munton and John Kirton (eds), *Canadian Foreign Policy: Selected Cases* (Scarborough: Prentice-Hall, 1992), 74. For former diplomat John Holmes, it was also a matter of national unity.
104 Peter V. Lyon, "The Old Commonwealth: The First Four Dominions," in Michael Howard and Roger Louis (eds.), *The Oxford History of the Twentieth Century* (Oxford: Oxford University Press, 1998), 300.
105 Holmes, "Le Canada dans le monde," 301–2.

106 James Eayrs, *In Defence of Canada: Growing Up Allied* (Toronto: University of Toronto Press, 1980), 150–151; and Gendron, 54.
107 André P. Donneur, "Les relations franco-canadiennes: Bilan et perspectives," *Politique étrangère* 38:2 (1973): 179–200.
108 See Kim Richard Nossal, "Succumbing to the Dumbbell: Canadian Perspectives on NATO in the 1990s," in Barbara MacDougall et al. (eds), *Canada and NATO: The Forgotten Ally?* (McLean Brassey's, 1992): 17–32; and Joseph T. Jockel, "Canada in a Twin-Pillared Alliance: The 'Dumbbell' May Just Have to Do," *International Journal* 46, no. 1 (Winter 1990–1): 8–26. Interestingly, Trudeau's reasons for partially withdrawing Canadian troops were similar to those leading to de Gaulle's 1966 decision. Recently available archives indicate that the French President's rationale rested on three arguments, two of which were of similar concern for Ottawa: "Les régimes communistes de l'Est devenaient moins menaçants. Les Etats-Unis risquaient de nous impliquer dans des conflits lointains, au Vietnam et en Chine, "d'où pourrait sortir une conflagration générale où l'Europe serait entraînée". Enfin, la France se dotait d'une arme atomique "dont la nature interdit qu'elle soit intégrée"." See Jean-Claude Casanova, "Alliance atlantique: en être ou pas?," *Le Monde* (21 May 2008).
109 Paul Létourneau and Michel Fortmann, "Canadian Defence and Security Policy," in Harold P. Klepak and Paul Létourneau (eds.), *Defence and Security: Eleven National Approaches* (Montreal: Méridien, 1990), 31.
110 Eddie Goldenberg, *The Way It Works: Inside Ottawa* (Toronto: McClelland & Stewart, 2006), 296.
111 David G. Haglund, "Relating to the Anglosphere: Canada, 'Culture,' and the Question of Military Intervention," *Journal of Transatlantic Studies* 3, no. 2 (Autumn 2005): 179 and 180.
112 Janice Gross Stein and Eugene Lang, *The Unexpected War: Canada in Kandahar* (Toronto: Viking Canada), 18.
113 Jocelyn Coulon, "Le Canada s'engage en Afghanistan," in Jocelyn Coulon (ed.), *Guide du maintien de la paix 2004* (Montréal: Athéna Éditions, 2003), 79–80.
114 As Minister Bill Graham stated at the time: "La France ne partage pas l'analyse voulant qu'une mission soit utile là-bas, parce que ce serait hors juridiction. Mais nous pensons que ce serait une belle occasion de collaborer avec l'OTAN." Presse canadienne, "Graham favorise une nouvelle forme de mission," *La Presse* (22 February 2003).
115 Alec Castonguay, "Afghanistan: Ottawa échoue à obtenir l'aide de Paris," *Le Devoir* (1 April 2008).
116 Bernard Descôteaux, "L'escalade afghane," *Le Devoir* (4 April 2008).
117 The phrase was used by socialist leader Jean-Marc Ayrault during the legislative debate on France's new military commitment in Afghanistan. See Elizabeth Pineau, "Nicolas Sarkozy multiplie les rapprochements avec Washington," *Le Monde* (3 April 2008).

118 Jacques Roy, "Fin du 'ni-ni': un changement compréhensible," *La Presse* (13 April 2008).
119 Black, *Direct Intervention*, 193.

11 From King to Kandahar: Canada, Multilateralism and Conflict in the Pacific, 1909–2009

JOHN MEEHAN
AND DAVID WEBSTER

"This, I think, is an excellent and very necessary step. I would rather have charge of such a Department than any other of the Government, and believe it would be made of infinite service to the country. Perhaps some day the opportunity will come."[1]

Such was Mackenzie King's reaction to Ottawa's decision in early 1909 to establish the Department of External Affairs. At the time of the announcement, King, then deputy minister of Labour under Wilfrid Laurier, was in Shanghai as one of five British delegates at an international opium conference. His remarks were prophetic given his later role as secretary of state for External Affairs for most of his long tenure as prime minister. As he toured India, China and Japan, King sensed much ignorance towards Canada and urged a bold assertion of dominion interests due to American competition and British aims. His nationalist ire was particularly kindled when a poorly informed American China-hand asked if Canada might be absorbed one day by the United States. The time had come for Canada to assume its nationhood, an indignant King responded, shedding its colonial status to "work out our own foreign policy ... from a national view-point."[2]

The birth of Canada's diplomatic service thus coincided with the first visit of a Canadian public figure to Asia. Yet King's Pacific tour set the tone for much ambiguity to come. Like most Canadians, he had only a vague notion of the region, his treaty-port attitude toward China and nostalgic image of Japan influenced by missionary accounts and family ties.[3] Canadians tended to see Asia in vaguely-formed images of vast riches, "China's millions" ripe for salvation, turbaned snake charmers, picturesque grass huts and pith-helmeted adventurers able to tame and make sense of it all. To King, as to many policy makers since, Canadian interests in the Pacific were shaped largely by geopolitics, trade and immigration.

Fittingly, he reacted in ways that reflected Canada's position within the British Empire and its position relative to the emerging American empire. Espousing the myth of a limitless Asian market, he was shocked by Canada's inept trade agent at Shanghai and urged that a proper commercial office be set up there. On immigration, he tried in vain to replace the head tax against Chinese with a "gentlemen's agreement" like that negotiated with Japan after the anti-Asian riot in Vancouver of 1907. Having led a royal commission into the latter, King was aware of the diplomatic realities involved. Unlike China, Japan was a powerful ally due to the Anglo-Japanese alliance (1902), its victory over Russia in 1905 and Canada's accession the following year to the Anglo-Japanese Treaty of Commerce and Navigation (1894). Significantly, King held out little hope for joint action in Asia. He found his first experiment in multilateralism a "very doubtful" one, its tedious format and political posturing far less effective than bilateral talks.[4]

Such inauspicious beginnings aptly characterized Canada's experience of multilateralism in the Pacific. As it responded to later crises in the region, Ottawa remained focused on the North Atlantic triangle, often viewing Asia as an afterthought. This was particularly apparent in times of conflict such as the Sino-Japanese hostilities of 1931–45, the Korean War, the conflict in Indochina and struggles for independence in and around Indonesia. In each case, Canada sought to leverage its position within alliances, often bending to trade concerns in dealing with a region that few Canadians knew firsthand. Its policies toward the Pacific, such as they were, were often marked by a credibility gap between commitments to global security, on the one hand, and attention to trade and geopolitical concerns, on the other. While much has been written on Canada's role during the Korean and Vietnam wars, few have examined its reaction to conflicts involving two other major countries in the Pacific.[5] Despite the differences in the Japanese and Indonesian cases, there was a remarkable continuity in Ottawa's responses from prewar to postwar periods. As in more recent Asian conflicts, its policies revealed a focus on geopolitics and trade, a gap between rhetoric and reality, and an overall Eurocentrism due to public ignorance toward the region.

CANADA AND THE SINO-JAPANESE CONFLICT

From the beginning, as King's tour indicated, Canada's Pacific ties were shaped by multilateralism. Its presence in the region occurred within the context of a larger Anglo-Saxon missionary and trade enterprise, Canadians serving alongside counterparts from Britain, the United

States and Australia. French Canadians, though under-represented in business, made significant contributions to Catholic missions in the region, often working with French missionaries, with whom they were at times confused. Inspired by myths about the region, most traders and missionaries saw an unlimited potential for making profit and saving souls. Despite his criticism of the more zealous among them (and his wariness of colonialism and multilateralism), King hoped Canada might benefit from its central position within the imperial network. By this stage, oceanic telegraph cables and shipping lines such as Canadian Pacific, with its gleaming *Empress* liners and "All Red Route," were a tangible British link to Asia by way of Canada.

To the extent that Canadians thought about Asia, they did so through the prism of the North Atlantic triangle. Significantly, John Bartlet Brebner, who coined this popular construct in Canadian diplomacy, first applied it to Ottawa's role in Pacific affairs during the interwar years. As Brebner noted, King's predecessor as prime minister, Arthur Meighen, favoured including the United States in a multilateral system of Pacific security over renewing the bilateral Anglo-Japanese pact. This was achieved at the Washington conference of Pacific powers (1921–22). King continued such promotion of Anglo-American harmony in Asian affairs. Advocating greater autonomy for the dominions at the imperial conferences of 1923 and 1926, he oversaw Ottawa's diplomatic debut in the region with the opening of a legation at Tokyo in 1929, Canada's third such diplomatic mission (after Washington and Paris). King hoped this "window on Asia" would promote trade and help implement a newly revised gentlemen's agreement. He shrugged off critics who feared the move duplicated the work of trade offices, active in the region from Kobe to Shanghai to Batavia, and might be misconstrued by the "Oriental mind" as a sign of imperial disunity.[6]

A far more serious threat to the North Atlantic triangle was isolationism. Many in Canada shared u.s. wariness of collective security, notably the mutual defence provisions of Article X of the League of Nations Covenant. Canada was a member of the body, unlike the United States, but often distanced itself from European concerns. One of its envoys to Geneva portrayed Canada as a "fire-proof house" far from the lethal feuds of the old world. In Asia too, many shared misgivings about the League, albeit for different reasons. With the defeat of Japan's racial equality clause at Versailles, the body seemed to represent Western interests. For their part, Chinese and Korean nationalists lost hope in the new internationalism. It had not prevented Japan from taking the Shandong peninsula and consolidating its interests in Korea and Manchuria.[7]

Ottawa's initiative in the Pacific, alas, was poorly timed. Within a month of the arrival of Herbert Marler, Canada's first minister to Japan, the stock market collapsed in the United States, sending shock waves through the global economy. Elected in 1930 on a platform of blasting into foreign markets, R.B. Bennett's Conservatives soon warmed to the Tokyo legation, seeing a role for it and the trade offices in depression diplomacy. Trade missions to Asia and plans for wheat sales to China yielded few results, however, and the trade commissioners resented Marler's attempts to coordinate their activities. Moreover, as such officials warned, goodwill was undermined by Canada's perceived double standard in the region. On the one hand, Ottawa cultivated good relations with Japan through the gentlemen's agreement and the decision to open its legation at Tokyo. On the other, it was unwilling to revise the Chinese Immigration Act (1923) that effectively barred Chinese from entry to Canada. Missionary sympathies with Korean and Chinese nationalism did not lead to an anti-colonial policy on the part of Canada. Indeed, Canadians, when approaching Asia, tended to see themselves as part of the British Empire. Meanwhile, rising protectionism put added strain on Anglo-American relations, especially after Washington imposed the Smoot-Hawley tariff (1930) and Britain endorsed imperial preference at the Ottawa conference of 1932. At the latter, Bennett alienated the United States but also shocked his British guests with his brash and erratic manner. His approach to the League similarly lacked coherence and direction just as the body faced its most serious crisis. After decades of rivalry with China and Russia in Manchuria, Japan seized the latter region in late 1931, responding to its own isolationist forces promising more radical solutions to domestic woes.[8]

The Manchurian crisis (1931–33), viewed by many as the true starting point of the Second World War, tested the limits of the North Atlantic triangle. As the dispute wore on, Canada sought an elusive middle ground between British conciliation and a growing American intransigence toward Japan. Britain's foreign minister, Sir John Simon, invoked pro-Japanese public opinion, Britain's vulnerability in Asia and dominion attitudes. The American secretary of state, Henry Stimson, yielded to public pressure, issuing a note in January 1932 that affirmed China's territorial integrity, the open door principle of equal economic opportunity there and the non-recognition of territorial gains. The message met with a chilly response in London, where officials claimed not to have been consulted beforehand. With little grasp of world affairs, Bennett turned to O. D. Skelton, the under-secretary of state for External Affairs he had inherited from King. Though the prime minister at times seemed inclined to bold forms of collective security, Skelton advised him against joint action without leadership from Britain and the United States.[9]

Within this diplomatic context, trade interests and public opinion further shaped Canada's response. The crisis revealed a rift in the public and press between defenders of collective security, on the one hand, and opponents of communism, on the other. Some, such as the Winnipeg *Free Press* and Toronto *Star*, called for sanctions against Japan, deploring Bennett's wait-and-see approach after hostilities reached Shanghai in early 1932. Others, including business leaders, some missionaries and the conservative press, doubted the League's relevance, saw Japan as a bulwark against communism and echoed British justifications of Tokyo's aims. As advocates on both sides noted, Japan had been Canada's fourth largest customer before the depression, importing $38 million in goods in 1929 with a surplus of $24 million in Canada's favour. The *Financial Post* claimed the League was unlikely to act since its members would not go to war over Manchuria. Bennett's secretary of state, C.H. Cahan, echoed this view when he addressed the League in late 1932. His speech, widely seen as pro-Japanese, caused a stir at Ottawa, where officials, unlike Simon, had not been invited to read it beforehand. Skelton promptly clarified matters with Washington but the affair revealed Ottawa's poor communications with Geneva as well as the impact of trade on relations with Japan. Like Cahan, Marler reflected Canada's business elite in his doubts about the League, his sympathy for Japan and his belief that recognition of Manchukuo, Japan's puppet state in Manchuria after 1932, was simply a matter of time.[10]

Japan stormed out of the League in February 1933, following the latter's adoption of the Lytton report recommending non-recognition of Manchukuo. Bennett then considered joining a British arms embargo against both Japan and China but the scheme was soon abandoned due to lack of American support. Such a reversal indicated Ottawa's shift towards Washington in the North Atlantic triangle, a stance reinforced by the poor state of coastal defences. Tensions increased in 1934 when a Japanese foreign ministry official declared Japan's right to unilateralism and, later that year, when Britain concluded it could not afford a simultaneous war in Europe and Asia. When the new U.S. president, Franklin Roosevelt, inquired of Stimson on how best to bring London around on Asia, the former secretary of state claimed Canada was "the key log in the jam" and suggested a trade agreement with Ottawa as the first step in improving ties with Britain. A deal was reached upon King's return to power in 1935 but the situation in Asia declined rapidly. By early 1936, Japan had withdrawn from the London naval talks, abandoning the Washington system of Pacific security, and narrowly quelled a military coup in Tokyo. The revolt greatly troubled King, already fearful of a "terrible combination" of Germany, Italy, Japan and possibly Russia. As if to realize his fears, Japan concluded a pact with Germany later that year, prompting Canada to double its naval budget.[11]

The renewal of Sino-Japanese hostilities in 1937 altered the balance but not the basic reliance of Canada upon the North Atlantic triangle in Pacific affairs. When the undeclared war erupted that summer, King was in London, where he strongly opposed a Pacific defence pact proposed by Australia and New Zealand at the imperial conference. Confident he had avoided any commitment to imperial defence, he proceeded to Berlin where he met with Adolf Hitler who impressed him as "a very great man [and] mystic." Ottawa's neutrality was tested in August, when Marler's successor, Randolph Bruce, was misquoted as justifying Japan's aims and Britain's ambassador to China was injured in a Japanese attack near Shanghai. Yet, in King's view, the main threat was not Japan's aggression but Britain's possible resort to coordination through the Empire and the League, which King saw as a forum for conciliation not enforcement. He clearly advised against any semblance of a Commonwealth bloc or Canadian lead there, even suggesting that Canada offer its seat on a Far Eastern advisory body to Australia. For its part, London was divided over how to respond to America's new-found resolve, as outlined by Roosevelt's speech at Chicago in October in which he called for a global quarantine of aggressor states. In the end, Britain deferred to an upcoming meeting of Pacific powers at Brussels, recommending it consider conciliation not sanctions, and canvassed the dominions and Washington for their views.[12]

King saw London's message as the most important one he had received since its request in 1922 (which he had denied) for troops to fight in Turkey. Viewing this as the latest challenge to autonomy, he looked to public opinion as well as American attitudes. By this stage, Ottawa faced growing criticism over the gap between its neutrality and its apparent complicity with Japan's war efforts. According to its own figures, the Japanese invasion of China had coincided with the largest rise in exports to Japan since the Kanto earthquake of 1923. Exports of lead and scrap iron had doubled since 1936 and those of nickel more than tripled, making Canada Japan's main supplier of nickel and probably of aluminum and lead. Calling for decisive action at Brussels, women, farmers, labourers, students, Chinese groups, city councils and even the Alberta legislature sent resolutions to King. Though inspired by similar movements in the United States and Britain, their calls for a boycott and embargo failed to convince most Canadians, whose sympathy for China did not extend to agreement on sanctions against Japan. To such activists, King depicted himself as a true pacifist in avoiding measures that might lead to war. Offering no public reply to Roosevelt's quarantine speech, he portrayed the upcoming conference as an exercise in conciliation, not coercion. Much to King's satisfaction, U.S. secretary of state Cordell Hull echoed this view during his visit to Canada in late October.[13]

To London's relief, the North Atlantic triangle seemed in agreement against sanctions. The Brussels conference, which opened in November 1937, proved a dismal failure. Japan refused to attend, Britain looked to the United States and the American delegation appeared to have no instructions. Canada advised its envoy to avoid giving any impression of an Empire bloc, to refuse invitations to act as chair and to avoid making any proposals, such action being up to the great powers. Even British officials admitted that it would be "veritable madness" for Canada to impose sanctions in advance of the United States. In the end, the delegates passed a motion, drafted by the Americans, reiterating the principles of non-interference and conciliation embodied in the Washington treaty. After this exercise in futility, Japan proceeded in its conquest of China, taking Nanking and major cities in the south in 1938. By early 1939, Ottawa faced renewed pressure for an embargo, the impetus coming this time from London. Fearing for Britain's interests in East Asia, its ambassador at Tokyo, Sir Robert Craigie, hoped Canada would support Britain and the United States when the time came to act against Japan.[14] His presumption that Canada would defend Anglo-American interests in the region outraged Skelton, who expressed Canadian isolationism in the following stark terms: "If we did not heed the cry of Chinese millions, I cannot conceive any great proportion of Canadians being moved to intervene in order to save the interests of United States Standard Oil companies in China or the interests of British merchants in Shanghai, who were so long anti-Chinese in their sympathies."[15]

The outbreak of war in Europe later that year forged an Anglo-American consensus in favour of sanctions against Japan. Within two weeks of declaring war against Germany on 10 September 1939, Ottawa passed an order-in-council requiring a permit for all exports of strategic metals, a step towards Allied coordination of trade. At first, only steel and scrap iron shipments were denied though, by year-end, Britain and the United States collaborated more closely on limiting alloy exports. When Washington allowed its commercial treaty with Japan to lapse in early 1940, Canada ended shipments to Japan of aluminum and zinc, then nickel and cobalt over the summer. Amidst outrage over Japan's attacks on Canadian missions in China, as well as its tripartite pact with Germany and Italy that September, Ottawa stopped exports to Japan of copper and lead and, bowing to pressure in British Columbia, began to register the 22,000 Japanese Canadians living there. The embargo was extended in early 1941 to include wheat, flour and wood pulp – prompting Japanese diplomats to claim the Canadian legation at Tokyo was no longer necessary due to the near cessation of trade – and Canada joined the U.S. and Britain in freezing Japanese assets after Japan's seizure of Indochina that July.[16] On London's urging, King did not appoint a minister to Tokyo, a post left vacant since Bruce's departure in 1938, and sent 1,975 soldiers to reinforce British troops at Hong Kong. Like Britain, Canada was on the sidelines during U.S.-Japan talks to avert a Pacific war but, through a technicality, was the first to declare war against Japan after its attack on Pearl Harbor on 7 December 1941. As in the past, conflict had brought the North Atlantic triangle together but Canada, like Britain, looked increasingly to the United States in responding to Japanese aggression and considering a postwar order in the Pacific.[17]

FROM INTERWAR TRIANGLE TO COLD WAR ALLIANCE

Canada's interwar experience shaped its postwar involvement in Asia. Its multilateral approach continued after the war, moving beyond the strictly Anglo-American context to broader military pacts, the United Nations and other international bodies. Within the North Atlantic triangle, its position shifted to reflect new realities, its foremost ally now the United States though Britain continued to exert an important influence. As the Cold War began to take shape, Canada turned increasingly to Washington in defining its role in Pacific affairs, yet it never fully adopted the perspective of its southern neighbour. Its policies in Asia, as Robert Bothwell has noted, differed from those of the United States in focus, importance and commitment. With less substantial interests in the region, Canada emerged from its more modest role in the Pacific war with a much smaller investment in East Asia and consequently a greater ease in accepting the "loss" of China to communism. Moreover, it was more willing to eschew unilateralism to support new multilateral institutions, soon depicting its presence at the creation of the United Nations at San Francisco in early 1945 as the birth of its diplomacy's golden age.[18] As a middle power, Canada endorsed the broad outline of American policies but sought unique ways of asserting its interests as a Pacific nation. During the occupation years, E. Herbert Norman, the noted Canadian diplomat and historian of Japan, worked closely with American officials but disagreed with them over how best to foster Japanese democracy. In particular, he went further than General Douglas MacArthur, the Supreme Commander of the Allied Powers, in advocating a significant role for the Japanese people in drafting a new constitution. Through its participation in the Far Eastern Advisory Commission formed in late 1945 (which later became the Far Eastern Commission) and the Tokyo trial, Canada saw that the occupation was essentially an American project. This was particularly apparent by 1947 when the United States adopted a "reverse course" in Japan, pardoning suspected war criminals and providing economic aid to rebuild its new Cold War ally. A Quebec court justice,

E. Stuart McDougall, served as a judge during the Tokyo trial but asked in early 1947 to be relieved of his duties due to concerns about the apparent exercise of victor's justice. When British officials echoed his misgivings that the judgment would "do credit to no nation," Ottawa sought to withdraw him for "health reasons" so as not to undermine American aims but McDougall remained until the trial ended in late 1948 out of a sense of duty. By this stage, Japan had a new constitution, largely drafted by American legal experts, and, by 1952, a peace treaty that transformed the former enemy into a key ally against communism in Asia.[19]

With Japan firmly in the American camp, Canada invoked its middle power status and Commonwealth ties to explore opportunities elsewhere in Asia. Though Japan continued to matter to Canadian policy makers due to its economic and strategic importance, new possibilities soon emerged. With the independence of India in 1947, Canadian diplomats, notably Escott Reid, touted a "special relationship" with the new state, a view that in retrospect appeared more fiction than fact. Still, scholars as eminent as John Holmes later referred to Canada's attempt to enter Asia "through India, Pakistan and Ceylon." With regard to Asia's most populous nation, China, relations were officially opened with the establishment of an embassy at Chungking in 1943 but the prewar legacy of inaction on immigration and Japanese expansion continued to plague relations. Canada's first ambassador, General Victor Odlum, was a strong supporter of Nationalist leader Chiang Kai-shek, though he soon lamented the American desire to control all trade with China, including in arms, during and after the war. With the United States, Britain and the Soviet Union vying for influence in China, he noted in his first despatch, "Canada is simply not in the picture. She is looked upon as being 'in the belly' of the U.S. ... or as a very minor tone in the British chorus." Odlum's successor after 1947, T.C. Davis, proved less adulating toward Chiang but was unable to stem Anglo-American divisions due to U.S. intransigence on China. With Britain ready to recognize the People's Republic of China, established in late 1949, his first secretary, Chester Ronning, urged Ottawa to follow suit. Yet the new government of Louis St. Laurent, bending to pressure from the United States and anti-communist sentiment in Quebec, reversed its early decision for recognition, setting an impasse on the question that remained for the next twenty-one years. As an External Affairs veteran later acknowledged, Ottawa had come so close to recognizing the PRC in 1949 that Ronning had been ready to select a site for the Canadian embassy in Beijing.[20]

The outbreak of the Korean War in June 1950 prevented any such overture. Indeed, China's aid to the north made it a *de facto* enemy of

Canada, whose support for a U.N. resolution condemning China as an aggressor led Beijing to order the closure of Canada's embassy in 1951. Korea became an ideological battleground in which anti-communism provided a needed focus for the North Atlantic triangle. Again working within this context, Canada participated in the war through the U.N., hoping to consolidate relations with the United States and Western Europe through the newly formed North Atlantic Treaty Organization (NATO). In such a way, as Steven Hugh Lee has observed, Canada's role in containing communism was inextricably linked to the promotion of its political and economic aims. Like Japan, it benefited diplomatically and commercially from the conflict, a sharp rise in military spending apparent shortly after the death in July 1950 of its great isolationist, Mackenzie King. St. Laurent would commit more than 25,000 troops to the war but he proceeded cautiously, attentive to factors he had stressed as External Affairs minister, namely national unity, multilateral commitments and relations with the U.S. Ottawa's outlook on Asia was shaped by its desire to use the U.N. and the Commonwealth to oppose communism, though the extent of its "diplomacy of constraint" on Washington later became the subject of historical debate. If imperial ties had bolstered Canada's place in the North Atlantic triangle prior to 1945, its multilateral approach to containing communism secured its position within the postwar order. Not coincidentally, many of those who had defended Japan during the 1930s as a bulwark against bolshevism invoked similar arguments against giving in to communism in Korea, Indochina and elsewhere. Even prior to the end of the Korean War in 1953, Canada hoped to counter communism not through regional defence pacts such as the Southeast Asia Treaty Organization (SEATO), but rather through its own multilateral network. In endorsing the Colombo Plan in 1950, for instance, it envisaged a new role for the Commonwealth in development, thereby hoping to stem the communist tide in the Pacific.[21]

CANADA AND CONFLICTS IN INDONESIA

Situated at the apex of East and South Asia, the intersection of American and British/Commonwealth spheres of interest, Indonesia provides a good example of the continued relevance of the North Atlantic triangle in Canadian thinking. Following a wartime Japanese occupation, Indonesian nationalists led by Sukarno and Mohammad Hatta declared independence two days after Japan's 1945 surrender. Canadian policy makers did not immediately notice events in Indonesia. As the Netherlands sought to reclaim its lost colony, Canada approved reconstruction loans for both the Netherlands and the colonial Dutch East Indies government, and armed one of the Dutch divisions that backed the attempted recolonization. Policy makers in Ottawa saw the Netherlands as a like-minded middle power and supporter of the "functional principle." On top of this community of interest were existing ties of wartime alliance, new ones of marriage and migration resulting from the liberation of the Netherlands by Canadian forces, and plans for future ties in a North Atlantic community. The East Indies loan aimed to help rebuild the triangular trade in which European trade deficits with the United States were financed by colonial raw materials exports. Conflict in Indonesia risked depriving the world of vital rubber, foodstuffs and mineral exports and destabilizing the peace so vital to trade. "Unrest in any part of the world which may become a threat to international peace and security is of direct concern to Canada, whose economy is so closely linked to international trade," the first External Affairs Department memorandum on Indonesia pointed out. Canadian policy makers also shared the stated Dutch goal of gradual progress towards a self-governing, federal Indonesia within a Netherlands-Indonesian Union. After all, the model was that pioneered by Canada within the British Commonwealth.[22]

The Dutch-Indonesian conflict drew United Nations attention, including the first appeal to the Security Council alleging a "breach of the peace" and the first UN-imposed timetable for decolonization. Embarking upon a Security Council term in 1948–49, Canadian officials faced three main issues: Palestine, Kashmir, and Indonesia. They worked to make the Security Council "the principal organ of conciliation" in the UN, and to develop King's conviction, dating back to league days, that the Council did not go beyond conciliation into considering enforcement measures. This Security Council term, and the successful mediation of the Indonesian question in particular, was the forum in which Canada developed, according to diplomat John Holmes, "the foundations for its reputation as a moderate mediatory power."[23]

Canadian actions on the Security Council were never designed in light of events in Indonesia. They aimed, rather, to uphold the functions Ottawa preferred for the UN, and to maintain unity within the Commonwealth and especially the emerging North Atlantic alliance. With Australia and India entering the lists as partisans of the Indonesian cause, unwelcome tensions flared within the Commonwealth, which Canada hoped to see develop into a "bridge" between the West and Asia. More significantly, differences over Indonesia threatened to derail the creation of the North Atlantic Treaty and offered a chance to shape that treaty to the liking of key figures within the Department of External Affairs. United States commitment to the principle of decolonization had not initially been allowed to derail tacit American consent for the basis of Dutch policy in Indonesia. In 1948, however, with the looming "loss" of China as background, the Sukarno-Hatta government crushed a Communist uprising. Overnight, it became a potential bastion against communism. American-backed Security Council resolutions condemned the Dutch and demanded an independent Indonesia. With North Atlantic Treaty talks moving towards conclusion, U.S. plans to exclude the Dutch from military aid provisions over the Indonesian issue were met with Dutch threats to stay outside the treaty. The progress of the North Atlantic talks shaped Canadian actions on Indonesia. Canada's Security Council delegation, on cabinet instructions, acted as the swing vote to defeat a 1948 Council order for Dutch forces to pull back. When the Netherlands refused to obey a Council timetable for Indonesian independence, with its officials muttering about staying outside the North Atlantic treaty and perhaps even leaving the UN, a Canadian-sponsored resolution found a middle path between U.S. and Dutch positions. This led to round-table talks among Dutch and Indonesian officials that produced an independent "United States of Indonesia" in federal union with the Netherlands by the end of 1949. In the process, officials struck a deal to assist the Dutch at the UN in exchange for Dutch support for the Canadian-backed Article 2 on economic and social cooperation in the North Atlantic Treaty.[24]

The incident remained central to Canadian diplomatic memory for some years, and underlay the decision to make Jakarta the site of Canada's first Southeast Asian embassy in 1953. With Canadian interests limited, External Affairs assigned the embassy a watching brief for the region. Its hoped-for purpose was new trade, symbolized by the choice to make the head of the trade commissioner service Canada's first ambassador. Despite a brief surge in wheat sales, those hopes did not materialize. As with Tokyo in 1929, the timing was poor. Indonesia's economy was in tatters, its scarce dollars earmarked for purchases other than Canadian goods, in an Asian economy still struggling to get back on its feet. Nor did Canada make Indonesia a priority. Ottawa disappointed American and Australian officials, for instance, when it turned down an Indonesian request for a Canadian or Commonwealth-led military training mission in favour of a similar mission to Luxembourg. The main ties came in the field of development aid. Canada's role in forming the Colombo Plan for Cooperative Economic Development in South and South-East Asia has been much exaggerated. Canadian contributions were limited and initially faced an "icy" attitude in cabinet. Prime Minister Louis St. Laurent wanted to reject participation in an Asian aid programme unless the United States was also involved. Ottawa finally agreed to join in order to offer a counter-attraction to communism in Asia, and in order to aid the reconstruction of global trading patterns. Indonesia joined the Plan in 1953. Japan followed the next year, conceding that its interest was to boost regional trade and Southeast Asian stability, "a very important factor in strengthening Japan politically and economically." Here were the beginnings of regionally-integrated economic thinking that flowed naturally from the "reverse course" in Japan.[25]

A second Dutch-Indonesian struggle, over control of the western half of the island of New Guinea, retained as a Dutch colony over Indonesian objections, spoiled hopes for orderly economic development in the region. When Diefenbaker toured Asia in 1958, he enjoyed a high-profile and pleasant trip to Malaya, recently independent within the Commonwealth. After grudgingly agreeing to a two-hour stop in Jakarta while his plane refuelled, he threatened at the last minute to stay on his plane rather than attend scheduled meetings, then "somewhat overwhelmed" the Indonesian prime minister with a lecture on the evils of communism and the virtues of foreign investment. The different treatments of Indonesia and Malaya mirrored a growing dichotomy in Canadian thinking between the model pro-Western Malayans and the overly emotional and vaguely untrustworthy Indonesians. Diefenbaker's cabinet awarded more money to Malaya and cut funds for Indonesia, Burma and other non-Commonwealth countries. The government also commercialized aid more than before. All Asian recipients were expected to take more of their aid allotment in the form of Canadian-grown wheat surpluses, which exceeded a billion bushels in 1957. Development aid through the Colombo Plan, originally conceived for Cold War reasons, took on a decidedly export-driven colour.[26]

Thwarted in its campaign to "recover" West New Guinea, Sukarno in 1960 broke diplomatic relations with the Netherlands and began a military build-up using Soviet sources. By 1962 Indonesia was the largest non-communist recipient of Soviet arms. The Netherlands appealed to its allies to slap military embargoes on Indonesia. John F. Kennedy's administration in Washington, concerned to keep Indonesia non-communist, sought a more conciliatory policy towards Jakarta. With another decolonization struggle causing angry exchanges between American and Dutch representatives at NATO meetings, Canada again sought the middle ground, acceding to the proposed NATO arms embargo, but defending the U.S. decision to continue supplying military goods and aid to Indonesia. Ottawa kept its head down on the issue, refusing Indonesian requests to mediate in order to avoid giving offence to the Netherlands. It was left to Kennedy's government to first force mediation, then impose an agreement that saw West New Guinea transferred to Indonesian rule via an interim UN administration.

With Lester Pearson as prime minister, Ottawa was less aloof when Indonesia posed a collective-security challenge in 1963–65. Britain shed its remaining Southeast Asian colonies in 1963, transferring them to reliable Malaya to create a new country, Malaysia. Seeing it as a stalking horse for British interests in the region, Indonesia refused to accept Malaysia's formation. As part of a policy of "confrontation," it carried out guerrilla attacks and left the United Nations when Malaysia won election to the Security Council. Here was a threat to collective security recalling the Manchurian crisis and Japan's withdrawal from the League in 1933. UN Secretary-General U Thant said the world organization was now in the worst crisis since its formation. Sukarno began to speak of forming a Conference of the New Emerging Forces, an alternative to the UN in New York. With a possible membership of China, Indonesia, North Korea, North Vietnam and possibly Pakistan, one Canadian diplomat wrote, "the Sukarno idea of a bad boys club competing with the UN" might take in a third of humanity and threaten the viability and universality of the United Nations.[27]

The Pearson government looked for ways to support Malaysia and its Commonwealth backers, without opposing the American policy of trying to use Indonesia as a barrier against communism and avoiding "a second Vietnam in Southeast Asia." It approved military aid to Malaysia, the first such Canadian aid in Southeast Asia, but resisted demands to announce an end to the small Canadian wheat aid grant for Indonesia. Still, Indonesian officials added Canada to the list of "imperialists with white skins" (albeit in last place, after New Zealand) and a semi-official newspaper reported that "a Canadian is not Canadian ... a Canadian is British." Canada maintained its contacts with the potential "modernizing elite" in Indonesia, however. After Sukarno was overthrown by his army commanders in 1965–66, Indonesians trained by Canadian technical advisors in the 1950s or at McGill University's Institute of Islamic Studies took up key positions in the "New Order" regime headed by General Suharto.[28]

The New Order's consolidation depended upon the massacre and arrest of over a million alleged communists and on extensive Western aid. It was, External Affairs decided, "patently in our interests that the new regime be able to consolidate its internal position and to pursue external policies it appears prepared to follow." Japan and the United States were the key backers of the new regime, once it demonstrated that it would take an anti-communist line in regional affairs and accept more foreign investment. The long-cherished Western goal for Asia, a crescent-shaped zone of non-communist stability surrounding China along the Pacific Rim, was closer than ever to realization as Indonesia entered the increasingly-integrated regional economy centred on Japan. Canadian support was limited at first, but accelerated once Pierre Trudeau took the reins as prime minister. Trudeau was more interested than his predecessors in the third world and in its economic development. Efforts to diversify trade as part of the "third option" featured a bid for closer ties to Japan and more trade with developing Asia. Here was a call to refocus Canadian attention across the Pacific, drawing upon the age-old ideas of Oriental riches. Canada was pursuing, one official said, "a conscious policy – rare for Canada in Asia – under which we wanted to bring China out of isolation, widen our relations with Japan, and promote stability throughout [Southeast Asia]." Setbacks in Vietnam were reducing American commitments in the region. The Trudeau government was willing to help fill the vacuum. Thus it identified Indonesia, "a nascent power among the non-Communist nations," as the first non-Commonwealth "country of concentration" for Canadian aid.[29]

Canadian aid was designed to "facilitate Indonesia's transformation from aid recipient to trading partner." The first big Canadian investment came from Inco, which opened a vast nickel mining operation with export development financing. "Indonesia has never seen so much money," one official told the Canadian ambassador. The Inco project would become a vital piece of the Canadian presence in Indonesia, enough to see Canada ranked number three among Indonesian foreign investors for a time. It offered a low-cost supplement to unionized mining operations in Ontario and Quebec, conveniently located for the Japanese market and thus easily integrated into regional production.[30]

When Indonesia had posed a security threat to Malaysia, Canada took a side. By 1975, when Indonesia launched a military invasion of the Portuguese colony of East Timor, Canada had substantial economic interests in Indonesia. The year saw the fall of Saigon and communist triumphs in Cambodia and Laos. When the social-democratic nationalist party Fretilin gained control in East Timor, it was easy for Indonesian officials to paint it as a potential Cuba. The spectre of an Indonesian invasion did not head off a Canadian $200-million credit extended when Suharto visited Ottawa in the summer of 1975. Canadian diplomats hoped an invasion would not be necessary, but most agreed that annexation by Indonesia was the best future for East Timor. The eventual Indonesian invasion cost the lives of a third of the Timorese population, but the Canadian ambassador was instructed to do no deploring. When the Timor invasion came to the United Nations, Canada abstained in General Assembly voting. Development aid in 1975–76 reached a record level of $36.7-million, placing Indonesia third among Canada's aid recipients. When Flora MacDonald, Conservative External Affairs minister in 1979–80, spoke of making human rights central in Canadian foreign policy, officials rejected applying that to the Timor case. "Frankly we would be dismayed if the Minister's admirable statement on human rights were ever to be interpreted as a mandate for taking up every lost cause in the world," one wrote. The "lost cause" thesis meant that the best thing to do was to forget the whole issue. Visiting Jakarta in 1983, Trudeau said East Timor "raised the problem of self-determination of peoples" but that "on balance we decided that stability of the region should be the foremost concern and thus had supported Indon[esia]."[31]

The end of the Cold War kicked away the ideological moorings for Western support of anti-communist dictatorships. As prime minister, Brian Mulroney delivered passionate declarations at 1991 summit meetings of the Commonwealth and *la francophonie* that Canada under his government would "no longer subsidize repression and the stifling of democracy." East Timor provided the first test case for the new rhetoric when Indonesian soldiers opened fire on a pro-independence march. Canada slapped a freeze on three planned future aid projects, but left existing aid untouched. Indonesia remained a trade priority, with two-way trade up 47% over the course of 1992. This trend only accelerated under the Chrétien government, which renewed aid to Indonesia and made it a target for the "Team Canada" trade promotion effort. As one of the low-cost anchors to the eastern Asia trading system, Indonesia remained important to Japan, the United States and European states. Canada did not wish to be left outside these trade opportunities. While the Cold War was over and Indonesia's strategic importance was gone, its economic importance continued to climb.[32]

A strong human rights lobby in Canada raised the political cost for the government of too close a rapprochement with Indonesia. When the 1998 Asian economic crisis toppled the Suharto dictatorship and temporarily removed the economic benefits of good relations with Indonesia, the Canadian government proved willing to seek a resolution of the East Timor issue, believing that regional security could be better served by removing a source of growing conflict. The shift also fit the needs of Foreign Minister Lloyd Axworthy's move towards a greater emphasis on "human security." East Timor for the first time fit the pre-occupations of Canadian foreign policy rather than acting as an obstacle to them. Indonesia's new "reform" government agreed to a 1999 referendum in East Timor to settle the issue one way or the other. After East Timorese opted for independence, however, militia groups backed by the Indonesian army launched organized mass violence to derail the results. This proved too much for many Western governments. Axworthy was one of the foreign ministers who played an active role in bringing an end to the violence. Where Canada had previously refused any form of linkage between trade and human rights, Axworthy now convened a meeting at the 1999 Asia Pacific Economic Cooperation summit to press Indonesia to accept an international stabilization force under Australian leadership.[33]

CONCLUSION

The story of Canada's relations with the Pacific illustrates how North Atlantic concerns mattered to the architects of its foreign policy. Throughout the interwar period, whenever Canada diverted its Eurocentric gaze to consider Asian affairs, it did so through the lens of the triangle. Under both Liberal and Conservative leaders, Ottawa looked to Britain and the United States in establishing its presence in the region and formulating a response to crises there. At first, this involvement was tentative and closely tied to British interests, an approach consistent with Canada's recent diplomatic coming of age and Canadians' identification as members of the British Empire. During the Manchurian crisis, Canada asserted its own interests, including trade and above all Anglo-American harmony in world affairs. This became increasingly difficult over the decade as Britain and the United States, like Canada and other powers, adopted a path of unilateralism and isolationism. After the outbreak of Sino-Japanese hostilities in 1937, the outline of a North Atlantic triangle re-emerged but with significant differences. It returned as a consensus by default that avoided conflicts where national interests were not perceived to be at stake. Moreover, it was an arrangement within which both Canada and Britain looked increasingly to the United States for leadership and direction.

The triangle did not entirely vanish after 1945. In South and Southeast Asia, indeed, there was a revival of Commonwealth thinking in Canada through the new emphasis on development. Canadian actions and attitudes showed continued North Atlantic thinking in the Indonesian independence issue. Here, Canada's main interest was to preserve harmony between the United States and the Netherlands and thus ease the formation of NATO. Canada attempted a middle path in the Indonesian-Malaysian conflict, perhaps the last stand of the idea of the Commonwealth as a joint actor in international affairs. Only when Indonesia began to pose a collective-security threat to the UN did Canada side fully with Malaysia. With a pro-Western government in power in Indonesia after 1965, trade came to the fore, overruling any thought that Canada should oppose Indonesia's invasion of East Timor. As in the case of relations with Japan before the war, Ottawa proved reluctant to take any step that might harm trade prospects with Indonesia. Canadian actions on East Timor, when they came, took place only in a narrow window when the Indonesia's economic and strategic value, high in 1975, had both declined sharply. Canada acted in conjunction with its allies in 1999. The North Atlantic triangle may have vanished by the 1960s, but the alliance thinking remained.

Canada's involvement in Asia, particularly in times of conflict, has been shaped by multilateralism. To put it starkly, there was no coherent

Canadian policy towards Asia, but rather a Canadian foreign policy applied to Asian cases. That policy, for most of the past century, has been driven by North Atlantic priorities. Canada's approach to non-communist eastern Asia, from its northern anchor in Japan to its southern anchor in Indonesia, concentrated above all on bridging differences between Canadian allies and contributing where possible to the overall goals of the Western alliance. Within those confines, successive Canadian governments have done what they could to take advantage of Asian trade opportunities.

The legacy of North Atlantic and Cold War ties has led to forms of alliance thinking that continue to affect Ottawa's response to crises, most recently in Afghanistan. As with Japan before 1945 and Indonesia in the postwar period, Canadian awareness of the country has improved only slightly from Gordon Sinclair's breathless account of 1932. Today's images of Afghanistan are not so much different from the Canadian journalist's portrait of "turbulent tribesmen" of "this warrior land ... where sniping is the favourite outdoor sport" who "live to plunder and kill," held back by British planes prone to bomb villages that become too troublesome. So too images of a vast Asian market remain similar to those of 100 years ago, and Canada balances alliance priorities. The journey from King to Kandahar has not been one of ever-greater awareness of Asia. For a nation aspiring to Pacific status, Canada's approach to the region has remained strongly North Atlantic.[34]

NOTES

1 King diary, 22 Feb.1909. Library and Archives Canada [hereinafter LAC], King Papers, MG26, J13. For more on King's tour see John Hilliker, "Mackenzie King on the Pacific Rim, 1909: Thinking about an East Asian Policy for Canada" in Dolores Elizalde, ed., *Las Relaciones Internacionales en el Pacifico (Siglos XVIII-XX): Colonizacion, Descolonizacion y Encuentro Cultural* (Madrid: Consejo Superior de Investigaciones Cientificas, 1997), 575–89.

2 As King reflected privately: "Let her remain part of the empire for the good of our own people; let her demand a position of equality with that of every other unit. Let her cease to think in colonial terms and to act in any way as with a colonial status. Let her become a nation or other nations will rob her of this right." King diary, 4 March 1909.

3 King's sister was married to the son of Horatio Nelson Lay, the legendary British trader and customs inspector at Shanghai. Alvyn Austin, *Saving China: Canadian Missionaries in the Middle Kingdom, 1888–1959* (Toronto: University of Toronto Press, 1986), 262.

4 Patricia Roy, *A White Man's Province: British Columbia Politicians and Chinese and Japanese Immigrants, 1858–1914* (Vancouver: UBC Press, 1989), 202–5; W. Peter Ward, *White Canada Forever: Popular Attitudes and Public Policy Toward Orientals in British Columbia* (Montreal and Kingston: McGill-Queen's University Press, 2002), 73–76; Serge Granger, *Lys et Lotus* (Montreal: VLB Editeur, 2005), 32; King diary, 26 Feb. 1909.

5 For more on Canada's role during the conflicts in Korea and Vietnam, see Steven Hugh Lee, *Outposts of Empire: Korea, Vietnam and the Origins of the Cold War in Asia, 1949–1954* (Kingston: McGill-Queen's University Press, 1995); Greg Donaghy, "Pacific Diplomacy: Canadian Statecraft and the Korean War, 1950–53," in R.W.L. Guisso and Young-sik Yoo, (eds.) *Canada and Korea: Perspectives 2000* (Toronto: Centre for Korean Studies, University of Toronto, 2002), 81–100; Dennis Stairs, *The Diplomacy of Constraint: Canada, the Korean War, and the United States* (Toronto: University of Toronto Press, 1974); Douglas A. Ross, *In the Interests of Peace: Canada and Vietnam 1954–1973* (Toronto: University of Toronto Press, 1984); Andrew Preston, "Balancing War and Peace: Canadian Foreign Policy and the Vietnam War," *Diplomatic History* 27 #1 (Winter 2003): 73–111; and Robert Bothwell, "The Further Shore: Canada and Vietnam," *International Journal* 51, no. 1 (2000–01): 89–114.

6 John B. Brebner, "Canada, the Anglo-Japanese Alliance and the Washington Conference", *Political Science Quarterly*, 50 (1935); W.L.M. King, "Canada's Legations Abroad," *Canadian Nation* 2, 1 (1929): 26; O.M. Hill, *Canada's Salesman to the World: the Department of Trade and Commerce, 1892–1939* (Montreal: McGill-Queen's University Press, 1977), 315; Canada, House of Commons, *Debates*, 30 Jan. 1928, 29. Canada had opened a high commission in London in 1880, a *commissaire général* in Paris in 1882, immigration and trade offices thereafter and, more recently, an advisory office at Geneva in 1924, but these lacked the diplomatic status of a legation.

7 John Meehan, *The Dominion and the Rising Sun: Canada Encounters Japan, 1929–1941* (Vancouver: University of British Columbia Press, 2004), 76–8; Margaret MacMillan, *Paris 1919: Six Months that Changed the World* (New York: Random House, 2001), 306–44.

8 Keenleyside report dated 30 Dec. 1936, RG25, G-1, vol. 1808, file 899, LAC; C.P. Stacey, *Canada and the Age of Conflict, vol. 2: 1921–1948* (Toronto: University of Toronto Press, 1984), 135–45; Michael Hart, *A Trading Nation: Canadian Trade Policy from Colonialism to Globalization* (Vancouver: University of British Columbia Press, 2002), 102–15.

9 See Christopher Thorne, *The Limits of Foreign Policy* (London, 1972), 141–43; Meehan, *Dominion and Rising Sun*, 55–69.

10 *Financial Post*, 21 Nov. 1931; Mack Eastman, *Canada at Geneva* (Toronto, 1946), 93; Marler to SSEA, 7 Feb. 1934, RG25, G-1, vol. 1606, file 786, LAC. For more on the Cahan affair, see Richard Veatch, *Canada and the League of*

Nations (Toronto, 1975); F.H. Soward, "Forty Years On: The Cahan Blunder Re-examined" in *BC Studies* 32 (Winter 1976–77): 126–38; Donald Story, "Canada, the League of Nations and the Far East, 1931–3: The Cahan Incident", *International History Review* 3, 2 (Apr. 1981): 236–55. For the full text of Cahan's speech, see Appendix II of R.A. MacKay and E.B. Rogers, *Canada Looks Abroad* (Toronto, 1938), 335–40.

11 Meehan, *Dominion and Rising Sun*, 95–97; T. McCulloch, "'The Key Log in the Jam': Mackenzie King, the North Atlantic Triangle and the Anglo-American Rapprochement of 1935–39," *London Journal of Canadian Studies* 20 (2004/2005): 47–50; King diary, 26 Feb. 1936.

12 John Meehan, "Steering Clear of Great Britain: Canada's Debate over Collective Security in the Far Eastern Crisis of 1937," *The International History Review* 25 (June 2003): 253–81; Stacey, *Canada and Age of Conflict*, 202–13; Meehan, *Dominion and Rising Sun*, 142–56; Bradford Lee, *Britain and the Sino-Japanese War, 1937–1939* (Stanford, 1973), 54.

13 King diary, 19 Oct. 1937; J.S. Macdonald memo, 16 Feb. 1938, RG25, D1, vol. 723, file 64, LAC; Canada, Dominion Bureau of Statistics, *Canada Year Book, 1938* (Ottawa, 1939), 580.

14 Meehan, *Dominion and Rising Sun*, 164–7.

15 Skelton to Bruce, 6 March 1939, RG25, D1, vol. 723, file 64, LAC.

16 Mockridge to Skelton, 27 Sept. 1939, RG25, G-1, vol. 1749, file 652B, LAC; SSEA to Wrong, 18 Oct. 1940, RG25, G-1, vol. 1953, file 836Y, LAC; McGreer to SSEA, 17 April 1941, MG26, J4, vol. 385, file 14, LAC.

17 King memo, 27 July 1941, MG26, J4, vol. 283, file 2963, LAC; Keenleyside memo, 5 Aug. 1941, MG26, J4, vol. 283, file 2965, LAC. King signed the declaration of war the night before Congress approved Roosevelt's message and Britain followed America's lead.

18 Lee, *Outposts of Empire*, 255–6; Robert Bothwell, "Eyes West: Canada and the Cold War in Asia" in Greg Donaghy, ed., *Canada and the Early Cold War, 1943–1957* (Ottawa: DFAIT, 1998), 60.

19 John Price, "E.H. Norman, Canada and Japan's Postwar Constitution," *Pacific Affairs* 74 (Fall 2001): 383–405; John Stanton, "Reluctant Vengeance: Canada at the Tokyo War Crimes Tribunal," *Journal of American and Canadian Studies* 17 (1999): 61–87.

20 John Holmes, *The Shaping of Peace: Canada and the Search for World Order 1943–1957*, vol. 2 (Toronto: University of Toronto Press, 1982), 177–8; Hilliker, *Canada's Department of External Affairs*, vol. I, 266; Odlum cited in Austin, *Saving China*, 274; Stephen Beecroft, "Canadian Policy towards China, 1949–1957: The Recognition Problem," in Bernie Frolic and Paul Evans, eds., *Reluctant Adversaries: Canada and the People's Republic of China* (Toronto: University of Toronto Press, 1991), 43–65; Meehan interview with Arthur Menzies, 16 July 2005.

21 Lee, *Outposts of Empire*, 74. For more on the debate regarding Canadian-American relations during the Korean conflict, see Stairs, *Diplomacy of*

Constraint; Robert Prince, "The Limits of Constraint: Canadian-American Relations and the Korean War, 1950–51," in *Journal of Canadian Studies*, 27, 4 (Winter 1992–93); and Donaghy, "Pacific Diplomacy," 81–5.

22 John Holmes, *The Shaping of Peace: Canada and the Search for World Order 1943–1957*, volume 2 (Toronto: University of Toronto Press, 1982), 177–8; "The Indonesian Question," memorandum by Arthur Menzies to USSEA, 31 Dec. 1947, LAC, RG25, vol. 5712, file 7-AT(s) [FP.2].

23 Alastair Taylor, *Indonesian Independence and the United Nations* (Ithaca: Cornell University Press, 1960); George Ignatieff, "General A.G.L. McNaughton: A Soldier in Diplomacy," *International Journal* 22 (1966–67): 402–14; Canadian UN delegation to USSEA, 7 Feb. 1948, LAC, RG25, vol. 4715, file 50054-40 [4]; King diary, 20 Feb. 1948; Holmes, *The Shaping of Peace*, 2: 69.

24 Cabinet conclusions, 23 Dec. 1948, LAC, RG2, A-5-a, vol. 2642; Australian high commission Ottawa report, 31 Dec. 1948, National Archives of Australia, A3100, G48/124; Dutch embassy Ottawa report, 14 Feb. 1949, *Officiële Beschieden betreffende de Nederlands-Indonesische Betrekkingen*, vol. 17, 561–2.

25 Memorandum for the PM, 16 May 1952, LAC, RG2, series 18, vol. 222, file I-18; SSEA's letter of instructions for Jakarta embassy, 19 Aug. 1953, LAC, RG25, vol. 6613, file 11129-40 [3.1]; Ademola Adeleke, *Ties without Strings? The Colombo Plan and the Geopolitics of International Aid* (Ph.D. dissertation, University of Toronto, 1996); Japanese government discussion paper, 12 Oct. 1954, LAC, RG25, vol. 11038-40 [18].

26 H. Basil Robinson, *Diefenbaker's World: A Populist in Foreign Affairs* (Toronto: University of Toronto Press, 1989); Theodore Newton, *South Seas Envoy: Memoirs of a Canadian ambassador*, unpublished manuscript, LAC, Theodore Newton papers, MG31 E74, 40; cabinet conclusions, 4 June 1959, LAC, RG2, A-5-a, vol. 2744, 1959/06/04; cabinet conclusions, 21 July 1960, LAC, RG2, A-5-a, vol. 2747, 1960/07/21; Michael Hart, *A Trading Nation: Canadian Trade Policy from Colonialism to Globalization* (Vancouver: UBC Press, 2002), 189.

27 Matthew Jones, *Conflict and Cooperation in Southeast Asia, 1961–1965: Britain, the United States, and the Creation of Malaysia* (Cambridge: Cambridge University Press, 2002); John Subritzky, *Confronting Sukarno: British, American, Australian and New Zealand diplomacy in the Malaysian-Indonesian confrontation, 1961–5* (Basingstoke: Macmillan, 2000); Canadian high commission Karachi telegram, 29 Sept. 1965, LAC, RG25, vol. 8861, file 20-INDON-1-3 [4].

28 Canadian embassy Washington to USSEA, 10 April 1964, LAC, RG25, vol. 8917, file 20-INDON-1-3-MLSIA [4]; Jakarta letter 104, 16 March 1965, LAC, RG25, vol. 8917, file 20-INDON-1-3-MLSIA [8]; *Indonesian Herald* editorial, 29 Jan. 1965; Bradley Simpson, *Economists with Guns* (Princeton University Press, forthcoming); David Webster, "Shaping Islam: the McGill Institute of Islamic Studies and cold war modernization," *International Journal of Canadian Studies* 32 (2005): 15–43.

29 John Roosa, *Pretext for Mass Murder: The September 30 Movement and Suharto's Coup in Indonesia* (Madison: University of Wisconsin Press, 2007); memorandum to the minister, 26 August 1966, LAC, RG25, vol. 10099, file 20-1-2-INDON; personal notes by Louis Rogers, director-general of Asian and Pacific Affairs, on visit to Southeast Asia, 6–14 June 1977, LAC, RG25, vol. 10861, file 20-INDON-2-2; *Foreign Policy for Canadians*, Pacific booklet (Ottawa: Dept. of External Affairs, 1970), 7; CIDA, *Canada and the Developing World* (Ottawa: Queen's Printer, 1970).

30 Briefing note for Suharto visit to Canada, cited in Sharon Scharfe, *Complicity: Human Rights and Canadian Foreign Policy, the Case of East Timor* (Montreal: Black Rose Books, 1996); Allan MacEachen speech in Jakarta, 25 Aug. 1976, External Affairs *Statements and Speeches* 76/25; Malia Southard, *Looking the Other Way: The Indonesian Bond, Partnership or Plunder* (Victoria: South Pacific Peoples Foundation, 1997); Jamie Swift, *The Big Nickel: Inco at Home and Abroad* (Toronto: Between the Lines, 1977); confidential memorandum on Inco operations, attached to Jakarta letter 280, 22 June 1971, LAC, RG25, vol. 10861, file 20-INDON-2-2.

31 Peter Johnston, *Cooper's Snoopers and Other Follies: Fragments of a Life* (Victoria: Trafford, 2002); Geoffrey B. Hainsworth, *Innocents Abroad or Partners in Development: An Evaluation of Canada-Indonesia Aid, Trade and Investment Relations* (Singapore: Institute of Southeast Asian Studies, 1986); David Morrison, "The Choice of Bilateral Aid Recipients," in Cranford Pratt, ed., *Canadian Development Assistance Policies: An Appraisal* (Montreal: McGill-Queen's University Press, 1994), 132; memorandum by W.T. Delworth, 9 Oct. 1979, LAC, RG25, vol. 8664, file 20-TIMOR [6]; "Twenty Years in East Timor: A Chronological Overview" [1994], DFAIT file 20-TIMOR, obtained through access to information requests.

32 Mulroney speech at Commonwealth heads of government meeting in Harare, Zimbabwe, 16 Oct. 1991; Chris Dagg. "Linking Aid to Human Rights in Indonesia: A Canadian Perspective," *Issues* 7 #1 (Winter 1993).

33 Canadian position paper on East Timor for APEC meeting, transmitted 7 Sept. 1999, DFAIT file 20-TIMOR; Ian Martin, *Self-Determination in East Timor: The United Nations, the Ballot, and International Intervention* (Boulder: Lynne Rienner, 2001); Geoffrey Robinson, *East Timor 1999: Crimes Against Humanity* (report for the UN High Commissioner for Human Rights, 2005).

34 Robert Bothwell, "Back to the Future: Canada and Empires," *International Journal* 59 #2 (Spring 2004); Gordon Sinclair, *Foot-Loose in India* (Toronto: McClelland and Stewart, 1966 edition), 1–27.

12 Chinese Shadows

FRED EDWARDS

In one of his best-known essays, *On Contradiction*, Mao Zedong said: "There are many contradictions in the course of development of every major thing."[1] Whether the chairman considered the Sino-Canadian relationship to be "a major thing" is a matter of conjecture, but it certainly has been rife with contradiction on the Canadian side. Some of these contradictions have been obvious, most notably the concurrence of racist immigration policies and missionary work in the late 19th and early 20th centuries. Others have been more subtle. After the Second World War, Canadian leaders enrolled the country in a powerful anti-Communist military alliance but also promoted diplomatic recognition and United Nations membership for the new People's Republic, a tricky combination that paralyzed independent policy making for two decades. Even after the normalization of bilateral relations in 1970, contradictions persisted. Was engagement with Beijing simply a matter of diplomatic realism or was there some broader national interest – trade, perhaps, or the building of a peaceful, rules-based international order, or the assertion of Canadian independence? Should Canada promote "Canadian values" – loosely defined as liberal democracy and human rights – and should these values have policy implications linked to the behaviour of China's Communist party dictatorship? As Mao said, contradictions are inevitable and we should not be surprised that they exist in the relations between two very different countries. Resolving them, though, has been made more difficult by the Canadian practice of relating to China largely on symbolic terms, a tendency reinforced by the – until recently – lack of real substance in the relationship. China variously has been a heathen land of lost souls, a gallant wartime ally, a spear point of militant communism, a counterweight to American influence, a tantalizing market. Rarely, in Canadian eyes, has China just been China.

Initial impressions were negative. Only a century ago, the British Columbia-based Asiatic Exclusion League proclaimed, "British Columbia people will not permit this country to be made a dumping ground of yellow cheap labour." A Vancouver Liberal MP said the province was meant to be "a white man's country. The majority of residents are utterly opposed to the present flinging wide the gates to Asiatics." Even Robert Borden, soon to be prime minister, was of the opinion that British Columbia should be "inhabited and dominated by men in whose veins runs the blood of those great pioneering races which built up and developed not only western but eastern Canada."[2] Not Chinese, in other words. The context of these unabashedly racist comments was the anti-Asian riots in Vancouver in September of 1907. They had broken out because white British Columbians felt that existing deterrents to Asian immigration were inadequate. Chinese immigrants had been subject to a head tax since 1885; it began at $50, had risen to $100 in 1900 and then leapt to $500 in 1903. Chinese voters were disenfranchised in B.C. and Saskatchewan – home to less than 1,000 Chinese – and Chinese workers earned a fraction of white wages. These measures had, however, failed to stop the modest trickle of Chinese immigrants. By 1911, the Chinese population was about 28,000 nationally, with 20,000 in British Columbia, enough for the Toronto *Globe* to warn of "national decay."[3]

Canada's restrictive immigration policies became an issue in the country's nascent foreign relations with China and Japan. They also collided with imperial concerns – one of the first examples of the complications in Canadian policy making stemming from the Dominion's status as a junior partner to a global power. The Anglo-Japanese alliance precluded any legislative restriction on the Japanese living in Canada; as late as 1922 the Supreme Court would overturn B.C. legislation on those grounds. After the Vancouver riots, Prime Minister Wilfrid Laurier cabled his regrets to the Japanese emperor; China got no similar apology. Canada would, though, negotiate a "gentleman's agreement" with Japan to limit immigration to 150 persons a year. Labour Minister Mackenzie King, representing Canada at the International Opium Commission meeting in Shanghai in 1909, approached Chinese authorities about the possibility of instituting a passport system that would allow Ottawa to limit the number of Chinese immigrants and also abolish the head tax. The Qing dynasty and the Liberal party of Canada both fell from power in 1911 before any agreement could be reached. The Chinese consul in Vancouver raised the issue again after the First World War. By this time, however, political turmoil in China persuaded Ottawa that no Chinese government would be capable of enforcing an accord, setting the stage for the Chinese Immigration Act of 1923. This bill eased Liberal consciences by abolishing the head tax but imposed such severe restrictions on admittance as to virtually eliminate Chinese immigration – census figures show that all of eight Chinese immigrants arrived between 1924 and 1940. King, now prime minister, tried to make this sordid act sound noble: "I could never see how Canada, from any self-respecting point of view, could impose a poll tax on working people coming from another country, and at the same time have its population subscribe to funds for missionary purposes to teach the heathen the most elementary principles of Christianity."[4]

Despite his hypocrisy, King here touched on the original contradiction – one might say the original sin – in Canadian-Chinese relations, the combination of good works overseas and blatant racism at home. By the early 20th century, there were about 3,300 Protestant missionaries in China, 1,800 of them British, of whom a quarter were Canadian. Alvyn Austin, in his history of Canadian mission work in China, notes that as a proportion of its population, Canada sponsored more missionaries than any other nation.[5] The first wave of volunteers was motivated by the opportunity provided by British-led globalization "to evangelize the world within a generation." The English missionary James Hudson Taylor, who founded the China Inland Mission and recruited the first group of Protestant Canadian missionaries, told a conference in Niagara-on-the-Lake in 1888 that "there is a great Niagara of souls passing into the dark in China ... A million a month are dying without God!" The desire to save souls in a heathen land was widely shared. In September of that year, when Taylor's party was preparing to depart from Toronto for the transcontinental train trip to the West Coast and the boat voyage to China, University of Toronto President Daniel Wilson addressed an enthusiastic crowd of 2,000 at the YMCA's Association Hall. "It must be a source of happiness to those present," he said, "to know that God has honoured the city by choosing so many of its young people to go out and preach the gospel to the heathen."[6]

The heathen, though, were not particularly receptive. Conversion rates were low and violence against missionaries was common. In Sichuan province, two-and-a-half decades of work by Canadian Methodists among a population of 12 million people produced a "Christian community" of about 14,000, of whom less than 250 were actually baptized.[7] Austin notes that "anti-Christian antipathy permeated all levels of society." Local gentry and officials felt threatened by foreigners who could both invoke the gospel and summon British gunboats when they encountered resistance. The wary and superstitious common people, the *laobaixing* (literally, the old hundred surnames), regarded the pale-skinned foreigners as not quite human.[8] Perhaps they were ghosts, perhaps demons; it was a subject of discussion in the teahouses. Exploiting the Chinese language's protean punning capability, a ubiquitous placard titled "Death Blow to Corrupt Doctrines" played on the common pronunciation of the words for "lord" and "pig." Thus the word for heavenly lord (*tianzhu*) became "heavenly pig," and the placard, which regularly appeared before anti-missionary riots, claimed that the perverted foreigners worshipped pigs. Anti-Christian feeling was hardly surprising, since missions tended to spread with the "unequal treaties" that foreign powers imposed on China. As such, it can be seen as an expression of Chinese nationalism.

The taunts and casual violence the early missionaries were subjected to encouraged a shift from pure evangelizing toward the provision of educational and medical services. Working in mission compounds with schools and hospitals was safer than the earlier practice of sending individuals or small groups into the hostile countryside. Medicine and education also were effective ways for missionaries to ingratiate themselves into Chinese society. The first Chinese convert in the Canadian-run northern Henan mission was a man who had a cataract removed.[9] The United Church's board of foreign missions noted later that Henan "was opened by the point of a lancet."[10] The emphasis on education and medicine coincided with the development of the "social gospel," which widened the scope of religious activity from saving souls to alleviating the effects of poverty and injustice. In 1907, the journal *Missionary Outlook* described Christianity as "a social religion concerned ... with the quality of human relations on this earth."[11] By 1919, the main Protestant denominations, the Methodists, Presbyterians and Anglicans, supported two universities, 270 schools and 30 hospitals.

Even the more secure setting of schools and hospitals, however, could not protect missionaries from waves of anti-foreign violence. Inland missions were evacuated at regular intervals as missionaries fled to the foreign concessions on the coast to escape mobs infuriated by some foreign outrage. By the mid-1920s, nationalist sentiment was coalescing around the Kuomintang, or nationalist party, led by Chiang Kai-shek since the death of founder Sun Yat-sen in 1925.[12] In 1926, Chiang led his forces out of Guangdong province in the south with the goal of reuniting the country and establishing an effective national government, a task he completed the following year when he marched into Beijing. This "northern expedition" unleashed a new spasm of nationalist violence against foreign missionaries and more than 8,000 were evacuated to the coast.

The rise of Chinese nationalism accentuated the contradictions between the evangelizers who wanted to save China and the social gospellers who wanted to serve China. One flashpoint was the role of Chinese Christians within the church. In Sichuan, Chinese Christians broke away from the Canadian-run West China mission. They set four goals: to destroy church imperialism; to recover religious autonomy; to love God, and to love China. The general assembly of the Church of Christ, a grouping of Chinese Presbyterians and Congregationalists, pointedly declared that the message of Christ must not be delivered "with pride of race or overbearing manner, not tied to alien civilizations or outworn dogmas ..."[13] Dismayed by these and similar events, Rev. Harvey Grant of the United Church, who served in Henan, expressed openly imperialist sentiments during the 1927 evacuation: "We are proud to be British citizens these days ... it may be necessary for G.B. and other countries who are following her lead to speak loudly with guns before the desired end is reached ..."[14] Nearby in Kaifeng, however, Anglican Bishop William White was ready to accommodate Chinese nationalism. He called the domination of the Chinese church by foreign missionaries "the greatest single obstacle to Christianity in the minds of the thinking classes, for the strong nationalist spirit of present China is violently anti-foreign and therefore anti-Christian. Until this stigma ... can be removed, the Church in China cannot be the Church of the Chinese nation."[15] Five years later, the associated boards for foreign missions of the United States and Canada issued a sombre report titled *Re-Thinking Missions* that clearly expressed a loss of confidence in the missionary enterprise. Most missionaries, it said, were "of limited outlook and capacity." It lamented that their "vision of the inner meaning of the mission has become obscured by the intricacies, divisions, frictions and details of a task too great for their powers and their hearts."[16]

A missionary connection runs through later Canadian foreign policy and often is cited when Canada and China are described as having a "special relationship."[17] Yet the missionary endeavour was neither successful on its own terms of winning converts nor popular with the Chinese people. Indeed, the word "missionary" remains something of an epithet in China, as Professor Charles Burton discovered in 2005 when he interviewed Chinese participants in the Canada-China bilateral human rights dialogue and one complained that "the Canadians have a 'missionary attitude.'"[18]

Anti-Chinese racism and the missionary movement were conflicting expressions of currents within contemporary Canadian society. In terms of formal foreign policy, China ranked low in Canadian priorities during the 1920s and 30s. After becoming prime minister in 1923, Mackenzie King favoured American-style isolationism, as did his chief foreign policy adviser, O.D. Skelton. Furthermore, Canada enjoyed good relations with Japan, China's chief tormentor. Trade with Japan more than doubled in the 1920s before the onset of the Depression, and spiked again in the late 1930s as Tokyo stocked up on Canadian metals to build its war machine.[19] As Japanese aggression against China intensified in the 1930s, Canada favoured appeasement and profitable trade.

Pearl Harbor changed everything. Not only did it turn Nationalist China into a wartime ally, it injected a powerful new factor into Canadian policy making – the United States. After the Japanese chased Britain from its Chinese and Southeast Asian redoubts, America led the Allied war effort in the Far East, emerging in 1945 as the dominant regional power, a status it still holds. Canada's tepid pro-Japanese position in the 1930s had mirrored London's but now every Canadian action would have to be considered in light of Washington's reaction. Unsurprisingly, American debates about China policy began to be echoed in Canada. Some Canadians, notably Ambassador Victor Odlum, became staunch supporters of Chiang and the Kuomintang. Others, including Odlum's successor T.C. Davis, were appalled by the corruption and inefficiency of Chiang's regime. James Endicott, a former missionary, personified the debate, embarking on an ideological journey that would take him from being a personal adviser to Chiang's quasi-fascist New Life Movement to winner of the Stalin Peace Prize in 1953 for his support of the Chinese Communists. As Chiang's prospects deteriorated after 1947, a consensus began to emerge among Canadian officials that Ottawa should recognize the new Communist regime when it was established. Indeed, cabinet agreed in principle on 16 November 1949 to recognize the People's Republic of China, just slightly more than a month after it was founded. The Department of External Affairs even took an option on a potential embassy site in Beijing in February 1950, and Chester Ronning, another former missionary, conducted negotiations with Chinese officials in the spring of 1950 about establishing relations prior to formal recognition.

Diplomatic recognition and admitting the People's Republic to the United Nations were consistent with the "new internationalism" that emerged in Canadian foreign policy after the Second World War. Compared with King's isolationism or the eager imperialism of earlier generations, this new stance was sophisticated and complex, perhaps too much so for a minor power. While aligning itself firmly with the U.S.-led alliance of western democracies, Ottawa also favoured peaceful engagement with potential adversaries within a rules-based international system. To External Affairs Minister Lester Pearson and his senior advisers, a policy of isolating Communist China would only serve to increase regional tension and undermine the United Nations, the very body Canada was counting on to provide a forum for peaceful conflict resolution.

Washington saw things differently. Although equally frustrated with Chiang and not lacking in advocates for engagement with Mao's

Communists, the United States faced the bitter prospect of seeing a country it had supported through long years of war sliding into the Communist camp at the very time the Soviet grip on Eastern Europe was tightening. A populist anti-Communist movement led by Wisconsin Senator Joseph McCarthy also deterred American policy makers from abandoning Chiang and recognizing Mao's Communists as the legitimate government of China. Ottawa was in no position to ignore American opinion. Not only was the United States the dominant power in Asia and leader of the broad western alliance, rapid continental economic integration in North America made Canadian policy makers uniquely sensitive to the potential material hazards of defying Washington. The reach of American opinion was further augmented by the development of a continental media market, notably television. There was firm domestic opposition as well. The federal Conservative party and the powerful premier of Quebec, Maurice Duplessis, were opposed to recognition and UN membership for the People's Republic, as were influential cabinet ministers like C.D. Howe and Jimmy Gardiner. Even Chinese Canadians, generally pro-Kuomintang and free since 1947 from the restrictions of the Chinese Immigration Act, opposed recognition. In this risky political and diplomatic climate, and in the absence of any compelling national interest to act quickly, Prime Minister Louis St. Laurent felt it best to wait.

For the newborn People's Republic, diplomatic relations outside the socialist camp were a low priority. Despite Mao's declaration of the founding of the PRC on 1 October 1949, fighting on the mainland continued, and would continue until 1954. Tibet and Taiwan were not secure. Military involvement in support of the Vietnamese and/or Korean Communists was a possibility – we now know that Mao and Stalin discussed the Korean issue as early as January 1950.[20] Beyond that, Mao had an ambitious domestic agenda to create a socialist society. Even states that promptly recognized the new government in Beijing were kept waiting. Britain, concerned about the security of Hong Kong, recognized the People's Republic in January 1950 but an office of chargé d'affaires was not established in Beijing until 1954; an exchange of ambassadors would take until 1972.

The outbreak of the Korean War on 25 June 1950 and Chinese intervention in October froze the United States and China into two decades of hostility and trapped Canadian policy within a prison of contradiction and indecision. The External Affairs Department – or at least parts of it – continued to recommend recognition but the political will to act was lacking. A repetitive pattern emerged: a trial balloon would be floated, domestic and foreign reaction would be gauged, and after anxious consideration the best course always seemed to be delay. In March of 1954, St. Laurent told the House of Commons that Canada eventually would have to recognize the government that the Chinese people had chosen. Confronted immediately with Conservative accusations of appeasement and a flood of letters from Quebec Catholics, he promptly apologized to the House for a poor choice of words. A year later, Pearson suggested during a speech in Vancouver that Canada soon would "have another and searching look at the problem."[21] Despite an initially muted U.S. response, External counselled against haste. Jules Léger, then under-secretary of state for External Affairs, said: "… it would seem the wisest policy to sit back for several months at least … and watch developments."[22] When the Americans did finally reply in December, Léger's caution seemed well warranted, as senior State Department official Walter Robertson warned of "disturbing consequences" if Canada continued down the recognition path.[23] In 1958, John Diefenbaker's foreign minister, Sidney Smith, raised the subject during a meeting with President Dwight Eisenhower and Secretary of State John Foster Dulles, only to be told that such an act risked the destruction of the United Nations. The Canadian tendency to retreat from the implications of its own commitment to peaceful engagement prompted R.L. Rogers to write in a departmental memo: "I think it is not to be expected that Canada will be found in the van of a movement for recognition or for seating Communist China in the United Nations. I think we must be prepared to follow a less heroic course, to be among the late-comers in recognition."[24]

Nor were Chinese actions helpful. Canadian policy makers could, and did, argue that Beijing's repeated shocks – intervention in Korea, shelling in the Taiwan Strait in 1954, the invasion of Tibet in 1959, war with India in 1962, a nuclear test in 1964, support for the Vietnamese Communists in the 1960s – proved that isolation only increased tension. Pearson made that point in a memo in May 1953: "Until Communist China is generally recognized we can see no end to the tension in the Far East."[25] Perhaps that was wise and prescient but Beijing's behaviour ensured that the political and diplomatic climate would remain hostile to a Canadian initiative.

Diplomatic impotence was one thing, commerce something else altogether. During this roughly two-decade period between 1949 and 1968, there was one significant development that owed more to robust Canadian grain production than to diplomatic boldness. Ironically, it occurred under the Conservative Diefenbaker, himself an opponent of diplomatic recognition. The late 1950s and early 1960s were famine years in China as Mao's Great Leap Forward, designed to propel the country into the ranks of the developed nations within a decade, failed spectacularly. Canada, on the other hand, was plagued by large agricultural surpluses that posed an economic and political problem for Diefenbaker and his Agriculture minister,

Alvin Hamilton. Anticipating American objections, Diefenbaker raised the issue of potential Canadian food exports to China during his 1958 meeting with Eisenhower and Dulles. The prime minister expressed his concern that restrictive U.S. legislation might prohibit the involvement of American firms or subsidiaries during key points in the trade process. Dulles, less worried about trade than broad geopolitical issues, assured Diefenbaker that special licensing procedures could overcome any difficulties. China started to buy Canadian wheat that same year but it was not until Hamilton took over the Agriculture portfolio in October 1960 that Canada adopted an aggressive strategy to open the Chinese market.[26] After the visit of a Canadian trade mission to Beijing, a Chinese team carrying $60 million arrived in Montreal in late November and bought 28 million bushels of wheat and 12 million bushels of barley. In March of 1961, the Canadian Wheat Board reported that the Chinese were prepared to make further massive purchases over the next two-and-a-half years "if flexibility in payment arrangements could be negotiated."[27] Hamilton was willing to grant credit but cabinet was opposed. It took Hamilton's threat to resign and the intervention of the prime minister to approve the proposed credit terms and save the sale.[28] Despite Dulles's earlier assurances, problems with the Americans remained. John Kennedy, who had campaigned as a militant cold warrior, was now president and not predisposed to enabling Canadian wheat sales to Communist China. An initial disagreement over the provision of oil from an American subsidiary to fuel the cargo ships was resolved quickly but then Kennedy balked at permitting the export of American-made grain unloaders, which were essential to the shipping process. In Diefenbaker's telling, Kennedy relented only after Diefenbaker threatened to go on national TV and radio to tell the Canadian people that Kennedy was "attempting to run our country."[29] Nor was that the end of it. In early 1962, Under-Secretary of State George Ball suggested that Canada should threaten to break off food deliveries over China's support of North Vietnam. Canada ignored the suggestion, and even continued grain exports after China attacked India, a fellow Commonwealth member, in 1962. China became the primary export market for Canadian wheat during the next decade, accounting for about a fifth of the country's cereal exports at a time when grain was Canada's second largest export commodity. With the China market accounting for almost 30 percent of Prairie farmers' annual income,[30] it is hardly surprising that the sales were a fantastic political success, securing Conservative support in the western provinces for a generation. They also proved something else: when tangible national interest was involved, Canada was willing to risk American disapproval in order to expand contact with China.

Diefenbaker, however, never considered reviving efforts to establish diplomatic relations, although in his memoirs he does mention that

Canada's failure to act promptly before the Korean War was "unfortunate" and a "mistake."[31] The return of the Liberals to power in 1963 revived the old Hamlet routine. External Affairs conducted policy reviews in 1963, 65 and 66 and there were minor Canadian initiatives in 1964 and 1966, but Pearson, more cautious as prime minister than he had been as foreign minister, remained reluctant to act. Still, the world was changing. France recognized China in 1964. Even the Americans began to rethink their policy. In 1966, the Senate Foreign Relations Committee held hearings on China and heard arguments suggesting that China could be contained without isolation. In the State Department, William Bundy, Joseph Sisco and Arthur Goldberg became converts to a two-China policy and even engaged in an odd bit of reverse lobbying, urging Canada to promote this approach with the Johnson administration as a way of outflanking Dean Rusk, the intransigent secretary of state. The Liberal party also was embarking on a transition. Pearson turned 70 in 1967 and potential successors such as Paul Martin Sr. and Pierre Trudeau felt it was time for change, as did the party as a whole. The 1966 Liberal conference voted for immediate recognition and UN admission. Martin, urged on by Trudeau and with the wary support of Pearson, abstained rather than voting no when Albania's annual motion to seat the People's Republic and expel the Taiwan-based Republic of China was put before the General Assembly that year. Typically, Ottawa braced for the reaction to what was the first significant change in the Canadian position since 1949. Nothing much happened. Even so, China was in no position to respond. Mao had embarked on his final revolutionary adventure and plunged the country into the Great Proletarian Cultural Revolution, paralyzing the government apparatus.

The arrival of Pierre Trudeau as prime minister in April 1968 cut through the contradictions and timidity that had paralyzed Canadian policy toward China since 1949. Trudeau brought with him a new style and sensibility – more independent, more truly global, less Atlanticist. He also had rare personal experience, having visited China in 1949 and 1960, and was something of an admirer of "one of the most significant revolutions in the history of the world and the extension of basic human amenities to hundreds of millions of persons to whom they had been denied for millennia."[32] Almost immediately he announced his intention to recognize the People's Republic "as soon as possible and to enable that government to occupy the seat of China at the UN, taking into account that there is a separate government in Taiwan."[33] His words set in motion a two-year process that ended in October of 1970 with a four-paragraph communiqué announcing the terms of the new relationship. The most contentious issue in the negotiations, and the main reason they took so long, was Taiwan. From the start, Beijing insisted on its "three constant principles": that Canada recognize the People's Republic as the sole legal government of China; recognize Taiwan as an inalienable part of China and sever all relationships with the Taipei government; and support PRC representation at the United Nations. Beijing's goal was not so much a formal relationship with Canada – desirable as that might be – as it was winning international legitimacy and building a majority in the United Nations General Assembly so it could take over the China seat. The Canadians eventually came up with some face-saving wording – that Ottawa "took note" of the Chinese claims – but still had to abandon Taiwan. This did not trouble Trudeau much. Taiwan, he and his foreign policy adviser Ivan Head wrote later, "was seen for what it was, a harsh dictatorship based on capitalistic principles."[34]

The Trudeau breakthrough represented the belated triumph of ideas Canadian diplomats had been advocating since 1949: that foreign policy should be based on facts and not ideological affinity, and that engagement was more effective than isolation in dealing with nations with different social and political systems. "A China open to the world," Trudeau and Head wrote, "… could be expected over time to adjust its political, economic and social practices to bring them into harmony with international norms."[35] Even so, the Sino-Canadian relationship remained almost entirely symbolic. As long as Mao was alive and committed to building a Communist society, there was little scope for utilizing the usual Canadian tools for deepening ties – aid, trade, investment, immigration, tourism. Paradoxically, the Sino-American relationship would develop much more quickly. Richard Nixon's surprise visit in 1972 – "the week that changed the world," in Margaret MacMillan's phrase[36] – led to the almost instant creation of a de facto Beijing-Washington alliance against Moscow. This vital security dimension permitted two countries with different social and political systems to engage each other in a substantive way that was impossible for Canada.

Mao's death in 1976, the rise of Deng Xiaoping and the subsequent implementation of economic reforms and loosening of social controls created new opportunities for Canada. A more market-oriented Beijing, too, was eager to expand trade as a way of dealing with the large annual deficits created by ongoing Canadian grain exports. The Canada-China Trade Council (now the Canada China Business Council) was established in 1978 and new agreements on trade and economic co-operation were signed the following year. In 1980, Canada granted China preferential trade status. Aid money began to flow to China, almost quadrupling during the 1980s. Conditions seemed ripe for a major expansion in economic relations. It did not occur. The reason can be traced to the mid-1980s economic boom in the United States and the signing of the Canada-u.s. Free Trade Agreement in 1988. For Canadian business, the familiar and rich

U.S. market remained a much safer bet than China. The U.S. share of total Canadian exports rose from 75 percent in the mid 1980s to 84 percent a decade later.[37] So while Canadian-Chinese trade did grow and China became Canada's fifth largest trading partner by 1995, Canada's share of Chinese imports was less than one percent.[38] The real disappointment, though, was political.

Trudeau had said that engagement would bring China "into harmony with international norms." In early June 1989, however, China's reformist leadership reverted to Stalinist form to crush the student-led pro-democracy movement that had blossomed in Tiananmen Square. Prime Minister Brian Mulroney, who had approvingly noted the "discreet monograms" on the socks of then Premier Zhao Ziyang during a visit to Beijing in 1986, was "shocked and sickened" by the images on his television.[39] He summoned the Chinese ambassador to express his disgust and recalled the Canadian ambassador from Beijing. He banned high-level contacts and supported sanctions by the G7. To the opposition Liberals and New Democrats, this was not enough. One contentious item was a $100 million federal loan to help China buy telephone cable and switching equipment from Canadian companies. The loan had been approved in the wake of a June 30 policy statement by External Affairs Minister Joe Clark, giving the Export Development Corp. authority to do business with China under an existing $2 billion line of credit. When the news of the loan came out, there was an angry reaction in the Chinese Canadian community that spread to the opposition parties.[40] Clark defended the loan with a classic restatement of the engagement policy: "We have seen elsewhere in the socialist world that the modernization of these societies can serve to advance political change." The Canadian government, he continued, saw "no gain to the cause of reform in China to be had from a policy which is 'anti-China.' A poorer and more isolated China is not in the broad interest of the Chinese people."[41]

A similar drama was played out later in the summer when a second loan – $130 million for a hydroelectric project in Hubei – became public. "Secret loans to the Chinese government for major projects violate the very essence of the commitment made by Parliament to condemn the Chinese government's action," Liberal leader John Turner argued. "Such loans are not only dishonest and hypocritical, they reflect moral turpitude on the part of the government."[42] A further loan, $28 million for a chemical plant, followed in December, and in mid-January Ottawa said it was willing to allow the World Bank to consider a $25 million loan to Beijing for earthquake reconstruction.[43]

Canada's ongoing commitment to engagement was evident during an odd ceremony that took place in Beijing's Great Hall of the People in

November of 1989. The Chinese government was marking the 50th anniversary of the death of Norman Bethune, the Canadian doctor who died while serving with Communist forces behind Japanese lines in northern China. The event had been planned months earlier as a grand celebration of Sino-Canadian friendship. After Tiananmen, however, it loomed as an embarrassment for Ottawa, especially as Bethune, in China, is an army figure and any ceremony was sure to have a strong contingent from the People's Liberation Army. Chinese soldiers, Tiananmen Square and smiling Canadian diplomats were very bad visuals for Mulroney's government. Still, Ottawa was looking for ways to contain the diplomatic damage from Tiananmen and did not want to cancel the ceremony. Canadians who worked for Chinese organizations in the Beijing area were rounded up and driven to the Great Hall and seated in the first five or so rows. The rest of the huge auditorium was filled by soldiers. Jiang Zemin, who had been named chairman of the Central Military Commission – supreme commander of the armed forces – just days before, led the official Chinese delegation accompanied by senior military officers, an ancient "comrade-in-arms" of Bethune, and Politburo member Li Ruihuan, who gave the major speech of the day. The only Canadians whose presence was officially acknowledged were two people from the Federation of Canada-China Friendship Associations, one of whom made a brief speech that obliquely criticized the Chinese government by referring to Bethune's respect for "all human life." The Chinese speakers, of course, praised Bethune as a great Communist.

Bruce Jutzi, then a councillor at the Canadian embassy, said later that Canada had informed the Chinese of its discomfort at being present at the Bethune event in any official capacity. The Chinese, he said, understood perfectly, and the two sides quickly came to an agreement that the event would be held with the Friendship Association people representing the Canadian side. Jutzi praised the Chinese officials he dealt with as competent and sophisticated in their understanding of Canadian political sensibilities. He also believed the ongoing presence of Canadians in Chinese work units during that difficult year furthered the process of engagement by preventing China's isolation.[44]

Official Canadian aid, which fell slightly in 1989–90, rebounded in the early 1990s and ministerial contacts resumed in 1991. Not long before leaving office in 1993, Mulroney invited Zhu Rongji, then a vice-premier, to dinner at 24 Sussex to send a signal "that Canada would be prepared to fully engage with China in the years ahead." He notes that the suggestion to extend the invitation came from Paul Desmarats, a powerful Quebec businessman with links to both of the major federal political parties.[45]

Tiananmen and the collapse of Soviet power in Eastern Europe later that year caused soul-searching in Beijing as well. Conservative intellectuals, presumably speaking with official sanction, denounced western support for the "peaceful evolution" of China away from communism and toward democracy and free-market economics. This was in fact one of the goals of western policy, even Canadian policy; it is what engagement was supposed to be about. For a time it appeared as though China might revert to a more conventional socialist state with a planned economy. It might well have had the 87-year-old Deng not had enough energy in 1992 to leave Beijing and embark on a tour of the special economic zones in the south where he praised the benefits of reform and advocated the creation of a "socialist market economy," a concept embraced at the Communist Party Congress later that year.

With political stability restored and further business-friendly reforms in place, China was perfectly situated to benefit from the quickening pace of economic globalization. Growth exploded – the numbers were so high that they were greeted with scepticism in many quarters.[46] For Canada, the long-elusive economic potential of the China connection seemed closer to fulfillment. Under Jean Chrétien, who became prime minister in 1993, Canada articulated a new activist China policy based on four pillars: peace and security, sustainable development, human rights and the rule of law, and economic partnership. While each pillar was supposed to be equal, economic partnership seemed to predominate as the Liberals resumed their long search for an economic counterweight to the United States. Chrétien travelled repeatedly to China, twice as leader of huge "Team Canada" trade missions. Bilateral trade worth $2 billion in 1989 expanded to $17.5 billion by 2001. As impressive as that was, it fell short of Chrétien's target for 2000 of $20 billion. Indeed, the expansion of economic relations pleased neither supporters nor opponents of deepening the China connection. Economic and business commentators lamented the fact that Canada's share of the Chinese market actually was decreasing as other countries moved more aggressively to exploit opportunities. In 2003, just after Paul Martin became prime minister, the Asia Pacific Foundation described economic relations as "underdeveloped."[47] In the opposite corner, human rights advocates and supporters of political reform felt Chrétien had abandoned Canada's liberal democratic values: what had happened to the "international norms" Trudeau had spoken of? In retirement, Chrétien has continued to deny that he subordinated values to trade. It was really just a matter of tactics: quiet persuasion worked better than confrontation. He fell back on the "e" word: "Engage them, don't insult them," he told delegates at the 2006 Liberal leadership convention. "I met 18 times with the president of China. I discussed human rights every time."[48] "There is a way to handle this problem," he said during a 2008 speech, "but at the same time not put the interests of Canada in a bad position."[49] Under Chrétien, Canada ceased to support the annual resolution at the UN Commission on Human Rights criticizing China's rights record, choosing instead to enter a human rights "dialogue" with Beijing in 1997. The dialogue process removed the issue from the public forum of the United Nations to private discussions between diplomats and experts. Human rights activists generally regard this approach – and China has been involved in similar dialogues with the EU, Australia, Brazil, Sweden, Norway, Great Britain and, intermittently, the United States – as a sham.[50] In 2005, the department of foreign affairs and international trade commissioned Professor Charles Burton of Brock University, a former diplomat who twice served in the Beijing embassy, to prepare a report on the process. He found that neither the Canadian nor Chinese participants were satisfied. Meetings were brief and shallow; uninformed participants "read scripts"; Canadians were simplistic and condescending; the Chinese nationalistic and "unwilling to be chastised over human rights any more."[51]

More than trade considerations muted Canadian criticism of China. The 1990s saw new tension emerge in the Sino-American relationship. With the common threat of the Soviet Union gone, China was the only plausible challenger to American regional hegemony, while America was the main barrier to Beijing's goal of re-establishing control over Taiwan. Furthermore, China had emerged from the tumultuous events of 1989 as the world's only significant Communist power, highlighting the stark ideological differences between Beijing and Washington. During the 1992 presidential election campaign, Bill Clinton criticized President George H.W. Bush for coddling the "butchers of Beijing."[52] Once in office, Clinton explicitly revealed the U.S. security commitment to Taiwan by deploying aircraft carriers in 1996 during provocative Chinese military exercises. Clinton's Pentagon identified China as a potential enemy and recommended refocusing U.S. defence priorities from Europe to the Pacific. The Clinton administration strengthened U.S. military co-operation with Japan and reached out to India and Vietnam – even North Korea – in what looked from Beijing like a strategy of encirclement. Washington also articulated a doctrine of "humanitarian intervention" that overrode the principle of national sovereignty and was applied in Kosovo, Haiti and East Timor. Beijing feared that in the future it might be used to justify intervention in Tibet, Xinjiang or Taiwan. China also was shaken by the bombing of its embassy in Belgrade in 1999, which most Chinese regarded as a deliberate attack.[53] Meanwhile, American academics and defence intellectuals penned books like *The Coming Conflict with China* and *The Clash of Civilizations* that openly predicted war.[54]

A familiar situation seemed to be developing: an America moving toward confrontation while Canada favoured peaceful engagement. In the

1950s, that had been a recipe for diplomatic paralysis in Ottawa. By the 1990s, however, anti-Americanism had become a popular and fairly painless political strategy, especially after the pro-American excesses of the Mulroney years. Trudeau had recognized China largely for sound foreign policy reasons, but was not blind to the benefits of appearing to act in defiance of the "elephant" to the south. Nor was Chrétien. His pro-China stance created symbolic distance between Ottawa and Washington, an electoral benefit at home and a useful tool in his China trade strategy. Chinese newspapers approvingly quoted Chrétien's complaints about the Americans' "cowboy-style attitude" after a Chinese interceptor collided with an American spy plane near Hainan Island in April 2001.[55] Later that year, Chrétien was featured on the front page of *China Daily* congratulating it on 20 years of publication.[56] Had any Canadian leader ever similarly congratulated *Pravda*?

The fact that *China Daily* chose to quote Chrétien indicates that Beijing also saw symbolic possibilities in the Beijing-Ottawa-Washington triangle. Beijing's good relations with peace-loving Canada and the EU were contrasted to its testy dealings with the hegemonic Americans. A staple of Chinese commentary in the late 1990s and early 2000s was that the natural trend in contemporary international relations was toward "multipolarity" but that the United States was trying to impose a "unipolar" system on the world.[57] The implication was that the differences between China and the United States were not about democracy or human rights, but about power. Beijing took great pleasure in the 2001 vote that saw the United States removed from the UN Commission on Human Rights. A *China Daily* commentary said the vote "was a timely warning for the United States that its arrogant, unilateral approaches have made it more and more unpopular among international communities [sic]." Significantly, the commentary chose to quote David Malone, a former Canadian ambassador to the UN, who referred to the Americans' "high-handed and disruptive behaviour."[58] Relations reached an apotheosis of sorts in 1998 when Zhu Rongji, now premier, referred to Canada as China's "best friend" in the developed world.[59] Beijing coined a grand new title for the China-Canada connection: the "Trans-Century Comprehensive partnership." That sort of talk ended when Stephen Harper became prime minister.

By 2006, the bilateral relationship had developed real substance. China was now Canada's second largest trading partner. Canadian exports nearly doubled between 2002 and 2006,[60] marking significant progress toward the long-desired goal of trade diversification. The People's Republic also was Canada's leading source of immigrants, accounting for 14 percent of newcomers between 2001 and 2006, more than 155,000 in 2006 alone.[61] Despite these concrete gains, Harper decided to mount a rhetorical offensive against China. He pushed all of Beijing's buttons in criticizing China's human rights record, meeting the Dalai Lama on Parliament Hill, loosening restrictions on contacts with Taiwan and airing concerns about Chinese industrial espionage. Harper and his ministers also dispensed with diplomatic language. After being snubbed by Chinese President Hu Jintao at the November 2006 APEC conference in Vietnam, Harper said: "I think Canadians want us to promote our trade relations worldwide, and we do that. But I don't think Canadians want us to sell out important Canadian values. They don't want us to sell that out to the almighty dollar."[62] His Multicultural Minister Jason Kenney, on the topic of visits by MPs to Taiwan, told a Vancouver audience: "Canada and Taiwan share the common value for democracy, and this should be respected ... Neither myself [sic] nor the Canadian government would need to apologize to anyone for visiting a democratically elected government."[63] Beijing, predictably, was outraged, referring to the Dalai Lama meeting as "disgusting conduct" and "gross interference in China's affairs."[64] A planned meeting of the Canada-China Strategic Working Group, a bilateral body created to build the two countries' "strategic partnership," was cancelled by the Chinese. This reaction must have been anticipated by Ottawa. The question is why Canadian policy changed.

Two symbolism-soaked reasons suggest themselves. The first is Canada's renewed emphasis on ideology. The Harper government has reversed Liberal priorities by subordinating trade and engagement to human rights and liberal democratic values. Human rights advocates generally approve. Charles Burton says the "quiet diplomacy" of the Liberals had provided "tacit sanction to China's violations of the rights of Chinese citizens" and "not led to any discernible progress in China's human rights record." Harper's "more frank and more public diplomacy" will, in his view, send a clearer message to Beijing about Canada's concerns over human rights, Tibet and worrisome Chinese activities in Sudan, Burma and Zimbabwe.[65]

The second factor is the Harper government's obvious desire to reharmonize Canadian and American policy, a tendency also evident in the Middle East and Central Asia. Reversing the longstanding Liberal policy of emphasizing Canadian sovereignty by distancing Ottawa from Washington, Harper seeks to expand Canadian influence by being seen as a reliable ally of the United States. He said this explicitly in the Canadian Alliance party's defence policy paper in 2003: "... [T]here is now no more important foreign policy interest for Canada than maintaining the ability to exercise effective influence in Washington so as to advance unique Canadian policy objectives."[66] This marks a return to the thinking of the 1950s, as do so many of Harper's policies.

Although the specifics of the Harper government's China policy run counter to the trend of the previous three decades, its overall approach is very much in the Canadian tradition. There is the familiar emphasis on symbolic gestures over substance; the assumption that Canada can influence Chinese behaviour; and the practice of speaking to Beijing to send signals to powerful allies. None of this is suitable in a relationship that, by any objective measure, has now become a "major thing." Perhaps one day Stephen Harper or a successor will recognize that and deal with China in a more substantive and realistic manner, but it seems a distant prospect.

NOTES

1 Mao Zedong, "On Contradiction" in *Selected Readings from the Works of Mao Tsetung* (Beijing: Foreign Languages Press 1971), 99.
2 Harry Con, et. al., *From China to Canada: A History of Chinese Communities in Canada* (Toronto: McClelland and Stewart 1982), 84–5.
3 Ibid., 94.
4 Charles J. Woodsworth, *Canada and the Orient* (Toronto: Macmillan 1941), 269–70.
5 Alvyn J. Austin, *Saving China: Canadian Missionaries in the Middle Kingdom, 1882–1959* (Toronto: University of Toronto Press 1986), 85.
6 Ibid., 9.
7 Board of Foreign Missions of the United Church of Canada, *Forward with China* (Toronto: Ryerson Press 1928), 252. The number of baptized was about 240.
8 Austin, *Saving China*, 73.
9 Ibid., 40.
10 United Church, *Forward with China*, 110.
11 Ibid., 87.
12 Most Chinese words in this paper are given in the modern Pinyin transliteration. These names, however, are more familiar to western readers in the older Wade-Giles system.
13 United Church, *Forward with China*, 345.
14 Austin, *Saving China*, 210.
15 Ibid., 211.
16 Ibid., 229.
17 For example, see Paul Evans and Yuen Pau Woo, "Canada and a Global China: From Special Relationship to Policy Partnership," Asia-Pacific Foundation, July 2004. Available at http://www.asiapacific.ca/analysis/pubs/other/globalchina.pdf.
18 Charles Burton, "Assessment of the Canada-China Bilateral Human Rights Dialogue," Report prepared for the Department of Foreign Affairs and

International Trade, available online at http://spartan.ac.brocku.ca/~cburton/Assessment%20of%20the%20Canada-China%20Bilateral%20Human%20Rights%20Dialogue%2019 APR06.pdf.
19 Woodsworth, *Canada and the Orient*, 182, 237.
20 John Lewis Gaddis, *We Now Know: Rethinking Cold War History* (New York: Oxford University Press 1997), 72–5.
21 Cited in Stephen Beecroft, "Canadian Policy Toward China, 1949–1957: The Recognition Problem," in Paul M. Evans and B. Michael Frolic, eds., *Reluctant Adversaries: Canada and the People's Republic of China, 1949–1970* (Toronto: University of Toronto Press 1991), 59.
22 Ibid.
23 Cited in Greg Donaghy and John Hilliker: "'Don't Let Asia Split the West': Canada and the People's Republic of China, 1949–1971," in *Documenting Diplomacy in the Twenty-First Century* (Washington: Department of State 2001), 84–99.
24 Beecroft, "Canadian Policy Toward China, 1949–1957," 60.
25 Cited in ibid., 55.
26 The importance of Hamilton's role is not universally accepted. In his history of the Canadian Wheat Board, William E. Morriss credits the board's own negotiators with opening the China market and disparagingly refers to "the myth of Alvin Hamilton as super-salesman." See *Chosen Instrument II: A History of the Canadian Wheat Board: New Horizons* (Winnipeg: Canadian Wheat Board), 23.
27 Patrick Kyba, "Alvin Hamilton and Sino-Canadian Relations," in Evans and Frolic, 170.
28 Diefenbaker explained his willingness to grant credit this way: "My experience was that when a Chinese gave his word, it was as good as his bond, apparently because of an adherence to the teachings of Confucius and Tao." John Diefenbaker, *One Canada: The Memoirs of the Right Honourable John G. Diefenbaker, Volume II, The Years of Achievement* (Toronto: Macmillan 1976), 179.
29 Ibid., 181.
30 Karen Minden, The *Politics of Cerealism: The Wheat Trade and Canadian-Chinese Relations* (Toronto: University of Toronto-York University Joint Centre on Modern Asia), 5, 14.
31 Diefenbaker, *One Canada*, 115, 177.
32 Cited in Ivan L. Head and Pierre Elliott Trudeau, *The Canadian Way: Shaping Canada's Foreign Policy 1968–1984* (Toronto: McClelland and Stewart 1995), 236.
33 Cited in B. Michael Frolic, "The Trudeau Initiative" in Evans and Frolic, *Reluctant Adversaries*, 192.
34 Head and Trudeau, *The Canadian Way*, 237.
35 Ibid., 227.
36 Margaret MacMillan, *Nixon in China: The Week that Changed the World* (Toronto: Viking 2006).

37 Diana Wyman, "Trading with a giant: An update on Canada-China trade," *Statistics Canada Canadian Economic Observer*, November 2007.
38 Brent Sutton and Zhili Ge, "Opportunities and Risks for Canadian Business in China: A Business Perspective on Policy Issues," Conference Board of Canada, 1996.
39 Brian Mulroney, *Memoirs 1939–1993* (Toronto: McClelland and Stewart 2007), 442, 665.
40 "Chinese community outraged by $100 million loan to Beijing," *Toronto Star*, 3 August 1989; "PM broke faith with the world over China loan, Turner says," *Toronto Star*, 17 August 1989.
41 "China loan will assist in reforms Clark insists," *Toronto Star*, 5 August 1989.
42 "Turner tells PM to drop hydro loan to China," *Toronto Star*, 13 September 1989.
43 "Canada willing to consider World Bank loan for China," *Globe and Mail*, 3 January 1990.
44 The author was present at the Bethune event and spoke later with Jutzi.
45 Mulroney, *Memoirs 1939–1993*, 996.
46 For example, Thomas Rawski, "What's happening to China's GDP statistics?" available at http://www.pitt.edu/~tgrawski/papers2001/gdp912f.pdf
47 "Bringing it to the Next Level," *Asia Pacific Bulletin*, 12 December 2003.
48 "Chrétien calls Harper's China policy 'immature,'" CTV.ca, available at www.ctv.ca/servlet/ArticleNews/story/CTVNews/20061202/chretien_harper_061202?s_name=&no_ads=
49 "Chrétien urges cautious approach," *Toronto Star*, 7 March 2008.
50 For example, see Philip Baker, "Human Rights, Europe and the People's Republic of China," *China Quarterly*, March 2002, 45–63.
51 Burton, "Assessment of the Canada-China Bilateral Human Rights Dialogue," 8, 13.
52 "Clinton campaign asks who's the real foreign policy risk," U.S. Newswire, 12 October 1992.
53 Many articles mentioned these themes. Some examples: "US hegemony shows new features," *China Daily*, 22 February 2001; "What decides Sino-US relations," *China Daily*, 30 May 2001; "Behind the abrupt warming in U.S.-Indian relations," *Beijing Review*, 21 June 2001.
54 The former by Richard Bernstein and Ross Munro, the latter by Samuel Huntington.
55 "PLANE: Hegemony widely criticized," *China Daily*, 7–8 April 2001.
56 "Messages from overseas," *China Daily*, 1 June 2001.
57 For example, "Global power, issues shifting," *China Daily*, 1 February 2001; and "Crazy for hegemony," *Beijing Review*, 24 May 2001.
58 "Globalization means one cannot go it alone," *China Daily*, 12–13 May 2001.
59 "'Canada is our best friend,' Chinese premier proclaims," *Toronto Star*, 21 November 1998.

60 Wyman, "Trading with a giant," 3.1
61 Statistics Canada, "Immigration in Canada: A Portrait of the Foreign-born Population, 2006 Census: Immigrants came from many countries." Available at http://www12.statcan.ca/english/census06/analysis/immcit/asia.cfm.
62 CBC, 15 November 2006. Available at http://www.cbc.ca/world/story/2006/11/15/harper-snub.html.
63 Chinese in Vancouver blog, http://chineseinvancouver.blogspot.com/2007/05/mps-free-to-visit-taiwan-needless-to.html
64 Aileen McCabe, "PM's Dalai Lama meeting 'disgusting conduct': China," CanWest News Service, 30 October 2007.
65 Charles Burton, "A 'Principled' Approach, Quiet Diplomacy and the Prime Minister's Message to Beijing," *Embassy newsweekly*, 14 November 2007.
66 *The New North Strong and Free: Protecting Canadian Sovereignty and Contributing to Global Stability*, Defence policy white paper of the Canadian Alliance, May 2003.

PART FOUR
Identity

13 The Transatlantic Romance of the North Atlantic Triangle: Narratives of Autonomy and Empire in Canadian Foreign Relations[1]

CARA SPITTAL

American President George W. Bush channelled Winston Churchill on 1 December 2004 when he stood on the historic Halifax Pier 21 to recall for his listeners what Canada and the United States had in common. He chose to evoke the collective cause of Americans and Canadians in the World Wars of the twentieth century, and so, grafted on to his calls for greater cooperation in his "War on Terror," was a plea that Canadians remember "the great principles of liberty derived from our common heritage," the underlying Anglo-Saxon alliance that is a permanent organic union.[2]

Stephen Harper invoked the spirit of Churchill, too, in a speech he delivered in January 2007 when he declared, "that history is built by layer upon layer of common experiences, shared values and ancient family ties." Like Churchill and Bush before him, Harper celebrated the "majestic past" that linked together the Anglo-Saxon races of the world "to the Tudors, the Plantagenets, the Magna Carta, habeas corpus, petition of rights [sic], and English common law ... all those massive stepping stones which the people of the British race shaped and forged to the joy, peace, and glory of mankind."[3]

Chris Sands, a senior fellow at the Hudson Institute in Washington, D.C., and one of the rare Canadian experts in the U.S. capital, echoed Harper's sentiments later that month when he paid homage to the historic ties that bind the special group of nations that share the English language and British tradition. He suggested that Stephen Harper's Conservatives were "Good Canadians," who, like the brave soldiers that joined their brethren from the United Kingdom and the United

States to defeat the Nazis, opted to fight the good war in Afghanistan and toe the American line in the Middle East.[4] The Liberals, by implication, were bad Canadians for refusing to either take part in Bush's war in Iraq or support the plan for ballistic missile defence.

All this talk of Britishness on the part of Sands, Bush, and Harper was meant to provide a historical imperative for the support of American foreign-policy decisions in Canada. Their calls for a moral, vigorous, and perhaps even an "Anglo-Saxon" foreign policy go back and back and back through successive layers of Canadian thinkers to the late-nineteenth century. Although British exceptionalism is now talked about in the more politically correct language of the "Anglosphere," a term coined by American public intellectual James C. Bennett to describe the shared customs, culture, and values of former members of the Commonwealth, Ireland and the United States, the "self-affirming narrative" of empire is more than a century old.[5] In Canada, it has been employed in many different historical contexts by Conservative political thinkers and politicians for the purpose of defining their partisan values and identities.

To be sure, the Conservatives are not alone in their expression of Canadian foreign policy in terms of competing partisan principles and values. As John English has shown, the Liberal narrative of national autonomy was forged in opposition to the Conservative bid for empire and goes back just as far. The narrative emerged at the turn of the twentieth century to abjure the Conservative inclination towards the British imperial dream and remains a fixture today when independence and autonomy means not from Britain but from the United States.[6]

Staying true to form, the Liberal Leader of Opposition, Stéphane Dion, has recently implied that Harper's foreign policy jeopardized Canadian sovereignty and dignity: "He admires George Bush a bit the way I admired Jean Beliveau when I was five. It's nonsensical how completely he copies him in everything – in the style, in the speeches on Iraq, in the way he muzzles his ministers, in the way he manages the press – he wants to be president."[7] The Liberal Deputy Leader, Michael Ignatieff, chimed in to insist that the Liberals were committed to a foreign policy founded on the principle of autonomy and the belief that "maintaining our national independence is our guiding national interest."[8]

Liberals and Conservatives have always talked about Canada's continental and imperial relations in the symbolic language of Crown, Empire, English common law, and national independence. Their respective partisan narratives were forged as weapons and used to battle for the middle ground of mainstream political discourse. Yet narratives of empire and autonomy were not simply rhetorical devices employed to trademark Liberal and Conservative candidates. They represented authentic and competing sets of political principles and values that were descriptive of the ways in which Grit and Tory thinkers imagined Canada and its place in the world, their own partisan identities, and the kinds of struggles in which they wished to engage.

The ritual debates between Liberal and Conservative political thinkers over Anglo-American-Canadian relations historically occur when broad swaths of the population are most unsure about the nation's political destiny. By juxtaposing the works of the key intellectuals engaged in these debates, this chapter peels back layers of partisan discourse developed over one hundred years of Canadian history. It is written in reverse chronological order for the purpose of uncovering the symbolic continuity and staying power of Grit and Tory national narratives. The approach is an exercise in archaeology that excavates partisan narratives of foreign policy from the most modern level on the surface through a descending order to the more ancient levels underneath.[9] In so doing, this chapter highlights the ways in which national narratives of autonomy and empire have always been articulated by political thinkers in terms of the Liberal and Conservative traditions of foreign policy and suggests they should be central to our understanding of the ways that English Canadians talk about Canada and its place in the world today.

NATIONAL NARRATIVES

Historians have only recently turned their attention to the question of how national narratives are shaped by and in turn make their imprint on foreign policy in Canada. Some scholars have explored the extent to which social life is "storied" and have suggested that narrative is an ontological condition of social life. Their research demonstrates that people construct multiple and changing identities by locating themselves in a repertoire of stories; that experience is constituted through narrative; and that people are guided to act in certain ways on the basis of the prejudices and ideals that they derive from the social, political, and cultural narratives available to them.[10] On a much larger scale, national narratives embed identities in historical and spatial relationships and provide the ideal evaluative frameworks against which interest groups can define imagined principles and values.[11]

In Canada there are many national narratives that deserve scholarly attention. One of the most important varieties is the French Canadian – a label that conceals many contradictory sub-narratives. The impact of French Canadian narratives on foreign policy is explored elsewhere in the volume; this chapter focuses primarily on the narratives produced in the English Canadian context.[12] Since English Canada's politics, economy, and culture were overwhelmingly influenced by its unequal and historic imperial and continental partnerships with the United States and Great Britain, it makes sense that Grit and Tory political thinkers forged their partisan identities by continually turning to the competing themes of autonomy and empire. Seen from this angle, national narratives of autonomy and empire were fashioned by partisan thinkers not only to impart views of Canada's relations with the British Empire and with the United States that coincided with the differing sets of prejudices that they claimed to have, but also to serve explicit political goals.

THE 1960S: PETER C. NEWMAN VERSUS GEORGE PARKIN GRANT

The 1960s mark an important turning point in the ways that Canadians talked about foreign policy. It was a time in which the national narrative of Queen, Commonwealth, and British parliamentary tradition exceeded its geopolitical relevance. The decline of the narrative was made clear after the Conservative Prime Minister John George Diefenbaker's fall from power in 1963. Diefenbaker's conception of Canada was rooted in traditional conservative ideas about transatlantic connections to the British Crown and Empire. Unlike Stephen Harper, whose neo-conservative philosophy is a product of the steady rise of American right-wing ideology, much of Diefenbaker's foreign policy was shaped by a deep-seated fear of the influence of American power on Canadian cultural, political, and economic life. Despite their differences, however, the two Tories told similar stories about ancient family ties and the integral role that Anglo-Saxon institutions, ideas, and values have played in civilizing the world.

After Diefenbaker became prime minister on 21 June 1957, it was only a matter of time before his vision of Canada's identity and its role in world affairs was made manifest on the international stage. Indeed, in the first major speech he delivered on his World Tour of 1958, Diefenbaker spoke in proselytizing tones about what he deemed to be a "renaissance" of the extended British family of nations. At the time, he thought little of how French Canadians might respond to his inflation of Canada's British identity. For him, the importance of the British connection to the English Canadian voters he knew and understood was all too clear. Diefenbaker spoke of the Commonwealth as an institution that would work alongside the United Nations to spread morality, peace, prosperity, and the capitalist ethos across the globe. "No other institution in the modern world" he proclaimed, "has the same global unity in the things of the spirit and the economic potential to preserve and defend the heritage of freedom."[13]

To be sure, Diefenbaker's national narrative was never really relevant to French Canadians who envisaged Canada as a separate and distinct nationality.¹⁴ In addition to fumbling on the domestic front, Diefenbaker failed as a diplomat as well. In the midst of the Cold War, his goal to forge "personal" relationships with non-aligned nations and take a leadership role in directing the affairs of the Commonwealth did not sit well with Canada's Anglo-American allies.¹⁵ Despite the fact that a number of trade-promotion programs had failed throughout the 1950s, his attempts to strengthen Commonwealth ties by transferring 15 percent of Canada's trade from the United States to Britain rendered him an embarrassment in Whitehall. Diefenbaker's public attempts to block Britain's application to join the European Economic Community created still more tension in his relationship with Prime Minister Harold Macmillan. At a time when the British were finally acknowledging their dwindling power, and working to strengthen their position in the newly integrated Europe, Diefenbaker's sentimental overtures to the old imperial connection mattered little.¹⁶

For many Canadians, most notably Liberal leader Lester B. Pearson, it was clear that the United States had become the central determinant of Canadian external relations. Pearson capitalized on Diefenbaker's failure to grasp the new North American bent of Canadian external affairs by openly siding with the American President, John F. Kennedy, on the issue of housing nuclear weapons on Canadian soil. During the federal election of 1963, one of the most important planks of the Liberal platform was the claim that with Pearson in charge, Canadians would witness the dawn of "a new era of good feeling" in Canadian-American relations.¹⁷ Pearson's decision to hitch himself to Kennedy's rising star paid off. On 22 April, when he was sworn in as Prime Minister, Pearson began the task of dealing with the trials, tribulations and the vast economic benefits of being the leader of a nation that was slowly coming to terms with its position as a junior partner of the United States.

Pearson came out of a tradition in Liberal foreign policy that was much more congenial to the forces of continentalism than that of the Conservatives – a point not lost on Canadian journalist and author, Peter C. Newman. Newman saw deep historical patterns in the Diefenbaker-Pearson war over foreign policy. "There is really a difference" between the Grits and the Tories, he contended: "First, you have to remember where the two old parties come from. Then you have to see which way they still jump when someone pricks them for words like inflation, tariff, Quebec, Yankee, Crown, or Empire." For Newman, "the disciples of the two old parties talk the same political language" but "they don't really think or feel the same way about the same things." While the Tories "have their origins in the Family Compact, Orange Order, Sir John A Macdonald, the Queen and her Empire" the Liberals "look to the Clear Grits of Ontario, the Quebec *rouges* and anti-monarchist rebels of 1837" for the conceptual roots of their credo. At bottom, according to Newman, the rhetoric of the Tories and Grits was rooted in competing versions of Canadian history and in "entirely different sets of prejudices."[18]

Newman's invocation of the historic struggle of the Tories and the Grits tapped a vein of latent but pervasive ontological angst in the English Canadian psyche. Years spent writing about political discord as if it were a "blood sport" taught him that "loyal Grits and loyal Tories" would always "damn each other's politics with the gusty passion of a Sicilian vendetta" at times when public opinion was most divided about where Canada stood in the world.[19] He had grounds, too, for thinking that Canada's historic imperial and continental partnerships were best expressed in the symbolic language of Queen, Church, Parliament, Yankee, and anti-monarchical rebel and couched in terms of warring partisan narratives of empire and autonomy. At a time when public concern about the potentially harmful effects of the rapid dismantling of the British Empire and increasing economic integration with the United States was widespread, it was only natural for Newman to frame the partisan political battle in terms of the Anglo-American-Canadian relationship.[20]

Like Pearson, Newman saw that Diefenbaker's talk of old imperial connections was no longer effective in the 1960s. The Liberal narrative of Canadian history as an inevitable progression from a backwards, colonial entity to a modern industrial and autonomous nation is the common thread that runs throughout his writing. As Robert Wright has shown, Newman's first book, *Flame of Power* (1959), put a Canadian spin on the themes of individual achievement, self-reliance, and laissez-faire capitalism.[21] His "power men" were pragmatic English Canadian industrialists whose empirical reason fuelled their compulsive drive for business success.[22] The old imperial connection and the cultural baggage it left behind did not belong in Newman's vision of an independent and self-made postwar Canada.

For this reason, Newman believed that the British Empire was no longer capable of exerting a fierce gravitational pull on Canadian politics. While Diefenbaker engaged in his spiritual communion with the quaint rural people who lived in "the soon-to-be-abandoned waypoints" that spotted the prairies, "the new generation was immune to his political magic":

To them, he was just another old guy, and if they knew him at all, it was as a duffer out of the history books, possibly the one who drove in the Last Spike. Dief had been born when Queen Victoria was on the throne. This was the

Swinging Sixties, when the pill was not something you took for headaches and "drugs" were not what your doctor gave you. He was trying to remain relevant in a spinning world of moon shots and mass protest. As he stood there uncomfortable and unrecognized, John Diefenbaker looked a million years old and I felt sorry for him.[23]

In Newman's national narrative, Diefenbaker is portrayed as being out of touch with a new generation mesmerized by American consumerism and mass culture. His fellow Tories thought so, too. In September 1967, Diefenbaker was summarily banished from his role as Tory leader – spurned by the Party that he had rescued from political oblivion a decade earlier.

Canadian philosopher and professor of religion George Parkin Grant knew well that that Diefenbaker's fall marked the death knell of the old Tory narrative. While political thinkers like Newman rejoiced in the dawn of the modern industrial era and the triumph of the postwar liberal consensus, Grant mourned the twilight of conservative nationalism in Canada. His *Lament for a Nation* (1965) was a scathing indictment of the emerging American empire, a critique of the destructive impact of modern life, and a testament to the failure of the Canadian experiment in creating a North American alternative to the American republic.

Grant's conception of the role of the Tory narrative in sustaining public conceptions of the good was central to his philosophy.[24] He lamented the notion that the last bastions of conservative and even socialist ideology in North America had been subsumed by the postwar liberal consensus. The idea itself was not new. Five years earlier, the American sociologist Daniel Bell declared that alternative political philosophies had been reduced to insignificance because Western democratic politics and capitalism had triumphed.[25] In this Grant found no cause for celebration. For him the defeat of conservatism in Canada meant the collapse of the moral force of British power into the "flabbiness and chaos" of American liberalism. It meant the replacement of the Protestant ethic by an increasingly technological system of corporate enterprise. It meant that the nation would descend into a nihilistic existence that had no "fixed points of meaning." It meant, above all else, that the very substance of Canadian life was tied inextricably to the fortunes of the United States.[26]

For Grant, the fault lines running underneath conservative nationalism emerged during long reign of Liberal Prime Minister Mackenzie King. In the decades before King's rise to power, Grant argued, "the character of the country was self-evident." Canadians were British, "a unique species of North American."[27] Things changed when King and his band of Liberal technocrats came to power; because they believed that British power threatened Canadian sovereignty, they actively sought to destroy the country's "indigenous" institutions and "old culture." And so the Liberals became agents of the American empires, worshippers at the church of "liberal technology," and proponents of mass culture and conformity.[28]

To Grant, the journalists and intellectuals whose Liberal propaganda remained hidden behind the mask of impartiality were just as bad. Their calls to "stop being British if you want to be a nationalist" were the hallmarks of the era.[29] In Grant's apocalyptic scenario, the incompatibility of American liberalism and conservative nationalism made the country's disintegration inevitable. Yet by peeling away another layer of history and going back to the 1940s and 50s, the partisan struggle going on between Grit and Tory political thinkers over Canada's destiny suggests that King's liberal consensus was always up for debate.

THE 1950S AND THE 1940S: FRANK H. UNDERHILL VERSUS DONALD CREIGHTON

The years between the Second World War and the 1960s have usually been viewed as an era of postwar liberal consensus made possible by widely diffused prosperity, creeping Americanization, and fears of Communist subversion.[30] To be sure, the implications of the rise of American power and its impact on Canada were only just beginning to be discussed. As Robert Bothwell explains, "in 1945 Canada had only recently become a sovereign state, and it had taken Canadians some time and considerable mental effort to get used to the fact."[31] Some political thinkers guarded the newly acquired sovereignty and fretted over any hint that it might be compromised; others agonized about what the acquisition of this new sovereignty might mean. In this way, despite outward appearances of sanguinity, the postwar period was an ontological quagmire when it came to talking about the English Canadian identity – past, present, and future.

The best-known critic of the Conservative vision was a prototype of the imperial Canadian. Frank H. Underhill was obviously Anglo-Saxon. He was educated at the University of Toronto, a graduate of Oxford University, and an officer in the First World War. Despite all this, however, Underhill rejected the notion that Canada was a conservative nation, whose European heritage was a key element in its identity. During the war he witnessed the folly of European imperialism first hand. Upon resuming his career as a Canadian historian at the University of Saskatchewan, Underhill touted the North American aspect of the Canadian identity and repudiated Conservative readiness to participate in a common Commonwealth foreign policy.

Underhill was embarrassed by the cyclical anti-Americanism that so many Tory leaders strategically whipped up during federal elections so that they could rescue Canada from its North American destiny. To him, the same debates about the Canadian identity had been going on since Confederation. In "studying the development of our Canadian nationality since 1867," he argued, "one comes to feel more and more like a squirrel running forever inside a revolving cage and never getting anywhere."[32] In 1891, the Tory slogan was "A British subject I was born, a British subject I will die." In 1911 it was much the same: "No truck or trade with the Yankees."[33] Even in the postwar world, the Tory Party appeared as it had in the glory days of the British Empire: like the "alumni association of a school whose members meet together periodically on ceremonial occasions to engage in certain rituals, to listen to a speech from the headmaster, and to enjoy themselves by free indulgence in nostalgic sentiments."[34]

In the mid-1950s, Underhill could see that the Tories were once again being "swept up by storms of neurotic emotion" that usually accompanied periods of uncertainty in Canada. Before the Second World War, he claimed that Canada's survival as a sovereign nation depended on its ability to balance itself "in a triangle of forces in which Britain was at one corner and the United States at the other corner of the triangle." From Lord Durham's Report in 1839 to the outbreak of war in 1939, Canada evolved from a British colony to an independent North American nation because it successfully positioned itself at the lesser point of an "isosceles triangle," with "both Britain and the United States pulling roughly the same weight."[35] By the 1950s, however, he saw the balance of power definitively shift from London to Washington. And much like his fellow Liberals, in Underhill's eyes this wasn't necessarily a bad thing; the [end of] the British century of Canadian history and the dawning of the North American century might inspire widespread national neuroses but it could also provoke the kind of change which would force Canada to chart its own geopolitical trajectory.

Underhill spent his career trying to remedy Canada's postcolonial inferiority complex. In "Canada and the Canadian Question 1954" he argued that the nation should stop lamenting the encroachment of American culture, politics, and economy on national life and learn to create "a better *American* way of life."[36] Yet while he was bent on pushing a North American variant of Liberalism, Underhill was no revolutionary. In his emphasis on peaceful evolution rather than revolution, slow constitutional change rather than national self-determination, Underhill's colony-to-nation narrative was more Gladstonian than Jeffersonian. He envisaged Liberalism as a tool with which the educated elite could champion gradual constitutional social reform for the greater good. The short stories he wrote about Liberals like Goldwin Smith and Edward Blake underscored the importance of liberal intellectuals in cultivating the "national spirit" and teaching the masses that there is "a truer ground on which to unite." Canada need not be an adjunct of the British or American empires, Underhill contended, when it had the potential to become an independent nation and an "equal partner" within the triangular relationship.[37] Thus, while North America appeared largely in the foreground of Underhill's imaginings of the Canadian identity, the English liberal tradition figured prominently in the background.

In the end, however, it wasn't the underlying contradictions in Underhill's ideas about the Canadian liberal tradition that troubled his Tory contemporaries; it was his unwitting acceptance that the United States was eclipsing Great Britain in its influence on Canada and the world in general. While Liberals like Frank Underhill and Peter Newman damned the Tories as relics of the Edwardian era, an alternative to the Liberal narrative of Canadian history was emerging in the political wilderness.

In the 1950s, Tory politicians like Gordon Churchill, Davie Fulton, and Donald Fleming were desperate to redefine "The New Conservatism" and reinsert their version of history into mainstream political discourse. Churchill and Fulton corresponded with historians like Donald Creighton to hone their narrative skills.[38] Disraeli, Burke, and Hogg, Sir John A. Macdonald and Sir Robert Borden were quoted on topics like the importance of religion as the basis of civil society, the "natural conservation" of symbols and traditions, the creed of continuity, the Queen, the Commonwealth, the self-made Canadian citizen, and the separate and distinct "Dominion of the North."[39] At a time when Canadians were just beginning to respond to the changes wrought by modern life and mass culture, the Tories located themselves firmly on the right side of the partisan struggle between the forces of good that that chose to uphold the moral foundations of society and the forces of evil that spurned the British tradition in the name of the crass forces of continentalism.[40]

If Underhill spent his academic career embedding the story of liberalism into the annals of history, Canadian historian Donald Creighton dedicated his to uncovering the defects and limitations of the Grit narrative and replacing it with a conservative alternative. Carl Berger has likened the romantic aspects of Creighton's histories of Canada to a "Wagnerian Opera," in which "great men were not merely human beings," but also "personified elemental forces, principles and ideas" – an instructive comparison. As Berger has shown, Creighton's story of the development of the northern dominion, from its origins in the commercial empire of the St Lawrence River to its realization in the nation-building policies of Sir John A. Macdonald, formed the core of his ideas about Canada's development as a unified, competitive, and separate entity in North America.[41]

Creighton's was a conscious political strategy to open public memory and recuperate pieces of the forgotten past in order to expose and replace the Grit narrative of Canadian history. He refuted what he deemed to be Liberal mystifications of the Canadian experience and inserted in their place the Tory story of national development. The Liberal narrative, Creighton argued, had been perfected by a "generation of publicists, journalists, and professors – the Canadian nationalists of the 1930s – who arose to extol the sufficiency and normality of North Americanism."[42] The stories about Canada's delivery from its colonial status always began with tales about "great Liberal reformers" like Robert Baldwin, Edward Blake, and Wilfrid Laurier – three nation builders "whose generalized features bore a remarkable resemblance to the sober, earnest, volubly virtuous ... William Ewart Gladstone." The stories always ended with the great works of William Lyon Mackenzie King, the politician and thinker who single-handedly "affected his people's final deliverance through the Statute of Westminster."[43]

Like Underhill, Creighton blamed the poverty of national politics and intellectual life on a postcolonial complex. Yet there would be no gradual constitutional evolution from colony to nation in the final version of his story of Canada, only the nightmarish scenario of a far more sinister form of colonial servitude under the thumb of the American empire.[44] In his eyes, Canadians passively bought into the American assertion that the Cold War was "a struggle between free enterprise and communism, between Christianity and irreligious determinism ... between two conflicting 'ways of life.'" After Mackenzie King sold the nation's soul to the American devil during the Second World War, Creighton believed that it was only natural that Canadians themselves would embrace American consumer culture. In so doing, they uncritically imbibed "a North American view of the world, mass produced in the United States."[45]

In a story about Canada and its place in the world that bears a striking resemblance to what would later become George P. Grant's and John Diefenbaker's, Creighton envisaged a world with a "multiple balance of power" in which multinational institutions like the Commonwealth and the UN would offset the power of the American and Soviet empires. "It was Great Britain," he urged, that "set India free and established democracies in Asia." And it was "the subsequent agreement of 1949, which permitted these new Asian nations ... to retain their historical affiliation," that revealed the Commonwealth once again as the greatest living example of the free association of peoples."[46]

Creighton's attempt to rearticulate the Tory national narrative in the context of the Cold War was of great import to the Conservative Party at the time. In 1956, Progressive Conservative Member of Parliament Davie Fulton wrote a thank-you letter to Creighton for the contribution he made to "the understanding of Canadian political history, the correction of a false mythology" and for providing members of his own party with "a clearer understanding... of the basic principles of their party."[47] Fulton was desperate. For twenty-one years the Conservative Party had unsuccessfully attempted to re-polarize Canadian politics by inserting its national narrative into mainstream political discourse. The weakness of the Tories in the mid-twentieth century has been attributed to internal party struggles, failed leadership, and their inability to create a national coalition of support.[48] Yet at a time when the Canadian economic and political system was shifting from a client-type colonial relationship with England to one with the United States,[49] it was the Liberal narrative that best reconciled the symbolic importance of Canada's British past with the reality of its North American present.

THE 1930S AND THE 1920S: OSCAR DOUGLAS SKELTON VERSUS STEPHEN LEACOCK

The tensions within the Liberal narrative, between its appreciation of Canada's real and symbolic ties to Great Britain and its recognition of the increasingly North American character of Canadian economic, cultural, and political life, were integral to its success. In 1939, a picture was taken of Mackenzie King greeting King George VI and Queen Elizabeth as they embarked on their triumphant North American tour. In it he is wearing the official regalia, happily soaking up the pageantry of the royal spectacle.[50] King loved the pomp and ceremony that surrounded his British heritage. In reality, however, he believed that "the universe looked best when viewed through a triangular lens."[51] Thus, while King recognized the importance of paying homage to the Empire when it came to the conduct of Canadian external affairs and safeguarding his political fortunes in English Canada, he had few doubts as to the central role that the United States would play in Canada's future.

The contradictions in the Liberal narrative and King's own persona were played out in his relationship with his under-secretary of state for External Affairs, Oscar Douglas Skelton. In contrast to King, who literally wore his transatlantic loyalties on the embroidered sleeve of his British court uniform, Skelton thought of Canada as a North American nation. At turn-of-the century Queen's University and later at the University of Chicago, he was schooled in the "North American creed" and the idea that "the continent was the crucial fact of Canadian economic life."[52] Skelton is referred to as the "the father of the Liberal narrative,"⁵³ and for good reason. His *Life and Letters of Sir Wilfrid Laurier* is a story in which the Liberal narrative of Canadian nationhood unfolds during what he describes as "the most creative and most formative period in the nation's history... the years when the Dominion was attaining at once industrial maturity and national status."⁵⁴

The renunciation of the Conservative readiness to participate in a common imperial foreign policy is a theme that runs consistently through his writing. Skelton was a student of the English school of liberalism. The Liberals, according to Skelton, "found their models and inspiration ... in the men who fought the battles of orderly freedom and responsible government" and against what they deemed to be Tory "privilege and self-interest." "On individual freedom alone," Skelton believed "could a sound national political system be built up," just as "on colonial freedom alone had it been possible to build up the imperial system."⁵⁵ As a result of the economic boom, Skelton believed that a home grown nationalism would emerge to trump the colonial state of mind.⁵⁶

Skelton contended that the dream of imperial federation was based on sentiment alone. He was for national autonomy, cosmopolitanism, and the high standards of civilization and culture and not the facile prejudices and fantasies of imperialism.⁵⁷ Norman Hillmer has shown that Skelton's career as an academic and as under-secretary of state for External Affairs was geared towards negotiating freer trade and stimulating political cooperation with the United States. Skelton was a proponent of the trend towards North Americanism, a movement that emerged in Canada during the first four decades of the twentieth century in the hopes of "distancing the country from the trap of British imperialism and European militarism."⁵⁸ The North Americans, he believed, had worked out a superior, more civilized system of communication and cooperation that should serve as a model for interstate relations. The two North American peoples had more in common together than they had with Britain. The argument for imperial federation was in this sense outmoded: "it was a product of its time of transition, uneasy answers to the promptings of the slow-rising spirit of nationhood."⁵⁹

From Skelton onwards, scholars of the Liberal school have argued that Canada bridged the gulf between a stagnant colonial status and a progressive nationhood during the days of Wilfrid Laurier. Certainly, Laurier's time in office coincided with a point in Canadian history when the country attempted to bring its politics, culture, and economy into line with the demands of modernity. "Optimism," according to Robert Craig Brown and Ramsay Cook, "was said to be the ruling passion."⁶⁰ And yet the debate over the destiny of British North America raged on – perhaps more because of the boom than in spite of it.

The proliferation of writing on the subject of imperial federation in the first decades of the twentieth century deflates the notion that the movement was so easily overshadowed by a swelling of Canadian nationalist sentiment.[61] At the time, Stephen Leacock was one of the most interesting contributors to the Tory narrative of the imperial idea. Although Leacock is generally known for his *Funny Pieces* and *Sunshine Sketches*, a biting critique of contemporary Canadian life pervades the more melancholic aspects of his work.[62] Leacock's satire honed in on what he deemed to be the unmitigated drive for material wealth in the first decades of the twentieth century. As a Tory of the old school in outlook and political affiliation, Leacock believed that the traditional decencies and duties of an agricultural society were the proper basis for society. His satirical portrayal of the impact of commercialism and corruption was thus an argument for the preservation of the values of history, morality, and humanity. Like his hero, Charles Dickens, Leacock "called amid a squalid industrialism for the colour and kindness of a slower age."[63]

Leacock's *Sunshine Sketches of a Little Town* is a comic rendering of the Ontario experience of small-town life during the heyday of the British Empire. The people of the fictional Mariposa are the typical rural fare – slightly conceited and charmingly provincial. Leacock's Mariposa is a utopia of sorts – a hallowed spot which the tide of industrialism has almost completely passed by. It follows, then, that the most interesting parts of the book are the ones in which the small town is corrupted by the influence of modern industrialism. In the sketch, "The Speculations of Jefferson Thorpe," for example, the effects of the financial and industrial boom on rural areas in Canada resemble that of a "B" horror movie: the town goes mad, the young bank teller commits suicide, and the laconic barber, Jefferson Thorpe, loses all of his possessions.[64]

The climax of *Sunshine Sketches* occurs in an exposé of the course of a general election in Mariposa. The chapters are historically grounded in the federal election of 1911, during which Leacock campaigned vigorously for Robert Borden's Tories against Laurier's policy of tariff reciprocity with the United States.[65] Although quite aware that national elections turned on issues of patronage, tribal loyalty, and religion, and that the party politics of the day were often unprincipled and highly pragmatic, the narrator's repetition of the Tory mantra that pervaded the election underlines his rhetorical bias: "I only knew that it was a huge election and that on it turned issues of the most tremendous importance, such as whether or not Mariposa should become part of the United States, and whether the flag that had waved over the school house at Tecumseh Township for ten centuries should be trampled under the hood of an alien invader, and whether Britons would be slaves..."[66] To be sure, Leacock takes a dig here at the dramatic language used to describe Britain the good and America the bad. Yet the distinctly Tory prejudices against which he measured the modern Canadian experience are clearly connected to the imperial cause and articulated in a particular kind of language.

The national narrative tied up in stories like *Sunshine Sketches* reveals a hankering for a kinder, gentler Canada – a vast expanse of land peopled by the self-made yeoman who put the good of the community before his own, attended the local church, and educated his children to revere the Queen, the flag, the constitution, and the vast expanse of the British Empire. And so, as the story goes, the British connection would remedy the continental pull that threatened Mariposas across Canada, and redress what the Tories feared was an increasingly imbalanced Anglo-American-Canadian relationship.

The relationship between Leacock's satirical treatment of modern Canadian life and the ideas of Canadian imperialism still resonant in the first decades of the twentieth century is made plain in his essay, *Greater Canada, An Appeal: Let Us No Longer Be a Colony* (1907). As the title suggests, Leacock believed that in order for the colony to realize itself as a "Greater Canada," it must either retain a separate but equal status as a member or the British Empire or "become something infinitely less."[67] "Canada as a colony was right enough in the days of good old Governor Simcoe," Leacock contended, "when your emigrant officer sat among the pine stumps of his Canadian clearing and reared his children in the fear of God and in the Love of England." The Canada of Laurier looked much different. "There is no pause upon the path of progress," he maintained, "there is no stagnation but the hush of death."[68] The "hush of death" to which he referred would be the result of the unbridled conquering of the land without the necessary cultural, historical, and spiritual balance that only the Empire could provide. Leacock called for the British to admit Canadians to the councils of Westminster and allow them to contribute to and have a say in the running of imperial defence.

It never happened, of course. Leacock's was a powerful vision, but it clashed with the experience of hundreds of thousands of Canadian veterans who left 60,000 of their number in Flanders Fields. By the end of First World War, the movement for imperial federation was overshadowed by the increasingly prevalent suspicion of the Old World and all its empires.[69] Yet the British Empire of 1918 and even 1945, in its period of most rapid decline, was a very different thing than the Empire of 1899.

THE 1890S: GOLDWIN SMITH VERSUS GEORGE MONRO GRANT

Sir Wilfrid Laurier was Prime Minister in 1899 – a time in which walking the tightrope between national autonomy and active participation in the British Empire could make or break a federal politician regardless of his political affiliation. With a career in federal politics that spanned from 1887 to 1919, Laurier might have presided over the greatest economic boom in Canadian history, but he was also witness to a period of extreme crisis and self-doubt in Canadian national life. The optimism with which he and the nation greeted the creation of the new nationality in 1867 had been overshadowed by a pessimism that arose in response to economic depression and threats of federal disintegration. Anxiety over being annexed to the United States contributed to the uncertainty of the decades after Confederation. Responsible government had been won, and so too had the right of Canadians to govern their own economic relations, but the nature of the relationship of the free dominions of the Empire to the mother country had yet to be determined.[70]

Laurier learned the hard way that tampering with the English Canada's British identity was political suicide. In the 1890s, when he was Leader of the Opposition, Laurier adopted a policy of unrestricted reciprocity with the United States in an effort to stave off further economic decline and national decay.[71] In doing so, he inadvertently revived the flagging career of the old Conservative leader, Sir John A. Macdonald, who, out of sheer opportunism, loudly decried Laurier's policy as yet another attack on the very structure of the country.

As in so many other federal elections, the great debate surrounding the contest of 1891 began with the respective merits of commercial policies but was soon boiled down to a question of national identity. The Tories denounced the Grit bid for free trade as the first step towards economic and political annexation and the breaking of the British connection. Macdonald cleverly fought and won the election with an emotional appeal to the "The Old Flag, The Old Policy, The Old Leader." The slogan encapsulated the three key tools of federal election victory that remain relevant today: strong leadership, a "national" policy, and the regional and racial appeal encoded in the British flag.[72]

The symbolic language reflected a particularly Tory brand of Canadian imperialism that was prevalent at the time. As Carl Berger has shown, the imperial federation movement of the 1880s–90s was founded on admiration for the British constitution, respect for tradition and precedent, and an enduring criticism of liberalism that was tied up in a particular understanding of American social and political practices.[73] The argument for imperial federation, however, was much more than a homespun variant of Canadian nationalism; it also laid the foundations of the Tory national narrative.

When the movement for imperial federation first proclaimed its gospel, genuine fears that the motherland had failed to tend to the imperial estate were growing on both sides of the Atlantic. In Britain, ideas that the Empire was already over-extended in relation to the metropolitan country's economic strength were beginning to hold sway. By the early 1870s, however, the battle for mastery in Europe and the consequent scramble for colonial possessions tipped the balance of popular opinion in favour of expanding the British Empire. In Canada, the conviction that the colonies were the pillars supporting Great Britain's status as a great power raised the battle cry for imperial unity to a fevered pitch.[74]

Heaven, or at least circumstance, sent a Liberal protagonist into the Canadian forests – from Oxford, no less. Goldwin Smith, a British political thinker and historian of some renown, had experienced life in all three corners of the North Atlantic triangle, but ultimately ended up in Canada where he became the most vocal opponent of imperialism. As a "Little Englander of the Manchester School," Smith disliked foreign entanglements, was sympathetic towards republican institutions and the principle of national self-determination, and condemned pride in empire.[75] He wrote *Canada and the Canadian Question* in 1891 as a campaign document for Laurier's Liberals and in support the cause of commercial and eventual political union with the United States. In the book, Smith argued that Canada, separated by geographical barriers running north and south into four regions, each having free communication with the adjoining parts of the United States, was an artificial nation that was destined by its natural configuration to enter into political and commercial union with the United States.[76]

While Smith shared with the imperialists the typically nineteenth century view that the power to establish free political and social institutions was the special gift of the Anglo-Saxon people, he believed that the stubborn insistence on the British connection retarded cultural and economic life in Canada.[77] Rather than institutionalize the filial relationship, he proposed the establishment of "moral federation of the whole English-speaking race throughout the world" and the promotion of a "Parliament of Man" as a means of fostering interdependence amongst the Anglo-Saxon colonies.[78] Sentiment, in his eyes, was all that remained of Canada's connection with Britain.

George Monro Grant took the opposite position. Born in Nova Scotia and educated in Scotland at the University of Glasgow, Grant was a Presbyterian minister, the principal of Queen's College in Kingston, Ontario, and a man who sired multiple generations of Canadian political thinkers, George P. Grant and Michael Ignatieff among them. He was also one of Canada's most prolific imperialists. In contrast to Smith's conception of a loose morally based Anglo-Saxon Polity, Grant's vision of empire was of a great council of Anglo-Saxon nations which boasted a common sovereign, flag and language and would be a force for Christian civilization and peace in the world. Unlike the

Americans, who were content with their unfettered pursuit of material gain, Grant believed that the British had the loftier goal of bringing civilization and the word of God to Africa, India, and South-Eastern Asia. His sharp critique of American social, economic and political life was coupled with the argument that the Dominion must also shoulder the "White Man's Burden." Rather than choosing to reap the material benefits of commercial and political union with the United States, Canadians would "be citizens of the world" and actively "take part in an Empire that is of world-wide significance."[79]

Grant's mystical account of the forging of the Canadian nation takes the form of a national narrative complete with its own "standing army of engineers, axmen and brawny labourers" who would conquer the west to make way for Anglo-Saxon liberty and progress. Like the wilds themselves, Grant believed that Canada was a slow-growing entity: "The nation" he said, "cannot be pulled up by its roots, cannot be dissociated from its past, without danger to its highest interests."[80] For Grant, the reference to historical precedent was crucial. In his eyes, "More valuable than even the direct advantages of the imperial connection were the subtle, indirect influences that flow from our living in unbroken connection with the old land, and the dynamical if imponderable forces that determine the tone and mold the character of a people." "In our halls" Grant said, "is hung the armory of the invincible knights of old. Ours are the old history, the misty paths, the graves of our forefathers. Ours the names to which a thousand memories call. Ours is the flag. Ours the Queen whose virtues transmute the sacred principle of loyalty into a personal affection."[81]

While Grant held that his imperialism was born out of a deep and abiding loyalty to the motherland, his adversary, Goldwin Smith, claimed that the movement for imperial unity was merely a product of its time. For Smith, the visible weakening of imperial ties and the increasing independence of the colonies "gave birth, by recoil, to Imperial Federation."[82] Smith's argument is true, at least in part. From the late-nineteenth century onwards, Britain faced a broader range of enemies, no longer confined to Europe, and with greater military strength. Relative to countries like the United States and Germany, its industrial prowess was diminishing.[83] David Cannadine has revealed the extent to which the invention of British royal rituals in the nineteenth century corresponded to, and was a product of, the relative decline of the Empire.[84] In this sense, the glorification of British tradition, symbols, and values on the part of Canadian imperialists was a segment of the larger imperial show. Yet, even if we understand the Canadian movement for imperial federation in the context of the decline of the British Empire and the rise of American power, we must also consider it as a way of

335 Narratives of Autonomy and Empire

talking about Canada – a prism through which a particular group of Canadians saw themselves, the nation, and its place in the wider world.

At the time, the Conservative Prime Minister Sir John A. Macdonald was no supporter of the movement for imperial federation. In his eyes the British dominions could never be effectively represented by an imperial parliament or by the establishment of a federal legislature for the entire Empire. However, despite his differences with hardcore imperialists, Macdonald's was a truly Tory narrative. There is much more to his famous declaration "I am a British subject and British born, and a British subject I hope to die" than the pragmatic desire to satisfy English Canadian jingoes.[85] The stories he told about Canada were developed within the historical dimension for a reason. They did not attempt to gauge history or unjust government by any real or ideal principles of reason or law. Rather, the stories looked beneath institutions and legislatures in order to uncover Canada's ancient British ties. By locating the Conservative Party platform and his own political persona within the Tory national narrative, Macdonald consciously sought to appeal to an audience that shared his own prejudices and ideals about themselves and about the nation.

ECHOES: THE PAST IN THE CANADIAN PRESENT

Sir John A. Macdonald has been a mythical figure in the Conservative national narrative ever since. With varying degrees of success, subsequent leaders have invoked his ghost in order to show that they are true blue Tories, defenders of Canadian sovereignty, and mindful of the British tradition. Like Macdonald before him, in a speech delivered recently at the Albany Club, Stephen Harper announced his bid to reclaim the "real Canada" groaning under the "Liberal Shibboleth." "Conservatives," Harper claimed, "understand what the Liberals do not grasp – the difference between defending our values and interests and attacking those of the United States. Just as Sir John A. did. When he created our federation. Built our transcontinental railway. And sent the Northwest Mounted Police west to assert our sovereignty. Sir John gave 21st century Conservatives much to be proud of."[86] Harper learned from Sir John A. that "the ties which join [Canada] to the mother country are more flexible than elastic, stronger than steel and tenser than any material known to science." Just as Macdonald reconciled Canada's status as an independent North American nation with its colonial ties to Britain, so Harper would "bridge the gap between the old world and the new, and reunite the world with a new bond of comradeship."[87]

Harper talked about Canadian politics in terms of competing Liberal and Conservative national narratives for a reason. He draped himself in the moth-eaten robe of empire and, in so doing, meant to constitute the patriot and the good Canadian as one with traditional Tory values. He embedded the narrative in a partisan version of Canadian history and shaped it in accordance with a vision of Canada's relationship with Britain and the United States that coincided with a particular set of prejudices and political goals that Tories have always claimed to have. He made reference to Canadian politics in terms of competing Liberal and Conservative traditions because he knew that political debates over foreign policy are so often fought within the realm of history.

The two versions of Canadian history that Harper recognized go back through generation after generation of Liberal and Conservative political debate. In the quarrels that pitted Grits versus Tories, from Stéphane Dion and Stephen Harper, Peter C. Newman and George P. Grant, Frank H. Underhill and Donald Creighton, O.D. Skelton and Stephen Leacock, down to Goldwin Smith and George M. Grant, the continuity in the two very different stories about Canada and its place in the world are made plain. Some of the protagonists may be dead, but their ideas are not extinct. The Grits understand Canadian history as a journey from colony to nation; the Tories have historically understood Canada as being part of a larger empire. In both cases, the partisan narratives were understood in terms of Canada's imperial and continental relationships. The debates themselves were the mediums through which the English Canadian identity was negotiated forged and re-forged.

The study of Canadian external relations is incomplete without considering how partisan national narratives shape and have shaped the ways that political thinkers and leaders talk about Canada and its place in the world. The debate about the Canadian identity in terms of its relations with Great Britain and the United States has gone on for so long that the existence of the recurrent stories and symbols that make up the conversation are often taken for granted. The narratives of autonomy and empire and the symbolic language of Anglo-Saxon tradition and national autonomy are so deeply ingrained in mainstream political discourse and so often repeated by political thinkers who articulate what Canada is and who Canadians are to the world that the origins of the stories and the ways and means by which they were fashioned are never discussed. By pealing back layer after layer of partisan political debate over Anglo-American-Canadian relations, we can see the ways in which Grit and Tory stories about autonomy and empire shape one another, and in turn how they serve explicit political goals and make their imprint on Canadian foreign policy.

NOTES

1 Professor Robert Bothwell and Julie Gilmour assisted with the conception and evolution of this chapter. Many friends have also contributed to the final product. Robert Adamson, Alison Norman, Susana Miranda, Nathan Smith, Denis McKim, Norman Hillmer, Brad Miller, Yen Tran and Ariel Beaujot read various drafts and provided many helpful comments.
2 See John Geddes, "Bush's Halifax Speech Invokes Canadian Martial Spirit," *Historica, The Canadian Encyclopedia*. http://www.thecanadianencyclopedia.com/index.cfm?PgNm=TCE&Params=M1ARTM0012692.
3 Stephen Harper delivered this speech to the Sir John A. Macdonald dinner at the Albany Club, 11 January 2007.
4 See Luiza Ch. Savage's blog, Savage Washington for 18 January 2007: "What is a 'good Canadian,'" *Maclean's, Blog Central*, 18 January 2007: http://forums.macleans.ca/advansis/?mod=for&act=dip&pid=22606&tid=22606&eid=21&so=1&ps=0&sb=1
5 James C. Bennett, *The Anglosphere Challenge: Why the English-Speaking Nations Will Lead the Way in the Twenty-First Century* (Toronto: Rowman and Littlefield Publishers, Inc., 2004), 80.
6 John English, "In the Liberal Tradition: Lloyd Axworthy and Canadian Foreign Policy," *Canada Among Nations 2001: The Axworthy Legacy*, Fen Osler Hampson, Norman Hillmer and Maureen Appel Molot, eds. (Toronto: Oxford University Press, 2001), 89–106.
7 Quoted in Paul Wells, *Right Side Up: The Fall of Paul Martin and the Rise of Stephen Harper's New Conservatism* (Toronto: McClelland and Stewart, 2006), 279.
8 Michael Ignatieff, "A Foreign Policy for Canada," 24 June 2004: http://www.michaelignatieff.ca/en/about/speeches/899_a-foreign-policy-agenda-for-canada.
9 The approach is inspired by Norman Davies' *Heart of Europe*. "For most readers" Davies said, "it will be a journey from the known to the unknown and back again." Norman Davies, *Heart of Europe: A Short History of Poland* (Oxford: Clarendon Press, 1984).
10 See Steve Penfold, *The Donut: A Canadian History* (Toronto: University of Toronto Press, 2008); Christopher Dummitt, *The Manly Modern: Masculinity in Postwar Canada* (Vancouver: University of British Columbia Press, 2007); Magda Fahrni and Robert Rutherdale, *Creating Postwar Canada: Community, Diversity, and Dissent, 1945–75* (Vancouver: University of British Columbia Press, 2007); Leonard Kuffert, *A Great Duty: Canadian Responses to Modern Life and Mass Culture, 1939–1967* (Montreal & Kingston: McGill-Queen's University Press, 2003); H.V. Nelles, *The Art of Nation Building* (Toronto: University of Toronto Press, 1999); Norman Knowles, *Inventing the Loyalists* (Toronto: University of Toronto Press, 1997).

11 What I refer to as "national narratives," Margaret Somers calls "meta-narratives" in "The Narrative Constitution of Identity: A Relational Network Approach," *Theory and Society* 23, no. 5 (October 1994): 619–620. For examples on the ways in which national narratives and foreign policy intertwine in the United States, see Walter Russell Mead, *God and Gold: Britain, America, and the Making of the Modern World* (New York: Alfred A. Knopf, 2008); Robert Kagan, *Dangerous Nation* (New York: Alfred A. Knopf, 2006); Richard Slotkin, *Gunfighter Nation: The Myth of the Frontier in Twentieth-Century America* (New York: Atheneum, 1992).
12 See Robert Bothwell, *Alliance and Illusion* (Vancouver: University of British Columbia Press, 2007), 5–9; Robert Bothwell, *Canada and Quebec: One Country Two Histories* (Vancouver: University of British Columbia Press, 1998); Arthur Silver, *The French Canadian Idea of Confederation* (Toronto: University of Toronto Press, 1997).
13 John G. Diefenbaker, "Address to the Commonwealth and Empire Industries Association at the Albert Hall, London, England," 4 November 1958: Diefenbaker Canada Centre (DCC) Speeches Series Vol. 25, 722-5.
14 See Pierre Sévigny, *This Game of Politics* (Toronto: McClelland and Stewart Ltd., 1965), 7. For more on French Canadian nationalism during this period, see Michael D. Behiels, *Prelude to Quebec's Quiet Revolution: Liberalism Versus Neo-Nationalism, 1945–1960* (Montreal & Kingston: McGill-Queen's University Press, 1985).
15 For example, on 14 July 1962 Lord Amory told the Secretary of State for Commonwealth Relations that Diefenbaker's attempt to become "at once the leader of the 'middle powers' and a bridge between the West and the un-committed and underdeveloped world... has led from time to time to embarrassments over colonialism, disarmament, nuclear weapons, and nuclear tests." The National Archives of the United Kingdom (NAUK): CAB 21/5477.
16 It is well known that despite Diefenbaker's claims to the contrary, Anglo-Canadian relations were at a very low point during his time in office. British Prime Minister Harold Macmillan was often "annoyed" that his meetings with Diefenbaker were "a complete waste of time": NAUK: CAB 21/5558. See also Robert Bothwell, *Alliance and Illusion* (Vancouver, University of British Columbia Press, 2007), 144.
17 Robert Bothwell, *Alliance and Illusion*, 177.
18 Peter C. Newman, "Peter C. Newman's Handbook for Voters: How to Tell the Grits from the Tories," *Maclean's*, 5 May 1962.
19 Interview with Peter C. Newman, 12 April 2006; Ibid.
20 For an interesting discussion on the impact of consumer culture on postwar Canada, see L.B. Kuffert, *A Great Duty: Canadian Responses to Modern Life and Mass Culture, 1939–1967* (Montreal & Kingston: McGill-Queen's University Press, 2003). See also Phillip Buckner, ed., *Canada and the End of Empire* (Vancouver: University of British Columbia Press, 2005).

21 Wright notes a telling parallel between Newman's *Flame of Power* (1959) and Ayn Rand's bestselling novel *Atlas Shrugged* (1957). Robert Wright, "From Liberalism to Nationalism: Peter C. Newman's Discovery of Canada," *Creating Postwar Canada, 1945–75*, Magda Fahrni and Robert Rutherdale, eds. (Vancouver: University of British Columbia Press, 2008), 115.
22 Peter C. Newman, *Renegade in Power* (Toronto: McClelland and Stewart, 1963), 11; see also, Peter C. Newman, *Home Country: People, Places and Power Politics* (Toronto: McClelland and Stewart, 1973), 21–2.
23 Peter C. Newman, *Here Be Dragons* (Toronto: McClelland and Stewart, 2005), 190.
24 William Christian, *George Grant: A Biography* (Toronto: University of Toronto Press, 1993), 255.
25 Daniel Bell, *The End of Ideology: On The Exhaustion of Political Ideas in the Fifties* (New York: Collier, 1961).
26 George Grant, *Philosophy in the Mass Age* (Toronto: Copp Clark, 1959), 5–7.
27 George Grant, *Lament for a Nation: The Defeat of Canadian Nationalism*, 40th Anniversary Edition (Montreal & Kingston: McGill-Queen's University Press, 1997), 5.
28 Grant, *Philosophy in the Mass Age*, 5.
29 Grant, *Lament for a Nation*, 5.
30 For new scholarship that considers the ideological and cultural diversity of the postwar period, see Magda Fahrni and Robert Rutherdale, eds, *Creating Postwar Canada: Community, Diversity, and Dissent, 1945–75* (Vancouver: University of British Columbia Press, 2007); Nancy Christie and Michael Gauvreau, eds., *Cultures of Citizenship in Postwar Canada, 1940–1955* (Montreal & Kingston: McGill-Queen's University Press, 2003).
31 Bothwell, *Alliance and Illusion*, 4.
32 Frank H. Underhill, "Edward Blake," in *Our Living Tradition: Seven Canadians*, Ser. 1, Claude T. Bissell, ed. (Toronto: University of Toronto Press, 1957), 9.
33 Frank H. Underhill, "Canada and the North Atlantic Triangle 1954," in *In Search of Canadian Liberalism* (Toronto: The Macmillan Company of Canada, 1961), 258.
34 Ibid., 219.
35 Ibid., 256.
36 Ibid., 257–8. See also R. Douglas Francis, *Frank H. Underhill: Intellectual Provocateur* (Toronto: University of Toronto Press 1986), 164.
37 Frank H. Underhill, "Edward Blake," 11–12.
38 See Davie Fulton's letter to Donald Creighton: *The Conservative Position*: LAC MG 32/B 11/6.
39 Gordon Churchill's "The New Conservative Position: A Statement of Philosophy and Principles, LAC: MG 32/B9/107, Davie Fulton's "The Conservative Position Restated," LAC: MG 32/B11/6; Donald Fleming, "Distinctive Conservatism" DCC: Series XII Personal and Confidential; Donald Creighton,

340 Spittal

    Dominion of the North: A History of Canada (Toronto: Macmillan of Canada, 1957).
40 Campaign Speech Number 1-John Diefenbaker, Massey Hall, Toronto, April 25, 1957, DCC: Speeches Series/Election 1957.
41 Carl Berger, *The Writing of Canadian History: Aspects of English-Canadian Historical Writing Since 1900* (Toronto: University of Toronto Press, 1986), 215.
42 Donald Creighton, "Canada in the World," *Canada's Tomorrow: Papers and Discussions from Canada's Tomorrow Conference, Quebec City, November 1953*, G.P. Gilmour, ed. (Toronto: University of Toronto Press, 1954), 5.
43 Donald Creighton, "Sir John A. Macdonald," *Our Living Tradition-Seven Canadians*, Ser. 1, Claude T. Bissell, ed. (Toronto: University of Toronto Press, 1957), 50–51.
44 Donald Creighton, "The Colony of Great Britain and the United States." Creighton was taking his cue here from his friend, Harold Innis. See Innis, "Great Britain, the United States and Canada," 21st Cust Foundation Lecture, delivered at the University of Nottingham, 21 May 1948 in M.Q. Innis, ed., *Essays in Canadian Economic History* (Toronto: University of Toronto Press, 1956), 394–412.
45 Donald Creighton, "Canada in World Affairs: Are We Pulling Our Weight?" *Couchiching Conference*, Friday, 13 August 1954, LAC: MG 31/D77/11.
46 Donald Creighton, "Canada in the World," LAC: MG 21/D77/Vol. 11.
47 Davie Fulton to Donald Creighton, 23 January 1956: LAC MG 32/B/11/6.
48 See George Perlin, *The Tory Syndrome: Leadership Politics in the Progressive Conservative Party* (Montreal & Kingston: McGill-Queen's University Press, 1980), 195.
49 It was also an environment in which patronage-based party organizations were being superseded by well-oiled bureaucratic machines. For more on how the Liberal Party presided over Canada from 1930–1957, see Reginald Whitaker, *The Government Party: Organizing and Financing the Liberal Party of Canada, 1930–1958* (Toronto: University of Toronto Press, 1977).
50 See Anne De Courcy, *1939: The Last Season* (London: Thames and Hudson, 1989), figure 38.
51 Robert Bothwell, *Alliance and Illusion*, 47.
52 Norman Hillmer, "O.D. Skelton and the North American Mind," *International Journal* 60, no. 1 (Winter 2004/2005): 96.
53 Interview with Robert Bothwell, 25 April 2008; See also Carl Berger, *The Sense of Power* (Toronto: University of Toronto Press, 1970).
54 O.D. Skelton, *Life and Letters of Sir Wilfrid Laurier, Vol. II, 1896–1919* (Toronto: McClelland and Stewart Ltd., 1965), 1.
55 Ibid., 49.
56 Barry Ferguson, *Remaking Liberalism: The Intellectual Legacy of Adam Shortt, O.D. Skelton, W.C. Clark, and W.A. Mackintosh, 1890–1993* (Montreal & Kingston: McGill-Queen's University Press, 1993), 77.

57 O.D. Skelton, *The Day of Wilfrid Laurier Part III: The Growth of Nationality* (Toronto: Glasgow, Brook, and Co., 1921), 108.
58 Norman Hillmer, "O.D. Skelton and the North American Mind," 93.
59 O.D. Skelton, *The Day of Laurier*, 148.
60 Robert Craig Brown and Ramsay Cook, *Canada: A Nation Transformed* (Toronto: McClelland and Stewart, 1974), 3; See also Robert Bothwell, Ian Drummond, and John English, "The Great Boom of 1900–13," *Canada 1900–1945* (Toronto: University of Toronto Press, 1987), 55–84.
61 Carl Berger, *Sense of Power*, 6; See also Skelton, *The Day of Laurier*, 169.
62 See Alan Bowker, Introduction to *The Social Criticism of Stephen Leacock* (University of Toronto Press, 1973); Robertson Davies, "Stephen Leacock," *Our Living Tradition-Seven Canadians*, Ser. 1, Claude Bissell, ed. (Toronto: University of Toronto Press, 1957), 128–149, and Desmond Pacey, "Leacock as Satirist," *Queen's Quarterly* 58 (Summer 1951): 208–19.
63 Robertson Davies, "Stephen Leacock," 133.
64 Stephen Leacock, "The Speculations of Jefferson Thorpe," *Sunshine Sketches of a Little Town*, (New York: W.W. Norton, 2005,), 37–62.
65 Robert Craig Brown and Ramsay Cook, *Canada 1896–1921: A Nation Transformed* (Toronto: McClelland and Steward, 1974): 187.
66 Stephen Leacock, *Sunshine Sketches of a Little Town*, 127.
67 Stephen Leacock, *Greater Canada, An Appeal: Let Us No Longer Be A Colony* (Montreal: Montreal News Company Ltd., 1907): 3.
68 Ibid., 3.
69 For more on nationalism and imperialism in the days of Laurier and Borden, see Charles P. Stacey, *Canada and the Age of Conflict: A History of Canadian External Policies Vol. I: 1867–1921* (Toronto: University of Toronto Press, 1984), 52–172.
70 Barry Ferguson, *Remaking Liberalism* (Montreal & Kingston: McGill-Queen's University Press, 1993), 66–7.
71 See O.D. Skelton, *The Day of Wilfrid Laurier: A Chronicle of Our Own Times* (Toronto: Glasgow, Brook, and Co., 1916).
72 See John Duffy, *Fights of Our Lives* (Toronto: Harper Collins, 2002), 27. The poster can be viewed at the McCord Museum's homepage: http://www.mccord-museum.qc.ca/en/collection/artifacts/M965.34.8&section=196?Lang=1&accessnumber=M965.34.8&section=196.
73 See Carl Berger, *The Sense of Power* (Toronto: University of Toronto Press, 1970), 10–11.
74 Few historians have examined how far the transatlantic and continental exchange of ideas and affected the course of Canadian intellectual thought. Robert Kelley is the exception. See Robert Kelley, *The Transatlantic Persuasion: The Liberal-Democratic Mind in the Age of Gladstone* (New York: Alfred A Knopf, 1969).

75 Elisabeth Wallace, *Goldwin Smith: Victorian Liberal* (Toronto: University of Toronto Press, 1957), 133.
76 Goldwin Smith, *Canada and the Canadian Question* (Toronto: University of Toronto Press, 1971), 153.
77 For more on the passing of the Anglo-Saxon torch of liberty, see David Hackett Fisher, *Albion's Seed* (London: Oxford University Press, 1989). In a more thorough study of Goldwin Smith, it would make sense to place his writing alongside that of the American Transcendentalists. They too believed that North America would be the future seat of the Anglo-Saxon "race." See, for example, Ralph Waldo Emerson's *English Traits* (Cambridge, Mass.: Belknap Press of Harvard University Press, 1966), 168–170.
78 Smith, *Canada and the Canadian Question*, 210–11.
79 George Monro Grant, "The Case for Canada," Published by the *Imperial Federation League*, 30 January 1891; See also Grant, *Ocean to Ocean: Sanford Fleming's Expedition Through Canada in 1872* (Toronto: James Campbell and Sons, 1873), 7.
80 George Monro Grant, *Ocean to Ocean*, 358.
81 Ibid., 368.
82 Goldwin Smith, *Canada and the Canadian Question*, 204.
83 David Reynolds, *Britannia Overruled* (London: Longman, 1991), 1–3.
84 See David Cannadine, "The Context, Performance and Meaning of Ritual: The British Monarchy and the 'Invention of Tradition,'" c. 1820–1977," *The Invention of Tradition*, Eric Hobsbawm and Terence Ranger, eds. (Cambridge: Cambridge University Press, 1983).
85 Donald Creighton, *The Old Chieftain* (Toronto: University of Toronto Press, 1998), 206.
86 Stephen Harper's speech at the Sir John A. Macdonald dinner at the Albany Club of Toronto, 11 Jan 2007.
87 Address by the Prime Minister at the Canada-UK Chamber of Commerce, 14 July 2006: http://pm.gc.ca/eng/media.asp?id=1247.

14 And the Beat Goes On: "Identity" and Canadian Foreign Policy

DAVID G. HAGLUND

INTRODUCTION

Annual holidays can be nearly as useful as centennial observations for renewing debate over the Canadian "national identity," and this year's Victoria Day celebration has provided a handy entrée into my chapter's inquiry on the part played by identity in the shaping of the country's foreign policy. At the outset, three observations need to be made about the nexus between identity and foreign policy. First, this is an old line of inquiry, even if conducted in the past under different terminological cover. Secondly, it is a never-ending interrogation. And thirdly, scholarly study of it comes pretty close to being a mug's game, given the ambiguousness of identity and the heated discussions in Canada (as indeed, elsewhere) as to what "really" causes foreign policy to take the form, and reflect the interests, that it does.

So daunting is the task, that one might be excused for simply jumping ship, and leaving its co-helmsmen, Robert Bothwell and Jean Daudelin, with a more navigable craft to take to the editorial seas; for of all the things that might be said of those tempted to chart the course of uncertain identity through the turbulent currents of foreign policy, perhaps the wisest would be the injunction, "don't sail in those waters." However, not being the captain of my fate in this endeavour, I stay on board, and take up a challenge that looks, at first blush, to be particularly problematical in the Canadian context, and not just at the level of federal politics, either.[1] In reality, as we shall see, Canada's case is hardly unique. Most countries have undergone, and continue to undergo, rigorous self-examination of their foreign policies from the coign of vantage of their identity. But if Canada's case is not unique, it remains nevertheless intriguing, for reasons I shall seek to establish in this chapter.

This gets us back to the opening point about the most recent Victoria Day, that of 2008. *Globe and Mail* columnist Jeffrey Simpson touched a nerve when he offered the advice that we should all enjoy this long weekend in May – "and resolve that it will be the last" such associated with Queen Victoria. Keep the holiday, but change the name, urged Simpson, who implored Canadians to demonstrate a sense of national maturity by parting company from the tiny handful of political entities (the Cayman Islands and "a few places in Scotland") that continue to remember a long-dead British monarch in this way. But while his dudgeon might be so easily (and often) elevated when he contemplates vestiges of Canada's colonial past in need (or so he maintains) of expunging, Simpson finds himself much more hard-pressed to suggest a suitable replacement name, and his perplexity stems directly from his well-grounded sense that taking the measure of the "national" identity is next to impossible. "[A]ny attempt," he laments, "to personalize commemorations in a country as politically correct as Canada, where apologies for just about everything done wrong here and abroad are so prevalent, would be denounced as not being sufficiently 'inclusive,' too disrespectful of diversity, inadequately mindful of the prerequisites of gender, ethnicity, race, religion, disability, sexual preference, political party, eye colour, hairstyle, historical experience, individual suffering, appropriation of voice."[2]

Nor was it necessarily much easier to gauge the national identity in an earlier, and presumably simpler (because not "politically correct") era – not if one of the country's ablest chroniclers of foreign policy, John Holmes, is to be believed. In a speech to the American Historical Association, meeting in Chicago in December 1962, Holmes despaired of the frequency with which concerns about identity continued to crop up in Canadian foreign policy discussions. In his view, appeals to this abstract concept, identity, were as troublesome as they were unnecessary, given that Canada's "role" in world affairs could be fairly accurately understood by the right kind of professional diplomatist, possessed with insight into the opportunities as well as constraints presented to Canada by dint of its relative standing in the international society of states. If only matters could be left to those professionals. Unfortunately, he told his audience, the "zeal with which a distinct foreign policy was pursued was not unrelated to the constant compulsion Canadians felt to preserve and assert their identity."[3]

Not only has the span of time not made the task of linking identity with foreign policy any easier than it ever was, but the span of distance also reveals the manifold dimensions of the challenge. Elsewhere in the world, or at least in the Western hemisphere, a Holmesian sense of annoyance about identity's trespassing into the political realm can be detected, for instance in the frustration of the Peruvian novelist Mario Vargas Llosa, who deplores a Latin American obsession with identity as "a useless enterprise, dangerous and impossible, because identity is something possessed by individuals and not collectivities, at least once they've transcended tribal conditions ... But, as in other parts of the world, this mania for determining historico-social or metaphysical specificity for an agglomeration has caused oceans of Latin American ink to flow, generating ferocious diatribes as well as interminable polemics."[4]

But if identity is a concept with which it is impossible to live, it also appears to be a category that is well-nigh unavoidable in the analysis of international relations, whether from the point of view of the diplomatic historian or the political scientist; and since we cannot make it go away, we might as well try to make sense of it. Thus the tack I take in this chapter will be to treat identity as if it really can be a meaningful indicator of foreign policy orientations and options. In so doing, however, I by no means wish to suggest that Canada's (or any other state's) identity is ever knowable, in any "scientific" or "objective" sense; I simply mean to suggest that it is more than legitimate, it is essential, to take into consideration debates about postulated identity, when one seeks to understand why and how foreign policy is made. Simply because debates about identity are never-ending is no reason to exempt this essentially contested category of analysis from scholarly examination.

In what follows, I am going to argue that identity-based arguments about Canadian foreign policy have taken two primary forms: 1) arguments predicated upon deductions made from an assessment of Canada's relative capability (i.e., its "power" or standing in the international system); and 2) arguments based upon inductions developed as a result, largely, of the country's "cultural" makeup (with this latter being interpreted either in terms of "national character," or of "transnational collective identity"). Discussion of both means of contemplating the identity-foreign policy nexus necessarily takes place against a theoretical and conceptual backdrop that accords much importance to "strategic culture" as well as to identity, in both its national and transnational manifestations. This backdrop figures centrally in this chapter's analysis.

STRATEGIC CULTURE: CAUSE OR EFFECT?

Political scientists, probably more so than historians, are subject from time to time to being swept along by the winds of theoretical fashion. And for those political scientists who, like myself, evince an interest in foreign and security policy, prevailing gusts have been transporting a rubric *du jour* called strategic culture. For all its flaws, this rubric can nevertheless serve to help us see more clearly than we might otherwise some connections worth establishing between identity and foreign policy, and not just in Canada's case. Its single biggest drawback, of course, is that no one can agree on how to define it. Part of the problem stems from its two parental elements, "strategy" and "culture," neither of which could be considered a simple concept, with culture being particularly troublesome from the definitional standpoint. Not for nothing did Raymond Williams wryly comment that the word had to rank as one of the two or three most difficult in the English language.[5]

Still, it is a rare (and almost always a vapid) concept in international relations that commands easy agreement as to its definition, so we can overlook this deficiency and turn to some more useful matters appertaining to strategic culture. And even if we cannot agree on a definition, we can at least identify two major definitional contenders, and thereby establish useful conceptual boundaries for strategic culture. On the one side are writers such as Alastair Iain Johnston, who has proffered the most ambitious and sophisticated definition, in referring to strategic culture as "an integrated system of symbols (i.e., argumentation structures, languages, analogies, metaphors, etc.) that acts to establish pervasive and long-lasting grand strategic preferences by formulating concepts of the role and efficacy of military force in interstate political affairs, and by clothing these conceptions with such an aura of factuality that the strategic preferences seem uniquely realistic and efficacious."[6]

On the other side are such writers as Colin Gray, who eschews the causal precision of Johnston and settles instead for a definition of strategic culture that holds it to be at one and the same time both cause and effect – or, to put it as he puts it, "context." In a rejoinder to Johnston, who placed him on his target list of analysts whose usage of strategic culture was deficient from the causal perspective, Gray responded that the best that could be hoped for was to regard the concept as "the world of mind, feeling, and *habit in behaviour*."[7] Later, Gray would return to the charge, and dismiss those who sought to endow the concept with causal prowess as dreamers who simply did not or would not realize that "scholarship on strategic culture ... is bound to fail when it ventures far beyond our culture-bound common sense and positivistically seeks a certain general wisdom."[8]

The contest between Johnston and Gray is useful in illuminating one important way in which strategic culture might be brought into the discussion of Canadian foreign policy, with a view to elucidating how the latter might be linked to identity. The protagonists were really quarrelling over the relative priority to be accorded two kinds of what political scientists like to call "variables," independent ones (i.e., causes) and dependent ones (i.e., effects). Diplomatic historians may be a bit more Laodicean when they turn their thoughts to matters of causality, but they have their own words for expressing the same idea as that motivating the social scientists, and it is a rare historian who would profess disdain for, or even indifference to, the job of trying to argue a persuasive connection between social phenomena, even if at times the enterprise is couched in terms of "understanding" rather than of "explanation."[9] Although Gray seeks to utilize his concept in a way that is both causal and consequential, Johnston wants strategic culture to be the thing that generates results, and not the result itself.

In contrast to either of these analysts, especially Johnston, is Robert Kagan, who conceives of strategic culture as being unambiguously and emphatically consequential. Though Kagan's is not the first name that comes to mind when one seeks to show how identity might have a hand in shaping *Canadian* foreign policy, his words are well worth pondering even if they were primarily directed at a transatlantic and not a North American policy debate. I refer to his celebrated essay, *Of Paradise and Power*, published in article form the year before the current Iraq war began, and reproduced in an expanded monograph as the fighting was set to commence in early 2003. To be sure, Kagan was not discussing Canada in his controversial book. Still, what he had to say about the difference in strategic identities as between America and its continental European allies is of direct bearing on our inquiry into Canadian foreign policy. For what Kagan was promoting was the idea that a country's strategic culture is inextricably bound up with its position in the international pecking order. Thus, he holds strategic culture to be (though he does not use these exact words) a quintessentially "dependent variable," standing for effect not cause, and being entirely explicable in terms of something else – relative capability. This accounts for America's being "from Mars" and quick to countenance martial solutions to security challenges, while Europe is (mainly) "from Venus," and reluctant to frame responses in the same way as its whilom friend across the Atlantic.[10]

IDENTITY AS ROLE: WHERE YOU STAND DEPENDS UPON WHERE YOU FIT

Robert Kagan's theoretical orientation demonstrates affinities with a perspective known variously as "structural realism" or "neoclassical realism." Since it is accepted that realism, no matter how it is modified, is far from a dominant (or, to some, even respectable) paradigm in Canada,[11] it might seem odd if not jarring to associate the Kagan view of strategic culture with a Canadian foreign policy "identity." Yet in so many ways, the Kagan perspective turns out to be clearly Canadian, for what it boils down to is the claim that one can pretty much deduce a country's foreign policy orientation from its relative power, that is from where it fits in the international hierarchy.

In a prescient article that deserves much more attention than it has received, Maureen Molot observed nearly two decades ago that the literature on Canadian foreign policy has been dominated by one particular issue, the country's place in the world, conceived in terms of its *relative capability*. "Concern with Canada's status within the global system has produced a Canadian foreign policy tradition diverse in its philosophical perspective yet rather narrow in the range of issues it has examined… [I]t reflects a fixation with either power or the lack thereof which needs some rethinking."[12]

Molot's admonition is well aimed. Indeed, it is more than a bit ironic that John Holmes, who did so much himself to shape a generation's thinking on Canadian foreign policy, should have complained back in 1962 about the intrusion of identity into the sacred realm of foreign policy, for the burden of much of Holmes's contributions was to suggest that Canada had, by dint of its place in the international structure, a particular "role" to play, one associated with its status of "middle power." And for analysts who imagine that strategic culture has to be inferred from relative capability, role is simply another way of expressing (or "operationalizing") the notion of identity.[13] The role of middle power was not the only identity to be generated by this consequential assessment of strategic culture, but it was the most enduring one, providing many Canadians with a comprehension of not only where the country stood vis-à-vis other states but how it should comport itself on the world stage.

More than a few Canadians (though not Holmes) took this role-mediated identity a bit farther than the facts allowed, and to these commentators on, as well as some practitioners of, the country's foreign policy, the middle would become invested with a significant normative content, such that Canada was said to possess a degree of rectitude held to be lacking in the diplomacy of "greater" (and therefore somewhat degenerate) powers. These observers regarded the middle as bespeaking a blissfully selfless, and decidedly superior, orientation toward the world, founded on the assertion that virtue and power had to be inversely related. According to this perspective, Canada's natural allies and the target of its diplomacy should be those similarly "sized" countries who, by dint of their power standing, constitute a priori what one wag labelled the "GGG," or "group of good guys."[14]

This approach did not just exercise the ire (and irony) of critics who rejected its sanctimoniousness. As well, this normatively laden understanding of middle-power diplomacy (lampooned skilfully by John Holmes as "middlepowermanship") was also dismissed as a category error based upon a fundamental misconception of power.[15] To the critics, there was simply no necessarily inverse relationship between virtue and power, and it was wrong-headed to try to "secure by empirical means ... an independent foundation for a normative dedication to the pursuit abroad of the collective international good."[16] Not only that, but Canada's unveiling of the middle-power concept was not noticeably idealistic, being at the outset intended instead to confer advantage upon it in a world in which the middle power was argued not to reside in the midst of the pack, but rather to stand just a notch below the great power(s), and therefore to be entitled, on the basis of something known as the "functional" principle, to privileges and ranks not enjoyed by the vast majority of states. In sum, middle power, far from connoting selfless politics, was a claim to preference, as originally promoted by Canadian policy makers during and immediately following the Second World War.[17]

There was nothing especially Canadian about the functional principle, which had its roots in 19th-century international-organizational thrusts; but the principle did attain a Canadian pedigree during the early interwar years, when governments in Ottawa (and not only those presided by Liberals) would invoke it as a means of buttressing a case for special ("functional") consideration within the Empire in respect of matters involving the Americans – a people whom Canadians, to the frequent irritation of the British, claimed to have peculiarly refined capacities to understand and interpret. Although deployed at the start of the 1920s in a bid (successful) to get Britain to scrap its bilateral alliance with Japan, the functional principle is most remembered for its second manifestation, during and following the Second World War, when Ottawa insisted that voice and status should be commensurate with each ally's contribution to the war effort and to the building of postwar order.

As Tony Miller explained so well, the functional principle was distinct conceptually from the doctrine of functionalism: the former was expressive of "possession goals" of policy (i.e., egotistical objectives), the latter of "milieu goals" (i.e., world-order objectives). The former was a means of enhancing Canadian influence, while the latter constituted a path toward the construction of a more peaceful world, in the event through international economic and social cooperation. "In 1945 two functionalist traditions, analytically distinct, coexisted in Canada. They subsequently merged, so that the functional principle acquired a connotation of disinterested internationalism that it has not subsequently shed ... The fusion of the functional principle with functionalism helps sustain the conviction that what is good for Canada is good for humanity."[18]

Canada, it transpired, would do well by doing good. And though functionalism as a foreign policy doctrine and identity may have put emphasis upon social and economic cooperation, it would be in the military sphere of peacekeeping that Canada earned its highest accolades in functionalism, as a good international citizen.[19] While peacekeeping was an activity marked by no little preference for cutting an ideological figure distinct from the country's principal NATO partners, especially the United States, it was often overlooked that the country was able to do as well as it did by (and through) peacekeeping precisely because it was such a competent ally, recognized both for its military expertise and the geopolitical company it kept within the alliance.[20]

Peacekeeping may have been the most enduring identity to be associated with strategic culture as consequence, but it was not the only one. Also important was a much earlier identity, that of victim, which really achieved its fullest airing at the start of the 20th century, and if it would subsequently diminish, in inverse proportion to the increase in the country's capabilities, it would never totally disappear from the arsenal of policy roles, where it remained a constant reminder that status still does count (a point to which I return at the conclusion of this chapter).[21]

As it has been with middle power, so too with victimhood: it can yield an easy correspondence between identity and morality. At the same time, foreign policy identity as deduced from system structure can provide empirical as well as normative instruction, endowing content to a strategic identity formed, so to speak, by the system itself. This is what Robert Bothwell had in mind when he commented upon the geo-pedagogical impact of the Cold War on Canadians, to wit that it gave them "a place that was never a mystery, though it was occasionally in question. The end of the Cold War, by contrast, forced Canada and its citizens to conceive new roles in a different world."[22] As noted above, Maureen Molot was similarly on the mark in stressing the outsized part played by assessments of relative capability in the scholarship on Canadian foreign policy. By and large, what I have in this section labelled the *deductive*, or consequential, approach to strategic culture results in a Canadian foreign policy identity that can look to be relatively stable. Can the same degree of stability, however, be associated with *inductive* approaches to strategic culture? Not really, and in the following sections of this chapter I try to show why identity, when regarded as a "causal" element in its own right, can be counted upon to make the study of Canadian foreign policy a much more complicated (but not less interesting) enterprise.

IDENTITY AND THE CONSTRUCTIVIST CHALLENGE IN IR

Many who study foreign policy object to assertions that a country's "interests" (and to be more precise, its "national interests") are and deserve to be of paramount importance when policy makers attempt to direct the affairs of state and an uncertain, confusing world. Although there is certainly a trend among those who study Canadian foreign policy (you might almost call it a tropism) to give a fairly wide berth to discussions of the national interest, as if such talk must be *infra dignitatem* among civilized folk, it should not be imagined that in other lands the national interest is regarded as a non-problematical construct, either for analyzing or for making foreign policy.

Those who like to take critical aim at this hoary analytical device will have no shortage of targets. It has often been said to suffer from vagueness and indeterminacy, and the proof of its unreliability as a guide to policy inheres in its uncanny ability to point simultaneously to any number of policy paths, so long as they are all trod in behalf of that national interest. Moreover, because for some analysts the national interest is said to be defined in terms of power, it violates the principle of social-science parsimony, thereby raising hob with Occam's razor, which warns of the folly of "multiplying essences" (or, defining one complicated concept by reference to a second, equally complicated concept). It has even been branded an outright lie, on the basis that there never has been such a thing as a collective interest attributable to the "nation" (state, really), but only a set of discrete partisan interests, based on section, class, ethnicity, gender, life-style, and so forth. Finally, some who may have been prepared to concede usefulness to the concept in an earlier time are now wont to defect from it, dismissing its value either because the world has changed and states (i.e., those entities that serve as the referent for the national interest) have lost competency in the new era of globalization, or because particular states have become so altered by the processes of "post-modernism" that they can no longer hope to lay claim to a collective (national) interest.

Although considered by many to be an outmoded – even worse, a "realist" – contrivance, the concept of the national interest has been attracting supporters lately from an unexpected quarter known as "social constructivism," a name given to a fairly new epistemological approach that has taken international relations by storm over the past dozen or so years.[23] This is not the place to summarize the content of social constructivism. Suffice it to note that what has been called the "constructivist turn" in international relations theory was partly a function of epistemological trends more broadly within the human sciences,[24] and partly the result of major transformations in the structure of the international system itself. In respect of the latter, the ending of the Cold War and demise of the Soviet Union obviously made life more complicated for those who had assimilated what Kenneth Waltz had to say about the basic stability of bipolarity.[25] Many assumed that the (temporary?) derailing of structural realism à la Waltz meant the end of realist so-called "hegemony" in international relations theory, hence the emphasis upon the "turn" the discipline was ostensibly in the process of making, away from realism and toward some other body of theory, constructivism to be precise, with adherents of this startlingly popular new approach insisting that only it could account for the phenomenon of *change* in international relations.

So the turn was argued to be very much a constructivist one, in which cultural variables were going increasingly to make themselves felt in states' decision making, post-bipolarity. And with culture's (re)appearance as a variable to reckon with came another concept that was bound to be important: identity.[26] This latter concept would be elevated to a central position in constructivist accounts of international outcomes, occupying for these theorists a position as central as that held by power for a certain kind of realist theoretician; identity would be the core organizing concept for realism's challenger, structuring cognition and prefiguring interests.[27] If some might have raised the quibble that this new core concept was itself riddled with ambiguity, the rejoinder came quickly that power's ambiguity had never stopped structural realists from placing *it* upon their theoretical pedestal.

No one has recounted better the ongoing utility of the national interest, from a social-constructivist perspective, than Jutta Weldes, for whom the construct remains of value because, "quite simply it is the language of state action."[28] Not only does the concept help central decision makers understand the ends of policy, but their appeal to it enables them to legitimate those ends, and thus mobilize the means required to attain them. In a word, it is a *sine qua non* of good strategizing. Unlike the realists, for whom the national interest is deduced from certain immutable assumptions about the international anarchical order, the social constructivists stress the interpretative ("intersubjective") creation of interest: "National interests ... are social constructions that emerge out of a ubiquitous and unavoidable process of representation through which meaning is created."[29] Most importantly, the constructivists stress the centrality of *identity* as the core building block of interest, national or otherwise.

Although they were writing about American not Canadian foreign policy, there is absolutely no reason to doubt that what Weldes and her co-author Christina Rowley had to say about identity applies equally to the study of both North American states' foreign policy:

Rather than taking interests as exogenously given, critical social constructivism understands interests as constituted in relation to identity. Critical constructivism foregrounds the role of identity – itself understood as constituted in and through representations – in the construction of state interests and thus of state action.... This means that the world is constituted (constructed) through meaningful practices and that people act on the basis of the meanings that 'things' have for them. These meanings are fundamentally cultural ...[30]

Lest it be thought that the theoretical disquisition above is not only a bit recherché but also is reflective of a kind of conceptualization that only political scientists might be capable of, it bears pointing out that it is not simply they, with their well-known penchant for concept-mongering, who seem to be fixated these days upon identity; if anything, the political scientists, in their embrace of inductivism, are coming closer to the diplomatic historians. For instance, in his recent study of Canadian diplomatic history in the four decades following the Second World War, Robert Bothwell not only gives obeisance to Canadians' "two identities – national and collective" as explanatory variables of great significance, he also invokes an even older core concept associated with the inductive approach to strategic culture, in insisting that "Canadian foreign relations ... have been shaped by the peculiarities of the Canadian national character in both its English and French versions."[31]

Bothwell's comment about Canada's having two identities ("national" and "collective") clashes with the above-cited assertion of Mario Vargas Llosa, regarding the impossibility of collectivities, once past the tribal state, possessing any identity at all. The Peruvian writer's scepticism on the matter of application may find an echo elsewhere,[32] but among social scientists who study the phenomenon, there is wide agreement that collectivities, and not just individuals, can and do possess this thing called identity.[33] The problem with employing identity as a means of comprehending foreign policy interests(s) lies elsewhere, and it is twofold. First, there is the familiar challenge of defining one's terms. Then, there is the question of the referent for the group identity. The trouble with distinguishing between a "national" and a "collective" identity is that these are, in reality, *both* collective identities; what I suspect Bothwell really means is that Canada's identity in the *inductive* sense can be taken to manifest itself in both national and transnational form. I discuss the national variant of identity in the following section, before turning in my penultimate section to an analysis of transnational identity and Canadian foreign policy.

NATIONAL IDENTITY AS NATIONAL CHARACTER?

How we are to think about Canada's national identity has to depend upon how we think about any state's national identity. And on this matter, the scholars are divided. Some argue that the "real" meaning of identity can only be a relational one; in other words, a state (nation) shapes its sense of what, or who, it is only because it is able to contrast itself with some significant "Other." Thus the most important component of national identity becomes simply a sense of difference, or apartness; indeed, to the extent (slight) that it is even possible to give specific content to the term, identity might be construed as the "state of being ... different from others in a particular circumstance. Identity involves the creation of boundaries that separate self and other."[34] There need be no imputation of any particular "essence" of the identity in question other than this: that it be different from its significant Other, which is typically located in the same neighbourhood. As one scholar sums up the thought, "[n]ational consciousness makes sense only in contrast to some other nation."[35]

Alternatively, some scholars prefer to grasp the essential qualities of the national collectivity in question, so as to employ these qualities as a prelude to explaining (and if ambitious, predicting) how "national character" must influence the shaping of foreign policy.[36] Now, it must be said that few scholars today are as bold as Robert Bothwell, in explicitly invoking national character,[37] which as an analytical concept has gone into deep eclipse after once having been very much *de rigueur*.[38] In fact, you could even say that national identity has been so eagerly embraced within the analytic ranks precisely because it connotes what was valuable in the older concept without being encumbered by the latter's normative baggage.[39] For national character has been attacked, under that name, by many who assume it must be packed with "essentialist" categories that lend themselves too easily to stereotyping and, in the worst of circumstances, even to being put at the service of oppressive regimes. The shunning of national character has been going on for decades,[40] but it should not be imagined the concept lacks its defenders, who insist that simply because it can be abused by mischievous people is no reason to discard it. And if the allegation against national character is a less *ad hominem* one, namely that it can be a somewhat fuzzy category of analysis, the defenders retort by asking which kinds of social scientific generalization schema might be any sharper?[41]

One of those defenders, Dean Peabody, insists that it is more than a bit absurd to reject national character in favour of equally ambiguous categories, e.g., social class. To Peabody, what is required is not to jettison, but to operationalize, the concept, which he takes as fundamentally representative of the "average (or central tendency) of the characteristics of individuals" within a given national polity.[42] Some writers like to conceive of national character as expressing a "modal personality," understood as a statistical notion for expressing personalities that appear with great frequency among a national population.[43] Truth to tell, there has been much disagreement as to what national character must mean, to say nothing of how it should be measured, although there would seem to be little to object to in one scholar's summation of it as a "coherent group of traits exhibiting some measure of permanence or continuity." That same scholar, Morris Ginsberg, went on to add that as social scientists became more adept at sampling public opinion (he wrote during the Second World War), it might be imagined that greater, scientifically valid, precision would come to be associated with those traits.[44] While not everyone thinks survey data is the only, or even the most reliable, measure of the national character, there are those who do elevate opinion polls to the status of the Holy Grail.

Prominent among those questing after scientific precision via the technique of polling is Michael Adams, who well illustrates how, in the Canadian context, the effort can combine both approaches – the relational and the essentialist – to inducing national character/identity. If it is true that the inductive road to identity is a bumpier one than the deductive one associated with inferring identity ("role") from assessments of relative capability, it is no less true that even the inductive road has some smooth patches. This is to say that establishing national identity through relational means is slightly less difficult than doing so by stressing essentialism, though often one finds, as with Adams's work, a combination of the relational and the essentialist. This is owing to the great gift that the existence of the United States provides to those who would set out to try to understand Canadian national identity: it enables them to proceed, on the basis of a logic *a contrario*, to establish what Canada must *be* by demonstrating what it is *not*. It is not the United States. It may be incorrect to claim that Canada is the world's original "anti-American" polity, but it is fair at least to give it pride of place among those locales that can be styled as "not-America."[45]

Nothing illustrates this better than Adams's best-seller of a few years ago, *Fire and Ice*, with its insistence that stories about American and Canadian "values" coming more to resemble each other were simply tales. The reality, Adams sought to convince his readers, was rather that the two countries were diverging in important aspects of their national characters, and though the book's ostensible focus was on *American* national character, it spoke volumes about Canada from what was being said about the United States, exemplifying wonderfully the *a contrario* approach. Using the lens of what he called "social values measurement," Adams sought to go to the crux of America's national character, and though he professes no animus against the United States, it is hardly surprising that so many of his American (and some Canadian) readers begged to differ, given his conclusion that Americans are "shutting themselves off from the world around them, becoming increasingly resigned to living in a competitive jungle where ostentatious consumption and personal thrills rule, and where there is little concern either for the natural environment or for those whose American Dreams have turned into nightmares."[46]

The Adams thesis has triggered a debate, as can be imagined. Against the argument of societal ("values") divergence, there is a counterargument that stresses either that the trend is toward convergence, or that there is simply no trend whatsoever worth observing in respect of the national characters of two peoples who resemble each other more than either resembles any other foreign nationality.[47] No one argues that Canada and the US have identical national characters, so the debate swirls around the degree of difference, and it is obvious, as Adams himself concedes, that ideology enters into how one interprets the "data," for he tells us that "[a]rguing about Canada and the United States is like arguing about the Bible: anyone can find a chapter and verse (or in this case, a statistic or policy outcome) to suit their ideological fancy."[48]

As fascinating as the debate is, it may not much matter, for there is a body of research that indicates that differences between peoples do not really need to be very large in order to be significant, in what Freud once termed the "narcissism of minor differences." A social-psychological approach known as "social identity theory" (SIT) basically posits that any difference, no matter how tiny, will suffice to instil in members of a group a sense of distinctive identity, almost always accompanied by a feeling of superiority, vis-à-vis members of the referent group (the Other), and this even if the distinctions between the "in group" and the "out group" may be so miniscule as to be barely detectable to others. Competition among what social psychologists label "minimal groups" is triggered by a cognitive need of peoples for collective self-esteem, and that cognitive need, in turn, is reinforced, in the sphere of international relations, by the mere existence of international anarchy.[49] Thus the emphasis upon identity (via assumptions about "national character") might be thought logically to lead to heightened interstate tension and ill-will, affecting Canada no less than others – and this because of what one writer terms, with allusion to Friedrich Nietzsche's "will to power," the phenomenon of interests demonstrating a "will to manifest identity."[50]

COMPLICATIONS OF TRANSNATIONAL COLLECTIVE IDENTITY

So far our exploration of how identity relates to Canadian foreign policy has taken us from the parsimony of the deductive approach (in which identity is linked to role, and the latter is inferred from relative capability) to the more complex realm of induction, in which national identity is equated with national character, with the latter supposedly revealed by reference to one's Other or by explication of one's own essential qualities (or by both). Things are about to get even more complicated, with the examination of another variant of collective identity that has also figured in the shaping of Canadian foreign policy, which we can label "transnational collective identity." This can take two primary forms, one of which has already been alluded to in the above-cited quote from Robert Bothwell regarding Canada's possessing both an English and a French "national" character. The impact of Canada's "French" identity upon the country's foreign policy is the subject of this volume's chapter by Justin Massie, and will not be discussed here.

Instead, what I will concentrate upon in this section are the contradictions that transnational collectivity identity poses for Canadian foreign policy. One of the contradictions might be said (save perhaps by extreme nationalists) to have beneficial effects, in that it arrests the tendency, discussed in the previous section, of the country's foreign policy going off the rails by according too much influence to egoism (or "collective self esteem"), which on the part of a relatively small country such as Canada can have a dangerous and not simply a ridiculous impact, if the stroking of the national ego (and the bashing of the significant Other) were to become so intense as to lead to the outbreak of interstate hostilities. The other major contradiction associated with transnational collective identity resides in the impact that the cultural variable known as "ethnicity" can and does have upon foreign policy making, at times by means of the pressures exerted upon central decision makers through assorted ethnic diasporas. In this section, I address in turn these two contradictions, one of which enhances the ability of policy makers to comprehend and act upon a "national interest," and the other of which renders such comprehension and action more difficult, and less possible. Thus transnational collective identity becomes the ultimate "spigot variable": turn it one way, and out will flow the water of policy coherence; turn it the other way, and out comes a stream of confusion.

From the point of view of national identity as revealed by national character, it might seem that Canada finds itself in an even greater geopolitical predicament than Mexico, once so famously described by an early 20th century dictator (Porfirio Díaz) as being "so far from God, and so close to the United States." Yet for all the attention accorded to the way in which the U.S., because of its role as Canada's Other, ineluctably must figure in discussions of national identity, it is equally if not more important to consider how America has been factored into the Canadian identity when this latter is contemplated not just from the perspective of national collective identity, but from that of *transnationalism* as well.

There are three principal ways in which transnational collective identity has had an impact upon Canadian foreign policy. The first and most important of these is to be encountered in the political dimension, and is embedded within the phenomenon of liberal democracy. Since the whole point about collective identity is that it is supposed to enable us to distinguish "ourselves" from those who are not in our group, it is absolutely essential to establish the conditions allowing us to "empathize" with others of our ilk, to try to see things the way that they see them, and accommodate their perspective on reality. In the words of one prominent constructivist theorist of international relations, collective identity entails our "positive identification with the welfare of another, such that the other is seen as a cognitive extension of the Self rather than as independent."[51] If we can achieve this positive identification, we can claim to have broadened our identity, beyond our individual psyche and our immediate circle of kinfolk. For some, such broadening is possible, but only up to – and stopping with – the collectivity known as the "nation."[52] Others, however, wonder why the feeling of "we-ness" cannot be extensible, transcending what they insist are the artificial confines of the nation (to reiterate, the state).

In the political dimension, the most potent transnational collective identity of which Canada has been a partaker (and which therefore has had great impact upon its foreign policy) has been that associated with the "democratic alliance,"[53] i.e., the transatlantic security community also known as "the West." The core assumption within the group, indeed the assumption that establishes it as a security community, is the conviction that among liberal democracies, resort to force (or even threatening such resort) is simply out of bounds as a means of conflict resolution; instead, members of the community resolve to settle conflicts arising between themselves in the same way that they resolve them domestically, by non-violent methods.[54] The corpus of theory that has been developed to account for this phenomenon is known as "democratic peace theory" (DPT) and though space does not allow an explication of the theory here,[55] it is important to note two major ways in which Canada's participation in this transnational collective identity influences the country's foreign policy. The first is self-evident, and crucial: membership in the democratic alliance resolves some of the dilemmas that would otherwise constantly attend Canadian relations with the United States. In short, it gives Canada freedom at times to resist American pressure without having to worry about paying the ultimate – or for that matter, any hefty – price for such resistance. The second implication is less obvious, but also important: it limits the burden that alliance membership might otherwise entail for Canada, and if it does not virtually guarantee that "limited liability" will be the operative principle governing Canadian commitments to allies, it certainly facilitates what has been a preference of policy makers for several decades – namely to make less of a commitment than alliance leaders would like.[56]

The second dimension of transnational collective identity of some significance in the crafting of Canadian foreign policy is associated with geography, and is subsumed in the conceptualization of the country as a "regional" actor, with North America said to be the territorial stage upon which foreign policy decisions of greatest importance get enacted. In part this is simply to state the obvious – that there are certain regional realities associated with economics and geography that have always to be heeded when policy is fashioned. But there have been moments when more than "objective" considerations have been under discussion, and when region has figured as a core component of identity in its own right. Admittedly, the present is not one of those moments, as once again it has become commonplace to hear and read references about the dangers of regionalism, often couched in terms of "continentalism."[57] As in the past, so too today, Canada's regional identity (or to phrase it more exactly, Canada's *non*-regional identity), is said to be up for grabs, and one short-term consequence of the Iraq war has been to convince some analysts that Canada might yet remain a "European" entity after all (this on the Kaganesque assumption that Europe equates with Venus, or peace).[58]

This debate, or what I have elsewhere termed a "geopolitical jamboree,"[59] can be expected to last for as long as Canada does. Thus it is well that we reflect upon the cyclical aspect of the discussion, for were we to cast our thinking back to the early years of the 20th century, we would be struck by the amount of intellectual energy being channelled into what was then being touted as a new and irenic contribution to global affairs, a breathtaking one at that – the "North American Idea."[60] To its proponents, the inspiring example of two North American lands settling their disputes via negotiation, not war, was capable of showing a war-prone Europe how it too might make the journey from Mars to Venus. In the bargain, the new-found North American identity would also elevate Canada's *rang*, by dint of the fortuitous conclusion that it, and *only* it, could play the indispensable role of linchpin, bonding North America with the British Empire/Commonwealth, in what would be (had it only succeeded) a geopolitical condominium more powerful than any international institution ever known, hence an unquestionable force for good in the world, to those (and there were many) who subscribed to the era's "linchpin mania."[61]

This notion, of an Anglo-Saxon condominium, leads us to the third and final way in which transnational collective identity might be said to influence Canada's foreign policy identity: ethnicity. In respect of ethnic identity, we are once more dealing with a "variable" that can exert its influence in two radically different ways. On the one hand, ethnicity looked in the past, never more so than at the dawn of the 20th century, as if it might provide the key to shaping the national interest, in a country in which the political elite styled itself as both British and imperialist.[62] The stylization could not last, and the cognitive "realm" of Canadian foreign policy would shrink, at least in terms of its ethnic content.[63] Partly, this was a result of domestic realities: the early 20th century was, after all, a time when a leading French sociologist could justifiably entitle a book about Canada's dual (English and French) character, *The Race Question in Canada*, with "race" standing for what today we know to be ethnicity.[64] Partly, it was a result of regional and extra-regional geopolitical developments, the former associated with the allure of a competing North American identity, the latter brought home in the extraordinary cost that an identity centred upon Britain and Empire could have for Canada, as demonstrated so graphically by the First World War. Not since that war has an appeal to the country's "British" (or "Anglo-Saxon") identity been able to exert such a pull on Canadian foreign policy, and though in recent years some analysts in the US and the UK have been heard to wax enthusiastically about an identity construct known as the "Anglosphere," appeals to this as a means of influencing *Canadian* foreign policy have had little traction.[65]

Instead, ethnicity as a vector of transnational collective identity has come to have a centrifugal rather than a centripetal impact upon foreign policy. In so doing, it has led in some respects to Canadian debates resembling those taking place in the United States, Michael Adams to the contrary notwithstanding. For in both polities, there is today great uncertainty as to the meaning that "multiculturalism" must have for the national interest.[66]

CONCLUSIONS

It might seem, from the discussion in this chapter, that the best thing we could do about our topic, identity and Canadian foreign policy, would be to tear a page out of the *Sopranos'* book, and forget about it. But we have no such luxury, for identity, like poverty, has an enduring quality. In this chapter, I have sought to make the best of a bad hand by trying to show how identity might be utilized as a foreign policy concept, with reference to contemporary discussions among theorists of international relations and foreign policy, especially those related to strategic culture.

Two implications of this chapter are worth stressing here. The first concerns the necessity to bring into the analysis the element of transnational – and not just national – collective identity. For though it surely is true that states can be and are eminently self-regarding entities, they are also "other-regarding" in being able (some of them at least) to resolve the cruellest dilemmas that anarchy would otherwise throw their way, by developing institutions for creative cooperation. Among such institutions, none can be of greater significance to Canada than the Western security community, which has done much to structure Canadian foreign policy identity for more than half a century.

Secondly, if the confusion of identity politics can be said to yield at least one invariant in the Canadian context, it is this: the United States will continue, in season and out, and irrespective of whether Canadians like or despise its president, to structure Canada's own national identity in a powerful fashion. It will do so in a manner, and for reasons similar to, the way in which Great Britain itself once structured *American* national identity, by serving as the significant Other. But there will be one big difference from the Anglo-American pattern, and it will stem from something introduced in this chapter's early pages: relative capability. Briefly put, it required a shift in the relative capabilities as between themselves and the British for Americans finally to abandon their long-standing habit of "tweaking the lion's tail," and through so doing establishing a sense of identity and importance, maybe not so much in the world's eyes as in their own. Because for so many years, Britain was *the* standard against which Americans measured their own worth, we sometimes forget why and how that measuring could work against the two constructing a more "healthy" bilateral relationship. What happened is that America outgrew Britain, and in so doing could outgrow its earlier practice of walking around with a geopolitical chip conspicuously balanced on its shoulder. It is hard to imagine, North American power differentials being what they are (and will remain), the Canadian chip similarly disappearing.[67] This is to say that we are unlikely ever to witness Canadian-American relations becoming as relatively trouble-free, from the perspective of identity, as British-American relations have become.

NOTES

1 As I write this, the Quebec government has just released the results of a study it commissioned into the province's "identity" – albeit not its foreign policy identity (at least not yet) – with the immediate result being to reignite the existential debate about what it "means" to be a Quebecker; see Rhéal Séguin, "Quebec's Day of Reckoning," *Globe and Mail*, 23 May 2008, A1, A14.
2 Jeffrey Simpson, "Why this Victoria Day Should Be Our Last," *Globe and Mail*, 17 May 2008, A21.
3 Quoted in Adam Chapnick, *Canada's Voice: The Public Life of John Wendell Holmes* (Vancouver: University of British Columbia Press, forthcoming).
4 Mario Vargas Llosa, "The Paradoxes of Latin America," *American Interest* 3 (January/February 2008): 7–11, quote at 8.
5 Williams, cited by William H. Sewell, Jr., "The Concept(s) of Culture," in *Beyond the Cultural Turn: New Directions in the Study of Society and Culture*, ed. Victoria E. Bonnell and Lynn Hunt (Berkeley: University of California Press, 1999), 35–61. For an extensive catalogue of culture's many, and at times contradictory, meanings, see A. L. Kroeber and Clyde Kluckhohn, *Culture: A Critical Review of Concepts and Definitions* (New York: Vintage Books, 1963).
6 Alastair Iain Johnston, *Cultural Realism: Strategic Culture and Grand Strategy in Chinese History* (Princeton: Princeton University Press, 1995), 36–37. Also see his "Thinking about Strategic Culture," *International Security* 19 (Spring 1995): 32–64.
7 Colin S. Gray, "Strategic Culture as Context: The First Generation of Theory Strikes Back," *Review of International Studies* 25 (January 1999): 49–69, quote at 58 (emphasis in original).
8 Colin S. Gray, "Out of the Wilderness: Prime Time for Strategic Culture," *Comparative Strategy* 26 (January-March 2007): 1–20, quote at 1.
9 For a stimulating discussion, see Marc Trachtenberg, *The Craft of International History: A Guide to Method* (Princeton: Princeton University Press, 2006).
10 Robert Kagan, *Of Paradise and Power: America and the New World Order* (New York: Alfred A. Knopf, 2003).
11 A recent study done of the theoretical inclinations of international relations specialists in Canada and the United States revealed that only 16 percent of Canadian professors labeled themselves "realists" (as opposed to 25 percent of American professors who did so). See Michael Lipson et al., "Divided Discipline? Comparing Views of US and Canadian IR Scholars," *International Journal* 62 (Spring 2007): 327–43, citation at 332.
12 Maureen Appel Molot, "Where Do We, or Should We, or Can We Sit? A Review of Canadian Foreign Policy Literature," *International Journal of Canadian Studies* 1–2 (Spring/Fall 1990): 77–96, quote on 86.
13 See Lisbeth Aggestam, "A Common Foreign and Security Policy: Role Conceptions and the Politics of Identity in the EU," in *Security and Identity in Europe:*

Exploring the New Agenda, ed. Aggestam and Adrian Hyde-Price (Houndmills: Macmillan, 2000), 86–115.
14 The wag was Denis Stairs, who made this observation in his rapporteur's notes presented to the first National Forum on Canada's International Relations, Ottawa, 22 March 1994.
15 John W. Holmes, "Most Safely in the Middle," in *Towards a New World: Readings in the History of Canadian Foreign Policy*, ed. J. L. Granatstein (Toronto: Copp Clark Pitman, 1992), 90–105.
16 Denis Stairs, "Will and Circumstance and the Postwar Study of Canada's Foreign Policy," *International Journal* 50 (Winter 1994–5): 9–39, quote at 17.
17 R. A. MacKay, "The Canadian Doctrine of the Middle Powers," in *Towards a New World*, 65–75.
18 A. J. Miller, "The Functional Principle in Canada's External Relations," *International Journal* 35 (Spring 1980): 309–28, quote at 321, 328.
19 See Robert C. Thomsen and Nikola Hynek, "Keeping the Peace and National Unity: Canada's National and International Identity Nexus," *International Journal* 61 (Autumn 2006): 845–58.
20 J. L. Granatstein, "Peacekeeping: Did Canada Make a Difference?" in *Making a Difference? Canadian Foreign Policy in a Changing World*, ed. John English and Norman Hillmer (Toronto: Lester, 1992), 222–36.
21 Victimhood can be at its most sublime when the country faces "oppression" coming from more than one quarter, and in this respect the quarrel over the shape of the boundary between Canada and the American holding of Alaska has to rank as one of the more enduring, and also noble, myths of Canadian foreign policy. It does so because it provides, even to this day, a heroic tale of Canadian pluckiness in the face of two great power bullies, one a threatening America, the other a duplicitous Britain. That the facts of the dispute, and for that matter international law as interpreted at the time, supported the American position and not the Canadian is of little moment, and that the British weighed in prudently, but not ineffectively, in Canada's favour, is seldom recalled. Instead, the image of a country effectively "sacrificed" on the altar of geopolitics lingers as a staple in Canadian foreign policy identity. See David G. Haglund and Tudor Onea, "Victory without Triumph: Theodore Roosevelt, Honour, and the Alaska Panhandle Boundary Dispute," *Diplomacy & Statecraft* 19 (March 2008): 20–41.
22 Robert Bothwell, *The Big Chill: Canada and the Cold War*, Contemporary Affairs no. 1 (Toronto: CIIA/Irwin, 1998), 109.
23 Illustratively, not too long ago I took part in the defence of a doctoral dissertation written by a student of international relations in my department, who at the time of the examination had just taken up his current position with the Royal Canadian Mounted Police. The dissertation was a constructivist analysis of trends in homeland security, prompting this examiner to remark that "when even the cops are constructivists, you know that you are confronted with a powerful new

paradigm." For the same thought, phrased in a less facetious manner, see Stephen M. Walt, "International Relations: One World, Many Theories," *Foreign Policy*, no. 110 (Spring 1998): 29–46.
24 Jeffrey Checkel, "The Constructivist Turn in International Relations Theory," *World Politics* 50 (January 1998): 324–48. Also see Terrence J. McDonald, ed., *The Historic Turn in the Human Sciences* (Ann Arbor: University of Michigan Press, 1996); Mark M. Blyth, "'Any More Bright Ideas?' The Ideational Turn of Comparative Political Economy," *Comparative Politics* 29 (January 1997): 229–50; and David Chaney, *The Cultural Turn: Scene-Setting Essays on Contemporary Cultural History* (London: Routledge, 1994).
25 Kenneth N. Waltz, *Theory of International Politics* (Reading, MA: Addison-Wesley, 1979).
26 See Sujata Chakrabarti Pasic, "Culturing International Relations Theory: A Call for Extension," in *The Return of Culture and Identity in IR Theory*, ed. Yosef Lapid and Friedrich Kratochwil (Boulder: Lynne Rienner, 1997), 85–104.
27 Ted Hopf, "The Promise of Constructivism in International Relations Theory," *International Security* 23 (Summer 1998): 171–200.
28 Jutta Weldes, "Constructing National Interests," *European Journal of International Relations* 2 (September 1996): 275–318, quote at 276.
29 Ibid., 283.
30 Christina Rowley and Jutta Weldes, "Identities and US Foreign Policy," in *US Foreign Policy*, ed. Michael Cox and Doug Stokes (Oxford: Oxford University Press, 2008), 183–209, quote at 186–87.
31 Robert Bothwell, *Alliance and Illusion: Canada and the World, 1945–1984* (Vancouver: UBC Press, 2007), 5, 9.
32 Similarly dubious about the utility of identity as a category of analysis in the group context are Rogers Brubaker and Frederick Cooper, "Beyond 'Identity'," *Theory and Society* 29 (February 2000): 1–47.
33 See William Bloom, *Personal Identity, National Identity and International Relations* (Cambridge: Cambridge University Press, 1990); and Shmuel Noah Eisenstadt and Bernhard Giesen, "The Construction of Collective Identity," *Archives of European Sociology* 56 (1995): 72–102.
34 Glenn Chafetz, Michael Spirtas, and Benjamin Frankel, "Introduction: Tracing the Influence of Identity on Foreign Policy," *Security Studies* 8 (Winter 1998/99–Spring 1999): vii–xxii, quote at viii.
35 Anna Triandafyllidou, "National Identity and the 'Other'," *Ethnic and Racial Studies* 21 (July 1998): 593–612, quote at 599.
36 Paul A. Kowert, "National Identity: Inside and Out," *Security Studies* 8 (Winter 1998/99–Spring 1999): 1–34.
37 One such scholar was Arthur Schlesinger, Jr., for whom national character raised important questions about the ability of America's creedal (constitutional) identity to withstand the challenge of a contemporary ethnic politics subsumed under the name "multiculturalism"; see his *The Disuniting of America: Reflections on a*

Multicultural Society, new and rev. ed. (New York: W. W. Norton, 1998), 169. Also see, on this theme, Samuel P. Huntington, "The Hispanic Challenge," *Foreign Policy*, no. 141 (March/April 2004), 30–45.

38 E. Adamson Hoebel, "Anthropological Perspectives on National Character," *Annals of the American Academy of Political and Social Science* 370 (March 1967): 1–7.

39 One of the first scholars openly to advocate replacing the label national character with that of national identity was Erik Erikson; see Bernard C. Hennessy, "Psycho-Cultural Studies of National Character: Relevances for International Relations," *Background* 6 (Autumn 1962): 27–49, citation at 28.

40 See in particular the critique unfurled in Hamilton Fyfe, *The Illusion of National Character* (London: Watts, 1940). Also see Kenneth W. Terhune, "From National Character to National Behavior: A Reformulation," *Journal of Conflict Resolution* 14 (June 1970): 203–63.

41 For a qualified endorsement of the continued applicability of national character, see Lloyd Jensen, *Explaining Foreign Policy* (Englewood Cliffs, NJ: Prentice-Hall, 1982), 53.

42 Dean Peabody, *National Characteristics* (Cambridge: Cambridge University Press, 1985), 44–5.

43 See Alex Inkeles and Daniel J. Levinson, "National Character: The Study of Modal Personality and Sociocultural Systems," in *The Handbook of Social Psychology* (2d ed.), vol. 4: *Group Psychology and Phenomena of Interaction*, ed. Gardner Lindzey and Elliot Aronson (Reading, MA: Addison-Wesley, 1969), 418–506.

44 Morris Ginsberg, "National Character," *British Journal of Psychology* 32 (January 1942): 183–205, quote at 183.

45 For this usage, only in the European not North American context, see Timothy Garton Ash, *Free World: America, Europe, and the Surprising Future of the West* (New York: Random House, 2004), 55–9.

46 Michael Adams, *Fire and Ice: The United States, Canada and the Myth of Converging Values*, with Amy Langstaff and David Jamieson (Toronto: Penguin Canada, 2003), 39.

47 For a rebuttal of the Adams thesis, see Reginald C. Stuart, *Dispersed Relations: Americans and Canadians in Upper North America* (Washington and Baltimore: Woodrow Wilson Center Press and Johns Hopkins University Press, 2007).

48 See his letter to the editor, *Literary Review of Canada* 16 (June 2008): 30–1. Adams was writing in response to an article the *Review* published the previous month, praising the Stuart book and, therefore, dispraising his own. For that review, see Edward Grabb, "Not So Different After All," *Literary Review of Canada* 16 (May 2008): 11–12.

49 Jonathan Mercer, "Identity and Anarchy," *International Organization* 49 (Spring 1995): 229–52. Also see Jennifer Crocker and Riia Luhtanen, "Collective Self-Esteem and Ingroup Bias," *Journal of Personality and Social*

Psychology 58 (January 1990): 60–67; Noel Kaplowitz, "National Self-Images, Perception of Enemies, and Conflict Strategies: Psychological Dimensions of International Relations," *Political Psychology* 11, 1 (1990): 39–82; Iver B. Neumann, "Self and Other in International Relations," *European Journal of International Relations* 2 (June 1996): 139–74; and Susan Oyama, "Innate Selfishness, Innate Sociality," *Behavioral and Brain Sciences* 12 (December 1989): 717–18.

50 Rodney Bruce Hall, *National Collective Identity: Social Constructs and International Systems* (New York: Columbia University Press, 1999), 38.

51 Alexander Wendt, "Identity and Structural Change in International Politics," in *Return of Culture and Identity in IR Theory*, 52. Also see this same author's *Social Theory of International Politics* (Cambridge: Cambridge University Press, 1999).

52 An excellent assessment of this variant of collective identity is Anthony D. Smith, *National Identity* (Reno: University of Nevada Press, 1991).

53 The concept comes from Thomas Risse-Kappen, *Cooperation Among Democracies: The European Influence on U.S. Foreign Policy* (Princeton: Princeton University Press, 1995).

54 See Emanuel Adler and Michael Barnett, eds., *Security Communities* (Cambridge: Cambridge University Press, 1998).

55 See Michael E. Brown, Sean M. Lynn-Jones, and Steven E. Miller, (eds.), *Debating the Democratic Peace* (Cambridge, MA: MIT Press, 1996).

56 For an analysis of how membership in a liberal-democratic alliance encourages limited liability, see David G. Haglund and Stéphane Roussel, "Is the Democratic Alliance a Ticket to (Free) Ride? Canada's 'Imperial Commitments,' from the Interwar Period to the Present," *Journal of Transatlantic Studies* 5 (Spring 2007): 1–24.

57 See Marie Bernard-Meunier, "The 'Inevitability' of North American Integration?" *International Journal* 60 (Summer 2005): 703–11; and Lawrence Martin, "North America's Era of Limitless Integration Draws to a Welcome Close," *Globe and Mail*, 3 June 2008, A19.

58 See especially Philip Resnick, *The European Roots of Canadian Identity* (Peterborough. ON: Broadview, 2005).

59 See my *The North Atlantic Triangle Revisited: Canadian Grand Strategy at Century's End*, Contemporary Affairs no. 4 (Toronto: CIIA/Irwin, Oxford University Press Canada, 2000), chap. 4.

60 In particular, see James A. Macdonald, *The North American Idea* (Toronto: McClelland, Goodchild & Stewart, 1917); and Donald M. Page, "Canada as the Exponent of North American Idealism," *American Review of Canadian Studies* 3 (Autumn 1973): 30–46.

61 The term is Robert Bothwell's. See his "Has Canada Made a Difference? The Case of Canada and the United States," in *Making a Difference?*, 8–9.

62 Carl Berger, *The Sense of Power: Studies in the Ideas of Canadian Imperialism, 1867–1914* (Toronto: University of Toronto Press, 1970).
63 By "realm" is implied a transnational collective identity, or as Kim Richard Nossal puts it, "a sphere or domain that is both a political space and an ideational construct of political identity and community that goes beyond the state as it is usually defined in international relations." See his "Defending the 'Realm': Canadian Strategic Culture Revisited," *International Journal* 59 (Summer 2004): 503–20, quote at 505.
64 André Siegfried, *The Race Question in Canada* (London: Eveleigh Nash, 1907).
65 David G. Haglund, "Relating to the Anglosphere: Canada, 'Culture,' and the Question of Military Intervention," *Journal of Transatlantic Studies* 3 (Autumn 2005): 179–98.
66 See David Carment and David Bercuson, eds., *The World in Canada: Diaspora, Democracy, and Domestic Politics* (Montreal and Kingston: McGill-Queen's University Press, 2008); and Denis Lacorne, *La Crise de l'identité américaine: Du melting-pot au multiculturalisme* (Paris: Fayard, 1997).
67 On the British role in shaping American national identity, see Walter Russell Mead, *God and Gold: Britain, America, and the Making of the Modern World* (New York: Alfred A. Knopf, 2008).

Contributors

ROBERT BOTHWELL is a Professor of History at the University of Toronto and Director of the International Relations Program at the University of Toronto.

DUANE BRATT is a Professor in the Department of Policy Studies at Mount Royal College in Calgary, Alberta.

JEAN DAUDELIN is an Assistant Professor of International Affairs at the Norman Patterson School of International Affairs at Carleton University in Ottawa.

GREG DONAGHY is Head of the Historical Section at Foreign Affairs and International Trade Canada and General Editor of the series, Documents on Canadian External Relations.

FRED EDWARDS is an editor at the *Toronto Star* and a former editorial adviser at *Beijing Review*.

JULIE GILMOUR is a Ph.D. candidate in the Department of History, and Instructor in the International Relations Program at Trinity College, University of Toronto.

DAVID G. HAGLUND is the Sir Edward Peacock Professor of Political Studies at Queen's University.

JUSTIN MASSIE is a doctoral candidate in the Department of Political Studies at Queen's University.

JOHN MEEHAN is Visiting Scholar, Asian Institute, Munk Centre for International Studies, University of Toronto.

KATHLEEN RASMUSSEN is a historian in the Office of the Historian, U.S. Department of State.

ROGER SARTY is a Professor of History at Wilfrid Laurier University.

WILLIAM A. SCHABAS is a Professor of Human Rights Law, National University of Ireland, Galway and Director, Irish Centre for Human Rights.

IAN SMILLIE is the Research Coordinator for Partnership Africa Canada and Chair, Diamond Development Initiative.

CARA SPITTAL is a Ph.D. candidate in the Department of History at the University of Toronto.

DAVID WEBSTER is Kiriyama Research Fellow, Center for the Pacific Rim, University of San Francisco.

GERALD WRIGHT currently teaches at the Norman Paterson School and is the chair of the Organizing Committee of the CIC Ottawa Foreign Affairs Program. In 1992–1993, he was Special Advisor to the Secretary of State for External Affairs.

Chronology of Canadian Political History

1 July 1867 – The British North America Act establishes the united Dominion of Canada, comprised of Canada East and West, New Brunswick, and Nova Scotia. Although accorded domestic autonomy, Canada still retains its colonial status in external affairs.

1867 – George-Etienne Cartier becomes Canada's first Minister of Militia and Defence.

1868 – The first Canadian immigration office is established.

1871 – As part of the British delegation, John A. Macdonald concludes the Treaty of Washington with the Americans to settle various differences between Great Britain and the United States.

20 July 1871 – British Columbia joins Confederation after numerous concessions, including a railway from central Canada to the Pacific coast.

1873 – Alexander Mackenzie's Liberals defeat Macdonald's Conservatives and form the government.

1 July 1873 – PEI joins Confederation.

1878 – John A. Macdonald and the Conservatives return to office.

1879 – John A. Macdonald institutes his National Policy, which encourages higher tariffs, the completion of the Trans-Canada railway, and the settlement of the west.

1880 – Alexander Galt is appointed to the position of High Commissioner to London.

1882 – Hector Fabre is appointed to France as an agent (later known as a High Commissioner).

1885 – Prime Minister Macdonald resists British appeals for the deployment of an official Canadian contingent to relieve British troops during the Sudan crisis.

1896 – Sir Wilfrid Laurier and the Liberal Party are elected to government. Joseph Pope becomes the first under-secretary of state for External Affairs

1899 – The outbreak of the Boer War causes tensions between French and English Canadians. In an attempt to preserve national unity, Laurier proposes a compromise; Canada will send 1000 volunteers who, once recruited and transported overseas, will be the responsibility of Britain.

1903 – A six person arbitration panel consisting of three Americans, two Canadians and one British representative is established to resolve the Alaska Boundary dispute. They decide in favour of the United States.

1904 – The Militia Act extends more control of the army to the Canadian government and opens the highest office to Canadians, as well as British officers. Additionally, the act leads to Canada's full assumption of its defence responsibilities.

1909 – As a preliminary step in the evolution of autonomous Canadian foreign policy, the Laurier government passes the External Affairs Act, and in doing so establishes the Department of External Affairs.

1909 – The Boundary Waters treaty marks a shift in Canadian-American relations towards accommodation, and establishes the six-member International Joint Commission.

1910 – Parliament passes the Naval Service Act, creating the Naval Service of Canada and the Department of Naval Service.

Chronology

1911 – Robert Borden and the Conservatives win the election because of discontent in Quebec over Laurier's Naval Service Act and unease in English Canada with reciprocity with the United States.

1912 – The positions of secretary of state for External Affairs and prime minister merge portfolios. The Naval Aid Bill is introduced, only to be defeated in the Senate in 1913.

1914 – Canada goes to war against Germany as a consequence of Britain's declaration of war.

1917 – At the Imperial War Conference, Borden introduces Resolution IX, calling for the full recognition of the dominions as autonomous states in the Commonwealth.

1 August 1917 – Borden institutes conscription with the passing of the Military Service Act, sparking uproar amongst French Canadians. After a divisive election, Borden is re-elected, leading a "union government" made up of Conservatives, and Liberals who had deserted Laurier on the issue.

1919 – Borden attends the Paris Peace Conference, and Canada signs the resulting Treaty of Versailles.

1920 – Conservative Arthur Meighen succeeds Borden as prime minister of Canada.

1921 – The Liberals under William Lyon Mackenzie King defeat Meighen in a general election and form the government.

1922 – Despite British appeals for assistance during the Chanak Affair, Mackenzie King remains detached, claiming that major questions of foreign policy must be settled by Parliament.

1923 – The Halibut Treaty with the United States, designed to protect the Pacific halibut fishery, is signed solely by a Canadian minister alone for the first time, and not a representative of the British government.

1 April 1925 – O.D. Skelton becomes under-secretary for External Affairs; his two primary objectives are the creation of an autonomous foreign service and the establishment of diplomatic missions abroad.

1926 – After a brief Conservative interlude under Arthur Meighen, William Lyon Mackenzie King leads the Liberal Party of Canada to a comfortable victory and regains office.

1926 – During an Imperial Conference, the Committee on Inter-Imperial Relations chaired by former British Prime Minister Lord Balfour concludes that the dominions are "autonomous Communities within the British Empire, equal in status, in no way subordinate one to another in any aspect of their domestic or external affairs…"

1927 – The first Canadian diplomatic post abroad, a legation, headed by a "minister" – Vincent Massey – and not an ambassador is established in Washington.

1930 – After nearly a decade of Liberal rule, Mackenzie King is defeated by R.B Bennett and the Conservatives in the federal elections.

11 December 1931 – The British dominions are granted their full legal freedom with the signing of the Statute of Westminster.

1932 – Members of the British Commonwealth convene in Ottawa for the first Imperial Economic Conference held outside of London, creating an empire-wide system of preferential tariffs.

14 October 1935 – Mackenzie King's Liberals defeat Bennett and the Conservatives.

11 November 1935 – President Franklin D. Roosevelt and Mackenzie King sign a trade agreement that bestows reciprocal most favoured nation status on all Canadian and American products and grants concessions on select Canadian natural resources.

17 November 1938 – In an act of Western solidarity, Canada and the United States, and Great Britain and the United States simultaneously sign separate commercial accords.

3 September 1939 – Great Britain declares war on Germany.

10 September 1939 – Following a vote in the Canadian House of Commons, King George VI signs a separate Canadian declaration of war.

August 1940 – Mackenzie King and President Roosevelt establish the Permanent Joint Board on Defence (PJBD), an advisory committee for continental defence, at Ogdensburg, New York, marking Canada's shift from the British to the American sphere of influence.

1941 – President Roosevelt and Mackenzie King conclude the Hyde Park agreement establishing a common continent-wide exchange of defence-related goods.

1943 – The Washington legation is raised to the status of Embassy.

July 1944 – A Canadian delegation attends the United Nations Monetary and Financial Conference during which the Bretton Woods Agreement is concluded.

April-June 1945 – At the United Nations Conference on International Organization in San Francisco, the Canadian delegation contributes significantly to the creation of the Economic and Social Council, and tries to safeguard the autonomy of smaller nations within the organization.

6 September 1945 – Igor Gouzenko, cipher clerk at the Russian embassy, reveals documents that expose Soviet spy rings in Canada.

27 June 1946 – The Canadian Citizenship Act is enacted.

13 January 1947 – St. Laurent defines the principles of an active Canadian foreign policy while delivering the Gray Lecture at the University of Toronto.

1 January 1948 – Canada signs the General Agreement on Tariffs and Trade (GATT), a global trade liberalization endeavour to reduce barriers to trade.

November 1948 – Mackenzie King resigns from political life and is succeeded as prime minister by Louis St. Laurent.

31 March 1949 – Newfoundland joins Confederation.

4 April 1949 – Canada signs the North Atlantic Treaty, establishing the North Atlantic Treaty Organization (NATO).

January 1950 – During the Commonwealth Foreign Ministers' Conference in Colombo, Ceylon, Pearson proposes the Colombo plan, Canada's first form of aid for Asia.

June 1950 – The Korean War begins; Canada supports UN intervention led by the United States.

September 1950 – Canada agrees to send troops and logistical support to the UN campaign in Korea.

1952 – Vincent Massey is appointed as the first Canadian governor general.

1954 – Canada agrees to participate in the three-member International Commission for Supervision and Control (ICSC) in Vietnam following the negotiation of the American-North Korean armistice.

1955 – Construction begins on the Distance Early Warning Line (DEW) along the 70th parallel in the Arctic.

1956 – Egyptian President Gamal Abdul Nasser unexpectedly nationalizes the Suez Canal, precipitating the joint Anglo-French-Israeli attacks by air, land, and sea.

4 November 1956 – Lester B. Pearson's resolution for an "international peace and police force" is passed by the UN General Assembly.

10 June 1957 – John Diefenbaker's Progressive Conservatives win a minority government.

24 July 1957 – Prime Minister Diefenbaker signs onto the North American Air Defence Command (NORAD) alliance.

October 1957 – Lester B. Pearson wins the Nobel Peace Prize for his role in resolving the Suez Crisis

1958 – Diefenbaker' Progressive Conservatives win the largest majority in national history.

20 February 1959 – The Canadian government announces the cancellation of the Avro Arrow, opting instead for nuclear-tipped U.S. Bomarc missiles.

March 1961 – At the Commonwealth Prime Ministers' conference in London, England, Diefenbaker is the only white prime minister to oppose South Africa's readmission to the Commonwealth.

1961 – Québec opens a *délégation-générale* in Paris.

18 June 1962 – The Progressive Conservatives are reduced to a minority government in the federal election.

22 October 1962 – The United States becomes embroiled in the Cuban Missile Crisis after American U-2 spy planes discover evidence of intermediate-range ballistic missiles (IRBMs) on the island.

24 October 1962 – Diefenbaker reluctantly agrees to put the Canadian Forces on alert.

February 1963 – The Diefenbaker government is defeated in the House of Commons.

8 April 1963 – In a federal election, Lester B. Pearson and the Liberals defeat the Conservatives and form a minority government.

January 1965 – The Canadian-American Auto Pact Agreement establishes free trade in the automotive industry between the two countries, reversing Canada's auto trade imbalance.

February 1965 – Quebec signs an *entente culturelle* with France.

April 1965 – In an address delivered at Temple University in Philadelphia, Pearson speaks in favour of the suspension of the United States' vigorous air strikes against North Vietnam.

1966 – Daniel Johnson and the Union Nationale party are victorious in the Quebec provincial election.

July 1967 – During a visit to Québec, Charles de Gaulle delivers a speech from Montréal city hall, during which he proclaims, "Vive le Québec libre!"

20 April 1968 – Pierre Elliott Trudeau becomes Prime Minister of Canada.

March 1969 – The Trudeau government reduces Canada's military commitment to NATO.

10 October 1970 – Canada recognizes the People's Republic of China, preceding American recognition by nine years.

1970 – The first intergovernmental body of *la francophonie*, l'Agence de cooperation culturelle et technique (ACCT), is established at a conference held in Niamey, Niger.

1970 – Former Under-Secretary of External Affairs Marcel Cadieux becomes the first Francophone ambassador to Washington.

May 1971 – Trudeau visits the USSR and signs a protocol on consultations with Leonid Brezhnev to establish regular meetings between the two countries.

August 1971 – Canada barely avoids the cancellation of the Auto Pact following the Nixon administration's proposal for protective economic measures.

April 1972 – Nixon makes his first presidential visit to Canada, during which he calls for an end to the Canadian-American "sentimental rhetoric" of the past.

October 1972 – Secretary of State Mitchell Sharp's "third option" paper proposes a Canadian policy to strengthen relations with the European Community (EC) and Japan.

January 1973 – Canada joins the new four-nation International Commission for Control and Supervision (ICCS) to monitor the cease-fire in Vietnam.

1973 – The Trudeau government establishes the Foreign Investment Review Agency (FIRA), a body whose mandate is to scrutinize applications for investment in Canadian.

1975 – Petro Canada is established as the first Canadian government-owned oil company.

1979 – The Progressive Conservative Alberta MP Joe Clark is appointed Prime Minister of Canada.

March 1980 – Trudeau's Liberals are re-elected to office.

1980 – The Department of Energy, Mines, and Resources enacts the National Energy Program (NEP) in the wake of the economic hardships of the 1970s.

1982 – Trudeau's successfully "patriated" Canadian Constitution Act, which incorporates the Charter of Rights and Freedoms into the constitution, is signed by Queen Elizabeth.

27 October 1983 – Trudeau embarks on a "Peace Initiative" trip across Europe, Asia, and the United States.

September 1984 – Brian Mulroney's Conservatives are elected to a majority government.

March 1985 – Prime Minister Mulroney hosts the "Shamrock Summit" with President Reagan.

January 1988 – Prime Minister Mulroney and President Reagan sign the legal text of the Free Trade Agreement, thereby committing to the elimination of virtually all tariffs by the end of 1998.

1988 – Canada and the United States sign an agreement on Arctic cooperation that requires American vessels to acquire Canadian signature before voyaging through the Northwest Passage.

September 1988 – Mulroney dissolves Parliament and calls an election over ratification of the Free Trade Agreement.

November 1988 – Mulroney's Conservatives retain a comfortable majority, and the FTA passes smoothly through the legislative process to become law.

1990 – Canada joins the Organization of American States.

September 1990 – Canada signs onto negotiations for a North American Free Trade Agreement (NAFTA), which incorporates Mexico into the Free Trade Agreement.

1993 – Former Justice Minister and Minister of Defence Kim Campbell succeeds Brian Mulroney as Prime Minister of Canada

July 1993 – The Distance Early Warning (DEW) line is shut down and replaced by the North Warning System (NWS), which became operational in 1994.

October 1993 – The Liberals led by Jean Chrétien win a secure majority and the Department of External Affairs is rechristened as the Department of Foreign Affairs.

1995 – The Canadian government offers a brigade, headquarters and over 1000 troops to the Stabilization Force in the Former Yugoslavia (SFOR).

1995 – The second Quebec referendum is narrowly defeated. [It's October not June]

1995 – Prime Minister Chrétien launches "Team Canada" trade missions around the globe in order to prevent over-dependency on the United States and ensure Canadian economic security.

July 1998 – The Rome Statute of the International Criminal Court is adopted.

11 September 2001 – Hijacked airplanes fly into the twin towers of the World Trade Centre in New York City and the Pentagon in Washington, D.C. A fourth airplane, allegedly destined for the White House, crashes into a field in Pennsylvania.

December 2001 – Canada and the U.S. agree to the "smart border declaration," which establishes a basis for greater cooperation between the two countries in areas related to economic and national security.

December 2002 – The Canadian government ratifies the UN Kyoto Protocol, committing Canada to a six percent reduction of greenhouse gas emissions from 1990.

February 2003 – Jean Chrétien announces that Canada will contribute troops to NATO's International Security Assistance Force (ISAF) in Afghanistan

March 2003 – The U.S. declares war Iraq on the grounds that the Saddam Hussein government has developed weapons of mass destruction.

2003 – Paul Martin succeeds Jean Chrétien as Liberal leader and prime minister.

August 2003 – A NAFTA panel rules that the 18 percent tariff imposed on softwood lumber by the United States is too high.

2004 – Paul Martin's Liberals are reduced to a minority government in the federal election.

August 2005 – Canada assumes responsibility from U.S. forces for the Provincial Reconstruction Team (PRT) in Kandahar City.

February 2006 – Conservative leader Stephen Harper becomes prime minister, defeating Paul Martin's Liberals in the federal election.

February 2006 – Stephen Harper sends a 2300-strong battle and reconstruction force into Kandahar, thereby committing Canadian troops to a dangerous combat role in the war in Afghanistan.

March 2006 – Harper flies to Afghanistan to pledge support to the mission; soon after, he extends the mission to 2009.

June 2006 – The Conservatives abandon the Kyoto Protocol in favour of a "made-in-Canada" approach to combating global warming and climate change.

July 2006 – Prime Minister Harper supports Israel's military retaliation against Hezbollah incursions into Israel from Lebanon.

September 2006 – The final legal text of the softwood lumber deal is signed by Canadian International Trade Minister David Emerson and United States trade representative Susan Schwab in Ottawa.

January 2007 – The U.S. government's Western Hemisphere Travel Initiative (WHTI) requires Canadians travelling to the United States by air to carry a passport.

Index

Acheson, Dean, 30, 33, 36–7n29, 238, 239
Adams, Michael, 355–6
Afghanistan: Canadian mission in, 9, 11, 13, 138, 139, 259, 288, 317–18; foreign aid to, 187, 197, 198, 200, 203; Soviet invasion of, 136
Alaska boundary dispute, 112–13
Alberta, and oil and gas industry, 210, 211–12, 214, 215, 216
Albright, Madeleine, 74
Andras, Robert, 174
Anglo-Japanese alliance, 112, 119–20, 123, 272, 273
anti-Americanism, 139, 245–6, 255, 259, 308, 355; and Conservative Party, 134, 323–4, 325, 327
anti-Communism, 28, 173, 223, 279, 280, 282, 283, 284, 298–9, 327
Arbour, Louise, 151
Arctic Waters Pollution Prevention Act, 147
Argentina, 7, 151, 217, 218, 221, 222

armed forces, Canadian, 138–9: air force, 120, 121, 123, 130, 131, 134; Canadian Expeditionary Force, 116–17, 119, 120, 126; and conscription, 117, 119, 123, 127; King's reorganization of, 121–3; and military mobilization of 1950s, 130–2, 138–9; militia, 113; and "Mobile Force" of 1960s, 134–5; navy, 114, 115, 118, 120–1, 122, 123, 126, 134; and peacekeeping, 13, 32, 67, 132, 136–7, 139, 145, 183, 258; and permanent allied force, 130; and Somalia incident, 137; Trudeau's cuts to, 135–6, 139; unification of, 135
Asia, Canada's relations with, 15–16, 271–88; and Cold War, 278–80, 286, 288; and Communism, 131, 275, 278, 279–80, 282–3, 284–5, 288; and Indonesian conflicts, 280–6, 287; and North Atlantic thinking, 272, 273–8, 280, 281–2, 287–8; and postwar

Japan, 278–9, 283, 284–5; and Sino-Japanese conflict, 272–8, 287. *See also specific countries*
Atlantic Charter, 86–7, 91
Atomic Energy of Canada Limited (AECL), 216–17, 225
Attlee, Clement, 164
Auriol, Vincent, 244
Australia, 92, 94, 117, 174, 276, 281, 286
Avro Arrow, 132, 133
Axworthy, Lloyd, 13–14, 74, 77, 154; and East Timor, 286; human security agenda of, 12, 14, 56, 61, 73–4, 152, 286; and landmines treaty, 14, 56, 73, 81n26, 137, 152; and "responsibility to protect," 14, 73, 145, 152

Baldwin, Robert, 327
ballistic missiles, 133; defence against (U.S.), 76, 318
Beatty, Perrin, 73
Beaudry, Laurent, 167
Beesley, J. Alan, 146
Bennett, R.B., 62, 89–90, 121, 123, 145, 274–5
Berlin Wall, fall of, 72, 136, 149
Bernier, Maxime, 76
Biafra, 50, 183–4
Black, Eldon, 241, 261
Blake, Edward, 326, 327
Boer War, 13, 21–2, 26, 112, 113, 114, 116, 252
Bomarc missiles, 66, 133
Borden, Sir Robert, 23, 25, 42, 62, 123, 127, 130, 294, 326, 330; and Canadian autonomy/national status, 115–18, 121, 128; and Canadian Navy, 115, 118, 120; and First World War, 115–18; and League of Nations, 144–5; and U.S.-British relations, 119–20

Bosnia, 73, 258
Bothwell, Robert, 350, 353, 354, 357
Boundary Waters Treaty, 143
Bourassa, Henri, 113, 115, 252
Brebner, John Bartlet, 273
Bretton Woods conference, 5, 7, 12, 93–4
Britain, 128, 247, 299; and Boer War, 13, 21–2, 26, 112, 113, 114, 116, 252; and relations with Japan, 112, 119–20, 123, 272, 273; and Second World War, 124–8; and Suez Crisis, 257. *See also* British Empire; Commonwealth
– Canada's relations with, 19–20, 34, 235, 237; and Canadian autonomy/independence, 23–5, 115–18, 121, 324; and collective identity, 243, 250, 252, 317–18, 320, 333–4, 336, 360; in colonial period, 21–3; and decline in trade, 101–2; and economic multilateralism, 91–102; and immigration, 250, 251; and NATO, 240–1; and postwar aid to Britain, 98–9, 101; and preferential tariffs/trade, 88, 89, 90, 99. *See also* Conservative Party narrative of empire; defence, and Canadian-British relations; Liberal Party narrative of autonomy
– and relations with U.S., 26, 27–8, 130, 361; and aid to Britain, 125–6, 128; and Alaska boundary dispute, 112–13; and Japan, 119–20, 122–3, 274–5, 277, 287; and special relationship, 236–8; and trade, 90, 91–2
British Columbia, 65, 124, 277, 294
British Commonwealth Air Training Plan (BCATP), 126
British Empire, 21–5, 26, 30, 142, 252. *See also* Commonwealth

British North America (BNA) Act, 87, 210
Bruce, Randolph, 276, 278
Burma, 283, 309; refugees from, 159, 176
Burney, Derek, 53, 54–5
Burton, Charles, 307, 309
Bush, George H.W., 307
Bush, George W., 81n26, 317

Cadieux, Marcel, 12, 35n10, 44, 47, 48–50, 51, 53, 54
Campbell, Kim, 73
Canada-China Trade Council, 303
Canada-Europe Framework Agreement, 241, 247
Canada Treaty Series, 143
Canada-U.S. Free Trade Agreement, 9, 13, 15, 55, 102, 248, 303–4; and oil and gas industry, 215–16, 226, 227
Canada-U.S. relations. *See* United States, Canada's relations with
Canada's International Policy Statement, 76, 138
Canadian Airborne Regiment, 137
Canadian Association of Petroleum Producers (CAPP), 210
Canadian Charter of Rights and Freedoms, 149, 153, 176
Canadian Expeditionary Force (CEF), 116–17, 119, 120, 126
Canadian International Development Agency. *See* CIDA
Canadian Nuclear Association, 217, 224
CANDU nuclear reactors, 15, 209–10, 217, 219, 221, 222, 225, 226
Caroline, sinking of, 142–3
Carroll, Aileen, 202–3
Carter, Jimmy, 70
Catley-Carlson, Maggie, 202
Chamberlain, Joseph, 113, 115

Chamberlain, Neville, 20, 124
Chiang Kai-shek, 279, 296, 298
China, People's Republic of, 16, 76, 282, 298–310; and Bethune tribute, 305; and Canadian nuclear technology, 15, 217; Cultural Revolution in, 67, 302; famine in, 300; foreign aid to, 186, 188, 189, 198; grain exports to, 274, 300–1, 303; human rights in, 8, 306–7, 308, 309; and Korea, 130–1, 279–80, 299, 300; loans to, 304; military aggression by, 300, 301; recognition of, 67, 68, 279–80, 298–303; and Tiananmen Square crackdown, 188, 304, 305; trade with, 15, 303–4, 306–7, 308; U.S. relations with, 298–303, 307–8
China, pre-revolutionary, 95, 271–2, 279, 293–8; missionary work in, 271, 272–3, 295–7; nationalism in, 296–7; and war with Japan, 272–8, 287
China Daily, 308
Chinese Canadians, 164, 272, 294–5
Chinese Immigration Act, 274, 295, 299
Chirac, Jacques, 257, 259
Chrétien, Jean, 241; and Afghanistan mission, 259; and criticisms of U.S., 308; and defence, 136–7; as foreign minister, 71; foreign ministers of, 73–5; and human rights in China, 8, 306–7; and relations with France, 248, 257; Team Canada missions of, 74, 286; and trade with China, 74, 306–7; and war in Iraq, 33, 258–9
Christie, Loring, 42, 121
Churchill, Gordon, 326
Churchill, Sir Winston, 25, 86–7, 97, 317
CIDA, 14, 51, 70, 73, 183–205, 223; aims and objectives of, 185–9; and

Bangladesh Railways project, 188; and "Better Aid Bill," 205; criticisms of, 185–6, 200; decentralization in, 200–2; and DFAIT, 184–5, 199, 200, 204; as government outlier, 200; history of, 183–4, 199; ministers and presidents of, 202–3; organization of, 184–5; proposed closure of, 200, 204; public profile of, 203–4; Senate report comments on, 200, 201–2, 204; *Sharing Our Future* report of, 149, 192, 197, 201, 204. See also foreign aid
Clark, Joe, 70; as foreign minister, 64, 71–2, 75, 188, 304
Clark, W.C., 96, 97–8, 100
Clemenceau, Georges, 144
Clinton, Bill, 81n26, 307
Cohen, Maxwell, 142, 143, 145
Cold War, 28, 55, 183, 187, 350, 352; and anti-Communism, 28, 173, 223, 279, 280, 282, 283, 284, 298–9, 327; and Canada's relations with Asia, 278–80, 286, 288; and NATO, 130, 131, 133, 135; and post-Cold War era, 72–6, 111, 136–9, 239, 350; revival of, 70, 136
Colombo Plan, 183, 280, 282–3
Committee of Imperial Defence (CID), 114–15
Commonwealth, 30, 67, 143, 198; and Asian conflicts, 280, 281, 286, 287; and Canadian identity, 126–8; Diefenbaker and, 320–1; and immigration policy, 173, 174, 175, 176; and Malaysia, 284; and narrative of empire, 320–1, 324, 326, 327; and nuclear technology aid, 224; and preferential trade, 89, 90; and South Africa, 65, 72; and trade with U.S., 96–7

Conference on International Economic Cooperation (CIEC), 69
Conference on Security and Cooperation in Europe (CSCE), 71, 149–50
Conservative Party, 9, 23, 36n27, 299, 300
Conservative Party narrative of empire, 16, 317–36; and Anglo-Saxon heritage/bond, 317–18, 320, 333–4, 336; as anti-American, 134, 323–4, 325, 327; and Commonwealth, 320–1, 324, 326, 327; and Creighton, 326–8, 336; and Diefenbaker, 320–3, 327; and G.M. Grant, 16, 333–4, 336; and G.P. Grant, 16, 323–4, 327, 336; and Harper, 317–18, 320, 335–6; and imperial federation, 332–3, 334–5; and Leacock, 330–1, 336; and Macdonald, 322, 326, 332, 335; and "New Conservatism," 326; origins of, 321–2; and vilification of King, 323–4, 327. See also Liberal Party narrative of autonomy
Constitution Act (1867), 87, 210
Convention on Future Multilateral Cooperation in the Northwest Atlantic Fisheries, 147
Co-operative Commonwealth Federation (CCF), 162
Copenhagen Document, 149–50
Creighton, Donald, 326–8, 336
Crerar, H.D.G., 125
Cuban Missile Crisis, 66, 134
Currie, Sir Arthur, 117, 126
Customs Act, 146
Cyprus, 32, 67

Dalai Lama, 309
Dallaire, Roméo, 137
Danchev, Alex, 236–8, 239
Davis, T.C., 279, 298

defence, 13, 111–39; under Borden, 115–20, 121, 128; under Chrétien, 136–7; in Cold War era, 128–36, 138–9; and Confederation, 112; and conscription, 117, 119, 123, 127; and Cuban Missile Crisis, 66, 134; under Diefenbaker, 31, 132–4; during First World War, 115–18, 121, 126, 128; and foreign affairs department, 111, 112; and interwar disarmament, 120–1, 128; under King, 120–9; under Laurier, 112–15; under Mulroney, 136; and 9/11, 137; of North America, 31, 131, 132–3, 239; and nuclear disarmament movement, 65, 66, 133–4, 138; and peacekeeping, 13, 32, 67, 132, 136–7, 139, 145, 183, 258; under Pearson, 134–5; in post-Cold War era, 136–9; during revolutionary period, 112; during Second World War, 124–8; under St. Laurent, 129–32; and Suez Crisis, 5, 15, 64, 132, 257; under Trudeau, 135–6. *See also* armed forces, Canadian; NATO; North American Air Defense Command
– and Canadian-British relations: and Alaska boundary dispute, 112–13; and Boer War, 21–2, 26, 112, 113; and British Navy withdrawal, 113; and Canadian autonomy/national status, 115–18, 121, 128; and Canadian militia, 113; during First World War, 115–18, 121, 126, 128; and Great Lakes defence, 114; under King, 121–5; and origins of Confederation, 112; and possibility of U.S. invasion, 112–13, 114–15, 118–19, 122; and proposal for imperial defence, 113; and Quebec, 113, 114, 115; during revolutionary period, 112; during Second World War, 124–8; and training of Commonwealth air crew, 126
– and Canadian-U.S. relations: and Alaska boundary dispute, 112–13; in Cold War era, 128–36; during First World War, 118–19; and Great Lakes defence, 114; and integrated war production, 125–6, 128; and Korean War, 130–1; and 9/11, 137; and Pacific coast concerns, 120, 122–3, 124; and Permanent Joint Board, 125, 129; and possibility of U.S. invasion, 112–13, 114–15, 118–19, 122; during Second World War, 125–6

Defence, Department of, 111, 120
Deng Xiaoping, 303, 306
Deschênes, Jules, 150–1
Development Assistance Committee (DAC), 187, 189, 197, 198, 199, 202, 203
Diefenbaker, John, 28, 50, 65, 258; and attachment to Commonwealth, 320–1; and Avro Arrow, 132; and defence, 31, 132–4; foreign ministers of, 65–6; and grain exports to China, 300–1; immigration policy of, 173–4; and loss of Conservative leadership, 323; and narrative of empire, 320–3, 327; national oil policy of, 212; and nuclear disarmament, 65, 66, 133–4; and recognition of China, 300, 301–2; and tour of Asia, 283
Dion, Stéphane, 16, 318, 336
diplomatic corps. *See* foreign service
disarmament: and Cold War era, 65, 66, 133–4, 138; and interwar era, 120–1, 128
Displaced Persons (DPs), 160–1, 163, 164–72; crisis of, 164–5; and

immigration policy, 161, 163, 164–72, 175, 176; and multi-ethnicity, 160, 171; and need for labour, 168–9; racism/prejudice towards, 160, 162–4, 169–71. *See also* immigration policy; refugee policy
Duff, Lyman, 144
Dulles, John Foster, 300, 301
Duplessis, Maurice, 63, 299

East Timor, 8, 189, 194, 285–6, 287, 307
Eisenhower, Dwight D., 134, 300, 301
Emerson, David, 62, 248
Endicott, James, 298
energy, and foreign policy. *See* nuclear energy; oil and gas industry
English-French relations: and First World War, 23, 252; and foreign policy, 9, 20, 21, 22–3, 24–5, 252–3; and Quebec separatism, 235, 241–2; and Second World War, 24–5. *See also* France, Canada's relations with; Quebec
Estai, 147–8
Europe, 128, 132, 136, 241, 247, 249–50, 347, 359
European Community, 132, 221, 247, 321
Export Credit Insurance Act, 247
Export Development Corp., 304
exports, to Britain and U.S. *See* multilateralism, economic
External Affairs, Department of, 19, 34n1, 79n3, 41; creation of, 19, 21, 42, 111, 112, 143, 271; legal advisor (*jurisconsult*) within, 143, 151; and its ministers, 62; Skelton's view of, 43; trade policy component of, 34n1, 54–5, 70; Trudeau's changes to, 10, 41, 50–1, 52, 53, 54, 56, 68, 70. *See also individual foreign ministers*

External Aid Office (later CIDA), 65, 70, 183

Fairclough, Ellen, 174
First World War, 13, 22–3, 25–6, 28, 87, 171, 252, 324, 331, 360; and Canadian autonomy/national status, 115–18, 121, 128; defence policies/actions during, 115–18, 121, 126, 128; U.S. entry into, 117, 118–19
Fleming, Donald, 326
Foreign Affairs and International Trade Canada (DFAIT), 61, 78, 79n3; and CIDA, 184–5, 199, 200, 204. *See also* External Affairs, Department of
foreign aid, 14, 65, 183–205; aims and objectives of, 185–9; and "basic human needs," 190, 196, 197, 198; and "Better Aid Bill," 205; channels for, 198–9; and commercial issues, 185, 187–9, 198; and democracy, 192, 193, 194–5, 196, 205; fads influencing, 189–97; and famine relief/poverty, 185, 186, 205; and food aid, 193–4; and gender issues, 195, 196; geographic distribution of, 197–8, 202–3; and governance, 194–5, 196, 197, 205; history of, 183–4, 199; and human rights, 187, 189, 193, 194, 196, 200, 205, 285–6; as "incoherent," 185, 189, 204–5; and integrated rural development, 190–1, 196; lack of focus in, 198; multilateral, 198–9; and NGOs, 198–9, 205; Pearson's role in, 183, 184, 185, 205; and political issues, 185, 186–7, 198; in post-9/11 era, 187; and prestige, 187, 198; and prioritization of issues, 195–6; and security issues, 185, 187; and

structural adjustment, 191–2, 194; and sustainability, 192–3, 197, 205; "three Ds" approach to, 200. *See also* CIDA
foreign direct investment (FDI), 209, 210, 211–13, 214, 226
Foreign Investment Review Agency (FIRA), 71, 212, 213, 214–15, 226
foreign ministers, 61–78; effectiveness of, 61–2; future of, 77–8; in late 1960s and beyond, 67–72; in post-Cold War era, 72–6; in postwar era, 63–7; prime ministers as, 62, 65, 111; and relationships with prime ministers, 64, 66, 68, 69, 71–2, 74, 76, 77–8; and relations with U.S., 66, 68–9, 71, 74–5, 76; roles of, 62; as separate portfolio, 62. *See also individual foreign ministers*
foreign policy, 19–34; and Canada as "middle power," 3, 9, 17, 145–6, 348–50; in colonial period, 21–3; and English-French relations, 9, 20, 21, 22–3, 24–5, 252–3; "Golden Age" of, 5, 9–11, 53; and human rights, 7–8, 13–14, 148–50, 154; and identity, 8–9, 16–17, 19–20, 21; and multilateralism, 4–5, 7, 8, 9; and North Atlantic Triangle, 3, 4–6, 7, 15–16, 240, 325; in postwar era, 28–32; pragmatism of, 6–8; transformation of, 10–11; and transition to independence, 23–5
foreign service, 41–57; under Cadieux, 48–50; and diplomatic dispatches, 49, 50–1, 53–4; early restrictions/tedium of, 44–6; establishment of, 62; exams of, 43–4, 51–2; francophones in, 44, 52; and generalists vs. specialists, 43, 48–9, 50, 52; later training program at, 46–7; and new generation of 1970s and beyond, 51–6; in postwar era, 48–52; and "public diplomacy," 55–6; rise and "decline" of, 41–2; and service delivery, 56–7; under Skelton, 42–4, 121; trade policy component of, 34n1, 54–5, 70; Trudeau's relations with, 10, 41, 50–1, 52, 53, 54, 56, 68, 70; as vocation, 49; and women, 43, 52

Fowler, Robert, 54, 152

France, 15, 33, 67, 69, 95, 112, 124; and Afghanistan mission, 259–60; fall of, 125, 126; and opposition to Canada joining G7, 6, 69, 235, 248, 260; and recognition of China, 302; and relations with Quebec, 235, 238–9, 241–2, 252–3, 256–7, 260; and Suez Crisis, 15, 257; and U.S. war on Iraq, 258–9; under Vichy government, 253

France, Canada's relations with, 15, 235–61; and Afghanistan mission, 259–60; and anti-Americanism, 245–6, 255, 259; and bilingualism/biculturalism, 253–4, 256, 257; and Canadian foreign policy, 253–5, 261; and Catholicism, 244, 252; and collective identity, 242–6, 250, 252, 255–6, 260; economic importance of, 241, 246–50; and Franco-Canadian investments, 248, 249, 261; and G7 membership, 6, 69, 235, 248, 260; and immigration, 250, 251; and international francophone culture/interests, 236, 242; and liberal-democratic values, 244–5; and national interest, 239–42, 246, 255–8, 260; and national unity, 239, 241–2, 246, 252–3, 255–8, 261; and NATO, 239–41, 254–6, 258; and postwar aid to France, 247;

and Quebec separatism, 235, 241–2, 256–7, 260, 261; and security issues, 239, 240–1, 243, 257, 261; sociopolitical/military importance of, 250–60; as special, 15, 236–8, 260–1. *See also* English-French relations; Quebec
Franck, Thomas, 154
Francophonie, La, 198, 236, 257, 286
Fulton, Davie, 326, 328

Gardiner, Jimmy, 99, 299
Gaulle, Charles de, 66, 235, 241–2, 244, 253, 254, 256, 258
General Agreement on Tariffs and Trade (GATT), 87, 91, 95, 97, 100–1, 214, 248
Geneva Conventions, 152; on Status of Refugees, 160, 161
Gérin-Lajoie, Paul, 202
Germany, 21, 24–5, 55, 112, 151, 247
Giscard d'Estaing, Valéry, 235, 248, 256
Glen, J.A., 169, 170
Goodale, Ralph, 225
Gordon, Walter, 212
Gotlieb, Allan, 12, 64, 79n12, 174; and new generation of diplomats, 51, 52, 53, 54, 55–6
Gouzenko, Igor, 129
Graham, Bill, 75, 154
Grant, George M., 16, 333–4, 336
Grant, George P., 16, 323–4, 327, 336
Gray, Colin, 346–7
Gray, Herb, 213
Green, Howard, 12, 50, 65–6, 74, 77, 133–4
Groulx, Lionel, 252
Group of Eight (G8), 56, 75, 77, 81n30, 198, 209

Group of Seven (G7), 53, 56, 70; and French opposition to Canada's joining, 6, 69, 235, 248, 260
Group of Twenty (G20), 56
Gulf War, 136, 259

Hadwen, J.G., 224
Haiti, 72, 75, 307; foreign aid to, 190, 191, 197, 198, 203
Harding, Warren, 120
Harkness, Douglas, 134
Harper, Stephen, 4–5, 9, 16, 34, 75–6; and Afghanistan mission, 138, 259–60; on Canada as "energy superpower," 14, 209, 227; foreign ministers of, 62, 76, 248; immigration policy of, 176; and narrative of empire, 317–18, 320, 335–6; and relations with China, 308–10; and relations with Europe/France, 241, 248, 250; and war in Iraq, 6, 33, 318
Hatta, Mohammad, 280, 282
Head, Ivan, 51
Heinbecker, Paul, 53, 55
Hellyer, Paul, 134
Helsinki Final Act/Helsinki Accords, 71, 149–50
Hickerson, Jack, 43, 44, 96
Hillier, Rick, 138
Hitler, Adolf, 276
Holmes, John, 3, 46, 102, 254, 258, 279, 281; on Canadian identity, 344, 348–9; and postwar refugee crisis, 165–6, 167, 176
Hoover, Herbert, 122
Howe, C.D., 90–1, 165, 166, 219, 299
Hu Jintao, 309
human rights: in China, 306–7, 308, 309; and foreign aid, 187, 189, 193, 194, 196, 200, 205, 285–6; and foreign policy, 7–8, 13–14, 148–50, 154

human security, as foreign policy, 12, 14, 56, 61, 73–5, 152, 286
Humphrey, John, 13, 148, 149
Hungarian Revolution, refugees of, 173, 176
Hussein, Saddam, 259

identity, Canadian, 8–9, 16–17, 343–61; of anglophones, 243, 250, 252, 317–18, 360; and Borden's fight for autonomy/national status, 115–18, 121, 128; as British colony, 19–23; and constructivism, 351–3; and ethnicity, 360; of francophones, 242–6, 250, 252, 255–6, 260, 360; and functionalism, 127–8, 281, 349–50; and geography, 359–60; Liberal and Conservative concepts of, 317–20; as liberal democracy, 358–9; medicare and, 135; as "middle power," 3, 9, 17, 145–6, 348–50; as "national" and "collective," 353; as national character, 353, 354–6; and peacekeeping, 139, 350; and relations with U.S., 127–8, 354, 356, 357–60, 361; during Second World War, 126–8; and strategic culture, 345–8, 350, 353, 361; and status in world, 348; and structural/neoclassical realism, 347–50; and transnational collective identity, 357–60, 361; as victim, 350, 363n21; and Victoria Day, 343, 344. *See also* Conservative Party narrative of empire; Liberal Party narrative of autonomy
Ignatieff, Michael, 318, 333
Ilsley, James, 94
I'm Alone, sinking of, 144
immigration, percentage of, by region, 250, 251
Immigration Act, 162–3, 169, 172, 174–5

immigration policy: British criticism of, 164; Commonwealth influence on, 173, 174, 175, 176; under Diefenbaker and Fairclough, 173–4; evolving humanitarian views on, 163–4; under Laurier and Sifton, 162; and plight of Displaced Persons, 161, 163, 164–72, 175, 176; and "points system," 174; in post-9/11 era, 175–6; postwar changes to, 168–71, 174–5, 176–7; and public racism/prejudice, 160, 162–4, 169–71, 172–3, 176; as restrictive/racist, 162–4, 166–7, 172, 176; UN influence on, 170–1, 174, 176. *See also* Displaced Persons; refugee policy
Imperial Conference of 1926, 42, 143
imperial federation, 332–3, 334–5
Imperial War Conference of 1917, 116–17
Inco, 285
India, 15, 95, 131, 190, 271, 281, 307, 327, 334; and Canadian nuclear technology, 15, 217, 221, 222, 223, 224; Chinese war with, 300, 301; independence of, 128, 279; nuclear tests by, 220, 221, 223, 227
Indochina: control/supervision commission for, 68, 131; French war in, 258, 272; refugees from, 70, 161, 175; truce commissions on, 31–2
Indonesia: as anti-Communist, 282, 283, 284; and East Timor, 8, 189, 194, 285–6, 287, 307; foreign aid to, 189, 198, 281–2, 284–6; independence of, 272, 280–2, 287; and Malaysia, 283–4, 285, 287; military build-up in, 283; and West New Guinea, 283

Industrial Cooperation Program (INC), 188
Inter-continental Ballistic Missiles (ICBMS), 133
Interdepartmental Committee on External Relations (ICER), 51
International Atomic Energy Agency (IAEA), 218, 219–20, 221, 225
International Commission of Control and Supervision (ICCS), for Vietnam, 68, 131
International Commission on Intervention and State Sovereignty (ICISS), 73, 152
International Court of Justice, 147–8, 152
International Criminal Court, 14, 56, 72, 73, 81n26, 151, 246
International Criminal Tribunals, 151
International Development Research Centre (IDRC), 183, 184, 185
International Joint Commission, 143
International Labour Organization (ILO), 145
international law. *See* law, international
International Monetary Fund (IMF), 12, 87, 91, 92, 93–4, 101, 191–2, 194
International Refugee Organization (IRO), 167
International Security Assistance Force (ISAF), in Afghanistan, 259
International Trade Organization (ITO), 91, 100, 101
Investment Canada, 215
Iraq, 136, 187, 197, 198, 203
Iraq, U.S. war with, 6, 9, 13, 75, 347, 359; as anticipatory self-defence, 142–3; Canada's refusal to join, 33, 245, 258–9, 318
Israeli-Palestinian conflict, 71–2, 76

Jamieson, Don, 70, 221–2
Japan, 271, 307; as anti-Communist ally, 279, 280; and attack on Pearl Harbor, 127, 278, 298; Canada's relations with, 272, 273–8, 284–5, 294, 297–8, 349; Canadian prewar trade with, 276, 277; and Colombo Plan, 283; and early tensions with U.S., 119–20, 122–3; and invasion of Manchuria, 5, 123, 274–5, 284, 287; in postwar era, 278–9, 283, 284–5; and relations with Britain, 112, 119–20, 123, 272, 273; and U.S.-British relations, 119–20, 122–3, 274–5, 277, 287; and war with China, 272–8, 287
Japanese Canadians, 277, 294
Jaruzelski, Wojciech, 7, 71
Jewish refugees, 159, 160, 163, 164, 167
Jiang Zemin, 305
Johnson, Lyndon B., 67, 302
Johnston, Alastair Iain, 346–7
jurisconsult (legal advisor to foreign affairs department), 143, 151

Kagan, Robert, 347–8, 359
Keenleyside, Hugh, 45, 46, 167
Kennedy, John F., 134, 283, 301, 321
Keynes, John Maynard, 87, 92, 93
Kimberley Process, 152
King, William Lyon Mackenzie, 6, 34, 48, 62, 63; as advocate of conciliation, 276, 281; and Asia, 271–3, 275–8; and Canadian autonomy/independence, 23–5, 42, 126–8, 271, 276; in Conservative narrative of empire, 323–4, 327; death of, 280; and defence, 120–9; and economic multilateralism, 91–102; and foreign service, 42–4, 45, 121; and functionalism, 127–8;

and Liberal narrative of autonomy, 328; and relations with China, 294–5, 297–8; and relations with French Canadians, 252–3; and reciprocity, 88, 90; and refugee policy, 164; and relations with U.S., 25–8, 124, 125–6, 127; and Roosevelt, 27, 124, 125–6, 127; and Sino-Japanese conflict, 275–8. *See also* multilateralism, economic

Kirsch, Philippe, 151
Kissinger, Henry, 68, 70
Korea, 63, 64; and China, 130–1, 279–80, 299, 300; and Japan, 273, 274. *See also* North Korea; South Korea
Korean War, 26, 29, 130–1, 272, 279–80, 299
Kosovo, 258, 259, 307
Kuomintang, 296, 298, 299
Kuwait, 136
Kyoto Protocol, 211, 225–6, 227

landmines, treaty on, 14, 56, 73, 81n26, 137, 152
Lapointe, Ernest, 252–3
Latin America, 65, 95, 175, 345
Laurendeau, André, 253
Laurier, Sir Wilfrid, 62, 119, 123, 130, 271, 294; and defence, 112–15; and foreign affairs, 21–3, 34; immigration policy of, 162; and narratives of autonomy and empire, 327, 329, 331–2, 333; and reciprocity, 88, 115, 330, 332; Skelton's biography of, 121, 329; and trade with France, 246
law, international, 13–14, 142–54; and Arctic sovereignty, 147; Bennett's use of, 145; and Canada-U.S. relations, 13, 142–4, 146–7; and Canadian autonomy in international affairs, 144–5; and Canadian law, 152–3; "Canadian school" of, 153–4; and *Caroline* incident, 142–3; and death penalty, 150; and *Estai* incident, 147–8; and human rights, 7–8, 13–14, 148–50, 154; and human security, 152; and *I'm Alone* incident, 144; and international criminal law, 150–1, 154; and Law of the Sea, 13, 146–7; and non-international armed conflict, 152; and treaties, 143; and war crimes prosecution, 142, 150–1

Law of the Sea, United Nations Convention on the, 13, 69, 146–7
Leacock, Stephen, 330–1, 336
League of Nations, 30, 45, 118, 121, 253; Japan's withdrawal from, 275, 284; and Monroe Doctrine clause, 144–5; and Sino-Japanese conflict, 273, 274, 275, 276, 281, 284
Léger, Jules, 35n10, 44, 223, 300
Lend-Lease Act (U.S.), 125, 128
Lewis, W.B., 219, 224
Liberal Party: nationalism of, 8–9, 31, 245; and relations with Alberta, 214; and relations with China, 302, 304, 306, 309
Liberal Party narrative of autonomy, 16, 317–36; as criticized by Creighton, 327; King's role in, 328; and Newman, 16, 321–3, 326, 336; origins of, 322; and Pearson, 321–2; and relations with U.S., 321, 322, 323–4, 325, 329, 333; and Skelton, 328–9, 336; and Smith, 16, 326, 333, 334, 336; and Underhill, 324–6, 327, 336. *See also* Conservative Party narrative of empire

Lloyd George, David, 117, 144
Lougheed, Peter, 214, 215, 216

MacArthur, Douglas, 278
MacDonald, Flora, 64, 70, 285
Macdonald, Sir John A., 119; and narrative of empire, 322, 326, 332, 335; National Policy of, 87, 88, 89, 212, 216; and reciprocity, 88, 332
MacDonald, Ramsay, 122
MacEachen, Allan, 12, 61, 68–70, 72, 73, 79n12, 80n13
MacGuigan, Mark, 70–1
MacKay, Peter, 76
Mackenzie, William Lyon, 142
Macmillan, Harold, 322
Malaysia, 283–4, 285, 287
Manchurian Crisis, 5, 123, 274–5, 284, 287
Manley, John, 12, 63, 74–5
Mao Zedong, 293, 298–9, 302, 303
Marler, Herbert, 273–4, 275, 276
Martin, Paul (Jr.), 75, 200, 306; and *International Policy Statement*, 76, 138
Martin, Paul (Sr.), 10, 50, 66–7, 186, 302
Massé, Marcel, 202
McCarthy, Joseph, 299
McDermott, Terry, 46–7
McDougall, Barbara, 12, 64, 72, 79n2
McDougall, E. Stuart, 279
McNamara, Robert, 134
McNaughton, A.G.L., 122–3
Mead, Walter Russell, 33–4
Meech Lake Accord, 256
Meighen, Arthur, 23, 24, 34, 42, 62, 120, 273
Militia Act, 113
Millennium Development Goals (MDGS), 196–7

Minna, Maria, 202
Mitterrand, François, 256
Mulroney, Brian, 308; and apartheid, 194; and CIDA, 201; and Clark, 71–2; and defence, 136; and East Timor, 286; foreign ministers of, 71–2, 79n2; and human rights, 189, 194, 286, 304; and oil and gas industry, 215–16, 226; and relations with France, 239, 248, 256; and Tiananmen Square crackdown, 304, 305
multilateralism, 4–5, 7, 8, 9; and anti-Communism, 280; and Canada-Europe relations, 246; and foreign aid, 198–9; and Law of the Sea, 146–7; meaning of, 86; and North American defence, 239
multilateralism, and Pacific conflict. *See* Pacific conflicts, multilateral approach to
multilateralism, economic, 13, 85–102; and access to international markets, 94–5; and Atlantic Charter, 86–7, 91; and bilateral trade proposal for U.S., 96; and British protectionism, 88, 97–9; and British trade initiative, 94, 95–6, 97–9; and Canadian protectionism, 87, 88, 89; end of, 101–2; and loans to Britain, 98–9, 101; and postwar economic reconstruction, 87, 91–2, 93–4; and postwar monetary stabilization plans, 87, 92–3; and preferential trade with Britain, 88, 89, 90; reasons for advocacy of, 91–3, 101–2; and reciprocity, 88, 89, 90; and U.S.-Commonwealth trade, 96–7; and wheat exports to Britain, 99
Munro, Gordon, 98, 99
Murphy, Charles, 62

narratives of autonomy and empire, 317–20, 335–6; Newman vs. G.P.

Grant, 320–4; Pearson vs. Diefenbaker, 320–3; Skelton vs. Leacock, 328–31; Smith vs. G.M. Grant, 331–5; Underhill vs. Creighton, 324–8. *See also* Conservative Party narrative of empire; Liberal Party narrative of autonomy
National Energy Program (NEP), 71, 211, 212, 213–14, 215, 216, 226, 227
nationalism, 29, 30, 35n10; and Canadian autonomy/independence, 23, 24, 29; of Liberal Party, 8–9, 31, 245
National Policy, 87, 88, 89, 212, 216
NATO, 5, 7, 12, 29, 30, 31, 66, 67, 68, 219, 280, 350; and Afghanistan mission, 138, 259; and Canada's relations with France, 239–41, 254–6, 258; and Canada's withdrawal from Europe, 136; and Canadian independence/identity, 239–41; and Cold War activity, 130, 131, 133, 135, 254; creation of, 129–30; and Indonesian independence, 281–2; and Korean War, 130; Pearson's role in, 149, 254–6; St. Laurent's role in, 63, 129, 255–6. *See also* North Atlantic Triangle
Netherlands, 95, 280–2, 283, 287
Newfoundland, 22, 31, 70, 218
Newman, Peter C., 16, 321–3, 326, 336
New Partnership for Africa's Development (NEPAD), 75
New Zealand, 117, 276, 284
9/11, terrorist attacks of, 14, 75, 137, 161, 237, 245
Nixon, Richard, 247, 303
non-governmental organizations (NGOS), 50, 53, 56, 75, 198–9, 205

Norman, E. Herbert, 278
North American Air Defense Command (NORAD), 31, 131, 132–3, 134, 219
North American Free Trade Agreement (NAFTA), 8, 55, 216, 226
North Atlantic Treaty Organization. *See* NATO
North Atlantic Triangle, 3, 4–6, 7, 15–16, 240, 325; and hostilities in Pacific, 272, 273–8, 280, 281–2, 287–8; and Manchurian crisis, 274–5, 284, 287. *See also* NATO
North Korea, 130, 136, 284, 307
nuclear energy, 14–15, 209–10, 216–27; as anti-Communist tool, 223; and Canada's membership in regulatory organizations, 218–21; and CANDU reactors, 15, 209–10, 217, 219, 221, 222, 225, 226; and CIRUS reactor, 223; and climate change, 224–6, 227; industry overview of, 216–17; and non-proliferation, 15, 210, 218–23, 227; and relations with developing world, 223–4; and uranium exports, 14, 209, 217–18, 219, 221, 223, 225, 226, 227. *See also* nuclear weapons
Nuclear Non-Proliferation Treaty (NPT), 218, 219, 220, 221–2
Nuclear Suppliers Group (NSG), 218, 219, 220–1, 230n43
nuclear weapons, 31, 136, 138; Canadian testing of, 66, 69, 133; and Green's disarmament activism, 65, 66, 133–4; and history of Canadian involvement, 218–19; non-proliferation of, 15, 210, 218–23, 227
Nuremberg trials, 142, 150, 151

Oda, Bev, 203
Odlum, Victor, 279, 298

Official Development Assistance (ODA). *See* foreign aid
oil and gas industry, 14–15, 209–16, 226–7; and Alberta government, 210, 211–12, 214, 215, 216; and Canada-U.S. free trade, 215–16, 226, 227; Canadianization of, 215, 226, 227; and economic liberalism, 215–16, 226, 227; and economic nationalism, 212–15, 216, 226, 227; foreign direct investment in, 209, 210, 211–13, 214, 226; history of, 211–12; and international oil prices, 213; jurisdiction over, 210–11; and National Energy Program, 71, 211, 212, 213–14, 215, 216, 226, 227; and relations with U.S., 14–15, 210, 211, 214–16, 226
oil embargo of 1973, and resulting energy crisis, 67, 213
Oliver, Frank, 162
Open Skies, Treaty on, 71, 80n18
Organisation for Economic Co-operation and Development (OECD), 187, 197, 198, 200–2, 224
Ottawa Treaty, to ban landmines, 14, 56, 73, 81n26, 137, 152
Ouellet, André, 73, 189, 196

Pacific conflicts, multilateral approach to, 15–16, 271–88; and Cold War alliances, 278–80; and Communism, 131, 275, 278, 279–80, 282–3, 284–5, 288; and Indonesian conflicts, 280–6, 287; and North Atlantic thinking, 272, 273–8, 280, 281–2, 287–8; and postwar Japan, 278–9, 283, 284–5; and Sino-Japanese conflict, 272–8, 287. *See also specific countries*
Pakistan, 190, 223, 279, 284; and Canadian nuclear technology, 15, 217, 221, 222, 224

Paris Peace Conference (1919), 119, 128, 144
Partial Test Ban Treaty, 66
peacekeeping, 13, 32, 67, 132, 136–7, 139, 145, 183, 258
Pearson, Lester B., 28, 34, 37n29, 50, 51, 53; and colonial France, 257, 258; and defence, 134–5; and foreign aid, 183, 184, 185, 205; foreign service career of, 44, 45, 46, 127; and Kennedy, 321; and Malaysia, 284; and medicare, 135; and narrative of autonomy, 321–2; as nationalist, 29, 35n10, 134; and nuclear weapons, 31, 134; and recognition of China, 298, 300, 302; and relations with U.S., 29–32, 321; social programs of, 10, 135; and speech on Vietnam War, 66
– as foreign minister, 6, 10, 12, 29–32, 33, 48, 50, 63–5, 77, 129, 298, 300; and foreign aid, 183, 184, 185, 205; and immigration agreements, 173; and Indochina truce commissions, 31–2; legacy of, 64–5; long tenure of, 11, 64; and NATO, 149, 254–6; and Nobel Peace Prize, 64, 145; on North Atlantic Triangle, 240; and recognition of China, 298, 300; and Suez Crisis, 64, 132, 257; and Universal Declaration of Human Rights, 7, 148–9
Permanent Joint Board on Defence (PJBD), 125, 129
Petro-Canada, 210, 212, 213, 214–15, 226, 227
Pettigrew, Pierre, 75–6
Pickersgill, Jack, 45
Pope, Joseph, 42
Program Against Hunger, Malnutrition and Disease (PAHMD), 194

Quebec, 162; and bilingualism/biculturalism, 253–4; and Canada's foreign policy, 63, 68; and Canada's relations with France, 241–2, 256; and Canada's wartime participation, 23, 24–5, 252; and early defence policy, 113, 114, 115; and recognition of China, 299, 300; referendum in, 73; relations of, with France, 235, 238–9, 241–2, 252–3, 256–7, 260; and Supreme Court's *Secession Reference*, 153; separatism/sovereignty movement in, 235, 241–2, 256–7, 260, 261; and U.S. war on Iraq, 245. *See also* English-French relations; France, Canada's relations with

Ralston, J.L., 121–2
Rasminsky, Louis, 87, 93, 94
Reagan, Ronald, 69, 71, 136, 214
Reciprocal Trade Agreements Act (U.S.), 90, 95, 96
reciprocity, 88, 89, 90, 115, 330, 332
Red Cross, International Committee of the, 152, 198
refugee policy, 14, 159–77; and acceptance of Displaced Persons, 160–1, 165–72, 176; and Canada's humanitarian reputation, 159–60, 167; economic factors in, 159–60, 162, 163, 171, 172, 175; and Geneva Convention, 160, 161; and Hungarian Revolution, 173, 176; and immigration policy, 161, 163–4, 165–72, 175; and need for labour, 168–9, 172, 179n29; in post-9/11 era, 161; and racism/prejudice, 160, 162–4, 169–71, 176; and refusal of Jewish refugees, 159, 160, 163, 164, 167; UN influence on, 170–1, 176; UN recognition of, 175. *See also* Displaced Persons; immigration policy

refugees: from Burma, 159, 176; definition of, 160; Displaced Persons as, 160–1, 163, 164–72; economic impact of, 159–60, 162, 163, 171, 172, 175; Geneva Convention on, 160, 161; from Hungary, 173, 176; from Indochina, 70, 161, 175; Jewish, 159, 160, 163, 164, 167; Mennonites and Doukhobors, 160, 163; racism/prejudice towards, 160, 162–4, 169–71, 176; from Uganda, 174; UN Convention on, 172, 174, 175

Reid, Escott, 35n10, 44, 47, 240, 279
"responsibility to protect," 14, 73, 145, 152, 154, 246
Rice, Condoleezza, 76
Riddell, R.G., 165, 167, 169, 176
Ritchie, Ed, 51
Robertson, Gordon, 46
Robertson, Norman, 35n10, 44, 46, 48, 127; and economic multilateralism, 94, 95, 96, 97, 99, 100
Robinson, Basil, 51
Roche, William James, 62
Romania, 217, 222, 223
Ronning, Chester, 67, 279, 298
Roosevelt, Franklin D., 25, 91, 113, 275, 276; and economic multilateralism, 86–7, 90; and King, 27, 124, 125–6, 127
Royal Canadian Air Force (RCAF), 120, 121, 123, 130, 131, 134
Royal Canadian Mounted Police (RCMP), 129
Royal Canadian Navy (RCN), 114, 115, 118, 120–1, 122, 123, 126, 134
Rusk, Dean, 66, 302
Russia, 33, 72, 112, 160, 209, 272. *See also* Soviet Union
Rwanda, 137, 151

Sarkozy, Nicolas, 257, 260
Secession Reference (Supreme Court of Canada), 153
Second World War, 24–5, 26, 28, 30, 46, 53, 66, 349; and British-U.S. relations, 238; defence policies/actions during, 124–8; Canada's entry into, 124–5; and economic multilateralism, 91–3; and Manchurian crisis, 274–5; and movement of Displaced Persons, 160–1, 165–72; and trade with Britain and U.S., 86, 90–1; and war crimes prosecution, 142, 150
Sharing Our Future (CIDA report), 149, 192, 197, 201, 204
Sharp, Mitchell, 67–8, 200, 220, 221
Shultz, George, 69, 71
Sifton, Clifford, 162
Simon, Sir John, 274, 275
Simpson, Jeffrey, 344
Sinai Peninsula, 32
Sino-Japanese conflict (1931–45), 272–8, 287
Skelton, O.D., 12, 48, 297; as biographer of Laurier, 121, 329; death of, 127; hiring of, 42, 121; and Liberal narrative of autonomy, 328–9, 336; and Manchurian crisis, 274, 275; and Second World War, 124; and shaping of foreign service, 42–4, 121; and Sino-Japanese conflict, 277
Smith, Goldwin, 16, 326, 333, 334, 336, 342n77
Smith, Sidney, 65, 300
Smoot-Hawley Tariff, 274
Somalia, 72, 137
South Africa, 65, 71, 94, 95, 151, 153, 194
Southeast Asia Treaty Organization (SEATO), 280
South Africa, Boer War in, 13, 21–2, 26, 112, 113, 114, 116, 252

South Korea, 130, 136; and Canadian nuclear technology, 217, 218, 221, 222
Soviet Union, 63, 136, 149, 160, 173, 241; collapse of, 192, 258, 305, 307, 352; and creation of NATO, 130, 131, 133, 135, 254; and Gouzenko defection, 128–9; and nuclear technology, 223. *See also* Russia
special relationships, between/among states, 236–8
St. Laurent, Louis, 20, 29, 50, 53, 224; and aid to Asia, 282–3; defeat of, 30; and defence, 129–32; as foreign minister, 10, 12, 63, 77, 129; and GATT negotiations, 100–1; and Korean War, 280; and national unity/identity, 63, 254, 255–6; and NATO, 63, 129, 255–6; and recognition of China, 279–80, 299–300; and relations with France, 239, 244–5, 254, 255–6
Statute of Westminster, 23, 87, 116, 327
Stimson, Harry, 274, 275
Strategic Defense Initiative (SDI), 71
Strong, Maurice, 183, 193, 199
Suez Crisis, 5, 15, 64, 132, 257
Suharto, 284, 285, 286
Sukarno, 280, 282, 283, 284
Sun Yat-sen, 296
Supreme Court of Canada, 144, 145, 149, 150, 151, 153

Taft, William Howard, 114, 115
Taiwan, 67, 217, 299, 300, 302–3, 307, 309
Taylor, James Hudson, 295
Thatcher, Margaret, 72
Thatcher, W. Ross, 168–9
Third Option, 4, 68, 102, 241, 247, 285

Tiananmen Square, crackdown on students in, 188, 304, 305
Tibet, 299, 300, 307, 309
Towers, Graham, 92, 98–9
trade, with Britain and U.S. *See* free trade agreements; multilateralism, economic
Trail Smelter Arbitration, 143
transatlantic free trade (TAFTA), 241, 249–50
Treaty of Paris, 142
Treaty of Utrecht, 142
Treaty of Versailles, 118, 128, 144, 145, 273
Trudeau, Pierre Elliott, 12, 28, 32, 258; and Asia, 284–5; and CIDA, 183; and defence, 135–6; foreign ministers of, 67–71; and Indonesia, 285, 286; and Law of the Sea, 147; on nuclear technology, 224–5; on nuclear weapons, 218–19; and oil and gas industry, 212–15, 216, 226, 227; and Reagan, 69, 71; and recognition of China, 68, 302–3, 304, 306, 308; and relations with foreign service, 10, 41, 50–1, 52, 53, 54, 56, 68, 70; and relations with France, 256, 257; and Third Option, 4, 68, 102, 241, 247, 285
Truman, Harry S., 130
Turner, John, 71, 304

Uganda, 174
Underhill, Frank, 240; Liberalism of, 325–6; and narrative of autonomy, 324–6, 327, 336; and North Atlantic Triangle, 4, 325
United Nations, 7, 12, 30, 64, 65, 70, 91, 128, 198, 218, 239; admission of new members to, 66; creation of, 278; and human rights in China, 307; and International Criminal Court, 151; and Korean War, 29, 130; and recognition of China, 298, 300, 302–3; and refugee/immigration policy, 170–1, 174, 176; and Rwanda, 137; and Yugoslavia, 136
United Nations Children's Fund (UNICEF), 191–2
United Nations Commission on Human Rights, 150, 307, 308
United Nations Convention on the Law of the Sea, 69; Canadian position on, 13, 146–7
United Nations Convention on the Rights of the Child, 149
United Nations Convention Relating to the Status of Refugees, 172, 174, 175; and later Protocol, 174, 175
United Nations Declaration on Friendly Relations, 153
United Nations Development Programme, 223–4
United Nations Economic and Social Council (ECOSOC), 170
United Nations International Refugee Commission, 165
United Nations Relief and Rehabilitation Administration (UNRRA), 165
United Nations Scientific Committee on the Effects of Atomic Radiation, 224
United Nations Security Council, 63, 74, 75, 151, 254, 281–2, 284
United Nations War Crimes Commission, 150
United States: anti-Communism of, 28, 298–9; and attack on Pearl Harbor, 127, 278, 298; as Canada's "Other," 354, 356, 357–8, 361; and Canada's relations with China, 16, 298–303; Canadian

immigration to, 26–7; and early tensions with Japan, 119–20, 122–3; and First World War, 117, 118–19; and Indonesian independence, 281–2; isolationism of, 125, 129; and later conflicts with China, 307–8; in NATO, 30; and nuclear non-proliferation, 222; and nuclear weapons, 31; and postwar refugee crisis, 164–5, 167, 172; and recognition of China, 298–9, 302; and trade with Commonwealth, 96–7; and war with Iraq, 6, 9, 13, 75, 347, 359; and withdrawal from Vietnam, 68. *See also* Britain, and relations with U.S.
– Canada's relations with, 25–34, 235, 237; and anti-Americanism, 139, 245–6, 255, 259, 323–4, 325, 327, 355; and Canadian autonomy/independence, 308, 309; and Canadian identity, 127–8, 354, 356, 357–60, 361; in Cold War era, 28–32; and collective identity, 317–18, 357–60; and early bilateral trade proposal, 96; and economic multilateralism, 91–102; and foreign ministers, 66, 68–9, 71, 74–5, 76; and free trade agreement, 9, 13, 15, 55, 102, 303–4; and international law, 13, 142–4, 146–7; and North American defence, 31, 239; oil and gas as factor in, 14–15, 210, 211, 214–16, 226; and reciprocity, 88, 89, 90, 115, 330, 332; and recognition of China, 298–303, 307–8; and war on Iraq, 33, 245, 258–9, 318. *See also* Conservative Party narrative of empire; defence, and Canadian-U.S. relations; Liberal Party narrative of autonomy

United States Agency for International Development (USAID), 190
Universal Declaration of Human Rights, 7, 148–9
uranium, 14, 209, 217–18, 219, 221, 223, 225, 226, 227

Vance, Cyrus, 70
Vanier, Georges, 44
Vargas Llosa, Mario, 345, 353
Verner, Josée, 203
Vietnam, 307; control/supervision commission for, 68, 131; and Indochina truce commissions, 31–2; U.S. withdrawal from, 68
Vietnamese Communists, Chinese support for, 299, 300, 301
Vietnam War, 50, 66, 67, 68, 272; and fall of Saigon, 285

war crimes, prosecution of, 142, 150–1, 278–9
Watkins, Mel, 212–13
West New Guinea, 283
Whelan, Susan, 202
White, Harry Dexter, 87, 92, 93
Wilson, Daniel, 295
Wilson, Michael, 217
Wilson, Woodrow, 25, 117, 119, 144
Winegard, William, 149
Woodsworth, J.S., 162, 163
World Bank, 91, 184, 190, 223; and structural adjustment, 191, 192, 194
Wrong, Hume, 35n10, 44, 45–6, 127, 170, 176

Yugoslavia, 72, 136, 137, 151

Zhao Ziyang, 304
Zhu Rongji, 305, 308